Did My Neurons Make Me Do It?

If humans are purely physical, and if it is the brain that does the work formerly assigned to the mind or soul, then how can it fail to be the case that all of our thoughts and actions are determined by the laws of neurobiology? If this is the case, then free will, moral responsibility, and, indeed, reason itself would appear to be in jeopardy. The authors here defend a non-reductive version of physicalism whereby humans are (sometimes) the authors of their own thoughts and actions.

In *Did My Neurons Make Me Do It?* Nancy Murphy and Warren S. Brown bring together insights from both philosophy and the cognitive neurosciences to defeat neurobiological reductionism. One resource is a 'post-Cartesian' account of mind as essentially embodied and constituted by action-feedback-evaluation-action loops in the environment, and 'scaffolded' by cultural resources. Another is a non-mysterious account of downward (mental) causation explained in terms of a complex, higher-order system exercising constraints on lower-level causal processes. These resources are intrinsically related: the embeddedness of brain events in action-feedback loops is the key to their mentality, and those broader systems have causal effects on the brain itself.

With these resources Murphy and Brown take on two problems in philosophy of mind: a response to the charges that physicalists cannot account for the meaningfulness of language nor the causal efficacy of the mental *qua* mental. Solutions to these problems are a prerequisite to addressing the central problem of the book: how can biological organisms be free and morally responsible? The authors argue that the free-will problem is badly framed if it is put in terms of neurobiological *determinism*; the real issue is neurobiological *reductionism*. If it is indeed possible to make sense of the notion of downward causation, then the relevant question is whether humans exert downward causation over some of their own parts and processes. If all organisms do this to some extent, what needs to be added to this animalian flexibility to constitute free and responsible action? The keys are sophisticated language and hierarchically ordered cognitive processes allowing (mature) humans to evaluate their own actions, motives, goals, and rational and moral principles.

Nancey Murphy is Professor of Christian Philosophy at Fuller Theological Seminary, Pasadena, California.

Warren S. Brown is Professor of Psychology at Fuller Graduate School of Psychology, Pasadena, California.

Did My Neurons Make Me Do It?

Philosophical and Neurobiological Perspectives on Moral Responsibility and Free Will

Nancey Murphy and Warren S. Brown

OXFORD
UNIVERSITY PRESS

OXFORD
UNIVERSITY PRESS

Great Clarendon Street, Oxford OX2 6DP

Oxford University Press is a department of the University of Oxford.
It furthers the University's objective of excellence in research, scholarship,
and education by publishing worldwide in

Oxford New York

Auckland Cape Town Dar es Salaam Hong Kong Karachi
Kuala Lumpur Madrid Melbourne Mexico City Nairobi
New Delhi Shanghai Taipei Toronto
With offices in
Argentina Austria Brazil Chile Czech Republic France Greece
Guatemala Hungary Italy Japan South Korea Poland Portugal
Singapore Switzerland Thailand Turkey Ukraine Vietnam

Oxford is a registered trade mark of Oxford University Press
in the UK and in certain other countries

Published in the United States
by Oxford University Press Inc., New York

ISBN 978-0-19-956823-9

Printed in the United Kingdom by
Lightning Source UK Ltd., Milton Keynes

Preface

When we set out to write this book we did not anticipate the time it would take. Neurobiological reductionism *has* to be false. If not, then what may appear to be a product of rational processes must instead be the consequence of causal processes in the brain. If this is the case, "arguments" for neurobiological reductionism are not in fact arguments but mere noises. And while we did not judge there to be a fully adequate response to this problem at the time we began our project (in the fall of 1998) we recognized a growing body of helpful resources in the literature. Each of us was focusing primarily on different sorts of developments: Murphy, the philosopher, on developments regarding anti-reductionism itself in both philosophy and the sciences; Brown, the neuropsychologist, on what we here designate anti-Cartesianism in the cognitive neurosciences. By this we mean critiques of approaches to mental phenomena that "locate" them "inside" the organism rather than recognize their co-constitution by the organism's action in the world, both physical and social. Thus, we believed that we could quickly stitch together resources of these two sorts and thereby solve outstanding problems in philosophy of mind. However, we found ourselves grinding to a halt again and again when the attempt led us to conclude that the philosophical problems themselves were formulated in slightly inappropriate ways; we had to spend months re-thinking the problems themselves before we could find meaningful points of contact between philosophy and science. We hope our readers will be patient enough to consider our contributions in this light—that is, allowing us to suggest reformulations of, and not just attempted solutions to, the assorted problems addressed herein.

The length and magnitude of the project has resulted in a tremendous number of debts. We here thank helpful critics who have commented on drafts: Leslie Brothers, Tom Clark, Frank Colborn, Owen Flanagan, C. Daniel Geisler, William Hasker, Malcolm Jeeves, Sir Anthony Kenny, Heather Looy, D. Z. Phillips, Rob Piehl, Alwyn Scott, Arthur Schwartz, Tom Tracy, and we are sure we are missing several. We are also indebted to our students at Fuller Seminary, in both the Schools of Psychology and Theology; and to several students at Boston University.

We are indebted to our own institution, Fuller Seminary, whose teaching load and sabbatical policy make research and writing possible. A small grant from the Templeton Foundation made further course reductions possible. Two conferences contributed to our work. The Center for Theology and the Natural Sciences in Berkeley named Murphy its J. K. Russell Fellow for the year 1999 and organized a conference in her honor on the topic of downward causation. The University of San Francisco (in conjunction with the Center for Theology and the Natural Sciences and the Vatican Observatory) sponsored a conference on reductionism and emergence in 2003, which enabled us to meet with a number of experts in the field. We wish to thank all of these institutions.

We thank Basil Blackwell for permission to reprint figures from Donald MacKay, *Behind the Eye* (1991); MIT Press for permission to reprint lengthy quotations from Alicia Juarrero, *Dynamics in Action: Intentional Behavior as a Complex System* (1999); and Oxford University Press for permission to reprint a figure from Joaquín Fuster, *Cortex and Mind: Unifying Cognition* (2003).

We owe special gratitude to several people. First, Robert Kane reviewed our manuscript for Oxford University Press, and while he did not recommend publication as it was, he sent not only detailed criticisms but also suggestions for improvement. We took his suggestions, and this has resulted in a much better book. Professor Kane was then gracious enough to take the time to re-read the manuscript; at that point he recommended it for publication. We are deeply grateful both for the suggestions for improvement and for his willingness to give the book a second chance.

We discovered Alicia Juarrero's writings after we thought we had finished our own. Her work on topics closely paralleling ours, but from the point of view of complex dynamical systems, struck us as revolutionary, and so we struggled to follow her footsteps across what we now call a "paradigm shift" from mechanistic to dynamical thinking. She was kind enough to read the entire manuscript, making helpful suggestions and correcting our errors.

Alwyn Scott, a specialist in nonlinear mathematics, contributed much in concrete suggestions and also by way of encouragement as we struggled with these issues. We mention him in particular, as he passed away while the book was in press. Two friends have provided inspiration of a different sort. Charles Townes and Ernan MacMullin are two deeply respected friends, who cannot imagine physicalism without reductionism. We have had them in mind all through the writing of this book. "If only this will convince Charlie or Ernan..."

Donald MacKay also had an important impact on our thinking. This influence goes back to a year Brown spent with him while he was formulating and giving his Gifford Lectures. These lectures became the basis for his *Behind the Eye*, to which we often refer in our book. MacKay inspired our understanding of mind as engaged in action–feedback–evaluation–action loops in the environment.

It will become apparent that we have drawn particularly on the ideas of a handful of other authors: Alicia Juarrero on downward causation in complex dynamical systems; Terrence Deacon on emergence and on symbolic language; Fred Dretske on beliefs as structuring causes of behavior; Ludwig Wittgenstein on language in action; Alasdair MacIntyre on moral responsibility; Robert Kane on free will. We will be happy if reviewers of the present volume conclude that we have done nothing more than to bring these giant contributions into conversation in such a way as to point the discussion of neurobiological reductionism in more fruitful directions.

Contents

Detailed Contents

List of Figures and Tables

Introduction: New Approaches to Knotty Old Problems

1 The Problem and Our Goals

It is an interesting fact about contemporary Westerners that we have no shared account of the nature of the human person. Even more interesting is the fact that many are unaware of the first fact.

What *are* humans? Are they complex biological organisms, or are they essentially non-material beings temporarily housed in physical bodies? Most neuroscientists hold a physicalist account of the person.[1] Most philosophers of mind are also physicalists. Dualists among philosophers tend to be motivated by religious commitments, yet physicalism is the position of choice among graduates of liberal Christian seminaries.[2]

In contrast, casual surveys of audiences we address (lay and professional, religious and secular) show that the majority hold either a dualist view (the person is body and soul or body and mind) or a trichotomist view (the person is body, soul, and spirit). We have addressed students who have no idea of what the traditional concept of *soul* involves, as well as others who cannot imagine "how I can be I if I have no soul".

---

[1] In sec. 3 and Ch. 1 we explain the meaning of "physicalism" in detail. For present purposes, take it to mean simply the denial that anything needs to be added to the living human body to constitute a human being. We shall argue emphatically that it does not mean that human behavior can be understood in terms of physics or even all of the physical sciences.

[2] Biblical scholars and church historians began arguing more than 100 years ago that dualism is *not* the position of the Hebrew or Christian Scriptures. See Warren S. Brown, Nancey Murphy, and H. Newton Malony (eds.), *Whatever Happened to the Soul?: Scientific and Theological Portraits of Human Nature* (Minneapolis: Fortress Press, 1998), ch. 1.

Most often these differences show up indirectly. The conviction with which many argue against abortion or embryonic stem-cell research is based on the assumption that what makes a bit of biological tissue a human being is the possession of a soul, and that the soul is present from the moment of fertilization. A current issue that highlights the differences is the cloning debate. Behind some of the more strident objections to human cloning is the unspoken assumption that a clone would have a body but no soul—it would be something like the zombies of science fiction and philosophical thought experiments.[3]

It is fortunate (in our view) that popularizations of recent developments in neuroscience and philosophy have begun to stimulate public discussion of these issues. However, many of the popularizers are not only physicalists but also ardent reductionists.[4] Their accounts of the neural (or genetic) bases for everything from mate selection to artistic appreciation and religious experience[5] rightly raise fears that science will overthrow cherished elements of our self-conceptions—fears about implications for rationality, free will, and moral accountability. The most radical reductionists deny the very existence of beliefs, intentions, and so forth (as ordinarily understood),[6] and even (perhaps) consciousness itself.[7]

The goal of this book is to show that such fears are groundless. There is no reason, in the name of science, to deny the most obvious features of experience (such as consciousness itself). In particular, we shall tackle the issue of the role of reason in human affairs—an issue addressed by philosophers as the problem of mental causation. Our thesis is that while human reasonableness and responsibility may be explained (partially) by

---

[3] One of the authors was contacted by someone from the media when Dolly was cloned. After his repeated attempts to provoke an expression of some sort of horror at the prospect of cloning humans, light dawned. "Do you read a lot of science fiction?" "Well, some." "Are you imagining that if we try to clone a human we'll clone a body but it won't have a soul? It will be like zombies in science fiction?" He replied, "Yes, something like that." "Well," I said, "don't worry. None of us has a soul and we all get along perfectly well."

[4] For an overview of forms of reductionism, see Ch. 2, sec. 1.2.

[5] See, e.g., V. S. Ramachandran, "The Science of Art: How the Brain Responds to Beauty", in Warren S. Brown (ed.), *Understanding Wisdom: Sources, Science, and Society* (Philadelphia and London: Templeton Foundation Press, 2000), 277–305; and Stephen Pinker, *How the Mind Works* (New York: W. W. Norton, 1999).

[6] Eliminative materialism is the thesis promoted by Paul and Patricia Churchland that "folk-psychological" concepts such as these will turn out not to map onto neuroscientific categories and will be eliminated. See, e.g., Paul M. Churchland, "Eliminative Materialism and the Propositional Attitudes", *Journal of Philosophy*, 78 (1981), 67–90.

[7] See Daniel C. Dennett, *Consciousness Explained* (Boston: Little, Brown, and Co., 1991).

the cognitive neurosciences, they cannot be explained *away*. Rather, we should expect scientific investigation of the brain to help us understand *how* humans succeed in acting reasonably, freely, and responsibly.[8] So the purpose of this volume is not to argue for a physicalist account of the person over against dualism. The question we explore is rather whether *nonreductive* physicalism is a coherent position. Many philosophers these days claim to be nonreductive physicalists; "reductionist" has become of a term of reproach in some circles. Yet it remains to be seen whether physicalists, whatever their intentions, can avoid the "nothing-buttery" of reductionism. If humans are *physical* systems, and if it is their brains (not minds) that allow them to think, how can it *not* be the case that all of their thoughts and behavior are simply the product of the laws of neurobiology?[9] How can it *not* be the case, as the epiphenomenalists argue,[10] that the mental life of reasoning, evaluating, deciding is a mere accompaniment of the brain processes that are really doing all the work?

If these questions cannot be answered, what happens to our traditional notions of moral responsibility, even of our sense of ourselves as *rational* animals? We hope in the following pages to shed some light on these issues. Thus, we set out to defend physicalism against charges that it inevitably leads to reductionist views of the person that conflict with our widely shared sense of ourselves as rational, free, and morally responsible beings.

2 Our Approach

Our goal here is not to argue *that* humans are rational and responsible. We could not make sense of what we are doing in writing this book if we did not assume common-sense views of the role of reason and reasons—that is, of our having good reasons for writing it and of our readers accepting our conclusions on the basis of reason. Rather, we hope to show *how* our

---

[8] The emphasis here on reason is not to deny other aspects of human life such as emotion. In fact, we shall argue that emotional response is an intrinsic part of human reasonableness and responsibility.

[9] Of course, many would assume environmental factors to be involved, but the usual reductionist response is to claim that the environment can affect the person only if mediated by neurobiology.

[10] In general, epiphenomenalism is the thesis that some feature of a situation arises in virtue of others, but has no causal efficacy itself. The favored example is a light blinking on a computer when it is in operation.

neurobiological equipment makes rationality, responsibility, and free will possible. In this task we intend to hold ourselves responsible to three sources of insight: science, philosophy, and ordinary experience (such as the facts that we are conscious and that our conscious plans have effects in the world).

The attempted integration of science and philosophy is, practically speaking, a consequence of the disciplinary perspectives of the authors (neuropsychology and philosophy). It turned out to be more difficult than we anticipated. We found in case after case that it was not possible to bring scientific insights to bear on the philosophical problems as they stood; instead, the science called the problems themselves into question. Our general conclusion, then, is that there are deeply ingrained world-view issues that complicate problems in the philosophy of mind. The two prominent ones are causal reductionism and the view of the mental as "inner". The result of our critique of these assumptions was often the reformulation of the problems.

This sort of reformulation depends on a shift in the understanding of the nature of philosophy. During the heyday of analytic philosophy one of the first lessons that undergraduates had to learn was to distinguish conceptual from empirical questions—a case in point being a distinction between questions about the meaning and use of concepts such as *mind, intention, free will* and empirical questions regarding cognitive functions and decision making. Part of the motivation for the distinction was, perhaps, the urgency of finding something for philosophers to *do* as science rapidly made further inroads into philosophy's traditional territory. Thus, (in part) the rationale for a distinction between the empirical and the conceptual: the conceptual could be preserved against scientific advance as the sole province of philosophers.

The beginning of the end of philosophy's analytic period is found in W. V. O. Quine's "Two Dogmas of Empiricism".[11] If the distinction between analytic and synthetic sentences cannot be drawn sharply, then neither can the distinction between conceptual analysis and empirical investigation. Quine's truth-meaning holism is based on the recognition that epistemological problems can usually be resolved in either of two ways: by revising our beliefs or by shifting the meaning and use of

---

[11]   W. V. O. Quine, "Two Dogmas of Empiricism", *Philosophical Review*, 60 (1951); repr. in *From a Logical Point of View* (Cambridge, Mass.: Harvard University Press, 1953), 20–43.

our words. Since Quine first delivered this address in 1950, a variety of developments in philosophy have confirmed his position. Thomas Kuhn's famous book made the point in a dramatic way that basic concepts in science undergo significant shifts, despite surface similarities in language.[12] In moral philosophy writers such as Charles Taylor and Alasdair MacIntyre have made it clear that basic concepts of the self[13] as well as the entirety of our moral discourse[14] have a history. MacIntyre and Stephen Toulmin have each in different ways provided insightful diagnoses and criticisms of modernity's attempt at ahistorical reason.[15]

Philosophers, then, cannot content themselves with doing conceptual *analysis*—they need to be aware of the changes that concepts have undergone in their history and understand the reasons for those changes—and more particularly, the need to be ready to change the way philosophical problems are formulated when they turn out to be based on outdated knowledge. This view of philosophy entails that philosophical arguments based on current linguistic practices are suspect. Paul Feyerabend pointed out that common idioms are adapted to *beliefs*, not facts, and the acquisition of new knowledge ought to be allowed to call such beliefs into question. Feyerabend says:

It would seem to me that the task of philosophy, or of any enterprise interested in the advance rather than the embalming of knowledge, is to encourage the development of such new modes of approach, to participate in their improvement rather than to waste time in showing, what is obvious anyway, that they are different from the status quo.[16]

---

[12] Thomas Kuhn, *The Structure of Scientific Revolutions*, 2nd edn. (Chicago: University of Chicago Press, 1970).

[13] See Charles Taylor, *Sources of the Self: The Making of Modern Identity* (Cambridge, Mass.: Harvard University Press, 1989).

[14] Alasdair MacIntyre, *After Virtue: A Study in Moral Theory*, 2nd edn. (Notre Dame, Ind.: University of Notre Dame Press, 1984).

[15] See Stephen Toulmin, *Cosmopolis: The Hidden Agenda of Modernity* (New York: Macmillan, 1990). A critique of the ahistorical aspirations of modernity has been a major theme of MacIntyre's writing at least since his "Epistemological Crises, Dramatic Narrative, and the Philosophy of Science": "Descartes' failure is complex. First of all he does not recognize that among the features of the universe which he is not putting in doubt is his own capacity to use the French and Latin languages ... and as a consequence does not put in doubt what he has inherited in and with these languages... These meanings have a history" (*Monist*, 60 (1977), 453–472; rep. in Stanley Hauerwas and L. Gregory Jones (eds.), *Why Narrative: Readings in Narrative Theology* (Grand Rapids, Mich.: Eerdmans, 1989), 138–157, at p. 144).

[16] Paul K. Feyerabend, "Materialism and the Mind–Body Problem", in *Realism, Rationalism, and Scientific Method: Philosophical Papers, Volume 1* (Cambridge: Cambridge University Press, 1981),

Arguments in favor of the accepted beliefs (e.g., dualism) on the grounds that the statement of a competing theory (e.g., physicalism) conflicts with common ways of talking are therefore circular. Similarly, arguments based on philosophical intuitions—on what can or cannot be conceived—are equally suspect, since conceivability is largely a product of linguistic practices. This post–analytic view of philosophy—philosophy "natural-ized"—demotes philosophers from the role of cultural magistrates and encourages them to investigate the frontiers of knowledge, looking out for ways in which traditional patterns of use may need to be modified.[17]

Thus, we pursue a three-way interaction among philosophy, science, and common experience. These three are already inextricably related: philosophy draws its materials from the language of everyday, yet earlier philosophical theories have shaped our current language, and language in turn shapes our most basic experiences. Science, too, draws its resources from culture, especially in areas such as cognitive science, whose objects include human beings. Furthermore, assessment of the relevance of science to cultural debates is an *interpretive* process. These three realms are inescapably interlinked, much as one might like to presume the indepen-dence of either philosophy or science.

The benefits of keeping all three sources in mind are many. Each provides a perspective on the same segment of reality, but these are different perspectives with different strengths and weaknesses. Science can help direct philosophical arguments away from implausible alternatives; we believe that the role of developments in neuroscience (e.g., functional brain imaging studies) in persuading many philosophers of mind to abandon dualism is one of the most important examples. Philosophical analysis helps with the interpretation of scientific findings: for example, pointing out that many purported sociobiological explanations of human altruism miss the mark because what one intends by "altruism" in the human sphere excludes anything that humans are determined to do exclusively by genetics. The whole of this volume represents an argument for the necessity of keeping

161–175, at p. 175. Cf. Richard Rorty, *Philosophy and the Mirror of Nature* (Princeton: Princeton University Press, 1979), 56.

[17] There is a congruence, which we shall not be able to pursue here, between this approach to philosophy and what is being learned about how the brain works. Science is just now getting beyond a peculiarly modern understanding of nature in terms of deterministic linear causal processes, which has been coupled with a parallel emphasis on linear algorithmic reasoning. The attempt to model the neural realization of human thinking using linear causal connections is thought by many to be a dead end.

common sense in mind when interpreting science. That is, re interpretations of science (whether neurophysiological or genetic) simply have to be false—if they are not, there is certainly no point in *arguing* against them!

A final note on methodology. We intend to avoid a tendency in much current literature to make over-hasty connections between robust human cognitive and behavioral phenomena (rationality, morality, free will) and the neurobiological level.[18] Our everyday talk about actions and intentions needs first to be analyzed into more basic cognitive prerequisites. For example, we shall claim that a sense of self is one of several cognitive prerequisites for moral responsibility. This sense of self in turn depends on more basic cognitive capacities such as narrative memory. Only when these more basic cognitive processes have been identified do we turn to neurobiology to see how much is known so far about the neural substrate that enables them.

3 Terminological Tangles

Before proceeding further, we need to explain (and perhaps defend) the very terminology we use. There is a welter of terms being used in current debates. We need to make some distinctions, in order to explain where we stand.

First, if "dualism" posits two components or substances (matter and mind) making up the person, then "monism" would seem to be the appropriate contrasting term. However, one can be a monist of either a mentalist/idealist sort or a materialist/physicalist sort. So let us take "physicalism" to be short for "physicalist monism".

In recent philosophical literature "physicalism" and "materialism" are *both* used to refer *both* to monist accounts of the *person* and to monistic *world views*. A materialist/physicalist account of the person does *not* entail a materialist/physicalist world view; in particular, it does not entail atheism.[19]

---

[18] For a critique of over-hasty resort to neuroscience see Leslie Brothers, *Mistaken Identity: The Mind–Brain Problem Reconsidered* (Albany, NY: SUNY Press, 2001).

[19] In fact, though, for many the denial of the existence of the human mind or soul seems to be unthinkingly equated with the denial of the existence of God. We suspect that this tendency is a result of the influence of the Greek and medieval notion of "the Great Chain of Being", in which human souls were placed above the great dividing line between matter and spirit, and thus (from a biblical perspective) equated all too closely with God. See A. O. Lovejoy, *The Great Chain of Being* (Cambridge, Mass.: Harvard University Press, 1936).

We choose to call our view of the person "physicalist" rather than "materialist", first, because it is in keeping with current philosophical usage, but second, because "materialism" has been used more often to designate a world view, and thus seems to carry additional atheistic connotations that we prefer to avoid.

The concept of *emergence* is often used in discussions of anthropology. Thus, some theorists call their positions "emergent materialism" or "emergent monism", which we take to mean *roughly* what we mean by "nonreductive physicalism". While "emergence" may seem intuitively better for conveying the intended meaning, philosophical discussions of emergence have a history of producing more heat than light. In contrast, discussions of reductionism and its contrary are much clearer, and furthermore, there is significant agreement in distinguishing various senses of the word (more on this in Ch. 2). Our conclusion will be that *causal* reductionism is the important threat to human self-understanding, and we shall argue that to counteract it, one needs to develop a concept of *downward* or *top-down causation*, which, in turn, needs to be understood in the context of dynamic systems. If we were to employ the term "emergent", we would speak not of emergent *entities* but rather of emergent *levels of causal efficacy*.[20] If "emergence" is so restricted in meaning, we believe, then "emergent monism" is entirely equivalent to our version of "nonreductive physicalism" with the stipulation that it is *causal* reductionism that is being denied.[21]

There are, in fact, a number of quite different conceptions of the person that go under the heading of "physicalism". One way to distinguish two important variants is by considering their different intellectual histories. One line of thought is described by Mary Midgley:

If certain confusions result from Descartes' having sliced human beings down the middle, many people feel that the best cure is just to drop the immaterial

---

[20] "Emergent entity" is ambiguous. Over time there are certainly emergent entities in one sense, such as organisms, and much of the point of this book is to take this fact seriously and recognize that these new entities have new causal capacities. This is not to say that there are emergent "metaphysical" or "ontological" entities such as minds.

[21] The concept of emergence is currently receiving renewed attention, and it may be that in a few years it will have a clear enough meaning to be useful. See, e.g., Terrence Deacon, "Three Levels of Emergent Phenomena", in Nancey Murphy and William R. Stoeger (eds.), *Evolution and Emergence: Systems, Organisms, Persons* (Oxford: Oxford University Press, 2007). Deacon here makes many points comparable to ours; see our Ch. 2, sec. 3.3.

half altogether ... The philosophers who favour this programme are known as Physicalists. Sometimes they promote it with brutal zest, sometimes quite apologetically and kindly.[22]

We hope not to be taken for physicalists of this type—not even of the kinder sort. Our account of physicalism, developed in the following chapter, arises not from the defeat of Descartes in the philosophy of mind, but largely from philosophy of biology—in particular from the recognition that the natural world needs to be understood as forming a *hierarchy of levels of complexity*. Quantum physics studies the most basic level (known to date) of this hierarchy, and sciences from atomic physics, through chemistry, and through the various levels of biology add to the picture. Cartesian dualism *minus* mind or soul is defective, in that it leaves humans nothing more than machines. Before we can begin to understand human beings, we need to appreciate the differences between mechanisms and complex organisms. Only by appreciating the developments from the levels of physics to the level of the ethological study of the higher primates do we place ourselves in position to ask intelligently whether a full account of human life requires the postulation of an immaterial mind or soul, and fully to understand what "remains" of a human being if there is no such thing. Thus, a better term for our position, were it not so inelegant, would be something like "nonreductive neurophysiologicalism", which would signal our emphasis on understanding human thought and behavior in light of their precursors in the animal world—a definitive rejection of the idea that humans can be understood in terms of the physical sciences alone. In this regard our position is comparable to that of John Searle. Searle calls his position "biological naturalism", objecting that the term "physicalism" already commits one to misleading conceptions of the world derived from Cartesian philosophy.[23] Owen Flanagan calls his position "subjective realism", in order to emphasize that the essence of an experience cannot be captured by a description of its neural realizer—it requires as well an account of how it feels to the organism that has it.[24]

[22] Mary Midgley, "The Soul's Successors: Philosophy and the 'Body'", in Sarah Coakley (ed.), *Religion and the Body* (Cambridge: Cambridge University Press, 1997), 53–68, at p. 53.

[23] John R. Searle, *The Rediscovery of the Mind* (Cambridge, Mass.: MIT Press, 1992), 1, 54–5.

[24] Owen Flanagan, *The Problem of the Soul: Two Visions of Mind and How to Reconcile Them* (New York: Basic Books, 2002), 88–97.

4 Overview of the Book

An underlying thesis of this volume is that, despite changes in physics, many in our culture are still functioning with a largely Newtonian understanding of causation, and, despite developments in philosophy of mind and the cognitive neurosciences, are still largely Cartesian in their understanding of the mental. The Newtonian element is the assumption that all complex entities or systems are either mere aggregates or mechanisms. Aggregates are collections of parts that do not interact (e.g., marbles in a bag). Mechanisms (e.g., mechanical clocks) are entities made of inert and separate parts that move one another in a determined order and are not themselves affected by their relations with the other parts. This assumption is at the heart of causal reductionism, the view that the behavior of the parts of an entity (or the laws governing the behavior of the parts) determines the behavior of the whole unilaterally.

One goal of this book is defeat of causal reductionism. That is, we need to show that there are systems that act as causes in their own right—not merely as an aggregate of micro-level causal processes. We shall argue that this top-down causation functions by means of *constraining* the behavior of its parts. In the hierarchy from leptons to human societies, there are new and different kinds of causal players at all levels: catalysts and convection currents at the molecular level, slime molds at the most primitive organic level, and, of course, organisms and humans. This would be common sense were it not for philosophers having convinced us that all of the causal work *must* be done at the level of subatomic physics.

The key to a shift in perspective is to turn attention from *things* to *systems*. The components of systems include processes. Processes become what they are (i.e., perform their function within the system) due to the way they are organized, related to other component processes. Systems are stable structures of processes that create their own components by constraining the degrees of freedom of processes so as to coordinate them with other processes. The coordination requires not just matter and energy, but also information. Thus, escaping the modern reductionist paradigm requires something like a *Gestalt* switch that recognizes, in addition to mechanisms, the existence of dynamical systems.

It is proving easier to exorcise the Cartesian ego—to get rid of Gilbert Ryle's "ghost in the machine"—than it is to close down the theater where the ego spent his time. The habits of thought developed during the Cartesian era still persist among those who have rejected mind–body dualism but simply replace talk of the mind or soul with talk of the brain. These habits are based on the notion that I—the *real* I—am "inside" my body, and that I have only mediated access to the world. In fact, when brain talk is substituted for mind talk, this is literally true; the brain *is* inside and really does not have any direct access to the world. This concept of mind includes the tendency to view the knower as passive, resulting in the neglect of the role of action in the life of the mind, and the neglect of the social constitution of mental life.

The *Gestalt* switch required to escape this misleading picture is related to the rejection of the mechanism; it is to understand the *mental* as pertaining to a higher-level *dynamical system* that is the brain in the body involved in interaction with the world, both physical and social. Thus, we shall argue for the essential action-relevance of perception and memory; mind is paradigmatically manifested in *informed* engagement in *action–feedback–evaluation–action* loops in the environment. The equation of mind with brain processes (alone) is an egregious form of reductionism.

Our approaches to the problems of rationality, language, responsibility, and free will depend on this combination of insights. We take rationality to depend most basically on downward causation from the environment reshaping neural networks, and, further, on the hierarchical ordering of cognitive processes such that higher-level evaluation selects among lower-level processes in accord with demands of the environment, both physical and social. Puzzles about language result largely from the inherited view that words get their meaning from inner mental acts. On our account, meaning is fixed by action in the social world. Morally responsible action is enabled by both rationality and sophisticated symbolic language, and first appears in the human species when it becomes possible to direct higher-order evaluative processes toward one's own cognitive and lower-order evaluative processes, influenced by the environmental scaffolding of moral language.[25] Free will we interpret as a matter of an agent's capacity, as a

---

[25] This is not to say that each morally responsible action requires such conscious reflection.

dynamic system, to redesign her own character through many instances of responsible action.

Our proposals build step by step in the pages that follow:

In Chapter 1, "Avoiding Cartesian Materialism", we explore the many ways in which Cartesian assumptions about human nature are embedded in most versions of physicalism. We criticize the tendency to substitute brain–body dualism for mind–body dualism, the assumption that emotion is opposed to rationality, the idea of mental processes as occurring in an inner space, no longer the "Cartesian theater" but nonetheless *inside* the head. In contrast, we emphasize that mind is embodied, not merely "embrained", and that mental events must be understood as *contextualized* brain events.

In Chapter 2, "From Causal Reductionism to Self-Directed Systems", we criticize overly simple accounts of causal processes, and make our case for the necessity of considering downward causation (the effect of the whole on its parts) as well as bottom–up causation (the effect of parts on the whole). The concept of downward causation, while commonly employed in the sciences, is highly suspect among some philosophers. On our account, downward causation involves selection or constraint of lower-level causal processes on the basis of how those lower-level processes or entities fit into a broader (higher-level) causal system. Countenancing downward causation is not equivalent to denying (all) causal determinism; the lower-level variants may be produced either deterministically or randomly.

In Chapter 3, "From Mindless to Intelligent Action", we build upon our account of complex causal processes by considering step by step the increasing abilities of organisms to respond to information about their environments in increasingly flexible ways, along with an account of the neural processes that make this flexibility possible. We shall see that the characteristics of goal-directedness and evaluation are present in even the most rudimentary biological activity; the distinctiveness of intelligent action lies in the organism's ability to detach itself from immediate biological and environmental stimuli and in the character of the evaluative processes involved. Such evaluation depends on hierarchical structuring of cognitive processes such that higher animals are able to make their own actions (and in the case of humans, their own cognition) the product of evaluation.

In Chapter 4, "How Can Neural Nets Mean?", we consider the charge that a physicalist cannot make sense of meaning. We argue that the supposed mysteries of meaning and intentionality are a product of Cartesian assumptions regarding the inwardness of mental acts and the passivity of the knower. If, instead, we consider the mental in terms of action in the social world, there is no more mystery to how the word "chair" hooks onto the world than there is to how one learns to sit in one. We consider what is known so far about the neural capacities needed for increasingly complex use of symbols. Symbolic language—in fact, quite sophisticated symbolic language—is a prerequisite for both reasoning and morally responsible action.

In Chapter 5, "How Does Reason Get its Grip on the Brain?", we turn to the role of reason in human thought and action. A powerful argument against physicalism is the lack, so far, of a suitable account of "mental causation", that is, of the role of reason in brain processes. The problem is often formulated as the question of how the mental properties of brain events can be causally efficacious. We reformulate the problem, instead, as two questions: How is it that series of mental/neural events come to conform to rational (as opposed to *merely* causal) patterns? And what difference does the possession of mental capacities make to the causal efficacy of an organism's interaction with its environment?

In Chapter 6, "Who's Responsible?", we turn to a central theme of the book, a philosophical analysis of the concept of morally responsible action. Here we adopt an account of moral agency worked out by Alasdair MacIntyre, premier moral philosopher of our day. Morally responsible action depends (initially) on the ability to evaluate one's reasons for acting in light of a concept of the good. We then investigate the cognitive prerequisites for such action, among which we include a sense of self, the ability to predict and represent the future, and high-order symbolic language.

Free will (in some sense) is taken as a prerequisite for moral responsibility. In Chapter 7, "Neurobiological Reductionism and Free Will", we address a small part of the tangled history of debates over the meaning and existence of free will. Our principal aim will be to eliminate one of the worries that seems to threaten our conception of ourselves as free agents: namely, neurobiological reductionism—the worry that "my neurons made me do it". We bring to bear our argument to the effect that organisms are (often) the causes of their own behavior (Chs. 2 and 3); that humans are capable of using and understanding the meaning of language (Ch. 4); that humans act for reasons, not merely on the basis of causes (Ch. 5); and that mature humans are able to act on the basis of moral concepts (Ch. 6). Next we bring resources of our earlier arguments to bear on a critique of some of the usual categories under which these issues have been debated.

We end with a very brief postscript on the practical implications of our work.

1

Avoiding Cartesian Materialism

1 Descartes's Legacy

We noted in the Introduction that one is bound to end up with a defective view of human beings if one begins with Descartes's dualism and simply subtracts the mind. The resulting position, aptly named "Cartesian materialism",[1] is inevitably reductionistic. A physicalist account that does justice to human life requires attention to mental phenomena, of course, but also requires attention to the body and to material reality in general. That is, if we have failed to update our account of *res extensa* (material substance) since the days of Descartes, it will be impossible to conceive of humans without minds (or souls) as anything other than machines.[2]

In this chapter we first consider Cartesian materialism and its critics, and then begin to set forth an alternative account of physicalism. We shall pursue our defense of the thesis that physicalism need not entail reductionism throughout this volume. In the next chapter we aim to identify assumptions about the material world as a whole that, if not questioned, make reductionism seem to be inevitable.

Galileo is famous for his role in the Copernican revolution, but he played a comparable role in a development that has had equally revolutionary consequences: the substitution of a corpuscular or atomist conception of matter for ancient and medieval hylomorphism (the thesis that all physical entities are composed of the complementary principles of *matter* and *form*).[3] Hence, the soul could no longer be understood as the *form* of the body. In

---

[1] Daniel Dennett, *Consciousness Explained* (Boston: Little, Brown, and Co., 1991). We are using the term more broadly than Dennett does.

[2] John Searle has argued this elegantly and effectively in *The Rediscovery of the Mind* (Cambridge, Mass.: MIT Press, 1992); see esp. p. 25.

[3] Another significant change was the reduction of Aristotle's fourfold theory of causes to what he called efficient causation—i.e., the rejection of the notions of material, final, and formal causes. See Ch. 2, sec. 1.3 below.

light of this metaphysical shift, both body and soul had to be reinvented. René Descartes obliged, devising a dualism more radical than Plato's.[4] Mind/soul (*res cogitans*) and body (*res extensa*) are two kinds of substance with nothing in common.

"Mind" and "soul" could be used interchangeably in Descartes's writings. In addition to its new metaphysical status as substance independent of matter, Descartes's notion of soul differed from his predecessors' in rejecting the Aristotelian notion of degrees or orders of soul. For Aristotle and his followers the vegetative or nutritive soul was that which animated the body, the sensitive or animal soul accounted for perception and emotion, and the rational soul accounted for intellect and will. Descartes saw no need for a soul to animate the body—it is a machine that works on its own. Both emotions and sensations were caused by the body, but consciousness of them was an aspect of cognition. So whereas earlier the mind had been one part or function of the soul, now mind, cognition, consciousness (thus expanded to include consciousness of sensation and emotion) became the soul's sole function.

Only in recent years have the connotations of "mind" and "soul" so diverged that "soul" is used exclusively in religious contexts. It is interesting to note that where earlier translators of Descartes's *anima* (Lat.) or *l'âme* (Fr.) used "soul", more recent translations substitute "mind".

Richard Rorty has called our attention to the peculiarities of the concept of mind that we inherited from Descartes. The mind is an *inner theater* in which there appear a variety of kinds of "ideas": beliefs, desires, intentions, occurrent thoughts, mental images, and "raw feels" such as pains and sensory images.[5] The peculiarity appears when we ask: "Appear *to whom?*" Theologian Nicholas Lash refers to this observer as "that obstinate and anxious little person, the Cartesian ego".[6] We shall see below that this inner spectator is more difficult to banish from our self-image than the Cartesian mind itself. The peculiar idea that the real I is an observer within the mind is one of Descartes's many legacies from Augustine, who described himself as wandering through the roomy chambers of his memory.[7]

---

[4] Plato described the person as an eternal soul imprisoned in a mortal body, but without Descartes's opposition of material and non-material.

[5] Richard Rorty, *Philosophy and the Mirror of Nature* (Princeton: Princeton University Press, 1979), 24.

[6] Nicholas Lash, *Easter in Ordinary: Reflections on Human Experience and the Knowledge of God* (Charlottesville, Va.: University Press of Virginia, 1986), 89.

[7] Augustine, *Confessions*, book X, ch. 8; see Phillip Cary, *Augustine's Invention of the Inner Self: The Legacy of a Christian Platonist* (Oxford: Oxford University Press, 2000).

The reconception of matter that served as the basis of early modern physics meant that bodies, too, had to be reconceived. Bodies are still material substances, but what does that mean? Not "matter" defined as that which has the potential to be activated by *form*. Descartes conceived of bodies as machines. This idea, now grown so familiar, may not seem strange until we consider animals. A colleague once pointed out that undergraduates can be brought to question their assumptions by asking two questions: (1) Do animals have souls? and (2) Are animals machines?

2 Cartesian Persons without Minds

There have been various sorts of monistic accounts of human nature throughout the modern period. Descartes's contemporary, Thomas Hobbes (1588–1679), was a materialist, who described thinking as motions about the head and emotions as "motions about the heart". George Berkeley (1685–1753) took the opposite tack and resolved all of reality into ideas (perceptions). Nonetheless, dualism has been a very common position throughout the earlier years of the modern period. Yet, ever since Descartes proposed the pineal gland as the locus of mind–brain interaction, the problem of the relation of the mind and body has occupied philosophers. Whereas for Aristotle and his followers the mind/soul was but one instance of form, in modern thought the mind becomes something of an anomaly in an otherwise purely material world of nature. Before, matter (at least as unformed, prime matter) had been conceived to be entirely passive. For early moderns, matter is also passive, inert. But now, instead of being moved by immanent forms, it is moved by external forces—physical forces. This creates a dilemma: hold on to the immateriality of mind, and there is no way to account for its supposed ability to move the body; interpret it as a quasi-physical force, and its effects ought to be measurable and quantifiable as is any other force in nature. But nothing of the latter enters into modern physics.

A variety of solutions to the problem of causal interaction have been tried. Psychophysical parallelism is the view that physical events cause physical events, mental events cause mental events, and that the *appearance* of causal interaction between the mental and the physical is an illusion created by the fact that there is a pre-established harmony between these two independent causal chains. This harmony is either established at the beginning by God or is the result of constant divine interventions. Gottfried Wilhelm Leibniz (1646–1716) was one proponent of this theory. The inspiration for his monadology is said to have come from observation that clocks on various towers throughout the city kept the same time yet had no causal influence on one another. This position was never widely accepted, and lost whatever appeal it had with the growing atheism of modern philosophy. As Owen Flanagan says, "to have to introduce God to explain the workings of the mind... is to introduce a big Spirit in order to get rid of the perplexities of a world of little spirits, and to magnify the complications one presumably set out to reduce".[8]

Another attempt to solve the problem of mental causation is epiphenomenalism. This is the theory that conscious mental life is a causally inconsequential by-product of physical processes in the brain. This position has two drawbacks. First, why should causation from the physical to the mental be thought any less problematic than that from the mental to the physical? Second, there seems to be overwhelming evidence for interaction. These objections are not thought fatal, however, and some say that there is now solid scientific evidence for the thesis.[9]

As a consequence both of the problem with mind–body interaction and of advances in the cognitive neurosciences, the balance has shifted in philosophy of mind from dualism to a variety of forms of physicalism. Logical behaviorism, widely discussed between the 1930s and the early 1960s, claimed that talk of mental phenomena is a shorthand (and misleading) way of talking about actual and potential behavior. Gilbert Ryle (1900–76) ridiculed the Cartesian mind as "the ghost in the machine", claiming that the view of the mind as a substance or object rests on a "category mistake" of assuming that because "mind" is a noun there must be an object that it names.[10] While Ryle's critique of dualism is widely

---

[8] Owen Flanagan, *The Science of the Mind*, 2nd edn. (Cambridge, Mass.: MIT Press, 1991), 64. Explanation of divine action in a post-Newtonian world *is* a problem, but it is not helped by adding minds/souls to the universe.

[9] Epiphenomenalism is one interpretation of research by Benjamin Libet on "readiness potential" in motor activity—although it conflicts with Libet's own interpretation. See discussions in, e.g., Ned Block, Owen Flanagan, and Güven Güzeldere (eds.), *The Nature of Consciousness: Philosophical Debates* (Cambridge, Mass.: MIT Press, 1997), *passim*. For a contrary view, see Flanagan, *Science of the Mind*, 344–8.

[10] Gilbert Ryle, *The Concept of Mind* (London: Hutchinson, 1949).

accepted as definitive, it has not proved possible to translate language about the mind into language about behavior and dispositions.

A still current option is the mind–brain identity thesis. There are various versions: the *mind* is identical with the brain; mental *properties* (such as the property of being in pain, or believing some proposition) are identical with physical properties; or mental *events* are identical with brain events. The first of these is an infelicitous expression of the identity thesis, since it makes the very mistake for which Ryle criticized the dualists.

An important distinction in philosophy of mind is that between "type identity" and "token identity". Token identity is the thesis that every particular mental event or property is identical with *some* physical event or other; type identity is a stronger thesis to the effect that for every individual (and perhaps for every conscious species) each type of mental event is identical with a type of physical event. So, for instance, a type of sensation, such as pain, is identical with a particular type of neuron firing. Type identity would entail the reducibility of the mental descriptions to physical descriptions: once we know that the "C-fibers" firing is what we mean by "pain", the mentalistic term can drop out of neurobiological language.[11] Owen Flanagan says:

The implication that follows from the latter assumption is this: if type–type identity theory is true then reduction of psychology to neuroscience will eventually be possible. It is easy to see why reduction requires that all the concepts of the science to be reduced be translatable into the concepts of the reducing science. These translations are called "bridge laws" and once they are in place reduction merely involves replacing, synonym for synonym. Type–type identity statements, of course, are precisely the necessary bridge laws.[12]

This strong identity thesis may be true (within a given species and even across species) in cases such as pain sensations, but it is not true of higher-order mental states. While it is likely true for a given individual that a particular mental state (such as thinking about Socrates) is realized by a similar pattern of neural activity each time it occurs, it is not the case that one person's thought of Socrates is instantiated or realized in the same pattern as someone else's. In fact, given that no two brains are exactly alike,

---

[11] We repeat this favorite example from the philosophical literature even though it is not technically correct; C-fibers only transmit information from the site of the injury to the brain.

[12] Flanagan, *Science of the Mind*, 218.

even those of identical twins, it is not clear what it could mean to speak of exactly the same brain state in two different people.

While token identity is a step in the right direction because it recognizes the variability in different brains—the multiple realizability of mental states—we believe that it, too, is reductionistic, in that it provides too *narrow* an account of mental events. We shall argue that a mental event is not even token-identical to a brain event, because the mental *qua* mental is essentially co-constituted by the context in which the mental/neural event occurs. Thus, a mental event must be understood as a *contextualized* brain event.

We believe that philosophy of mind has been spinning its wheels for years for want of a suitable *concept* to describe the relation between mental events and brain events. Until recently the options were causation (interactionism, epiphenomenalism), correlation (parallelism), and identity (mind–brain identity, event identity, property identity). It is widely recognized that the concept of *supervenience* offers interesting new alternatives to these three. "Supervenience" was first employed as a technical term in ethics, and its sense is best conveyed by R. M. Hare's original example:

let us take that characteristic of "good" which has been called its supervenience. Suppose that we say "St. Francis was a good man". It is logically impossible to say this and to maintain at the same time that there might have been another man placed in precisely the same circumstances as St. Francis, and who behaved in them in exactly the same way, but who differed from St. Francis in this respect only, that he was not a good man.[13]

Donald Davidson's suggestion that mental events (or properties) supervene on brain events seems a promising alternative to the claim that mental events are identical to brain events.[14] One clear advantage is that supervenient properties are taken to be *multiply realizable*. That is, there is a variety of life patterns that satisfy the concept of goodness; there is a variety of devices that realize the property of being a calculator. This fits nicely with the recognition that different thoughts are realized differently in different brains.

---

[13] R. M. Hare, *The Language of Morals* (Oxford: Oxford University Press, 1966), 145; originally published in 1952.

[14] Donald Davidson, *Essays on Actions and Events* (Oxford: Clarendon Press, 1980), 214.

While we believe that supervenience will turn out to be an essential concept for explicating nonreductive physicalism, the use to which it has been put by most philosophers of mind has proved to be unhelpful. Jaegwon Kim has been most prolific in seeking an adequate definition of "supervenience"; he puts it in terms of property covariation: if mental properties are supervenient on brain properties, then there can be no difference in brain properties without a difference in mental properties. He concludes, rightly, we believe, that if this is how "supervenience" is to be defined, then it does not aid in avoidance of causal reductionism.

Kim now believes that causal reductionism is inevitable: he argues that mental properties will turn out to be reducible to physical properties unless one countenances some sort of downward causation. But such downward efficacy of the mental would suggest an ontological status for the mental that verges on dualism.[15] However, as mentioned above, we find the concept of downward causation entirely unproblematic, and will show that it does not require any sort of psychophysical dualism.

We shall return to the topic of supervenience in Chapter 5. We shall argue that the standard account of supervenient mental properties perpetuates Cartesian views of the mind as "inner" and as essentially contemplative or passive. We propose instead that supervenient mental states be understood to be co-determined by subvenient neural events *along with* social, environmental, and historical *context*.[16]

3 Critiques of Cartesian Materialism

Cartesianism has been described as a pernicious doctrine, with "more lives than a cat", to be "tolerated to our detriment in even its mild forms".[17] We

---

[15] See Jaegwon Kim, "The Myth of Nonreductive Materialism", in Richard Warren and Tadeusz Szubka (eds.), *The Mind–Body Problem* (Oxford: Blackwell, 1994), 242–60.

[16] This is the point of our objection (above) to the token identity thesis.

[17] J. Aronson, E. Dietrich, and E. Way, "Throwing the Conscious Baby Out with the Cartesian Bath Water", *Behavioral and Brain Science*, 15/2 (1992), 202–3. Descartes is called the "father" of modern philosophy, and as often happens to fathers when their children seek independence, he is now blamed for most of the ills of modernity. We invoke Descartes's name often, but with the caveat that what matters most about Descartes's thought is those aspects that his followers found reason to adopt and develop.

consider here criticisms of some of the ways in which Cartesian assumptions tend to be transposed into physicalist terms—that is, properties or functions of Descartes's concept of mind are transferred without evaluation to the brain.

3.1 Brain–Body Dualism

One of the most obvious ways in which Cartesian dualism becomes transmuted into Cartesian materialism is in substituting the brain for the mind and then *opposing* it to the body. Philosopher David Braine points out that most materialist accounts carry over a dualistic pattern of analysis of what goes on in human life, making sharp distinctions between the mental and the physical aspects of life.[18] This results in a brain–body dualism patterned after earlier mind–body dualisms.[19] We see this in neuroscience as well as in philosophy. Neurobiologist Joseph LeDoux, despite his extensive treatment of the role in emotion of physiological systems throughout the body, adopts a convention of using the word "body" to refer to all of the body *except* the brain.[20]

While it is easy to make a case for the role of the whole body in perception, sensation, emotion, and intentional action, linguists George Lakoff and Mark Johnson argue that the structure of reason itself comes from the details of our embodiment. By careful analysis of the language of *time, causation, mind, morality,* and other concepts, they show that the same cognitive mechanisms that allow us to perceive and move around in the physical world also create our conceptual systems and modes of reason. The raw materials for all of our thinking, even philosophical categories, are metaphorical extensions of language developed for describing everyday bodily actions and experiences. Thus, they hypothesize that "an embodied

[18] The arbitrariness of our categorization of mental and physical was made evident to one author in reading labels on Chinese herbal remedies that recommend them for combinations of ailments such as headache, anxiety, and indigestion.

[19] David Braine, *The Human Person: Animal and Spirit* (Notre Dame, Ind.: University of Notre Dame Press, 1992), 23.

[20] Joseph LeDoux, *The Emotional Brain: The Mysterious Underpinnings of Emotional Life* (New York: Simon & Schuster, 1996).

concept is a neural structure that is actually part of, or makes use of, the sensorimotor systems of our brains. Much conceptual inference is, therefore, sensorimotor inference."[21]

Thus, neuroscientist Antonio Damasio is correct in saying: "It is not only the separation of mind and brain that is mythical; the separation between mind and body is probably just as fictional. The mind is embodied, in the full sense of the term, not just embrained."[22]

Donald MacKay illustrates the embodied nature of mind by means of a thought experiment in which you imagine that you have your own operating brain sitting on a table in front of you (still functionally connected to your body and nervous system).[23] In this thought experiment, you electrically stimulate your own brain in the primary visual area, and, of course, you will see flashes of light. MacKay believes that several questions can be answered by this simple thought experiment:

1. Where are you? *You* are sitting in front of your brain. You are not on the table in front of you. Therefore, all descriptions of human mental experience are about the whole embodied person, not about the brain as a separate organ. MacKay makes a general point concerning the use of any mentalist terms with respect to human behavior: we should attempt to exercise "semantic hygiene"; that is, we should use mentalist language only to describe what the whole person is doing or experiencing, not to refer to the activity of some part of the person (such as the brain). The brain is necessary for mind, but not sufficient. In our terms, applying mentalist language to the brain is a category mistake—another version of Cartesian materialism.

2. Where are the physical events that are creating your experience of lights flashing? They are in the part of the brain being stimulated.

[21] George Lakoff and Mark Johnson, *Philosophy in the Flesh: The Embodied Mind and Its Challenge to Western Thought* (New York: Basic Books, 1999), 20. For an example of inference based on metaphorical content, see Ch. 4, sec. 4.2.

[22] Antonio R. Damasio, *Descartes' Error: Emotion, Reason, and the Human Brain* (New York: G. P. Putnam's Sons, 1994), 118.

[23] Donald M. MacKay, *Behind the Eye*, The Gifford Lectures, ed. Valerie MacKay (Oxford: Blackwell, 1991), 5–8.

Thus, brain activity is necessary (but not sufficient) for your subjective mental experience of lights flashing. But to reiterate: the mental event of seeing–lights–flashing is a phenomenon attributable to you as a whole person.

3. Where are the lights as far as you are concerned? They are out in your immediate action–space. They are part of your map of the external world—the field with which you are currently interacting. Mental events, even if dependent on internal physiological events, are about the field–of–action (or about you–in–the–field–of–action).[24]

3.2 Emotion

Rightly *and* wrongly, Descartes is accused of valuing reason at the expense of emotion. Those who believe he ignored the emotional life are wrong: his last book was a treatise on the emotions entitled *The Passions of the Soul* (1649). He recognized that the emotions originate in the body, and saw their purpose as disposing the soul to want the things for which the emotions prepare the body. For example, fear moves the soul to want to flee.

Despite his recognition of important functions for the emotions, Descartes followed a long line of predecessors in Western thought in emphasizing the necessity for the control of emotion by reason. He argued that the chief use of wisdom lies in becoming masters of our passions.

Damasio titled his recent book *Descartes' Error*, and the specific error he attacks is the belief that "the mechanisms of reason existed in a separate province of the mind, where emotion should not be allowed to intrude". This psychological hypothesis had been transferred by neuroscientists to a conception of the brain, leading them to envision separate neural systems for reason and emotion.[25]

Damasio's engaging account of the evidence against the Cartesian assumptions that had influenced him (and continue to influence most of his fellow neuroscientists) begins with the famous case of Phineas Gage. Gage was a worker on the Rutland and Burlington Railroad, "the most efficient and capable man" in its employ. Outside of his work he was a

---

[24] Of course, there is the issue of the "internalness" of thinking, which we shall approach in Ch. 5 in discussing symbolic and off-line processes. We shall suggest that the capacity for off-line symbolic thought can be understood as piggy-backing on processes involved in ongoing adaptive action.

[25] A. R. Damasio, *Descartes' Error*, p. xi.

responsible family man and upstanding citizen. In 1848 Gage was setting explosives to clear a path for new track. He had drilled a hole and poured the explosive powder into it. Thinking that sand had already been poured over the powder, he began tamping the powder with a heavy iron rod. A spark ignited the powder, blowing the tamping rod up through his cheek and out the top of his head.

Gage was stunned by the event, but did not lose consciousness, and was fairly well recovered within two weeks. He maintained his general intelligence and had no obvious cognitive deficits. However, Gage's personality and character changed. After the accident he was unreliable and capricious, and often socially inappropriate in his behavior. He soon lost his job, left his family, and lost whatever fortune he had accumulated. He spent most of the rest of his life as a transient and a circus side-show attraction.

Recently Hanna Damasio and her colleagues reconstructed the path of the iron rod, based on damage to Gage's skull. It was clear in the reconstruction that the primary damage occurred in the orbital frontal cortex, mostly on the left side.[26] Neurological literature provides accounts of a number of cases in which damage to similar regions of the brain results in similar changes of behavior and character.

The significant fact about these cases for present purposes is that whereas the Cartesian account of the relation between intellect and emotion, transferred to a hypothesis about brain function, would lead us to expect the lack of practical wisdom manifest by these patients to result from deficits to the higher cognitive faculties, the reverse is true. In these cases intellect and other cognitive faculties are typically intact. So what, exactly, is lost? Antonio Damasio was able to demonstrate that the capricious, unwise, and socially inappropriate behavior was the result of a deficit in the elicitation of *emotions*.

Damasio and his colleagues had individuals with damage to the same orbital frontal brain area participate in a game that required participants to learn not to make choices that had the possibility of large monetary gains, but also might result in very large monetary penalties. Predictably, individuals with orbital frontal brain damage could not resist the temptation to make such risky choices, resulting in the loss of all of their monetary stake. It was also found that normal individuals with intact frontal lobes responded with

---

[26] Hanna Damasio *et al.*, "The Return of Phineas Gage: The Skull of a Famous Patient Yields Clues about the Brain", *Science*, 264 (1994), 1102–5.

bodily physical changes (i.e., autonomic responses) indicative of negative emotions whenever they even contemplated such inappropriate choices. However, individuals like Gage who had damage to the orbital frontal areas of the brain had no such autonomic/emotional responses. Without the restraining influence of these negative emotional reactions to mere contemplation of making inappropriate responses, these individuals made impulsive and risky choices. Thus, emotional responses related to contemplated behavior, manifest in what Damasio called "somatic markers", were shown to be what was lost in patients like Gage. Anticipatory emotional responses signal important knowledge about the likely consequences of our actions, and are therefore necessary for wise and rational behavior. More recent research suggests that damage to this same brain area (the orbital frontal area) also disrupts the ability to experience regret over past decisions and behavior.[27]

Recent work in neuroanatomy has added significantly to the story of somatic markers. This research has focused on Von Economo neurons—very large neurons with cell bodies in the limbic cortex (specifically the anterior cingulate gyrus and fronto-insular cortex) that have very long axons projecting throughout much of the cerebral cortex.[28] The insular cortex receives information about the state of the body (i.e., visceral/emotive information regarding heart rate, blood pressure, peripheral blood vessel dilation, muscle tone, etc.). This information is integrated in the cingulate and fronto-insular cortex and, according to the hypothesis of neuroanatomist John Allman, is spread throughout the cortex as a way of informing cognition about bodily states. Integration of information about bodily states with other forms of cognitive processing is important for comprehension of emotion and signaling to ourselves the social significance of action and perception. The anterior cingulate cortex and the fronto-insular cortex, where this integration of bodily information takes place, are both structures that have been found in neuroimaging studies of humans to be highly active during states of empathy, shame, trust, regret, detecting the mental and emotional states of others, and making moral decisions. What is most interesting about Von Economo neurons is the relative uniqueness

---

[27] Nathalie Camille et al., "The Involvement of the Orbitofrontal Cortex in the Experience of Regret", Science, 304 (2004), 1167–70.

[28] John A. Allman, K. K. Watson, N. A. Tetreault, and A. Y. Hakeem, "Intuition and Autism: A Possible Role for Von Economo Neurons", Trends in Cognitive Sciences, 9 (2005), 367–73.

of these neurons to the human brain. This type of neuron is found in great abundance in the adult human brain, but are few in number in human infants and apes, and non-existent in lesser primates. Thus, in humankind the limbic cortex is supplied with a large quantity of relatively unique neurons that communicate subtle properties of bodily emotional reactions to the entire cerebral cortex. Therefore, we adult humans have a unique ability to incorporate into our cognitive processes information about the subtleties of bodily reactions that adds intuitive awareness ("gut feelings") to our thinking and behavioral regulation. Allman has hypothesized that abnormality in the development of Von Economo neurons may be a cause of autism.[29]

These are but a few lines of research that contradict the traditional Western view of reason and emotion as separate and hierarchically related. Emotions are critical for the emergence of behaviors that would be deemed both rational and uniquely human.

3.3 The Mind/Brain as Inner Theater

A subtle form of mind–brain identification occurs when the "inwardness" of the Cartesian mind is transferred to the brain. Descartes described himself as a thinking thing, distinct from and somehow "within" his body. Thinking is a process of focusing the mind's eye; but focusing on what? On ideas in his mind. Thus there arose the image of the "Cartesian theater": the real "I" is an observer "in" the mind, looking at mental representations of what is outside. A related factor in Descartes's epistemological writings is his focus on the solitary knower: "I am here quite alone"; "I stayed all day shut up in a stove-heated room where I was completely free to converse with myself about my own thoughts."[30]

In contrast, Austin Farrer reminds us that the subject of experience is the whole person. In an imagined dialogue about Dick, who has just received a meaningful communication from Tom, he asks: Is it Dick the man or Dick the brain who understands the signal? When we think of the visual organs and the nerves connected to them we are tempted to ask where the signals go. "All the way in—to where? To where Dick is? But isn't Dick all over himself?"[31]

---

[29] Ibid.

[30] René Descartes, Meditations on First Philosophy, First Meditation; Discourse on Method, part 2.

[31] Austin Farrer, The Freedom of the Will, The Gifford Lectures (1957) (London: Adam & Charles Black, 1958), 90.

Ludwig Wittgenstein has long been thought to be concerned primarily with language, but some recent commentators see him as premier critic of the Cartesian image of the mind as inner theater. Wittgenstein's *Philosophical Investigations* begins with a passage from Augustine's *Confessions*, which philosophical theologian Fergus Kerr paraphrases as follows:

The text from Augustine's *Confessions*... registers a strong sense of how the self-transparent little soul looks out from its head, hears the adults making various noises, watches them (through its eyes) as they lumber towards some item of middle-sized dry goods, and then, suddenly, on its own, makes the connection, in its own mind, between the sounds the adults emit and the objects they touch. Augustine pictures his infant self as already aware of its own identity (what is going on inside its own mind) and of the essence of human language.[32]

Wittgenstein was equally intent on criticizing *materialist* versions of this picture: "The idea of thinking as a process in the head, in a completely enclosed space, makes thinking something occult."[33] "One of the most dangerous ideas for a philosopher is, oddly enough, that we think with our heads or in our heads."[34]

The problem with Augustine's and Descartes's "inside-out" approach to philosophy is that it set Descartes up for a pernicious sort of skepticism: how to know that any ideas in the theater accurately represent the world outside—since one can never get outside to check.[35] Many prominent features of modern thought can be explained as a consequence of this approach to mind. In particular, it explains the persistence of the "problem of other minds": how do I know that there is an "I" inside other human bodies, that they are not robots?[36]

Critics of the notion of the Cartesian theater are now numerous in philosophy. They are also beginning to appear in the cognitive neurosciences as

---

[32] Fergus Kerr, *Theology after Wittgenstein*, 2nd edn. (London: SPCK, 1997), 56.

[33] Ludwig Wittgenstein, *Philosophical Grammar*, ed. R. Rhees, trans. A. Kenny (Berkeley and Los Angeles: University of California Press, 1974), § 64.

[34] Ludwig Wittgenstein, *Zettel*, ed. G. E. M. Anscombe and G. H. von Wright, trans. G. E. M. Anscombe (Berkeley and Los Angeles: University of California Press, 1970), § 605.

[35] Wallace I. Matson points out that most modern philosophers have been inside-out thinkers; outside-in thinkers, in contrast, begin with an account of the world and at or near the end of that account they explain the human mind and its knowledge in terms developed in that account. See *A New History of Philosophy*, 2 vols. (San Diego: Harcourt Brace Jovanovich, 1987), ii. 275.

[36] Sec. 3.4 explores how this problem is reflected in current psychology.

well. Philosopher Daniel Dennett coined the term "Cartesian materialism" to refer to the view one arrives at "when one discards Descartes' dualism but fails to discard the associated imagery of a central (but material) theater where 'it all comes together'—as if somewhere in the brain the results of sensory perception are 'presented' for subjective judgment".[37] Dennett and neuroscientist Marcel Kinsbourne criticize this view, first because there is nothing in the functional anatomy of the brain that suggests such a general meeting place. Subjective mental states are not the operation of a single brain subsystem, but are patterns of greater or lesser neural activation broadly distributed across most (if not all) of the brain. Second, they believe that the concept of a central theater distorts research on the nature and timing of perception, response initiation, and consciousness. Perception is not the arrival of pre-processed information at some central brain location; nor does response organization and initiation begin at a central brain locus and proceed outward.

According to the Multiple Drafts model developed by Dennett and Kinsbourne, "there is not a single, definitive 'stream of consciousness', only a parallel stream of conflicting and continuously revised contents". "[A]ll perceptual operations, and indeed all operations of thought and action, are accomplished by multitrack processes of interpretation and elaboration that occur over hundreds of milliseconds, during which time various additions, incorporations, emendations, and overwritings of content can occur, in various orders."[38]

Gerald Edelman and Giulio Tononi have a very similar view.[39] They believe that consciousness is not linked to the activity of a single brain area, but is a functionally integrated network of neuronal activity that extends across widely distributed areas of the cerebral cortex. The stream of consciousness is embodied in dynamic, moment-to-moment changes in the patterns of these functionally interconnected networks.

---

[37] Daniel C. Dennett and Marcel Kinsbourne, "Time and the Observer: The Where and When of Consciousness in the Brain", *Behavioral and Brain Sciences*, 15 (1992), 183–247, at p. 185.

[38] Ibid. 185. While we do not wish to enter the debate on the adequacy and coherence of Dennett and Kinsbourne's model, the facts he points to regarding the editing of information before it is consciously perceived are important examples of top-down processes in the brain.

[39] Gerald M. Edelman and Giulio Tononi, *A Universe of Consciousness: How Matter Becomes Imagination* (New York: Basic Books, 2000).

Psychiatrist and neurobiologist Leslie Brothers objects to ways in which Cartesian *individualism* appears in neuroscientific research. Research on humans and other primates has often been pursued as though brains operate the same way in isolation as they do in social contexts. Brothers sees this as a consequence of the practical problem that social contexts are complex and make controlled experimentation difficult. More important, though, is the Enlightenment assumption that the individual is logically prior to the social group. Brothers's book is entitled *Friday's Footprint,* and her point is to induce something of a *Gestalt* switch for those who see Robinson Crusoe's solitary life as normal, if not normative. In fact, she argues, mental life is only possible *at all* as a result of socialization, language, conversation.[40] This is consistent with our emphasis throughout on the context-dependence of the mental.

While the Cartesian ego had to prove to itself that there are other minds, the social brain, apparently, cannot help but believe there are. Brothers summarizes research showing that humans and other social primates are neurobiologically equipped to perceive *persons*—that is, bodies-with-subjectivity.[41] Neurons in and near the amygdala respond selectively to faces and to hand and eye movements that signal others' intentions.

The role of the brain in recognizing persons is further supported by the fact that brain lesions sometimes produce "misidentification syndrome", in which patients may attribute one mind to several bodies or perceive a body as being taken over by an alien mind. Brothers concludes that just as we are unable to hear a word in a familiar language without perceiving the meaning, so our brains have developed in such a way that when we perceive features such as body appearance, body movement, voice, and face, we are compelled to experience them as indicative of the presence of a person who has subjectivity.[42]

An important Cartesian assumption was that people know only their own minds directly, and that all else is known by inference. Neuroscientist Marc Jeannerod adds evidence for our in-built capacities to perceive others'

[40] Leslie Brothers, *Friday's Footprint: How Society Shapes the Human Mind* (New York: Oxford University Press, 1997).

[41] For a helpful account of the nature of persons and the relation between a person and a body, see Lynne Rudder Baker, *Persons and Bodies: A Constitution View* (Cambridge: Cambridge University Press, 2000). Persons are bodies with a first-person perspective.

[42] Brothers, *Friday's Footprint,* 4–5.

intentions and also notes cases in which it is possible to misidentify one's own intentions. When we perceive others' intentions, it is by means of "mirror neurons": that is, populations of neurons in several brain areas that selectively encode postures and movements performed by conspecifics. Much of this population of neurons overlaps that in parts of the motor cortex that is involved in performing those same actions. Thus, the intentions of others are represented by means of the same neural activity as one's own intentions to act. So it is one thing to represent the intention, and another to identify whose intention it is. Only in particularly unusual circumstances do we fail to make the proper attribution, such as in schizophrenia, which sometimes involves a tendency to mistake others' perceived intentions for one's own.[43]

So we see here that in a variety of ways both philosophers and neuroscientists are calling into question the Cartesian image of the person as having its locus solely inside—whether inside the mind or the brain—and are emphasizing our immediate awareness of and participation in the world, especially the social world.

3.4 Cartesian Psychology

The tendency to identify the person with something inside the head appears in psychology as well. With the exception of radical behaviorism, the field of psychology has been strongly influenced by an implicit (and sometimes explicit) Cartesian psychology in which the "self" (or the "ego", or a "central processor", or some other internal entity) replaces the soul in a Cartesian philosophy. That is, the external world is presumed to be experienced by, and behavior controlled by, some form of inner agent. When the psychological properties of human functioning are presumed to be manifestations of the inner self, rather than identified with whole persons, the "person" (understood as the inner agent) becomes dissociated from his or her behavior. Focus on an inner self also leads to reduced awareness of the social embeddedness of the person, as well as an instrumental view of other persons and of communities as either helps or hindrances to self-actualization or self-expression. In most forms of psychotherapy,

---

[43] Marc Jeannerod, "To Act or Not to Act: Perspectives on the Representation of Actions", *Quarterly Journal of Experimental Psychology*, 52A (1999), 1–29.

for example, to find the source of a client's psychological problems, or resources for their resolution, attention is turned inward toward the self (that is assumed to be the *real person*), rather than outward to the person in his or her social environment. In this view, the underlying source of a psychological problem is not to be found in how the person, as an embodied agent, functions in the social world, but is related to inadequacy in some inner, more essential part of the person.

Jack Martin, Jeff Sugarmann, and Janice Thompson note the way in which this inner focus distracts clinicians and others from economic, social, and political issues:

A final feature of psychology's sociocultural blindness may be seen in the by now well-known penchant of many clinical psychologists to relocate what most reasonably might be understood as economic, political, and/or social difficulties in the minds, psyches, and personalities of individual clients. Thus, there is a tendency in the literature of clinical psychology to assume that particular events and experiences (often described as "traumatic") lead more or less directly and automatically to particular symptoms and syndromes (e.g., posttraumatic stress disorder). Paradoxically, not only does such a maneuver place the problem to be treated within the client (and therefore within the realm of psychological intervention and expertise), but the assumed lawfulness of the connection between traumatic event and resultant psychological condition also leaves little room for the possible exercise of agency on the part of the individual client... And, of course, the administration of individual treatments by expert psychological practitioners directs both attention and resources from the possible alleviation of larger political, economic, and social problems.[44]

It is not that there is nothing going on "inside" that is worth considering. A person's behavior is regulated and modified by action-related maps of the world that are interior in some sense and that include a representation of one's self in space and time. Humans also have the ability to run off-line action simulations or behavioral scenarios—that is, simulations of potential actions that do not get released into bodily behavior. Often these off-line processes involve simulated speech in the form of self-talk

---

[44] Jack Martin, Jeff Sugarmann, and Janice Thompson, *Psychology and the Question of Agency* (Albany, NY: SUNY Press, 2003), 23–4. These authors' emphasis on recognizing the causal role of personal agency (rather than merely a resultant of biological and environmental causes) is consistent with the view to be established in this volume.

or imagined conversations. The main point to be made is that maps of self-in-the-world, although they contain a representation of the self, do not constitute a Cartesian self, in that they do not constitute a separate inner agent. Similarly, the subjective experience of running an off-line behavioral scenario is not proof of an inner agent. Only the person as a whole is an agent. The maps and simulations come into play in order to regulate action of the whole person. When coupled with a Cartesian view of persons, subjective experiences of our inner workings come to be treated as evidence of a separate inner *agent*, rather than descriptions of the functioning of the person as a whole.

An example of the distinction we are trying to make can be found in recent critiques of the concept of a Theory of Mind (often abbreviated ToM). The idea behind ToM is that in social interactions we impute mental states to other individuals. We use these imputations to predict their likely behaviors or to explain the behaviors we see. The development of the concept of a ToM has spawned a plethora of research, particularly in developmental psychology. It has been estimated that 1 per cent of the academic publications in 2003 that refer to infants or children also refer to a ToM.[45] Much of this research has involved study of individuals with autism whose deficits in social interactions many believe stem from an inadequate ToM.[46]

The theory of a ToM (sometimes referred to as the "theory theory") has been criticized by a number of writers as essentially Cartesian. That is, the child is viewed as an inner agent that constructs "theories" about other persons during social interactions. These "theories" are about the knowledge, desires, beliefs, and intentions of other persons that are presumed to be hidden from view. In the case of either the theorizer or the person who is the subject of the theorizing, it is presumed that an independent agent exists *within* the person, whose dealings are private and reflected only vaguely in expressed behavior. The inner agent of one person must construct adequate theories about the hidden attributes of the other person's inner agent in order to behave appropriately.

[45] Vasudevi Reddy and Paul Morris, "Participants Don't Need Theories: Knowing Minds in Engagement", *Theory and Psychology*, 14 (2004), 647–65.

[46] S. Baron-Cohen, A. Leslie, and Uta Frith, "Does the Autistic Child Have a 'Theory of Mind'?", *Cognition*, 21 (1985), 37–46.

Pressed by such criticisms of the Cartesian nature of this "theory theory", the term "mentalizing" has been increasingly used as a substitute. "Mentalizing" has the advantage of allowing for the possibility that mapping the knowledge, beliefs, intentions, and so forth of other persons is a *process* done by whole persons. The difference is captured by the title of one critique of the theory of a ToM: "Participants don't need theories."[47] Human beings do not have separate agents somewhere in the head that construct theories, but are themselves very complex agents that have various skills for mapping, remembering, and interacting with the social environment. The distinction is subtle, but critically important for our understanding of humankind.

3.5 Brains in a Vat

Richard Rorty has written extensively on the effects in philosophy and in Western culture generally of ocular metaphors for knowledge and the image of mind as a passive reflector of representations. There was apparently no particular reason why these metaphors seized the imagination of the founders of Western thought. Why view theoretical knowledge, he asks, as "looking at something (rather than, say rubbing up against it, or crushing it underfoot, or having sexual intercourse with it)"?[48] Rorty promotes a pragmatic view of knowledge—knowledge is what it is best for us to believe—and recommends getting rid of the notion of representation.

The physicalist analogue of mind as passive contemplator of representations is caricatured in philosophers' thought experiments involving brains in vats, kept alive and ingeniously hooked up so that they receive stimulation as if they were embodied and acting in the world.[49] This image stands as the quintessential physicalist analogue of the view that minds are passive recipients, "inside" the body, receiving information, through questionable channels from the "outside" world. The movie "The Matrix" presents similar imagery.

---

[47] Reddy and Morris, "Participants Don't Need Theories".

[48] Rorty, *Philosophy and the Mirror of Nature*, 39.

[49] See, e.g., Hilary Putnam, "Brains in a Vat", in *Reason, Truth, and History* (Cambridge: Cambridge University Press, 1981), 1–21. Putnam uses the image to argue that the language used by such consciousnesses would not refer to things in the (real) world because the appropriate causal connections to those things would be absent.

The neuroscientific analogue to the image of mind as mirror is found in all attempts to understand the neural underpinnings of language, perception, or thought without taking account of human activity. Various recent thinkers in various ways have been moving away from accounts that attempt to understand cognition apart from action. Lakoff and Johnson, mentioned above, hypothesize that cognition depends on neural networks first developed to enable *activity in the physical world*. Cognitive scientist Michael Arbib uses the concept of a *schema* as a bridge between cognitive science and neuroscience. Arbib emphasizes that a schema is a unit of *action*, thought, and perception. For example, to have the schema for a house is to know how houses fit into other aspects of human life, to be able to recognize one when one sees it, and to know how to do things such as locate the front door. Cognition and action are made possible by combining elementary schemas into complex systems.[50]

Donald MacKay, who began his career as a physicist studying information systems and then turned to neuroscience, also emphasizes the intrinsic relations between action and cognition. Perception is an organism's way of matching its activities to the world in order to be able to achieve its purposes. Rather than reject the notion of representation, as Rorty does, MacKay redefines it in a way suited to an account of mind as active. He defines a representation as a "conditional readiness to reckon" with something in the environment. To illustrate what he means in the simplest way possible, he proposes an analogy:

Suppose you drive your car up a semi-circular drive into its garage. In the garage the front wheels will be at a certain angle to the chassis. This angle of the wheels *implicitly represents* the curvature of the drive. It has set up in the car what you could call, in an obvious sense, a "state of conditional readiness": the car is "conditionally" ready to follow the required path if and when it is set in motion ... So the setting of the wheel implicitly represents the curvature of the drive in view of the goal of following the path of the drive. If it were not that the car (or car plus driver) had a goal of following the drive, the angle of the wheels wouldn't represent anything. But given that this is a goal-directed system, the angle of the wheels represents a "conditional readiness" to match the shape of the drive. You

---

[50] Michael A. Arbib, *The Metaphorical Brain, ii: Neural Networks and Beyond* (New York: Wiley-Interscience, 1989).

don't need to have a little picture of the drive inside the car for this purpose, all you need is the appropriate constraint on its repertoire of action.[51]

For an equally simple example from neuroscience, consider the following. If a tone is regularly paired with a puff of air to the eye of a rat or a rabbit, the animal will, over time, learn to blink when it hears the tone. It has been possible to show that this learning depends on the growth of synaptic interactions between particular sorts of neuron in the brain.[52] Thus, its "knowledge" of the relationship between the tone and an air puff to the eye is not an iconic sensory representation or image,[53] but rather an altered conditional readiness to respond to tones by eye-blinks. The altered synaptic interactions serve as a *representation* of the connection in the animal's environment between the sound and puffs of air. There is no sense in which the synaptic changes *resemble* these environmental events. It is, rather, a representation in MacKay's sense of a conditional readiness to respond. An important advantage in neuroscience of substituting an account of representation in terms of causes and potential behavior for an account in terms of inner images is that it eliminates the (apparent) need to postulate an inner observer in the "theater" to perceive the image.[54]

A similar idea can be found in the theory of "affordances" developed by J. J. Gibson and elaborated by other theorists.[55] The theory of affordances is a view of perception and action that emphasizes agent–situation interactions. Affordances are action possibilities available in the environment with respect to a particular organism. For adequate behavior with respect to the environment, abstract neural representations of objects are not necessary, but only the direct detection of action possibilities (affordances). Stairs provide a simple example. Although we have accessible in our memories residual visual images and abstract symbols for staircases, the direct perception of a particular staircase is sufficient as an affordance to cause us successively to lift our legs the appropriate height when encountering steps in our pathway.

---

[51] MacKay, *Behind the Eye*, 66–7.
[52] D. G. Lavond, "Role of the Nuclei in Eyeblink Conditioning", *Annals of the New York Academy of Sciences*, 978 (2002), 93–105.
[53] An iconic representation is one that resembles that which it represents.
[54] We shall have more to say about representations in Chs. 3 and 4.
[55] James G. Greeno, "Gibson's Affordances", *Psychological Review*, 101 (1994), 336–42.

Raymond Gibbs has recently attempted to rethink the entire field of cognitive psychology from the point of view of embodiment.[56] For Gibbs, "human cognition is fundamentally shaped by embodied experience."[57] He emphasizes the importance of memories of bodily experience in "theoretical accounts of how people perceive, learn, think, experience emotions and consciousness, and use language".[58]

A contemporary author, Andy Clark, provides one of the most forceful statements of the intrinsic relation between cognition and action. Clark's book is subtitled "Putting Brain, Body, and World Together Again". Nicholas Humphrey writes that while there have been several revolutions in psychology in its short lifetime, "no theoretical insight has ever seemed so likely to change the landscape permanently as the one in this brilliant... book".[59]

Clark draws his evidence from disciplines as diverse as robotics, neuroscience, infant development studies, and research on artificial intelligence. His central point is that a version of the old opposition between matter and mind persists in the way we try to study brain and mind while excluding the roles of the rest of the body and the local environment. We need to think of mind primarily as the modulator and regulator of ongoing embodied activity, and this requires abandonment of the dividing lines among perception, cognition, and action. His motto is: minds make motions; mind is always "on the hoof".

Clark joins cognitive scientists of other stripes in rejecting a model of neural processing based on formal symbolic thought, but, unlike some others, he does not reject the notion of internal representations altogether. Nor does he downplay the role of language in human thinking. Rather, he emphasizes the ways in which our thinking depends on "external scaffolding". One example is the observation that we do complicated arithmetical problems with the aid of external props such as paper and pencil or calculators. To the extent that we are able to do mental arithmetic, it is because we have internalized these embodied activities.

---

[56] Raymond W. Gibbs, Jr., *Embodiment and Cognitive Science* (Cambridge: Cambridge University Press, 2006).

[57] Ibid. 3.   [58] Ibid.

[59] Nicholas Humphrey, back cover of Andy Clark, *Being There: Putting Brain, Body, and World Together Again* (Cambridge, Mass.: MIT Press, 1997).

Clark ends his work with an imagined dialogue between John and his brain that serves nicely to conclude this section. The brain says, "A complex of important misapprehensions center around the question of the provenance of thoughts. John thinks of me as the point source of the intellectual products he identifies as his thoughts. But, to put it crudely, I do not have John's thoughts. John has John's thoughts."[60] That is, it is the person as a whole who perceives and acts, with the help of neural machinery, just as hands and eyes help us to grasp and see.

3.6 Moral Solipsism

Moral philosopher Mary Midgley does an excellent job of summing up our complaints about current physicalist accounts of human nature that uncritically carry over Cartesian baggage, but adds a criticism of her own. Midgley is critical of the moral solipsism that derives from the central Enlightenment view of personal identity:

Crudely—and we have to be crude here to bring the matter out into the open—this view showed the essential self as consisting in reason. That meant an isolated will, guided by an intelligence, arbitrarily connected to a rather unsatisfactory array of feelings, and lodged, by chance, in an equally unsatisfactory human body. Externally, this being stood alone. Each individual's relation to all others was optional, to be arranged at will by contract. It depended on the calculations of the intellect about self-interest and on views of that interest freely chosen by the will. The dignity of the will rests in its ability to assert reason against passive feeling, which is seen as relatively subhuman, emanating from the body.[61]

Midgley notes that on the rare occasions when philosophers do discuss the mind–body relation, "they rarely consider anything in that 'body' below the level of the neck. Either they focus exclusively on the mind's relation to the brain, or, more generally, on its relation to the physical world tout court. Flesh and bones (and unsurprisingly, women's minds) are still relatively neglected subjects in the field."[62]

---

[60] Clark, Being There, 224.
[61] Mary Midgley, "The Soul's Successors: Philosophy and the 'Body'", in Sarah Coakley (ed.), Religion and the Body (Cambridge: Cambridge University Press, 1997), 53–68, at p. 56.
[62] Midgley, "The Soul's Successors", 67.

This notion of the independent rational will resulted ultimately in the "moral solipsism" of nihilist Friedrich Nietzsche and existentialist philosopher Jean-Paul Sartre—the view that we need to invent our own values. Midgley's own account of human nature and human morality draws deeply from ethology,[63] and more recent works provide further evidence for the fact that sociality is a feature already found in non-human primates and in animals such as wolves and dolphins that live in large family groups. Primate ethologist Frans de Waal describes caring behavior and rudimentary awareness of issues of fairness among primates.[64]

Alasdair MacIntyre, in his recent book *Dependent Rational Animals*, argues persuasively that humans are not left to choose from scratch their moral goals. Humans, like dolphins, come equipped by nature with the goals of survival and of flourishing in ways appropriate to their species. What distinguishes humans from the higher animals is that, given our sophisticated language, we alone have the capacity to evaluate and sometimes overturn our natural hierarchy of goals—for instance, when we choose to sacrifice our well-being and even our lives for an abstract goal.

This capacity for moral reasoning requires instruction. So, in addition to being physically dependent on others during childhood, illness, and old age, we are dependent for our flourishing, in this uniquely human way, on moral teachers—those who by incorporating us into a moral community, train us in the practice of moral reasoning.[65] One could say that the point of MacIntyre's book is to explode the Enlightenment myths of autonomy and moral solipsism. We rely upon and develop MacIntyre's account of moral responsibility in Chapter 6.

4 Conclusion

Our purpose in this chapter has been to marshal some of the most important critiques of theories of human nature that incorporate, paradoxically,

[63] See Mary Midgley, *Beast and Man: The Roots of Human Nature* (Ithaca, NY: Cornell University Press, 1978).

[64] Frans de Waal, *Good Natured: The Origins of Right and Wrong in Humans and Other Animals* (Cambridge, Mass.: Harvard University Press, 1996).

[65] Alasdair MacIntyre, *Dependent Rational Animals: Why Human Beings Need the Virtues* (Chicago: Open Court, 1999). We treat MacIntyre's work at greater length in Chs. 3, 4, and 6.

remnants of Cartesian dualism into physicalist accounts of human nature that are specifically intended to be anti-Cartesian (i.e., anti-dualist). We have taken considerable trouble to do this, in order to clear the way for a more viable account of physicalism. So our task in what follows is to try to avoid all of the Cartesian errors we have criticized here, primarily the attribution to the brain alone of all the characteristics of the Cartesian mind. We constantly need to remind ourselves (as well as our readers) that mental phenomena pertain to the entire person, both brain and body, in social relations (at least, past social relations if not present ones), and active (at least at times[66]) in the physical world. This is easier said than done—we are as much children of Descartes as are our readers.

We claim, in contrast, that mental states are *contextualized* brain states. In other words, brain states constitute specific mental states only insofar as they bear appropriate interactive relations to things in the world and to the agents' ongoing processes and actions.[67] The mental cannot be understood as a property of individual, isolated, passive brains. A mental state is a brain–body event relevant to or directed toward a social or environmental context—past, present, or imagined in the future.

All theories that consider the mental life to be exclusively in the brain, and thus to be set apart from ongoing bodily adaptive interactions with the environment, we believe to be a form of Cartesian materialism. Mentality originates in a form of adaptation and environmental interaction that allows for greater behavioral flexibility. Therefore, it is not ordinarily a matter of something in the brain attending to something else in the brain, but rather a process of the entire person focusing on some aspect of the environment (even if the relevant environment is only imaginative at the moment) in order to maximize behavioral flexibility. Mental life is in its rudimentary form the record of person–environment interactions (real or hypothetical). The human capacity for abstract self-representation and internal self-talk (which we shall consider below) allows persons to *imagine* behavioral scenarios involving the self acting in various contexts. It is this unique process of abstract and analogical behavioral adaptability that gives

---

[66] We consider internal mental events to be simulated forms of action-in-the-world. Thus, "at times" in this sentence means that sometimes the actions are internal simulations, and sometimes they are bodily actions.

[67] We shall explain in Ch. 5 how this account differs from the functionalists' *definition* of the mental in terms of causes and effects.

the subjective impression of a Cartesian theater. However, we believe that even this abstract imaginative process is best thought of as the whole brain/body running an off-line analog of real environmental interactions involving the whole person.

In what follows we lay the groundwork for a more positive form of physicalism. In Chapter 2 we criticize the other holdover from Cartesianism: an early modern reductionist view of matter. We pursue a critique of mechanistic accounts of organisms in Chapter 3. The reader may have noticed that we have devoted an entire chapter to views of the mind, but have barely mentioned consciousness. This would appear odd (to say the least) to Descartes, who *defined* the mental as the content of consciousness. This is the subject to which we turn at the end of Chapter 3.

2

From Causal Reductionism to Self–Directed Systems

1 Reductionism in the Hierarchy of Complex Systems

We often meet with incomprehension when we argue for a physicalist account of human nature, but then add that we are *not* reductionists. We have come to see that the problem is not simply that we have not yet worked out the details so as to be able to make our case quickly and intelligibly. Rather, we are encountering a world view—a set of interrelated assumptions about reality—that makes a nonreductive physicalist account of the person seem impossible. This reductionist world view, developed in concert with early modern physics, makes it genuinely inconceivable how, if our bodies are indeed ordinary parts of the physical world, human beings could be the one exception to the universal rule of the laws of physics.

Our plan in this chapter is, first, to survey some of the history of the development of this world view and note the crucial metaphysical assumptions that together make reductionism appear to be inevitable. These assumptions include the notion that reality can be understood as a hierarchy of complex systems, such that lower-level entities become components of the next higher level. Yet the higher-level systems tend to be seen not as entities with causal powers in their own right but as mere aggregates of the basic constituents. The "atoms" (in the philosophical sense of being the most basic components) are attributed "ontological priority" over the things they constitute. Thus, all causation is bottom-up—it is the atoms that do all of the causal work, and the supposed causal capacities of macroscopic entities are seen as epiphenomenal. When this picture is coupled with a further assumption about causation, a holdover from

Aristotle, that nothing can be the cause of itself, the conclusion is that humans and other organisms cannot be the causes of their own behavior or characters. The behavior must be caused either by their microphysical parts or by environmental influences translated into microphysical causes. The goal of this chapter is to argue against the assumptions of atomism and bottom-up causation. What is needed is a concept of top-down causation—an account of how the higher-level system (i.e., the broader, more complex system) exerts causal influences on its parts—such that a complex system can be seen as (in part) its own cause, and thus to prepare the way for an account of sophisticated organisms as *agents*.

Thus, in section 2 we survey a variety of resources that call into question the simplistic account of causation derived from early modern physics, and end with Robert Van Gulick's account of downward causation as selective activation of the causal powers of an entity's constituents. This account needs to be developed and defended against the objection that such selection among lower-level processes must necessarily be by means of the ordinary causal forces described by physics, and hence that physics determines everything after all.

To meet this challenge, we first draw together the conceptual resources developed over the past fifty years in cybernetics, information theory, systems theory, chaos theory, emergence theory, and nonlinear mathematics (sec. 3). These resources provide the raw materials that have already been synthesized in Alicia Juarrero's account of downward causation via "context-sensitive constraints" exercised by the whole of a complex adaptive system on its components (sec. 4).

In the process we shall argue that the change from an atomistic, mechanistic, bottom-up view of entities to a systems perspective requires something akin to a paradigm change or *Gestalt* switch. Causal reductionism is so deeply ingrained in modern thinking that it cannot be argued away. We hope, therefore, not to argue the determinist out of her position, but to induce a change of perspective by examining a very simple example of a complex dynamic system, an ant colony, and contrasting bottom-up and top-down accounts of its behavior. We then return to the metaphysical issues introduced at the beginning to see how far we have come.

In section 6, however, we acknowledge how much further we need to go. An ant colony evidences a level of complexity and integration compa-rable to a *very* simple organism. Thus, by the end of this chapter we shall have the conceptual resources at hand to begin to consider causation within the sphere of biology. In short, if the previous chapter's goal was to exorcise the remnants of Ryle's "ghost in the machine", the goal of this chapter (and the next) is to transform the machine into a biological organism.

1.1 World Views and Hierarchies

The notion of a hierarchy of *beings* is essential for understanding Western thought from Plato to the beginning of the modern era. This conception helps to explain everything from Classical Greek views of beauty to Augustine's notion of original sin. In this hierarchy of beings, humans were generally located in the middle, with divine and angelic beings above, animals, plants, and inorganic beings below. Causation was understood to be top-down, so the ability of mind to move matter in the microcosmic human being went without saying. The problem was to account for the role of the body—for example, the sense organs—in affecting mental life.

The Copernican revolution marked the beginning of the end of this world view: if the Earth is not the center of the universe, then Aristotle's account of motions—earthy objects moving downward to find their natural place—had to be rejected and replaced with a new science of motion. As previously mentioned, Aristotle's hylomorphism was replaced by an even more ancient account of matter, Democritus's atomism.[1] On this account, common-sense entities came to be seen as ontologically secondary when contrasted with the primary ontological status of the atoms.[2] In other words, "wholes" are mere aggregates and are therefore epiphenomenal—causally impotent by-products of the behavior of their parts.[3]

This doctrine of the primacy of atoms led to a decidedly different conception of the hierarchical ordering of the universe: a conception of a hierarchy of *complex systems*, reflected in a hierarchical ordering of the *sciences*. The concept of the hierarchy of the sciences is already found in the writings of seventeenth-century philosopher Thomas Hobbes. Hobbes took geometry to be the basic science, because he conceived of geometrical figures as describing paths of motion. Next is physics, the study of the

---

[1] See below, sec. 2.1, for an account of the replacement of Aristotle's fourfold account of causation by an account that recognizes only efficient causation.

[2] Edward Pols, *Mind Regained* (Ithaca, NY: Cornell University Press, 1998), 64.

[3] Alicia Juarrero, *Dynamics in Action: Intentional Behavior as a Complex System* (Cambridge, Mass.: MIT Press, 1999), 21.

effects upon one another of moving bodies. Motions of particles in the brain and heart are the subject matter of moral philosophy, and civil philosophy is the study of the motions of men (we use the masculine term advisedly) in commonwealths.[4] Today the hierarchy of the sciences is taken (unproblematically) to include various levels of physics, chemistry, and the many levels of biology, from molecular biology through scientific ecology. Whether the human and social sciences can be added to the hierarchy has remained a contentious issue, one closely tied to debates about dualism. A dualist account of human nature provided grounds for saying that the human sciences are entirely distinct from the natural sciences, and even require a different kind of method. It is noteworthy that Hobbes, one of the first of modern physicalists, had no hesitation in including what we would now call psychology and political science.

The important difference, for our purposes here, between the ancient and medieval hierarchy and its modern replacement is the inversion of causal priority. The medieval Christian version of the hierarchy of beings took God to be the first mover, whose action in the natural world was mediated by angelic control of the movement of the planets. Modern physicists up through Newton's day maintained a semblance of the earlier notion of divine causation by understanding matter to be inert and governed by the laws of nature, and understanding those laws, in turn, as expressions of God's will. Yet, invention of the concept of the laws of nature sowed the seeds of an inversion of the causal hierarchy. By Laplace's day, a century later, not only was it unnecessary to posit God's occasional readjustment of the cosmic system, but the laws of nature came to be understood as intrinsic to the natural world itself.

If the universe is indeed created by a divine intelligence, that intelligence's very idea of the material universe it wishes to create carries with it just those laws. In that sense the laws are necessary rather than contingent: the creation of the material universe is necessarily the creation of the laws that permeate it and define it.[5]

Laplace is famous for his determinism; while he expressed his views in epistemological terms (an intelligence that knew all the laws of nature and

---

[4] This is Wallace Matson's summary in *A New History of Philosophy*, 2 vols. (San Diego: Harcourt Brace Jovanovich, 1987), ii. 288.
[5] Pols, *Mind Regained*, 66. Note that this conception of the laws of nature as necessary has been rejected in recent discussions of the "anthropic principle".

the position of all the beings of which nature is composed would know all future states of the universe), we shall see that the problematic consequences of this world view have to do with causation.

The atomist–reductionist–determinist world view made sense in the early days of modern physics. For various reasons, but largely to find alternatives to Aristotelianism, there was a revival of interest in ancient writers. Most important for science was Pierre Gassendi's (1592–1655) revival of Epicurean atomism,[6] which went back originally to Leucippus and Democritus. The essential assumption is that everything that happens is a consequence of the motions and combinations of atoms. The indestructible atoms ("atom" meant uncuttable) are not affected by these interactions. The atoms' characteristics were speed and direction of motion (and sometimes shape). Already the Epicureans recognized the implications of their views for human freedom. Atomism applies to human bodies and also souls, since they held a materialist account of the soul. So human beings, too, are merely temporary combinations of atoms, and their behavior is a result of the motions of the atoms. The very influential Hobbes held a view scarcely distinguishable from this.

So the essential features of the atomism of both the Epicureans and early modern natural philosophers are the following:

1. The essential elements of reality are the atoms.
2. Atoms are unaffected by their interaction with other atoms or by the composites of which they are a part.
3. The atoms are the source of all motion and change.
4. Insofar as the atoms behave deterministically (the Epicureans countenanced spontaneous "swerves", but Laplace and his followers did not), they determine the behavior of all complex entities.
5. Complex entities are not, ultimately, causes in their own right.

When modern scientists added Newton's laws of motion, it was then reasonable to assume that these "deterministic" laws governed the behavior of all physical processes. In modern terms, all causation is bottom-up (causal reductionism), and all physical processes are deterministic, because the ultimate causal players (the atoms) obey deterministic, laws. The

[6] Richard H. Popkin, *The History of Skepticism: From Savonarola to Bayle*, rev. and expanded edn. (Oxford: Oxford University Press, 2003).

determinism at the bottom of the hierarchy of the sciences is transmitted to all higher levels.

1.2 The Many Faces of Reductionism

So far we have not defined "reductionism". This is because the term refers to at least five related but distinguishable elements in the reductionist program. We distinguish as follows:

1. *Methodological reductionism*: a research strategy of analyzing the thing to be studied in terms of its parts. This was *the* focus of early modern science. It is now recognized that it needs to be supplemented by approaches that recognize the role of environment (more on this in secs. 2–5).

2. *Epistemological reductionism*: the view that laws or theories pertaining to the higher levels of the hierarchy of the sciences can (and should) be shown to follow from lower-level laws, and ultimately from the laws of physics. This was the focus of twentieth-century positivist philosophers of science. It is now thought to be possible only in a limited number of cases, and how "limited" is still controversial. It is closely related to logical or definitional reductionism: the view that words and sentences referring to a higher-level entity can be translated without residue into language about lower-level entities. The lack of such translatability in many cases is one of the reasons for the failure of epistemological reductionism

3. *Causal reductionism*: the view that the behavior of the parts of a system (ultimately, the parts studied by subatomic physics) is determinative of the behavior of all higher-level entities. Thus, this is the thesis that all causation in the hierarchy is "bottom–up".

4. *Ontological reductionism*: the view that higher-level entities are nothing but the sum of their parts. However, this thesis is ambiguous; we need names here for two distinct positions:

4a. One is the view that as one goes up the hierarchy of levels, no new kinds of non-physical "ingredients" need to be added to produce higher-level entities from lower. No "vital force" or "entelechy" must be added to get living beings from non-living materials; no immaterial mind or soul is needed to get consciousness; no *Zeitgeist* to form individuals into a society.

4b. A much stronger thesis is that only the entities at the lowest level are *really* real; higher-level entities—molecules, cells, organisms—are only composite structures (temporary aggregates) made of atoms. This is the assumption, mentioned above, that the atoms have ontological priority over the things they constitute. We shall designate this position "atomist reductionism" to distinguish it from 4a, for which we shall retain the designation of "ontological reductionism". It is possible to hold a physicalist ontology without subscribing to atomist reductionism. Thus, one might want to say that higher-level entities are real—as real as the entities that compose them—and at the same time reject all sorts of vitalism and dualism.[7]

In one sense the whole of this book is addressed to defining the difference between ontological reductionism and atomist reductionism. Ontological reductionism is entirely unobjectionable.[8] In fact, this is simply what "physicalism" means as applied to the human person. Atomist reductionism is another metaphysical position; but apart from its original formulation by ancient philosophers and early modern scientists, its meaning is more difficult to specify without employing, as we have done, the nonsense phrase "really real". Our focus in attacking it will be its counter-intuitive consequence for understanding causation; on this view, our common-sense notion that macroscopic objects (rocks, horses, people, e.g.) exert causal effects on one another is only a manner of speaking, so all macroscopic causation is in fact by means of micro-to-micro-causal processes. All of the real causal work is done at the lowest level. A major task of this book, then, will be to argue for what ought to be an obvious fact: agents are the causes of their own behavior. Our direct focus in this chapter in particular and in the volume as a whole will be the defeat of causal reductionism.

1.3 Contemporary Challenges to the Atomist-Reductionist-Determinist World View

The tidy Laplacean world view has fallen apart in more ways than we can catalogue here.

[7] Francisco J. Ayala distinguished among methodological, epistemological, and ontological reduction in his "Introduction", in Ayala and Theodosius Dobzhansky (eds.), *Studies in the Philosophy of Biology: Reduction and Related Problems* (Berkeley and Los Angeles: University of California Press, 1974), pp. vii–xvi. Arthur Peacocke pointed out the ambiguity in the meaning of "ontological reduction" in his *God and the New Biology* (Glouster, Mass.: Peter Smith, 1986).
[8] That is, when it is applied only to the cosmos itself, and no illegitimate inferences are drawn from it regarding the source of the cosmos.

1.3.1. Where Have All the Atoms Gone?   We shall not attempt to give a full or up-to-date assessment of the fate of the atoms. Atoms modeled as tiny solar systems have given way to a plethora of smaller constituents whose "particle-ness" is problematic. It is unknown whether these will turn out to be composed of even stranger parts, such as strings.

1.3.2. The Effects of Wholes on Parts   The original assumption that the elementary particles are unaffected by their interactions has certainly been challenged by the peculiar phenomenon of quantum nonlocality. Particles that have once interacted continue to behave in coordinated ways even when they are too far apart for any known causal interaction in the time available. Thus, measuring or otherwise tampering with one particle affects its partner, wherever it happens to be.

It may also be the case that the downward causation, for which we shall argue below, is the effect of action of the broader system on the otherwise indeterminate events at the quantum level. All of this is controversial, but if it is the case, as widely supposed, that certain processes at the quantum level are genuinely (ontologically) indeterminate, then decoherence or measurement—the interaction of a particle with something else in its environment—is what causes a determinate state to emerge. Cosmologist George Ellis says:

> Most quantum states are entangled states. This means that instead of thinking of bottom-up action by invariant constituents, one must consider cooperative effects between the constituent components that modify their very nature. Because of quantum entanglement, it is difficult even to talk of individual properties of constituent parts. But if the constituent particles at the microlevel don't even have individual properties, a simplistic reductionist view is undermined.
>
> In practice in many cases, because of decoherence (induced by the top-down effect of the environment) the system may be regarded as composed of individual particles with well-defined properties. But this approximation is valid only because the interference terms are small. In principle the particles have no separate existence. It can be suggested that our worldview should take this seriously, if indeed we take quantum theory seriously.[9]

---

[9] George F. R. Ellis, "Quantum Theory and the Macroscopic World", in Robert J. Russell *et al.* (eds.), *Quantum Mechanics: Scientific Perspectives on Divine Action* (Vatican City State and Berkeley: Vatican Observatory and Center for Theology and the Natural Sciences, 2001), 259–91, at p. 270.

We shall see below that when we consider parts from levels of complexity above the atomic and subatomic, the possibilities for the whole to effect changes are dramatic, and the notion of a part shifts from that of a component *thing* to that of a component process or function.

1.3.3. Whence Motion?   Scientific ideas about the ultimate source of motion and change have gone through a complex history of changes—too many to catalogue here. For the Epicureans, atoms alone were the source of motion. An important development was Newton's concept of inertia: a body will remain at rest or continue in uniform motion unless acted upon by a force. In Newton's system, initial movement could only be from a first cause, God, and the relation of the force of gravity to divine action remained for him a problem. Eventually three other forces, electromagnetism and the strong and weak nuclear forces were added to the picture.

Big-bang cosmology played a role, too. The force of the initial explosion plays a significant part in the causes of motion, and it is very much an open question whether there can be an explanation of that singularity.

1.3.4. How to Define Determinism?   There is no consensus on what the concept of determinism amounts to. If it is merely the claim that every event has a cause, then it may be false or harmless for present purposes. (We discuss causation below.) Important sources of the general determinist thesis were theological: God's foreknowledge or God's will. Theological determinism will not concern us here except insofar as it entered into the physico-theology of the early modern natural philosophers.

For the Epicureans, determinism was in nature itself. After the invention of the concept of laws of nature, we have to distinguish between claims that things or events *in nature* determine subsequent events and the claim that *the laws of nature* are deterministic. Again, much has changed during the modern period. The concept of a law of nature began as a metaphor: God has laws for human behavior and for non-human nature. While it was thought that nature always obeyed God's laws, God presumably could change or override his own laws. As noted above, by Laplace's day the laws of nature were thought to be necessary. But today, with multiple-universe cosmologies and reflection on the anthropic issue (why does the universe have laws and constants, from within a vast range of possibilities, that belong to a *very* small set that permit the evolution of life?), there is much room, again, to imagine that the laws of our universe are contingent.

Jeremy Butterfield argues that the only clear sense to be made of determinist theses is to ask whether significant scientific theories are deterministic. This is more difficult than it first appears, however. It may appear that the determinism of a set of equations is simply the mathematical necessity in their transformations and use in predictions of future states of the system. One problem, though, is that "there are many examples of a set of differential equations which can be interpreted as a deterministic theory, or as an indeterminate theory, depending on the notion of state used to interpret the equations".[10] See also our discussion of chaos (sec. 3.2.2).

Second, even if a theory is deterministic, no theories apply to actual systems *in* the universe, because no system can be suitably isolated from its environment. The only way around this problem would be to take the whole universe as the system in question. If the idea of a theory that describes the relevant (essential, intrinsic) properties of the state of the entire universe and allows for calculation of all future states is even coherent, it is wildly speculative.

A third problem, argued by Alwyn Scott, is the fact that many important theories dealing with higher levels of complexity (such as those governing the transmission of nerve impulses) can be shown *not* to be derivable from lower-level theories, and especially not from quantum mechanics.[11]

1.3.5. What Are Causes? Jaegwon Kim concludes that, given the vast diversity in the ways we use causal language, "it may be doubted wheth-er there is a unitary concept that can be captured in an enlightening philosophical analysis".[12] In ancient philosophy there were at least three alternatives: Aristotle's fourfold account of final, formal, material, and efficient causes. We have already described the atomist position, both with

---

[10] Jeremy Butterfield, "Determinism", in Edward Craig (ed.), *Routledge Encyclopedia of Philosophy* (London: Routledge, 1998), iii. 33–9, at p. 38.

[11] Alwyn Scott, *Stairway to the Mind: The Controversial New Science of Consciousness* (New York: Springer Verlag, 1995), 52.

[12] Jaegwon Kim, "Causation", in Robert Audi (ed.), *The Cambridge Dictionary of Philosophy* (Cambridge: Cambridge University Press, 1995), 110–112, at p. 112.

and without swerves to provide for contingency and human freedom. All along, though, it has been questioned whether indeterminacy provides for anything interesting in the way of human freedom. So from as early as the writings of Carneades (c.213–129 BCE), it has been argued by a minority that humans (and perhaps other entities) have the capacity to cause their own actions. Later proponents include Thomas Reid, Samuel Clarke, and C. A. Campbell. Alicia Juarrero has made the point that while Aristotle is usually counted among those who recognize that animals are the causes of their own action, he did so only with great difficulty. Aristotle's problem was based on his concept of potency. There is the potential to be acted upon and also, for organisms, the potential to act on something else. Juarrero writes: "For organisms to act on themselves they would have to possess simultaneously both the passive potency to be acted on as well as the active potency to act upon (something else). Since nothing can simultaneously possess both potencies with respect to the same property, nothing can act on itself."[13] In order to reconcile this principle with the obvious fact that organisms are indeed active, he needed his fourfold account of causation: the organism's form (soul) moves its passive body in the pursuit of final causes. Given the rejection of all the rest of Aristotle's account of matter and causation, it is odd that this principle continues to be assumed by almost everyone in contemporary philosophy. Juarrero asks how else to account for the current reluctance to countenance anything like agent causation—that is, a reluctance to speak of organisms as the cause of their own behavior. It is assumed that either the environment or a part of the organism (now the brain, not the soul) or some combination must be the cause.

We submit that since the demise of the Newtonian world view, philosophical accounts of causation have not kept pace with science. If one still holds to all of the rest of the atomist–determinist world view of early modern science, it does indeed seem impossible to understand how something like an organism can be a genuine causal player in its own right.

1.4 Towards a Nonreductive World View

Vitalism is the thesis that living organisms have some special entity or force in addition to non-living matter. It is a translation into biological terms of the ancient idea of soul as the life force (anima in Latin), and has been

---

[13] Juarrero, Dynamics in Action, 17.

promoted throughout the modern period as an alternative to mechanistic conceptions of organisms. Attempts in philosophy of biology early in the twentieth century to provide an alternative to both mechanism and vitalism led to some creative critiques of reductionism. For example, American philosopher Roy Wood Sellars accepted the picture of nature as forming a hierarchy of levels of complexity and noted, in light of evolutionary theory, that these levels had emerged over time. Sellars criticized reductionists on the grounds that they overemphasized the matter of which higher-level entities are composed, in contrast to the organization. Recognition of the role of patterns and functions led Sellars to propose that new levels of causality emerge at higher levels of organization.[14]

Sellars's emphasis on organization, pattern, and function is an important step in the critique of causal reductionism, but it is not alone sufficient. A promising avenue for understanding what Sellars might mean by "new levels of causality" is in the development, over the past half-century, of the concept of *downward* or *top-down* causation. Philosophical theologian Austin Farrer was clearly groping for such a concept in his 1957 Gifford Lectures. Seeking a way to argue that higher-level patterns of action, in general, may do some real work, and thus *not* be reducible to the mass effect of lower-level constituents, he says that "in cellular organization the molecular constituents are caught up and as it were bewitched by larger patterns of action, and cells in their turn by the animal body".[15] However, Farrer's metaphor of higher-level organizations "bewitching" the lower-level constituents is the sort of talk that deepens the mystery, rather than clarifies it.

Neuropsychologist Roger Sperry argued for the replacement of reductionism in psychology by the "cognitivist paradigm". According to this new account, he says,

The control upward is retained but is claimed not to furnish the whole story. The full explanation requires that one also take into account new, previously nonexistent, emergent properties, including the mental, that interact causally at their own higher level and also exert causal control from above downward. The

---

[14] Roy Wood Sellars, *The Philosophy of Physical Realism* (1932; repr. New York: Russell and Russell, 1996); idem, *Principles of Emergent Realism: The Philosophical Essays of Roy Wood Sellars*, ed. W. Preston Warren (St Louis: Warren H. Green, 1970).

[15] Austin Farrer, *The Freedom of the Will*, The Gifford Lectures (1957) (London: Adam & Charles Black, 1958), 57.

supervenient control exerted by the higher over the lower level properties of a system ... operates concurrently with the "micro" control from below upward. Mental states, as emergent properties of brain activity, thus exert downward control over their constituent neuronal events—at the same time that they are being determined by them.[16]

The question remains of *how* it can be that mental properties exert downward control over their constituent neural events. Sperry sometimes speaks of the properties of the higher-level entity or system *overpowering* the causal forces of the component entities.[17] However, elsewhere in his writings Sperry refers to Donald Campbell's account of downward causation, which we explore below. In sections 3 and 4 we explore how a complex system becomes a cause in its own right.

2 Defending Downward Causation

If causal reductionism amounts to the assumption that causation is always bottom-up—that is, from part to whole—then the needed antidote is in fact something like the downward or top-down causation that Sperry set out to describe. At a small conference dedicated to this and related topics, the question constantly raised during coffee breaks was whether we were attempting to describe something that was ubiquitous and almost trivial, or something rare and mysterious. We have become convinced that it is ubiquitous and would not even be terribly interesting were it not for the hold that causal reductionism has on the imagination. It is obvious, is it not, that the environment (or the broader system of which the entity or system in question is a part) often has a causal effect on that entity or system? Is it not, therefore, also obvious that the behavior of an entity is often *not* determined solely by the behavior (or laws governing the behavior) of its parts? And is it not obvious that a sophisticated entity such as an organism has control of (some of) its own parts—the horse runs across the pasture, and all of its parts go with

---

[16] Roger W. Sperry, "Psychology's Mentalist Paradigm and the Religion/Science Tension", *American Psychologist*, 43/8 (1988), 607–13, at p. 609.

[17] Roger W. Sperry, *Science and Moral Priority: Merging Mind, Brain, and Human Values* (New York: Columbia University Press, 1983), 117.

it? If all of this is so obvious, why is causal reductionism still so widely assumed?[18]

Sellars commented in 1932 that reductionism is a result of the fact that "the ontological imagination was stifled at the start by [the picture] of microscopic billiard balls". The problem with having billiard balls in mind when thinking about causation is that billiard balls have so few ways of interacting causally, and no meaningful *structures* can be formed with them. So in this section we lay out a series of considerations to stimulate the imagination as to how causal accounts in terms of laws governing the micro-constituents of entities can and must be complemented (not ignored or refuted) by additional considerations.

2.1 Shifts in Science: From Newton to Prigogine

The progress of science from Newton's day to our own has, in many ways, required adjustment to earlier, simpler views of physical causation, and in understanding relations between higher and lower levels of complexity. We shall mention but two of these developments: thermodynamics and evolutionary theory.

If the image of microscopic billiard balls has been powerful in shaping the modern imagination, the metaphor of the clockwork universe has been even more so. Clocks are *mechanisms* in the sense that they are systems composed of solid, inert, and separable parts, such that when the system is put in motion, the parts move one another in a determined order.[19] Clocks are *designed*, as far as possible, so that their behavior is strictly determined by their parts and insensitive to environmental conditions. So in (old-fashioned) clocks we have (it seems) a perfect example of part–whole causation: the behavior of the whole is strictly, regularly, mechanistically determined by the behavior of its parts.

The development of thermodynamics in the nineteenth century introduced a very different sort of bottom-up causation. The temperature and

---

[18] We have anecdotal evidence that reductionism is no longer universally assumed. We have been surprised in the past few years to find students whose immediate reaction is anti-reductionist, and in fact we sometimes have to work to make reductionism plausible. We suspect that in this respect (as well as in many others) we are witnessing a subtle shift in philosophical assumptions. For an account of the relation between this transition and other "postmodern" developments, see Nancey Murphy, *Anglo-American Postmodernity: Philosophical Perspectives on Science, Religion, and Ethics* (Boulder, Colo.: Westview Press, 1998).

[19] Farrer, *Freedom of the Will*, 51.

pressure of a macroscopic volume of gas *are* determined by the behavior of the particles of which it consists, but in a very different sort of way than the clock. It depends only on their mean kinetic energy, not on the particular movements of particular particles. In this case, the higher-level (macroscopic) system is said to be *decoupled* from the lower. This decoupling justifies a change in level of discourse—one can speak of the macroscopic properties without reference to their atomic or molecular constituents. Notice how very different bottom-up causation via averaging across multiple lower-level states is from the kind of causation we see in mechanisms, in which the particular behavior of each part has a particular effect on the whole.

We noted (parenthetically) that the clock *seems* to be an ideal metaphor for the Newtonian universe, but thermodynamics reminds us that it is not. Newton's universe, once set in motion, should run forever, but clocks obey the second law of thermodynamics—they run down. So while we design them to be independent of the environment in certain respects, they are nonetheless essentially dependent on the environment in the sense of needing energy input.

Recognition of the law of entropy created a background that made biology appear problematic in a new way. Classical thermodynamics presented a universe with a history: over time systems change from order to disorder, and not the reverse. Yet another nineteenth-century development, Darwinian evolution, forced upon us a recognition of the extent to which complexity and order have *increased* over time. This is not, on the face of it, contrary to classical thermodynamics, since organisms are not closed systems. Yet, "by giving the environment in which an organism is located a central role as the agent of selection, Darwin's writings returned context to science for the first time in centuries".[20]

The shift from Aristotelian to modern physics involved the rejection of teleological explanation (final causes), but biology inevitably reintroduced the concepts of *function* and *goal-directedness*. We find goal-directedness both in human inventions and in the biological world. Machines are structured by agents in ways that harness the laws of nature in order to achieve some goal—for example, the laws of combustion to push the piston in a gasoline engine. It is not possible to say what a piston *is* without describing its *function* in the engine.

---

[20] Juarrero, *Dynamics in Action*, 4.

At the level of complexity in the natural world that we call *life*, the correlative concepts of purpose (or goal[21]) and function become essential for understanding causal processes. The most rudimentary goals of organisms are survival and reproduction; the causal histories of most biological structures can be understood only in terms of their function in light of one or both of these goals. Thus, the existence and structure of a given part of the organism cannot be understood merely in terms of the microprocesses by which it is constructed in the individual organism. We have to refer as well to the function it serves in the larger system, which is the organism as a whole (and perhaps to the system which is the organism as a whole in its environment). In the next chapter we consider a variety of levels of biological activity, and we shall see that goal-seeking processes are ubiquitous.

The existence of functional structures in machines, of course, is explained by the actions of purposeful agents. The existence of functional structures and processes in nature can be fully explained only by including the concept of *selection*. Philosopher of science Donald Campbell has crafted an account of how a larger system of causal factors can exert downward efficacy on lower-level entities by means of selection. His example is the role of natural selection in producing the remarkably efficient jaw structures of worker termites and ants:

Consider the anatomy of the jaws of a worker termite or ant. The hinge surfaces and the muscle attachments agree with Archimedes' laws of levers, that is, with macromechanics. They are optimally designed to apply maximum force at a useful distance from the hinge ... This is a kind of conformity to physics, but a different kind than is involved in the molecular, atomic, strong and weak coupling processes underlying the formation of the particular proteins of the muscle and shell of which the system is constructed. The laws of levers are one part of the complex selective system operating at the level of whole organisms. Selection at that level has optimised viability, and has thus optimised the form of parts of organisms, for the worker termite and ant and for their solitary ancestors. We need the laws of levers, *and organism-level selection* ... to explain the particular distribution of proteins found in the jaw and *hence* the DNA templates guiding their production ... Even

---

[21] Not, for the most part, *conscious* goals. Francisco Ayala distinguishes three categories of biological phenomena in which teleological explanations are pertinent: (1) when the purpose or goal is consciously anticipated by the agent, (2) in self-regulating systems, and (3) when structures are anatomically and physiologically constituted to perform a certain function. Francisco J. Ayala, "Teleological Explanations versus Teleology", *History and Philosophy of the Life Sciences*, 20 (1998), 41–50, at p. 46.

the *hence* of the previous sentence implies a reverse-directional "cause" in that, by natural selection, it is protein efficacy that determines which DNA templates are present, even though the immediate micro determination is from DNA to protein.[22]

Campbell provides this example to illustrate the following set of theses:

(1) All processes at the higher levels are restrained by and act in conformity to the laws of lower levels, including the levels of subatomic physics.

(2) The teleonomic achievements at higher levels require for their implementation specific lower-level mechanisms and processes. Explanation is not complete until these micromechanisms have been specified.

But in addition:

(3) (The emergentist principle) Biological evolution in its meandering exploration of segments of the universe encounters laws, operating as selective systems, which are not described by the laws of physics and inorganic chemistry, and which will not be described by the future substitutes for the present approximations of physics and inorganic chemistry.

(4) (Downward causation) Where natural selection operates through life and death at a higher level of organisation, the laws of the higher-level selective system determine in part the distribution of lower-level events and substances. Description of an intermediate-level phenomenon is not completed by describing its possibility and implementation in lower-level terms. Its presence, prevalence or distribution (all needed for a complete explanation of biological phenomena) will often require reference to laws at a higher level of organisation as well. Paraphrasing Point 1, all processes at the lower levels of a hierarchy are restrained by and act in conformity to the laws of the higher levels.[23]

Campbell says that he uses the term "downward causation" reluctantly, "because of the shambles that philosophical analysis has revealed in our common-sense meanings of 'cause'". If it is causation, he says, "it is the back-handed variety of natural selection and cybernetics, causation by a selective system which edits the products of direct physical causation."[24] Biochemist Arthur Peacocke has pointed out that downward causation

---

[22] Donald T. Campbell, "'Downward Causation' in Hierarchically Organised Biological Systems", in F. J. Ayala and T. Dobzhansky (eds.), *Studies in the Philosophy of Biology*, 179–86, at p. 181.
[23] Ibid. 180.   [24] Ibid. 180–1.

in the sense of environmental "editing" of lower-level causal processes is widely recognized in biology.[25]

While classical thermodynamics explains how an organism can maintain its structure by taking in energy from the environment, and while Darwin's account explains the selection among complex life forms, there was no explanation until a century later of how complex structures (organisms) could come into existence in the first place. Ilya Prigogine received the Nobel Prize in 1977 for solving this problem. We return to Prigogine's account of nonlinear, far-from-equilibrium systems below. It will be helpful beforehand to marshal some of the philosophical concepts needed to describe his work.

2.2 Resources from Philosophy of Science

While it may be the case that the attempt to analyze the concept of causation has reached an impasse,[26] resources for describing the causal complexities introduced by the progress of science have been accumulating. We consider some of these here.

2.2.1. Laws of Nature versus Initial Conditions   With the advantage of hindsight, the beginning of the end of causal reductionism can be seen already in Laplace's determinism: *given* knowledge of the position of all of the particles in the universe, all future states could be deduced. That is, as neopositivist philosophers of science of the mid-twentieth century pointed out, explanation of physical phenomena requires knowledge both of the laws governing transitions from one state to another and of the *antecedent* (or *initial* or *boundary*) conditions of the system.[27] It does not appear that these terms are adequately distinguished or used consistently across disciplines. "Initial conditions" suggests an element of time, and can be taken to refer to the state of a system prior to a particular transformation (at $t = 0$). "Boundary conditions" are sometimes defined as elements of a system's environment with which the system interacts; but in other cases the term also refers to the state or structure of the system itself. In the latter case, the initial conditions of a system are also (part of) its boundary conditions

---

[25] Arthur Peacocke, *Theology for a Scientific Age*, 2nd edn. (Minneapolis: Fortress Press, 1993), 53–9.

[26] Cf. Kim, "Causation", in Audi (ed.), *Cambridge Dictionary of Philosophy*, 12.

[27] Carl G. Hempel and Paul Oppenheim, "Studies in the Logic of Explanation", *Philosophy of Science*, 15 (1948), 135–76.

at $t = 0$. Note that the terms are used still differently in mathematics. We shall speak of initial conditions and use "boundary conditions" to refer to environmental conditions, while we use "structural conditions" to refer to structure internal to the entity or system itself.

Until recently, science has focused on the laws, and has taken the conditions to be unproblematic. In fact, the success of experimental science has depended on scientists' ability to control or systematically vary the conditions in order to perceive regularities in the behavior of the entities in question. In simple systems regularities will appear despite a wide variety of conditions. For example, the acceleration of a body in free fall is the same regardless of the height from which it is dropped. We can see, though, that it takes very little in the way of increased complexity to make the conditions critical. Consider the difference between a body in free fall and one rolling down an inclined plane. For the former, conditions such as air density and the shape of the object make negligible differences within a wide range of conditions. For an object rolling down an incline, however, conditions such as degree of tilt and smoothness of the surface make a great deal of difference, as does the shape of the object itself. These complications are well represented if we think of a pinball machine instead of billiard balls.

German philosopher of science Bernd-Olaf Küppers argues that the biological sciences have recently undergone a paradigm shift, due to recognition that complex systems such as living organisms are extremely sensitive to initial conditions, and, therefore, explanation of the causes of the conditions themselves is at least as important as investigation of the laws governing the processes that transpire within the organism. He argues, further, that while much of the progress of biological science now comes from understanding the physico-chemical processes that create the conditions upon which biological processes depend, there is an inherent limit to the reductionist program.[28] We pursue parallel arguments below, but for now the importance of the distinction between conditions and laws is simply that it provides a way of thinking about how top-down and bottom-up causation may be complementary: top-down determination

---

[28] Bernd-Olaf Küppers, "Understanding Complexity", in Robert J. Russell, Nancey Murphy, and Arthur R. Peacocke (eds.), *Chaos and Complexity: Scientific Perspectives on Divine Action* (Vatican City State and Berkeley: Vatican Observatory and Center for Theology and the Natural Sciences, 1995), 93–106, at p. 103.

of the various conditions is entirely compatible with the uninterrupted operation of lower-level laws, once those conditions are in place.

2.2.2. Triggering and Structuring Causes   Philosopher Fred Dretske has provided valuable terminology for understanding the relationship between causal laws and initial/boundary conditions. He distinguishes between triggering causes and structuring causes, as illustrated by the following example: "A terrorist plants a bomb in the general's car. The bomb sits there for days until the general gets in his car and turns the key ... The bomb is detonated (triggered by turning the key in the ignition) and the general is killed." The terrorist's action was the structuring cause, the cause of its being the case that turning the key sets off the bomb.[29] Another example: the design of the computer hardware and the programming of the machine are structuring causes that make it the case that a triggering cause, such as striking a key on the computer keyboard, will have the effect it does. In contrast to a computer, where predictability is essential, the pinball machine is structured so that approximately the same triggering cause (shooting the ball) will have strikingly different outcomes. We need not turn to such complex examples, however: our previous example of a marble rolling down an incline will serve as well. Cutting grooves in the surface is a structuring cause that determines, along with the law of gravity, the trajectory of the marble.

So for many purposes it is an oversimplification to represent a causal sequence simply as a series of events: $E \rightarrow E \rightarrow E$ as the modern paradigm assumes. Instead, we need to think of *two* series of events: those leading up to the triggering (T) of the effect (E) as well as those leading up to the condition under which T is able to cause E. Figure 2.1, adapted from Dretske, is intended to represent these intersecting strings of triggering and structuring causes. The Ts represent a series of causes leading up to the triggering of the effect E, while the Ss represent another series leading to the condition C such that T is able to cause E.

Attention to structural conditions and their causes helps make clear what Sellars was pointing to in emphasizing pattern and organization in addition to matter, and also what Sperry was attempting to articulate when he

---

[29] Fred Dretske, "Mental Events as Structuring Causes of Behavior", in John Heil and Alfred Mele (eds.), *Mental Causation* (Oxford: Clarendon Press, 1995), 121–36, at pp. 122–3.

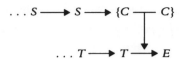

Figure 2.1. A series of structuring causes leading up to a condition such that a triggering cause is able to cause an effect.

pointed out that the behavior of higher-level entities cannot be understood without taking into account the spatio-temporal patterning of physical masses, and when he claimed, in addition, that such patterns exert causal influences in and of themselves.[30]

2.2.3. Defining Downward Causation   We have already made use numerous times of the concept of downward causation, and (in sec. 2.1) we introduced Donald Campbell's account of evolutionary selection as an instance. Recall that our goal in this volume is the defeat of neurobiological reductionism. To do so, we need to tackle causal reductionism itself, which we define as the assumption that the behavior of an entity is determined by the behavior (or the laws governing the behavior) of its parts. *Note that it is not determinism* per se *that is at issue.* Thus, we have looked at a variety of ways in which a causal account in terms of lower-level laws is inherently incomplete, and have suggested that downward causation will be a matter of fixing these other factors, not of violating or overriding the lower-level laws themselves.

In this section we present what we believe to be the best account of downward causation so far. By the end of this chapter we shall have drawn on resources from the interrelated areas of information theory, systems theory, complexity studies, and nonlinear dynamics, and will have endorsed Alicia Juarrero's account of whole–part constraint in dynamic systems as the best synthesis of this material and defense of the cogency of the concept of downward causation.

A word on terminology: while "top-down causation" and "downward causation" are the appropriate contrastive terms to "bottom-up causation", and while these are the terms currently used in the literature, they are, unfortunately, open to misinterpretation. This happens when one forgets that "higher" in this context refers to two systems, S and S', where S' is

[30] Roger W. Sperry, "The Import and Promise of the Cognitive Revolution", *American Psychologist*, 48/8 (1993), 878–85, at p. 880.

said to be a higher-order system because it incorporates S and relates S to its environment; in other words, because it includes S and the effect on S of boundary conditions not themselves constituent of S. The discussions of downward causation in philosophy of mind usually fail to take this into account. Mental properties are said to supervene on brain properties, diagrams are drawn with the mental properties *above* the brain properties, and then the question is posed as to how the mental property "up there" can influence the next brain property "down here". As we shall argue in Chapter 5, our account of the mental in terms of a brain event *in context* emphasizes that the sense in which a mental event or property is "higher" is in fact that it participates in a broader, more complex causal or semantic system. Thus, while we continue to speak here of "downward causation", we would be less subject to misunderstanding if we employed Juarrero's "whole–part constraint" throughout.[31]

The concept of downward causation is used extensively in psychology, cognitive science, and related disciplines. In fact, it is critical in the interpretation of biological data at all levels of complexity. A recent survey of research articles published over the prior five years yielded 286 articles in the biomedical literature and 182 articles in the psychological literature that used the term "top-down". In the vast majority of these articles, the implication was that phenomena at some higher level of organization of a complex system had a downward causal influence on the events that were being studied at a lower level. Top-down processes have been used to explain energy metabolism in a complex system such as mitochondria or entire cells,[32] the influence of working memory on the attention-related activity of neurons of the temporal lobe of the brain,[33] the recovery of three-dimensional volume information from more elementary two-dimensional images in visual perception,[34] the modulation of conscious auditory perception by

---

[31] Arthur Peacocke has adopted this convention as well. See *inter alia* "God's Interaction with the World: The Implications of Deterministic 'Chaos' and of Interconnected and Interdependent Complexity", in Russell *et al.* (eds.), *Chaos and Complexity*, 263–87.

[32] M. D. Brand, "Top-Down Elasticity Analysis and its Application to Energy Metabolism in Isolated Mitochondria and Intact Cells", *Molecular and Cellular Biochemistry*, 184 (1998), 13–20.

[33] L. Chelazzi, J. Duncan, E. K. Miller, and R. Desimone, "Responses of Neurons in Inferior Temporal Cortex during Memory-Guided Visual Search", *Journal of Neurophysiology*, 80 (1998), 2918–40.

[34] C. Moore and P. Cavanagh, "Recovery of 3D Volume from 2-Tone Images of Novel Objects", *Cognition*, 67 (1998), 45–71.

volition,[35] and expectancy-based illusions of differences in the perceived weight of objects.[36] Indeed, there is a major debate between particle physicists and solid-state physicists over whether particles in very complex systems (from superconductors to ordinary crystals) obey new, emergent, and nonreducible laws—that is, whether elementary particles are subject to top-down influences that cannot be explained at the level of the particles themselves.[37] Thus, from particle physics to cellular metabolism, to subjective judgments, top-down influences created by properties of more complex systems have proved necessary to explain the available scientific data.

Alwyn Scott helps us to see how pervasive downward causation must be. As one goes up the hierarchy of complex systems, the laws at each level permit larger and larger numbers of entities, states, and processes. For example, if a protein could be composed of (only) 85 amino acids (actually some have 200), the number of proteins allowed by the laws of chemistry would be 10^{110}, which is equal to the mass of the universe measured in units of the mass of a hydrogen atom times the age of the universe measured in picoseconds.[38] Biochemistry itself can never explain why the world contains the proteins it does, since it explains equally well why we could have had a vast number of sets of entirely different ones. We need top-down accounts that involve information about what existing proteins do in organisms' bodies in order to explain why these ones exist and others do not—we need to know their *functions* in larger systems.

As one goes up the hierarchy of complexity, the numbers of possibilities increase. It is estimated that given the number of neurons in a human brain and the number of synapses, there are $10^{10^{14}}$ possibilities for different brain-functional configurations.[39] Neither genetics nor any other branch

---

[35] D. A. Silbersweig and E. Stern, "Towards a Functional Neuroanatomy of Conscious Perception and its Modulation by Volition: Implications of Human Auditory Neuroimaging Studies", *Philosophical Transactions of the Royal Society of London*, Series B: *Biological Sciences*, 351 (1998), 1883–8.

[36] R. R. Ellis and S. J. Lederman, "The Golf-Ball Illusion: Evidence for Top-Down Processing in Weight Perception", *Perception*, 27 (1998), 193–201.

[37] George Johnson, "Challenging Particle Physics as Path to Truth", *New York Times*, 4 Dec. 2001; reproduced by Metanexus Newsclippings, <www.metanexus.net.>

[38] Scott, *Stairway to the Mind*, 29. Physicist Walter Elsasser coined the term "immense" for numbers larger than 10^{110}. Scott says (p. 20): "Why is this definition of interest? Because one generally assumes that any finite number of items can be put on a list and examined, one by one. For an immense number of items, however, this is not possible … [A]ny computer that could ever be built … would not have enough memory capacity to store an immense list. Even if a single atom were used to remember each item on the list, it would still be far too long."

[39] Owen Flanagan, *Consciousness Reconsidered* (Cambridge, Mass.: MIT Press, 1992), 37.

of biology can explain why the few billions of human brains that have ever existed have been as they have been and not otherwise. The role of top-down causation in shaping the brain is, of course, a central interest of this book.

While the concept of downward causation is used extensively in the literature of science, it appears to have received little attention in philosophy of science since the publication of Campbell's essay in 1974. Recall that Campbell's account combined bottom-up production of genetic variation with feedback from the environment exercising a selective effect on those variants. Figure 2.2 represents these processes.[40]

Recently Robert Van Gulick has written on downward causation, spelling out in more detail an account based on selection. He makes his points about top-down causation in the context of an argument for the nonreducibility of higher-level sciences. The reductionist, he says, will claim that the causal roles associated with special-science classifications are entirely derivative from the causal roles of the underlying physical constituents. Van Gulick replies that the events and objects picked out by the special sciences *are* composites of physical constituents, yet the causal

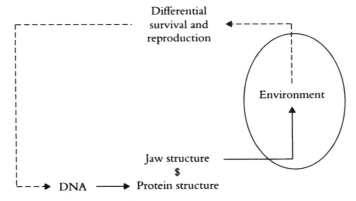

Figure 2.2. A representation of Campbell's account of downward causation. The solid arrow represents the bottom–up causation from the biological level; the dollar sign represents the fact that the jaw structure *supervenes* on the protein structures produced by the genome; the dashed arrow represents the downward causation (selection) from the environment.

[40] Using $ to represent supervenience may be our greatest contribution to philosophy: it resembles an *S* for "supervenience" and is a key on the computer for which (American) philosophers otherwise have little need.

powers of such objects are not determined solely by the physical properties of their constituents and the laws of physics. They are also determined by the *organization* of those constituents within the composite. And it is just such patterns of organization (i.e., sets of boundary conditions, structures) that are picked out by the predicates of the special sciences. These patterns have downward causal efficacy, in that they can affect which causal powers of their constituents are activated. "A given physical constituent may have many causal powers, but only some subsets of them will be active in a given situation. The larger context (i.e. the pattern) of which it is a part may affect which of its causal powers get activated... Thus the whole is not any simple function of its parts, since the whole at least partially determines what contributions are made by its parts."[41]

Such patterns or entities are stable features of the world, often in spite of variations or exchanges in their underlying physical constituents. Many such patterns are self-sustaining or self-reproducing in the face of perturbing physical forces that might degrade or destroy them (e.g., DNA patterns). Finally, the selective activation of the causal powers of such a pattern's parts may in many cases contribute to the maintenance and preservation of the pattern itself. Taken together, these points illustrate that "higher-order patterns can have a degree of independence from their underlying physical realizations and can exert what might be called downward causal influences without requiring any objectionable form of emergentism by which higher-order properties would alter the underlying laws of physics. Higher-order properties act by the *selective activation* of physical powers and not by their *alteration*."[42] None of this involves either *violation* of the laws of physics or *causal overdetermination*, because it all has to do with selecting and channeling physical processes, not interrupting or overriding them.

2.3 Prospect

We have presented Van Gulick's account of downward causation, which we believe is correct, but unlikely to convince the determinist. It is open to the following objection. Van Gulick says that the larger context of which a physical constituent is a part "may affect which of its causal powers

---

[41] Robert Van Gulick, "Who's in Charge Here? And Who's Doing All the Work?", in Heil and Mele (eds.), *Mental Causation*, 233–56, at p. 251.
[42] Ibid. 252.

gets activated".[43] The reductionist will ask *how* the larger system affects the behavior of its constituents. To affect it must be to *cause* it to do something different from what it would have done otherwise. Either this is causation by the usual physical means, or it is something spooky. If it is by the usual physical means, then those interactions must be governed by ordinary physical laws, and thus all causation is bottom-up after all. This is the challenge. In the next section we provide resources for understanding the stable patterns, broader causal systems, to which Van Gulick refers, and then in section 4 present Juarrero's solution in terms of *constraints*.

3 Toward an Understanding of Self-Directed Systems

We reported above (sec. 2.2.1) on Küppers's claim that a paradigm shift has occurred in biology, in which the heretofore taken for granted initial and boundary conditions of living systems have become the focus. We claim that a comparable shift is occurring in a variety of fields. It is a shift from mechanistic to systems thinking. It rejects the earlier bias in favor of concrete entities over processes; it recognizes that complex wholes can be more than aggregates. It employs the concepts of boundary conditions, structures, information, feedback, and downward causation. There are two pressing questions. One is the question with which we ended the previous section: how do downward causes cause? The other is: how do complex systems (apart from human creations) come into existence? In this section we present a variety of perspectives on complex systems, including responses to the question of how such systems organize and direct themselves.

3.1 Feedback and Information

Many of the complex systems we shall be concerned with below operate on information as well as on energy. Thus, we include a brief excursus on the topic of information. Information transmission (in the ordinary sense, as opposed to that of "information theory"[44]) requires a four-part system: a sender, a receiver, a channel, and a referent—something for the

[43] Ibid. 251.
[44] Information theory is a mathematical theory concerned purely with measuring quantities of information, usually thought of in terms of reductions of uncertainty.

information to be *about*. So a thermometer whose mercury level is at the mark labeled 80 is a (potential) sender of information, and someone who looks at it is a (potential) receiver. The receiver need not be conscious: a thermometer can transmit information to a switching mechanism or some other device. For the person looking at a thermometer, the channel includes the light rays reflected from the surface of the instrument and the visual apparatus of the observer. The referent is the level of heat in the room. It is common to say that a unit (or flow) of information is *realized* by some state (or process) of the physical system. Alternatively, we may say that the property of being a unit of information *supervenes* on the state of a physical system (we spell this out in detail in Ch. 5, sec. 2.3). A supervenient state is multiply realizable; that is, the same information state can be realized by a variety of different devices—there are in fact a wide variety of kinds of thermometers.

Donald MacKay points out that there are systems that run on both energy and information. That is, there are systems, both natural and of human design, that need a certain amount of information in order to fulfill a particular function. MacKay emphasizes that chains of cause and effect can be traced at either the supervenient information level or at the subvenient energy level. So, for example, the operation of a thermostatically controlled heating system can be explained in terms of information flow or in terms of mechanics and electrical circuits, and "there is not the slightest hint of rivalry between that (information engineering) explanation and the explanation that a physicist would give of what every element in the loop is doing".[45] The concept of an information-using system means that systems can be goal-directed—systems whose behavior is modified in light of information regarding their success or failure in pursuit of their goals. A thermostatically controlled heating system is a simple example. MacKay represents such systems using Figure 2.3.

This system incorporates the causal concepts discussed in the previous section. The thermostat is *structured* (i.e., its *structural conditions* have been designed) so that it is *triggered* by changes in the temperature of its environment (*external boundary conditions*) to perform its *function*: namely, to act in such a way as to pursue the *goal* of keeping the room temperature

---

[45] Donald M. MacKay, *Behind the Eye*, The Gifford Lectures, ed. Valerie MacKay (Oxford: Blackwell, 1991), 47.

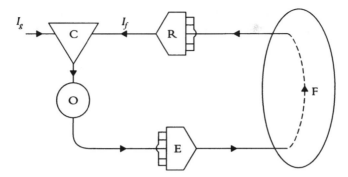

Figure 2.3. The simplest model of an information-using and goal-directed system. Here the action of the effector system, E, in the field, F, is monitored by the receptor system, R, which provides an indication I_f of the state of F. This indication is compared with the goal criterion I_g in the comparator, C, which informs the organizing system, O, of any mismatch. O selects from the repertoire of E actions calculated to reduce the mismatch. *Source*: MacKay, *Behind the Eye*, The Gifford Lectures, ed. Valerie MacKay (Oxford: Blackwell, 1991), 47.

within certain boundaries. There are several levels of *downward causation* here. First, consider the furnace as a causal system, S. This system has two possible states: on or off. Information about the design of the furnace and the physics upon which it operates explains what is going on in each of these states. However, only with knowledge of the larger system, S', which includes the furnace and the thermostat, do we know what causes S to be on or off.

S' is an information-using system designed to receive and use information about its environment. The capacity to respond to information about the environment, not just to ordinary causal influences, makes for a more interesting sort of downward causation. While the furnace has only two possible states, on and off, the thermostat and furnace together have something like 41 relevant operational states (I_g). The whole system can be turned on or off, and if it is on, the temperature can be set anywhere from 45 to 85 degrees. Physics and a combination of mechanical and electrical engineering can give a complete causal account of everything that happens in the furnace, the thermostat, and the room (S''), but nothing in physics or engineering can begin to explain why the temperature is set at 70 degrees. So human action, a third level of downward causation, is needed to explain why S'' is in the state it is. MacKay says: "A characteristic thing about all the systems we have been discussing—automatic pilots, thermostats and the like—is that they have something ending in free space. The thermostat has a knob waiting for the housewife to come and set it."[46] This feature is represented in Figure 2.3 by the fact that there is no indication of how I_g gets set.

Living organisms, of course, do not have knobs waiting to be set. Here we make a connection with Campbell's downward causation via selection in the evolutionary process. Homeostatic feedback processes that regulate the operation of an organism's metabolism and behavior have built-in goal states (e.g., keeping body temperature within a narrow range). These goal states have been set by eons of selection: organisms with inappropriate values fail to survive or to reproduce as efficiently. To represent this double feedback we replace the DNA and the jaw and protein structures of Figure 2.2 with a copy of Figure 2.3. Figure 2.4 shows the role of downward causation in specifying the features of DNA that result in the homeostatic mechanism within the organism having the goal state it does (I_g). The organism's DNA also influences its organizing system (O), as well as its effector system (E) such as its jaw structure with its effects in the environment.

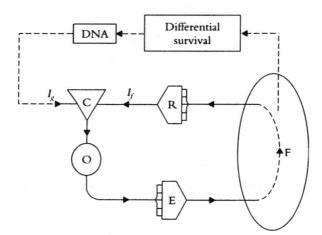

Figure 2.4. The simple information-using and goal-directed system enhanced by an indication of how evolution serves to set the goal criterion, I_g, by means of genetic preservation (DNA) of goals leading to differential survival.

[46] MacKay, *Behind the Eye*, 49.

3.2 Cybernetics, Systems Theory, and Complexity Studies

We have been emphasizing the importance of pattern and structure in causal systems. The world is full of systems that maintain stable patterns despite constant change in the matter of which they are composed and despite perturbations. A very simple example of a self-sustaining pattern is the whirlpool that forms when water is let out of the sink. The matter that forms it (the water) is constantly changing, yet the shape of the whirlpool remains nearly constant and will form again if it is perturbed. An organism is a prime example of a self-sustaining structure. The minimum capacities for an organic system to count as living are self-maintenance and reproduction. Self-maintenance in response to injury generally involves repair of the structure using materials taken from elsewhere in the organism and ultimately from the environment. The human organism is a relatively stable structure despite the fact that the matter of which the body is composed is almost entirely replaced after seven years.

Cybernetics, systems theory, and, more recently, theories of complex systems, all in related ways shift attention from the matter of which a system is composed to its structure, the functions of its parts, its means of interacting with its environment, and the information transfers involved therein. Before looking at these contributions, consider the shift in perspective represented in the following statement:

Causal explanation is usually positive. We say that billiard ball B moved in such and such a direction because billiard ball A hit it at such and such an angle. In contrast to this, cybernetic explanation is always negative. We consider what alternate possibilities could conceivably have occurred and then ask why many of the alternatives were not followed, so that the particular event was one of the few which could, in fact occur ...

In cybernetic language, the course of events is said to be subject to restraints, and it is assumed that, apart from such restraints, the pathways of change would be governed only by equal probability.[47]

The term "cybernetics" was coined by Norbert Weiner in 1947, and is based on the Greek word *kubernētēs* (helmsman). Cybernetics is the attempt to describe in general terms the sorts of systems (such as the thermostat in the preceding section) that run on information as well as energy.

---

[47] Alan B. Scrivener, "A Curriculum for Cybernetics and Systems Theory", <http://www.well.com/user/abs/curriculum.html> (accessed 19 Nov. 2004).

3.2.1. Systems Theory   The development of systems theory is traced to Ludwig von Bertalanffy, also writing in the 1940s. This is the attempt to describe in abstract terms the organization of systems, independently of their substance and spatio-temporal scale. Cybernetics and systems theory are closely related; if there is a distinction to be made, it is that the latter places greater emphasis on structure, while the former emphasizes process, function, and control.

The basic concepts of systems theory include, of course, the concept of a *system* itself. A system is distinguished from an aggregate in that the properties of components of a system are *dependent* on their being a part of the system in question. For example, a component may be described in functional terms—the coil in a thermostat is not a thermometer unless it is appropriately integrated into the device as a whole.

Juarrero makes a distinction between the concepts of *organization* and *structure*. The structure of a (physical) system is its physical configuration, but its organization (the important concept for describing systems) is given in relational terms. Thus, the structure of an organism changes as it grows, while its basic organization (at least after the embryonic stage) does not. The identity of a system over time is dependent on identity of organization, not of structure.[48]

Notice the shift in ontology here. The components of a (physical) system are not the material ingredients, but components described in relational (e.g., functional) terms. From a systems perspective, a mammal is composed of a circulatory system, a reproductive system, and so forth, *not* of carbon, hydrogen, and calcium. The "motions" of the atomists' "microscopic billiard balls" have dropped out of the account entirely. The organismic level is entirely *decoupled* from the atomic level.

All systems have *boundaries,* without which the system could not be recognized or defined. Systems may be defined as *open* or *closed*. An open system needs to be characterized not only in terms of its own organization but also in terms of its transactions with its environment. The elements of the environment with which it interacts may be called its *external structure* or its *boundary conditions*. *Inputs* and *outputs* may be material, energetic, or informational.

As noted above, systems are related hierarchically. The system that is *S* in its environment is a higher-order system, *S'*. There is an important

[48] Juarrero, *Dynamics in Action*, 109–10.

difference between what Howard Pattee calls *structural* and *control hierarchies*. Juarrero says: "When levels of *structural hierarchies* do not interact, they can be described by dynamical equations that deal with only one level at a time. In *control hierarchies,* on the other hand, the upper level exerts an 'active authority relation' on the components of the lower level."[49] She quotes Pattee:

In a control hierarchy, the upper level exerts a specific, dynamic constraint on the details of the motion at the lower level, so that the fast dynamics of the lower level cannot simply be averaged out. The collection of subunits that forms the upper level in a structural hierarchy *now also acts as a constraint on the motions of selected individual subunits. This amounts to a feedback path between levels.* [The description of] the physical behavior of a control hierarchy must take into account at least two levels at a time.[50]

More often, though, three levels are involved, the focal level (e.g., an organism), its components (e.g., its nervous system), and its interactions with the environment.

Systems vary in regard to degrees of integration (i.e., tightly or loosely causally interacting parts; greater or lesser interaction with the environment),[51] stability (degree of fluctuation around a constant value); and resilience (ability to absorb changes and still persist).[52]

3.2.2. Nonlinearity and Chaotic Systems   Some systems can be modeled by means of linear equations, others only by nonlinear equations. A linear system is one in which the sum of two causes yields an effect that is the sum of the two individual effects. A nonlinear system is one in which this is not the case. These are called "nonlinear" because the equations needed to model their transformation from one state to the next are nonlinear. That is, one starts from an initial state x_0 and uses the equation to calculate x_1, but then x_1 is fed back into the equation to calculate x_2. A significant example is the "logistic equation", $x_{n+1} = kx_n(1 - x_n)$.

[49] Ibid. 114.
[50] Ibid. quoting Harold Pattee, "The Physical Basis and Origin of Hierarchical Control", in *idem* (ed.), *Hierarchy Theory* (New York: George Braziller, 1973), 77; Juarrero's emphasis.
[51] Nancey Murphy and George F. R. Ellis, *On the Moral Nature of the Universe: Theology, Cosmology, and Ethics* (Minneapolis: Fortress Press, 1996), 26.
[52] Juarrero, *Dynamics in Action*, 111.

"Chaos theory" is now almost a household word, so we shall not spell out details. Chaotic systems are nonlinear systems that can be modeled by the logistic equation when the constant k falls within the range 3.57–4. Such systems (many of which are biological) are said to be maximally sensitive to the value of initial conditions. Because of the level of sensitivity involved, differences in two systems' initial conditions that are too small to measure will still make significant differences in how the two systems evolve over time. Thus, such systems are intrinsically unpredictable.[53]

Does this mean that chaotic systems are indeterministic? The best answer seems to be: there is no way to know. Some have argued for indeterminacy on the basis of unpredictability, but this is to confuse the epistemological order (what can be known) with the ontological order (what makes things happen). A contrary move has been to point out that the logistic equation is a deterministic equation and to argue from this to the determinacy of the systems. This, too, is a mistake (see sec. 1.3.4 above). The equation is a *model* of the system that predicts *general* features of the behavior of such systems (such as the major fluctuations seen in insect populations). The equation does not address causation (there is nothing in it that feeds or kills insects). So the mathematical determinateness of the equation has no implications for the causal processes of the system.

Furthermore, because of the great fluctuation in chaotic systems and their intrinsic unpredictability, there is no way to *test* whether the (deterministic) equation is in fact an adequate model of the system. Robert J. Russell and Wesley Wildman put it this way: universal determinism in nature is usually taken as a metaphysical assumption. Given the growing consensus that (at least) some quantum effects are indeterministic, it ought to be treated instead as a metaphysical *hypothesis*. The role of chaos theory, then, is to introduce a fundamental limitation on our ability to test the determinist thesis. This is the limit on the extent to which it can be known that "a chaotic dynamical system in mathematics, with its 'deterministic'

---

[53] Alwyn Scott (personal communication) points out that Henri Poincaré predicted unpredictable systems over a century ago: perfect knowledge of laws of nature with only approximate knowledge of initial conditions (even though very close) will result over the long term in *very* inaccurate predictions. In 1972 Edward Lorenz confirmed Poincaré's expectation using computer models for weather prediction. The title of his lecture was "Predictability: Does the Flap of a Butterfly's Wings in Brazil Set Off a Tornado in Texas?" See Henri Poincaré, *Science and Method* (1903) (Chicago: St. Augustine's Press, 2001); and E. N. Lorenz, *The Essence of Chaos* (Seattle: University of Washington Press, 1993).

equations, provides the right explanation for 'randomness' in a natural system".[54]

Thus, one conclusion to draw from chaos theory is a recognition of the extent to which universal causal determinism *is* merely a metaphysical assumption. The ability to model systems that appear to behave randomly by means of a deterministic equation looked like confirmation for the determinist, but has instead opened our eyes to the many systems in nature whose determinism *or indeterminism* can never be known. The fact that some chaotic systems are sensitive to initial conditions specifiable only at the quantum level suggests that insofar as the quantum events are indeterminate, so is the macroscopic system. We shall argue in Chapter 7 that the free-will question should not be taken to depend on an answer to any *general* sort of determinist thesis. Our consideration of chaotic systems here is but one reason for saying that one has to ask what in human behavior is supposed to be determined *by what*. Thus, while there are ingenious arguments for free will based on chaos theory, we do not believe that whether chaotic systems are determinate or indeterminate is the important question.

What is important for our purposes here is the change in form that explanation takes in dynamic systems. Chaos theorists have developed the notion of a *strange attractor*. Change in a simple system with only two variables can be plotted as a moving point on a graph. For example, the movement of a pendulum involves two variables, velocity and spatial position, so its activity can be represented as a spiral toward the center, as in Figure 2.5. The width and velocity of its movement begin high and gradually drop to zero if no force is applied.

From such considerations the concept of *state space* was developed in order to visualize the behavior of a dynamic system. This term refers to an *abstract* space whose coordinates are the degrees of freedom of a system's behavior. If we plot changes in the system over time, the moving point creates a "shape" in state space. Some shapes are simple: the shape for a pendulum on a clock in constant motion is a circle. Slightly more complex is a torus (a doughnut shape). The shapes for chaotic systems are much more strange. The region in state space traversed by the system is called an *attractor*, since the system will return to it if it is perturbed. Because the

---

[54] Wesley J. Wildman and Robert John Russell, "Chaos: A Mathematical Introduction with Philosophical Reflections", in Russell *et al.* (eds.), *Chaos and Complexity*, 49–90, at p. 82.

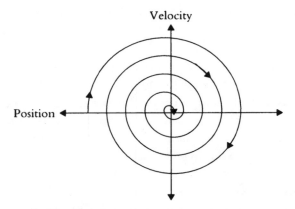

Figure 2.5. Graphic representation of the state space of a very simple dynamic system—a pendulum.

attractors representing the behavior of chaotic systems are strange shapes, they are called, imaginatively, *strange attractors*.

A further conceptual development for describing the behavior of dynamic systems is that of an *ontogenic landscape*. Juarrero says:

> If a system accessed every point or region in its phase space with the same frequency as every other (that is, randomly) its ontogenetic landscape would be smooth and flat. A completely flat, smooth initial landscape would portray an object with no propensities or dispositions—that is, with no attractors ... In contrast, the increased probability that a real system will occupy a particular state can be represented as wells (dips or valleys in the landscape) that embody attractor states and behaviors that the system is more likely to occupy. The deeper the valley, the greater the propensity of its being visited ...
>
> Topologically, ridges separating basins of attraction are called *separatrices* or *repellers*. Sharp peaks are *saddle points* representing states and behaviors from which the system shies away and in all likelihood will not access; the probability of their occurrence is lowered or eliminated altogether ... Separatrix height represents the unlikelihood that the system will switch to another attractor given its history, current dynamics, and the environment. The steeper the separatrix's walls, the greater the improbability of the system's making the transition. On the other hand, the deeper the valley, the stronger the attractor's pull, and so the more entrenched the behavior described by that attractor and the stronger the perturbation needed to dislodge the system from that propensity. The broader the floor of a basin of attraction, the greater the variability in states and behaviors that the attractor allows

under its control. The narrower the valley, the more specific the attractor, that is, the fewer states and behaviors within its basin.[55]

3.2.3. A Paradigm Shift in Science   How far we have come from Descartes's hydraulic animal bodies and Newton's clockwork universe! The universe is now seen to be composed not so much of objects as of systems. The components of the systems themselves are not atoms but structures defined by their relations to one another and to their environment, rather than by their primary qualities. James Gleick says: "Simple systems give rise to complex behavior. Complex systems give rise to simple behavior. And most important, the laws of complexity hold universally, caring not at all for the details of a system's constituent atoms."[56]

Concepts of causation based on mechanical pushing and pulling have been replaced by the concept of attraction in phase space. In such a picture, the stark notions of determinism and indeterminism are replaced by the notions of probability, propensity, and constraint. We can now see what Scrivener means in saying that the new mode of explanation is negative: it is a matter of understanding the restraints that have reduced the possibilities for the pathways the system may follow.

Alwyn Scott, a specialist in nonlinear mathematics, states that a paradigm change (in Thomas Kuhn's sense) has occurred in science beginning in the 1970s. He describes nonlinear science as a meta-science, based on recognition of patterns in kinds of phenomena in diverse fields. This paradigm shift amounts to a new conception of the nature of causality. He says:

Key concepts of nonlinear science are at least threefold. First, there is low-dimensional *chaos,* comprising several unexpected ideas that arise from the sensitive dependence of a nonlinear system on its initial conditions—popularly known as the "butterfly effect". Second, there is the localization of dynamic variables in energy-conserving (Hamiltonian) systems, a phenomenon exemplified by the *solitary wave,* in which mass and energy form a self-consistent dynamic structure (a new particle-like "thing"), and the *soliton* which maintains its shape and speed even after collisions with other solitons. Third, there is the *reaction–diffusion* process, under which a moving disturbance—like a candle flame or a nerve

---

[55] Alicia Juarrero, *Dynamics in Action: Intentional Behavior as a Complex System* (Cambridge, Mass.: MIT Press, 1999) Reprinted with kind permission by MIT Press. © MIT 1999, 156.
[56] James Gleick, *Chaos: Making a New Science* (New York: Penguin, 1987), 304.

impulse—releases the energy that is necessarily consumed by associated dissipation. These three phenomena are central components of modern nonlinear science.[57]

3.3 Emergence

We stated in our Introduction that we take emergence theses to be the flip side of anti-reductionist theses, but choose to speak in terms of anti-reductionism rather than emergence because philosophers have done a better job of defining and distinguishing types of anti-reductionist arguments than they have of emergentist theses. Nonetheless, there are valuable resources to be mined from this literature and interesting parallels with developments in the foregoing section.

Achim Stephan describes three phases in the development of the concept of *emergence*. The first was in the work of J. S. Mill and George Lewes in the nineteenth century. Mill was interested in effects that were the "resultant" of intersecting causal laws; Lewes used the term "emergent" for such effects.

The second phase is better known. This was a discussion in the philosophy of biology beginning in the 1920s; "emergent evolutionism" was proposed as an alternative to vitalism, preformationism, and mechanist–reductionist accounts of the origin of life. The authors usually cited are C. Lloyd Morgan, Samuel Alexander, and C. D. Broad in Britain; however, there were also significant contributions made by American philosophers Roy Wood Sellars, A. O. Lovejoy, and Stephen C. Pepper.[58]

Jaegwon Kim writes that by the middle of the twentieth century emergentism was often trivialized, if not ridiculed, in philosophy as a result of the anti-metaphysical stance of logical positivism and analytic philosophy.[59] Stephan attributes the eclipse of the discussion particularly to the neopositivists Carl G. Hempel, Paul Oppenheim, and Ernst Nagel.

---

[57] Alwyn Scott, "The Development of Nonlinear Science", *Revista del Nuovo Cimento*, 27/10–11 (2004), 1–115, at 2.

[58] Achim Stephan, "Emergence—A Systematic View on its Historical Facets", in Ansgar Beckermann, Hans Flohr, and Jaegwon Kim (eds.), *Emergence or Reduction?: Essays on the Prospects of Nonreductive Physicalism* (Berlin and New York: Walter de Gruyter, 1992), 25–48, at p. 25. Stephan actually divides this movement into two phases, before and after 1926, but we do not see his reason for doing so.

[59] Jaegwon Kim, "Being Realistic about Emergence", in Philip Clayton and Paul Davies (eds.), *The Re-Emergence of Emergence* (Oxford: Oxford University Press, 2006), 190.

The third stage of the discussion began in 1977 with Mario Bunge's and Karl Popper's applications to the mind—brain problem. Other contributors here include psychologist Roger Sperry and philosopher J. J. C. Smart.[60]

Various types of things have been classified in the literature as emergent: laws, effects, events, entities, and properties.[61] Robert Van Gulick makes a helpful distinction between emergentist theses that pertain to objective real-world items and those that appeal to what we as cognitive agents can or cannot know. He further distinguishes, on the objective, metaphysical side, between two main classes of emergents: properties and causal powers or forces. Within the category of epistemological emergentist theses he further distinguishes between those that pertain to prediction and those that pertain to understanding. All of these sub-categories come in stronger or weaker forms.[62]

As already noted, we agree with Van Gulick in seeing emergentist theses to be roughly equivalent to anti-reductionist theses. If this is the case, and if we are right in identifying the defeat of causal reductionism as the central issue, then the form of emergence to look for will be one that has to do with causation. In any case, we can rule out as relatively uninteresting any epistemological thesis. We know of cases where we can neither predict outcomes nor explain known facts (explain in the sense of "retrodiction" from laws and initial conditions) simply because the level of complexity or the need for fine-scale measurements goes beyond human capacities. If we attempt to evade this problem by invoking an omniscient predictor, we are unable to *apply* the criterion because we have no way to settle disputes about what the omniscient one would or would not know.

An ontological or metaphysical definition, then, is desirable. But as between causal factors and properties, it seems best to focus on causal factors, because having causal powers seems to be the best *criterion* we have for the existence of a distinct *property*. As between causal forces and causal powers, we cast our vote for powers because the postulation of new causal forces, over and above those known to physics, would seem to violate the causal closure of physics. So we conclude that what the emergentist needs to show is that as we go up the hierarchy of complex systems we find entities that exhibit new causal powers (or, perhaps better, participate in

[60] Stephan, "Emergence", 26.   [61] Ibid. 27.

[62] Robert Van Gulick, "Reduction, Emergence and Other Recent Options on the Mind/Body Problem: A Philosophic Overview", *Journal of Consciousness Studies*, 8/9–10 (2001), 1–34.

new causal processes or fulfill new causal roles) that cannot be reduced to the combined effects of lower-level causal processes.

We believe that Terrence Deacon has provided a suitably precise account of emergence that meets our desiderata. His account employs many of the causal complexities we have canvassed above: the role of initial conditions and structures, function, selection, feedback, information, and nonlinearity. According to Deacon, emergent phenomena are often described as having novel properties not exhibited by their constituents and as exhibiting regularities that cannot be deduced from laws pertaining to the constituents. However, it is usually claimed that the physical laws governing the constituents are not superseded or violated in emergent phenomena. "What is not provided by these physical properties and laws and is critical to emergent properties is an additional account of the *configurational regularities affecting constituent interactions.*"[63] A related point concerns "holistic" properties—that is, higher-order ensemble properties of systems. The existence and relative autonomy of holistic properties and of a kind of top-down influence over the properties and dynamics of system constituents remains both the key defining character and the most criticized claim of arguments for emergence.

Deacon develops existing accounts of emergence by tracing ways in which "*nature can tangle causal chains into complex knots. Emergence is about the topology of causality*" (p. 94). He finds three levels of complexity in causal tangles, and consequently defines three levels of emergence.

What needs explaining is how some systems come to be dominated by higher-order causal properties such that they appear to "drag along" component constituent dynamics, even though these higher-order regularities are constituted by lower-order interactions. The secret to explaining the apparently contrary causal relationships is to recognize the central role played by *amplification processes* in the pattern formation occurring in these kinds of phenomena. Wherever it occurs, amplification is accomplished by a kind of repetitive superimposition of similar forms. It can be achieved by mathematical recursion in a computation, by recycling of a signal that reinforces itself and cancels the background in signal processing circuits, or by repetitively sampling the same biased set of phenomena in statistical analyses. In each case, it is the formal or configurational regularities that serve as the basis for amplification, not merely the "stuff" that is the medium in which it is exhibited.

---

[63] Terrence Deacon, "Three Levels of Emergent Phenomena", in Nancey Murphy and William R. Stoeger (eds.), *Evolution and Emergence: Systems, Organisms, Persons* (Oxford: Oxford University Press, 2007), ch. 4. Further citations are given parenthetically in the text.

Amplification can be a merely physical process or an informational process (the latter usually depends on the former). Its role in the analysis of emergence is in explaining how certain minor or even incidental aspects of complex phenomena can come to be the source of its dominant features.

(p. 95)

Deacon uses the "amplification logic" as a guide to distinguish emergent systems. The most useful architectural feature is whether this causal architecture is recurrent or circular across levels of scale. More specifically, Deacon analyzes relationships of recursive causality in which the feedback is from features of a whole system to the very architecture of its components and how these levels interact. "My question is: What happens when the global configurational regularities of a locally bounded open physical system are in some way fed back into that system via effects propagated through its 'environment'" (p. 96). The three categories of emergence Deacon describes exhibit nonrecurrent-, simple-recurrent-, and recurrent-recurrent-trans-scale architectures.

Deacon applies the terms "first-order emergence" or "supervenient emergence" to systems in which lower-order *relational* properties are the constitutive factor determining some higher-order property. An example is the turbulence of large bodies of liquid. While physics can provide a good theoretical description of the properties of turbulence (and in this sense the system is "fully reducible"), the higher-level descriptions are applicable not to single water molecules, but to the relational interactions of the aggregate. What is more, that the supervenient property is more than descriptive is suggested by the fact that it is precisely the supervenient property (rather than the properties of the constituents) that represents the contribution of a particular aggregate to some larger system. Thus, while the sensitivity of a synaptic receptor to a neurotransmitter (resulting in the opening of ion channels) might (someday) be fully reducible to a description at the level of atoms and molecules (and thus be an example of *mere* first-order emergence), it is the aggregate behavior of the changes in ion channels due to contact with neurotransmitters that constitutes the contribution of the receptor system to the properties of information exchange between neurons.

Second-order emergence occurs when there is temporal development, or symmetry breaking, in a system.

There is a simple self-similarity to liquid properties across time and position that is further "smoothed" by entropic processes. In contrast, there is a self-differentiating feature to living and mental processes, which both retains and undermines aspects of self-similarity. This characteristic breakdown of self-similarity or symmetry-breaking is now recognized in numerous kinds of complex phenomena, including systems far simpler than living systems. These complex emergent phenomena share this characteristic of change of ensemble properties *across time,* and are often computationally unpredictable. So it would be useful to distinguish first-order emergence from these more complex forms of emergent phenomena in which the cumulative stochastic canceling of configurational interactions exhibited by simple entropic systems is undermined, and where this contributes to development and change of both micro- and macro-properties across time.

(p. 99)

Chaotic and self-organized systems fall into this category. In chaotic systems certain higher-order regularities become unstable, and "an unpredictability of higher-order dynamics results ... [T]his unpredictability derives from the fact that the regularities at lower levels have become strongly affected by regularities emerging at higher levels of organization. This can happen when configurational features at the ensemble level drastically change the probabilities of certain whole classes of component interactions" (p. 101).

Whereas first-order emergent systems can be adequately described without taking their history into account, second-order systems cannot, because of their sensitive dependence on initial conditions and because perturbations are likely to be amplified rather than smoothed out as the system evolves. Systems characterized by second-order emergence undergo recursive feedback that is self-undermining, causing prior states to be irreversibly superseded. Supervenient emergent properties have become self-modifying, resulting in supervenient emergence of new supervenient phenomenon.

Third-order emergent systems involve, in addition, some form of information or memory. "The result is that specific historical moments of higher-order regularity or of unique micro-causal configurations can additionally exert a cumulative influence over the entire causal future of the system. In other words, via memory, constraints derived from specific past higher-order states can get repeatedly re-entered into the lower-order dynamics leading to future states, in addition to their effects mediated by second-order processes" (p. 105–6). Third-order emergence involves an even more complex form of development or evolutionary history in that memory allows for the current system state to be modified by a preserved record of a previous system state. Thus, the system is not only subject to change based on immediate feedback, but is subject to changes from records of past states relevant to the current state (e.g., records preserved in DNA or patterns of synaptic efficiency). Thus, there is both amplification of global influences and reintroduction of them redundantly across time and into different realizations of the system.

The representation relationship implicit in third-order emergent phenomena demands a combination of multi-scale, historical, and semiotic analyses. Thus, living and cognitive processes require introducing concepts such as representation, adaptation, information, and function in order to capture the logic of the most salient of emergent phenomena. This makes the study of living forms qualitatively different from other physical sciences. It makes no sense to ask about the function of granite. Though the atoms composing a heart muscle fiber or a neurotransmitter molecule have no function in themselves, the particular configurations of the heart and its cell types additionally beg for some sort of teleological assessment. They do something for something. Organisms evolve and regulate the production of multiple second-order emergent phenomena with respect to some third-order emergent phenomenon. Only a third-order emergent process has such an intrinsic identity.

So life, even in its simplest forms, is third-order emergent and its products can't be fully understood apart from either history or functionality.

(p. 106–7)

Third-order emergence constitutes the origination of information, semiosis, and teleology in the world. It is the point where physical causality acquires (or rather constitutes) significance.

In sum, third-order (evolutionary) emergence contains second-order (self-organizing) emergence as a limiting case, which in turn contains first-order (supervenient) emergence as a limiting case. For this reason it is insufficient to describe mental phenomena as merely supervenient on cellular-molecular interactions. The many levels of embedded evolutionary emergent processes characteristic of brains is what enable them so rapidly to selectively amplify such a vast range of possible forms of activity.

Deacon emphasizes that "[n]o novel types of physical causes are evoked by this conception of emergence, only novel types of configurations and what might be described as 'configurational causes' " (p. 109). This concept of emergence does, however, "offer an amendment to two major oversim-plifications about the nature of causality, that causes have simple location and that causes always flow upward and outward in scale" (p. 109).

The form of emergence that Deacon describes is increasingly being recognized as necessary for the understanding of brain process. Remarkably, this is true even within the field of computational neuroscience, where the computational task might presume reduction of cognitive processes to the parameters of computational formulae. However, O'Reilly provides the following perspective in a recent review of the computational modeling of processes of the frontal lobe that are involved in higher-level cognition:

The promise of biologically based computational models is that they can actu-ally break open these mysteries by describing the underlying mechanisms in precise computational detail and showing that they are indeed capable of the functions attributed to the [prefrontal cortex]. The success of this approach does not mean that we need to think of humans as robots. Instead, these models show that many subtle factors interact in complex ways to produce the emer-gent phenomenon of cognitive control, which cannot be simply reduced to its constituents.[64]

Thus, current progress in computational modeling of the functions of the frontal lobe of the brain strongly suggests that higher-level cognitive prop-erties are emergent and not reducible to the properties of the constituent parts that yield the parameters contributing to the models.

3.4 Far-from-Equilibrium Dissipative Systems

We noted in section 2.1 that the solution to the problem of how complexity could come into existence in an entropic world had to await the work of Ilya Prigogine and colleagues in the 1970s. Prigogine's contribution was to describe how nonlinear systems could jump to a higher level of complexity; the key is their being open systems far from thermodynamic equilibrium. When a system is near equilibrium (e.g., water in a pan), fluctuations are dampened out (i.e., the molecules bounce around in such a way that the whole pan-full remains stationary). If the system is taken far from equilibrium (e.g., by heating the bottom of the pan), there may be a sudden change from random motion to order (convection cells appear).

[64] Randall C. O'Reilly, "Biologically Based Computational Models of High-Level Cognition", *Science*, 314/5796 (6 Oct. 2006), 91.

Such orderly processes are called "dissipative systems". The system emerges when previously uncorrelated particles or processes suddenly become coordinated and interconnected. One of the simpler examples of such systems is an autocatalytic process. This is a circular process in which one molecule acts as a catalyst in the synthesis of another, and then the second acts as a catalyst to synthesize more of the first.

The answer, then, to the question of how order can increase in the biological world despite entropy is via a hierarchy of self-organizing systems. The first-order system is a set of coordinated particles or processes. A second-order system is one that organizes a number of first-order systems, and so on.

So here are resources for answering the first question with which we began this section: how do complex systems come into existence? The next step is to consider how and in what sense these systems are causal players in their own right, partly independent of the behavior of their components, selectively influenced by the environment, and capable of pursuing their own goals.

4 Self-Causing Systems

We discovered Juarrero's *Dynamics in Action* after completing a draft of this book. Hers is an impressive volume, covering in its own way most of the same issues as ours. Her focus is action theory; her thesis is that human action cannot be understood given current accounts of causation (as bottom-up and mechanistic) and of explanation (as subsumption under universal laws). Drawing upon resources from information theory, systems theory, and non-equilibrium thermodynamics, she proposes that the theory of complex adaptive systems can serve as a "theory constitutive metaphor" for reconceptualizing the causes of action. In light of this metaphor she addresses the role of intention in action (i.e., why the mental *qua* mental matters), and argues that actions can be understood only on a narrative-hermeneutical model. She ends with reflections on free will and how best to increase and maintain optimal space for personal agency.

The particular value of Juarrero's work for our project is twofold. First, she draws together and amplifies the assorted resources we proposed in the preceding sections for explaining and defending downward causation. This requires a synthesis of insights from systems theory, nonlinear mathematics, and emergence theory. Second, in our first approach to this book we had assumed that the defeat of neurobiological reductionism depended only on the development and defense of an adequate concept of downward causation. Juarrero convinced us that it requires in addition an account of how a complex system, as a whole, can be the cause of its own behavior, and even to a degree the maker of its own components. She called our attention to the assumption, a holdover from Aristotle, that nothing can be the cause of itself. As we noted above (sec. 1.3.5), this assumption accounts for the reluctance to view an organism as the cause of its own behavior. We shall argue (in Ch. 7) that it also accounts for reluctance to recognize that humans eventually become the causes of their own moral character. That is, in addition to establishing the downward efficacy of the environment and the downward efficacy of the system itself on its parts, it is necessary to show that the system itself can be a (relatively) autonomous causal player at its own level in the hierarchy. This is to anticipate, in the case of humans, an argument that we are not merely products of environment plus biology, but are causal players in our own right, and this in such a way as (potentially) to be the most significant creators of ourselves. We are (somewhat) autonomous, self-directed shapers of our own future character and behavior.

But we get ahead of the story. Before making the case for human self-direction and self-creation we need much simpler models of self-directed systems, for which we turn to Juarrero's work. In sum, Juarrero says: complex adaptive systems are characterized, first,

by positive feedback processes in which the product of the process is necessary for the process itself. Contrary to Aristotle, this circular type of causality *is* a form of self-cause. Second, when parts interact to produce wholes, and the resulting distributed wholes in turn affect the behavior of their parts, interlevel causality is at work. Interactions among certain dynamical processes can create a systems-level organization with new properties that are not the simple sum of the components that create the higher level. In turn, the overall dynamics of the emergent distributed system not only determine which parts will be allowed into the system: the global dynamics also regulate and constrain the behavior of the lower-level components.[65]

---

[65] Juarrero, *Dynamics in Action*, 5–6. Further citations are given parenthetically in the text.

Notice that the focus here is on systems, rather than things, and that the systems are nonlinear. The nesting of a system in its environment opens the way for control hierarchies with both bottom-up and top-down causation—inter-level causal loops (cf. Deacon on second- and third-order emergence).

Juarrero's work on self-causing systems draws from Prigogine's research on far-from-equilibrium dissipative systems. She says:

Because self-organizing systems are dynamic processes ... reification is inappropriate. Self-organizing structures are not concrete things. Dissipative structures and autocatalytic webs are meta-stable networks of transformations, nested, hierarchical arrangements of *organizational* patterns: "structures of process".

(p. 124)

4.1 How Do Downward Causes Cause?

Juarrero describes the role of the system as a whole in determining the behavior of its parts in terms similar to Robert Van Gulick's account of the larger pattern or entity selectively activating the causal powers of its components. Juarrero says:

The dynamical organization functions as an internal selection process established by the system itself, operating top-down to preserve and enhance itself. That is why autocatalytic and other self-organizing processes are primarily informational; their internal dynamics determine which molecules are "fit" to be imported into the system or survive. (p. 126)

She addresses the crucial question of how to understand the causal effect of the system on its components. Her answer is that the system *constrains* the behavior of its component processes. The earliest use of the concept of constraint in science was in physics, as in the motion of a pendulum or an object on an inclined plane. Thus, we would say, the concept was comparable to that of Dretske's structuring causes. It suggests, Juarrero says, "not an external force that pushes, but a thing's connections to something else by rods ... and the like as well as to the setting in which the object is situated" (p. 132). More generally, then, constraints pertain to an object's connection within a larger system or its embeddedness within an environment. They are relational properties rather than primary qualities in the object itself. Objects in aggregates do not have constraints; constraints exist only when an object is part of a unified system. When two objects or systems are correlated by means of constraints, they are said to be *entrained*.

From information theory Juarrero employs a distinction between *context-free* and *context-sensitive constraints*.[66] First, an example of each. In successive throws of a die, the numbers that have come up previously do not constrain the probabilities for the current throw; the constraints on the die's behavior are context-free. In contrast, in a card game the chances of drawing an ace at any point are sensitive to history; if one ace has been drawn previously, the odds drop from 4 in 52 to 3 in 51. A nonlinear system is one that imposes contextual constraints on its components. What has gone on before constrains what can happen next; the history of such a system is essential to its characterization (compare this to what Deacon says about second- and third-order emergence). Juarrero says: "The higher level's self-organization is the change in probability of the lower-level events. Top-down causes cause by changing the prior probability of the components' behavior, which they do as second-order contextual constraints"(p. 146).

Another example is an autocatalytic process. If molecule A catalyzes the synthesis of B, and B the synthesis of A, the quantities of both A and B will increase, first slowly and then more rapidly, until the components of A, B, or both are used up. The total state of the system depends on its history. Each synthesis of a molecule of A slightly increases the probability, for each component of B, that it will find the other component(s) and a molecule of the catalyst at the same time. Note the consonance of Juarrero's claim with what we referred to above as the paradigm change involved in dynamic systems theory. The sort of causation involved here is not forceful or energetic. It operates by reducing the number of ways in which the parts can be arranged and function. It is a matter of changing the shape of a system's phase space.

Juarrero's reply to an imagined objection is worth quoting in full:

I have analyzed interlevel causality in terms of the workings of context-sensitive constraints and constraint as alterations in degrees of freedom and probability distributions. It might be objected, however, that "alteration" presupposes causality and so the entire project is guilty of circularity. In reply, consider the following: assume there are four aces in a fifty-two card deck, which is dealt evenly around the

---

[66]   The distinction is from Lila Gatlin, *Information and Living Systems* (New York: Columbia University Press, 1972).

table. Before the game starts each player has a 1/13 chance of receiving at least one ace. As the game proceeds, *once* players A, B, and C have already been dealt all four aces, the probability that player D has one automatically drops to 0. The change occurs because within the context of the game, player D's having an ace is not independent of what the other players have. Any prior probability in place before the game starts suddenly changes because, by establishing interrelationships among the players, the rules of the game impose second-order contextual constraints (and thus conditional probabilities).

... [N]o external force was impressed on D to alter his situation. There was no forceful efficient cause separate and distinct from the effect. Once the individuals become card players, the conditional probabilities imposed by the rules and the course of the game itself alter the prior probability that D has an ace, not because one thing bumps into another but because each player is embedded in a web of interrelationships.

(p. 146)

A common objection to the idea of downward causation is that it is a confusion to speak of the whole causally affecting its parts because the whole is nothing other than its parts. For example, Mario Bunge writes that wholes cannot act on their parts because a level of organization "is not a thing but a set and therefore a concept... All talk of interlevel action is elliptical or metaphorical."[67] Juarrero replies that such an objection betrays philosophers' refusal to acknowledge self-cause as well as a tendency toward reification, "an ontological bias that favors concrete things over processes and relations, substances over properties" (p. 129). We note, as well, the assumption of atomist reductionism betrayed in Bunge's claim that wholes are merely sets rather than real existents.

4.2 Autonomous Systems

One of the most important facts that Juarrero recognizes is the way in which the binding of components into a dynamic system limits the components' degrees of freedom, but *the system as a whole gains a broader causal repertoire.* "The higher level of organization, whether thermodynamic, psychological, or social, possesses a qualitatively different repertoire of states and behavior than the earlier level, as well as greater degrees of freedom" (p. 145). The

---

[67] Mario Bunge, *Ontology, ii: A World of Systems* (Dordrecht: D. Reidel, 1979), 13–14; quoted by Juarrero, *Dynamics in Action*, 129.

emergence of relatively autonomous levels of organization results in the emergence of relatively autonomous qualities, which represent new kinds of causal factors (p. 129). This increase in degrees of freedom at the system level, due to context-sensitive constraints at the level of the components, will be essential for understanding language (see our Ch. 4) and almost every aspect of human behavior, both individual and social.

Equally important: a complex adaptive system represents the emergence of a system with the capacity to control itself. Such systems are goal-directed, at the very least to the extent that they are organized in a manner to pursue their own self-maintenance. As already emphasized, they exert constraints on their own components. Finally, they are capable of selecting the stimuli in the environment to which they will respond, making them semi-autonomous from environmental control as well (p. 143). *They become (in part) their own causes.*

5 From Mechanisms to Ant Colonies

In the foregoing sections we have laid out resources, from simple to complex, for answering the question: how can it *fail* to be the case that the behavior of an entity or system is entirely the product of the behavior of its parts? However, the step-by-step organization of this material, while necessitated by the linearity of writing, is not likely to be effective in convincing the skeptical reader. Reductionism is a world-view issue; it is, in Ludwig Wittgenstein's terms, part of the riverbed that channels one's thinking. It takes more than the force of an argument to shift the banks of the river. Thus, we have claimed, the shift from a reductionist to an anti-reductionist perspective is a paradigm shift. These shifts are sometimes likened to a *Gestalt* switch, in contrast to the acceptance of the conclusion to an argument. In the case of a visual *Gestalt*, a figure, once seen as a chalice against a dark background, suddenly appears as two faces in profile. While it may not help to be told that the drawing *really is* two faces, one can highlight features ("see, here is one nose") that will cause the shift. Thus, the purpose of this section is to offer an example on the borderline between mechanistic and dynamic systems that can be seen both reductively and nonreductively, and to attempt to highlight features that will trigger a paradigm shift in the reader.

5.1 A "Simple" Complex System

The challenge for this section, then, is to find an example that is comprehensible enough to allow for comparison between the explanatory power of the old reductionist paradigm and the new systems paradigm. Our ultimate goal in the book as a whole is to understand the complex dynamic systems that are human beings with their immense neural complexity enmeshed in an immensely complex cultural environment. Such systems are beyond human capacity to describe fully. However, Juarrero has already applied her work on dynamic systems to the topics of meaning, intentional action, rationality, and free will; we shall note her contributions in the remaining chapters of this book as we pursue the same issues.

So the goal of this section is, on the one hand, very modest: to provide an easily grasped example of a dynamic system. On the other, it is very ambitious, as noted above, in that we hope to provoke a shift in perspective from the reductionist paradigm that has dominated modern thinking. A suitable candidate for comparing reductionist and systems accounts is the description of ant colonies found in Steven Johnson's book, *Emergence: The Connected Lives of Ants, Brains, Cities, and Software.*[68] The book's title suggests that its outlook will be anti–reductionist, yet it is replete with claims such as the following: self-organizing systems are

bottom-up systems, not top-down... [T]hey are complex adaptive systems that display emergent behaviors. In these systems, agents residing on one scale start producing behavior that lies one scale above them: ants create colonies; urbanites create neighborhoods; simple pattern-recognition software learns how to recommend new books. The movement from low level rules to higher-level sophistication is what we call emergence. (p. 18)

The crucial question, then, is whether the term "emergence" is a vacuous compliment paid to particularly *interesting* instances of bottom-up causal processes.

Harvester ant colonies consist of a queen surrounded by interior workers deep inside the burrow and other worker ants that only enter chambers near the surface. The worker ants are specialized: some forage for food, others carry away trash, and still others carry dead ants away from the

---

[68] Steven Johnson, *Emergence: The Connected Lives of Ants, Brains, Cities, and Software* (New York: Simon & Schuster, 2001). Citations are given parenthetically in the text.

colony. Deborah Gordon has shown that the ants manage to locate the trash pile and the cemetery at points that maximize the distances between cemetery and trash pile, and between both of these and the colony itself.[69] Johnson says, "it is as though they've solved one of those spatial math tests that appear on standardized tests, conjuring up a solution ... that might easily stump an eight-year-old human. The question is, who's doing the conjuring"? (p. 33).

Ant colonies show other sorts of "intelligent" behavior. If the colony is disturbed, workers near the queen will carry her down an escape hatch. "A harvester ant colony in the field will not only ascertain the shortest distance to a food source, it will also prioritize food sources, based on their distance and ease of access. In response to changing external conditions, worker ants switch from nest-building to foraging, to raising ant pupae" (p. 74). Colonies develop over time. Successful colonies last up to 15 years, the lifespan of the queen, even though worker ants live only a year. The colonies themselves go through stages: young colonies are more fickle than older ones. Gordon says: "If I do the same experiment week after week with older colonies, I get the same results: they respond the same way over and over. If we do the same experiment week after week with a younger colony, they'll respond one way this week, and another way next week, so the younger colonies are more sensitive to whatever's different about this week than last week" (p. 81). Younger colonies are also more aggressive. "If older colonies meet a neighbor one day, the next day they're more likely to turn and go in the other direction to avoid each other. The younger colonies are much more persistent and aggressive, even though they're smaller" (p. 81).

While these shifts in the colonies' "attitudes" over time have yet to be explained, the coordination of the functions of the worker ants, such as changing from foraging to nest building, has been. Ants secrete pheromones that serve as chemical signals to other ants. E. O. Wilson has shown that fire ants have a vocabulary of ten signals, nine based on pheromones.[70] These code for task recognition, "I'm on foraging duty"; trail attraction, "There's food over here"; alarm behavior; and necrophoric behavior, "Let's get rid of

---

[69] Deborah Gordon, *Ants at Work: How an Insect Society is Organized* (New York: Free Press, 1999).
[70] Edward O. Wilson and Bert Holldobler, *The Ants* (Cambridge, Mass.: Harvard University Press, 1990).

these dead comrades" (p. 75). Gradients in pheromone trails make it possible to indicate directionality. The explanation for the colony's ability to adjust task allocation according to colony size and food supply depends on the ants' ability to keep track of the frequency of encounters with other ants of various types. So, for example, "[a] foraging ant might expect to meet three other foragers per minute—if she encounters more than three, she might follow a rule that has her return to the nest" (pp. 76–7).

Johnson intersperses his account of ant behavior with reports on computer simulations of ants learning to follow a pheromone trail, of ant colonies discovering food sources, and other "artificial life" programs. These programs employ very simple rules governing the interaction of the components with their neighbors, yet produce remarkably sophisticated "behavior".[71] All of this is taken to be exemplary of what Johnson calls the "bottom–up mind-set" (p. 64) and he attributes it to (among others) the development of systems theory, cybernetics, and chaos theory. Surely this is confirmation for the reductionist agenda: it appears that the behavior of the colony as a whole can be explained by means of a set of genetically endowed behavioral rules governing the action of the individual ants. The challenge for us, then, ignoring Johnson's bottom–up language, is to see whether the account developed in this chapter of a self-organized system that involves a dynamic interplay between bottom–up causation and the exertion of downward constraint over its components is a better description than what the reductionist has to offer solely in terms of bottom–up causation.[72]

It is knowledge of some of the ant rules that gives the impression that the behavior of the colony is entirely determined bottom-up. Here is a typical objection to claims regarding downward causation in which we have supplied alternative terms relevant to this particular case. William Hasker writes:

---

[71] Interspersing formal *models* of ant behavior based on simple rules adds to the illusion of bottom–up determinism until we take into account that the *relevant* system is not the run of the computer program but the program *plus* the the programmers who tinkered with the rules until they found some that worked for their purposes.

[72] In fairness to Johnson, we need to point out that he is using "bottom-up" and "top-down" in different senses from ours. For him the contrast to "bottom–up" is not whole–part constraint but a higher-order *element* of the system governing the lower-level elements. That is, it is the democracy of the ant colony that he is celebrating in the absence of a queen that *rules* it. So it is not clear whether he is in the reductionist or the anti-reductionist camp. This is why his book serves as such an appealing test case.

I take this to mean that the interaction between the specific physical system [the colony] and others [e.g., other colonies] leads to different results than would occur if the system in question were left undisturbed, or were interacting in some other "broader causal system." Presumably, however, the interactions between the system and the other, surrounding systems will still occur according to the standard physical laws [standard ant rules]. In principle, then, all the events that occur are explainable in bottom-up fashion—that is, they are explainable mechanistically [in neural-molecular terms]. The notion that "downward causation" interpreted in this way represents an *alternative* to mechanism [microphysical causation] is sheer confusion.[73]

That is, one can imagine that each ant has built-in laws governing its behavior, and one can imagine a molecular-neural level account: "smell of fourth forager within one minute causes return to the nest." So the typical causal agent is not "the system as a whole" or "the environment" but a few molecules of a pheromone embedded in the ant's receptor system. If one had all of the information about the rules, the initial placement of the ants, and the pheromone trails, one could predict or explain the behavior of the whole colony.

5.2 The Paradigm Shift

Let us now consider an alternative, systems-theory description of the phenomena. The colony as a whole is certainly describable as a system. It is bounded but not closed; it is a self-sustaining pattern. The shift in perspective required by a systems approach is to see the colony's components as a set of interrelated functional systems—not a queen plus other *ants,* but rather an *organization of processes* such as reproduction, foraging, nest building. It is a system that runs on information. The colony is a self-organized system: it produces and maintains its own functional systems, in that the relations among the ants constrain them to fulfill the roles of queen, forager, and so on. All have the same DNA; differentiation occurs only in the context of the colony. In addition, it has a high degree of autonomy *vis-à-vis* the environment.

Insect populations are a favorite example in the chaos literature, but a better example for such purposes is a species like grasshoppers, whose

---

[73] William Hasker, "Reply to My Friendly Critics", *Philosophia Christi,* 2/2 (2000), 197–207, at pp. 198–9.

populations fluctuate widely from year to year, yet in generally predictable manners (e.g., seven-year cycles).[74] The ant colony is a nonlinear system but, in contrast, remarkably stable under most conditions. The gradual changes typical of colonies over their 15-year life cycles (from erratic to stable, from aggressive to non-aggressive) can be described in Juarrero's terms as the gradual change in the *ontogenic landscape* constraining their behavior: over time deeper valleys and higher separatrices develop, making erratic behavior less likely.

The colony displays a number of emergent, holistic properties. In addition to its relative stability there is the "intelligence" that Johnson describes in the placement of the trash pile and cemetery, the ability to prioritize food sources. It displays what Deacon calls second-order emergence, in that there are simple-recurrent feedback loops across levels. Accidents of the environment such as location of food sources affect the foraging system as a whole, which in turn constrains the behavior of individual ants; individual ants, of course, do the work of the foraging system.

The crucial shift in perspective, as we noted above, is from thinking in terms of causes (nothing will happen unless something makes it happen) to thinking in terms of both bottom-up causes *and* constraints (a variety of behaviors is possible, and the important question is what constricts the possibilities to give the observed result). It is a switch from viewing matter as inherently passive to viewing it (at least the complex systems in question) as inherently active. In contrast to the *assumption* that each lower-level entity will do only one thing, the assumption here is that each lower-level entity has a repertoire of behaviors, one of which will be *selected* due to its *relations* to the rest of the system and to its environment. In fact, ant behavior, when extracted from its environment (colony), is a good visual model: drop an ant on the table and it runs helter-skelter. It can be coerced into going one way rather than another (context-free constraints), but in the colony it also responds to context-sensitive constraints that entrain its behavior to that of other ants in ways sensitive to history and higher levels

---

[74] Fluctuation of this sort is an indication that the constant k in the logistic equation, describing the population changes over time, falls within the critical range 3.57–4 (see sec. 3.2.2 above). This means that the population one year is highly sensitive to the population level of the year before. The difference between grasshoppers and ants is that the ant colony places constraints on its members, creating more constancy over time. The ant colony is a dynamic system operating top-down to preserve and regulate itself, for example, by switching ants from foraging duty to raising pupae when food is plentiful.

of organized context. From this point of view, the genetically imprinted rules in the individual ants' nervous systems are not (primarily) to be understood as causal laws; they are receptors of information regarding such things as the density of the forager population. The holistic property of the system—forager density—increases the probability that a given forager will encounter more than three other foragers per minute, and thus increases the probability that the ant in question will return to the nest. It is a non-forceful constraint on the ant's behavior that is causal.

5.3 How to Choose?

Because the ant colony is at the border between a dynamic and a non-dynamic system (due to the relatively low level of interconnection among its components), it is possible to view it in either of two ways. The standard reductionist model assumes that the ants are like atoms, whose behavior is determined solely by internal rules, *and whose characteristics are not affected by relations within the colony.* If one knew all the rules, the initial placement of the ants in their physical environment, and especially the placement of pheromone molecules, it would be possible to understand the operation of the entire colony. The basic causes are neural and molecular. The alternative is to assume that the ants themselves are tiny dynamic systems with an array of potential behaviors, which are constrained in response to information about global states of the entire dynamic system, conveyed via pheromones.

Is it possible to choose one perspective over the other? Certainly the reductionist account cannot be *disproven;* one can always argue that if we just knew *more* about the ants' nervous systems, their locations in the colony, the location of pheromone molecules… It is possible, however, to provide some grounds for choosing the systems account. First, note that the reductionist account, as we have presented it, begs the question in assuming that ants themselves obey fixed, deterministic rules and are unchanged by their interactions with other ants and the environment. The systems theorist can argue that the ants are better characterized in dynamic terms. Martin Heisenberg has performed experiments studying the irregular patterns of turns in the flight of flies.[75] These are called "body

---

[75] Martin Heisenberg, "Voluntariness (*Willkürfähigkeit*) and the General Organization of Behavior", in R. J. Greenspan *et al.* (eds.), *Flexibility and Constraint in Behavioral Systems* (Hoboken, NJ: John Wiley & Sons, Ltd., 1994).

saccades" (saccades are sudden and rapid shifts of eye fixation). Heisenberg has studied the causes of body saccades with respect both to external stimuli and to events in the nervous system. This research involves tethering the fly in such a way that it can still engage in normal flying behaviors. The fly's attempts at changing direction in flight are registered by the torque imposed on the tether. In this manner all stimuli available to the fly can be systematically controlled and manipulated, and differences between activity and reactivity can be easily distinguished. Since the fly is in a fixed location, events in the nervous system can also be simultaneously recorded.

Based on these experiments, Heisenberg comes to several conclusions. First, the behavior of the fly is "voluntary"; that is, when all environmental stimuli are held constant, changes in direction of flight are spontaneous and endogenous in origin. While manipulation of the visual environment of the fly may cause the fly to make compensatory adjustments, the direction of flight is otherwise endogenously generated. Second, homeostatic states (appetites and avoidances) only modulate but do not cause behavior. Finally, the body saccades of the fly can best be understood as a means of "trying out" behavior. A saccade is made, then its relationship to intended outcomes is evaluated from sensory feedback.

Based on this research (including observations of the activity of the nervous system) Heisenberg proposes that within the nervous system of the fly there exists a weighted matrix of probabilities of potential behaviors. The behaviors represented in the matrix are relatively fixed in form (although these may be modified by rudimentary forms of learning). The matrix of potential behaviors is "sampled" by some process (that may or may not be genuinely random—it is unknown at this point.[76]) Behaviors with larger weights are much more likely to be sampled and executed, but other behaviors with lower weights can occur. Weights in this matrix are changeable, depending on appetites, drives, and avoidances. Behaviors that are sampled are tried out in action, and, as a consequence, the probability matrix itself changes. A behavior that results in positive feedback hollows out the ontogenic landscape, making a repeat more likely; a negative outcome flattens the landscape, increasing the probability that the insect will try something different in the future. Thus, while genetics

---

[76] The fact that we do not know and do not *need* to know whether it is random or deterministic is an important point; see sec. 5.4 below.

determines the behaviors available, the weighting of potential behaviors related to particular motivational states (appetites or avoidances) and the criteria for evaluation—and so the behavior itself—are not fixed. Rather, behavior is continuously variable depending on sampling from a historically influenced matrix of behavioral probabilities, trying out, and feedback from execution. This account suggests that the behavior of organisms even as simple as insects is neither deterministic nor purely random, as though it were based on indeterministic quantum events. Emission of behavior is based on something more like the rolling of weighted dice, with the weights constantly changing as a result of changing needs on the part of the organism and a history of feedback from the environment. (This will be important in our consideration of free will in Ch. 7.)

So the behavior of individual insects is readily describable in dynamic terms, even that of the simple fruit fly with 250,000 neurons (which happens to be the same as the ant). This leaves us, again, with two narratives, two descriptions. Are there any other considerations to bring to bear? Note that the reductionist's question is: if you take all the *components* and place them in exactly the same positions in the environment and allow the system to run again, will the entire system follow exactly the same path? The reductionist assumes that it *must* do so unless there is some source of genuine indeterminacy involved at the bottom level. The systems theorist asks a different question: given that no two complex systems (e.g., two ant colonies) are ever identical, why is it the case that, starting from so wide a variety of initial conditions, one finds such similar patterns emerging? That the world is full of such phenomena is now a widely recognized fact, but it is counter-intuitive on a bottom-up account. Johnson provides an imaginary model that better depicts what one would expect in a bottom-up world.

Imagine a billiard table populated by semi-intelligent, motorized billiard balls that have been programmed to explore the space of the table and alter their movement patterns based on specific interactions with other balls. For the most part, the table is in permanent motion, with balls colliding constantly, switching directions and speed every second. Because they are motorized, they never slow down unless their rules instruct them to, and their programming enables them to take unexpected turns when they encounter other balls. Such a system would define the most elemental form of *complex* behavior: a system with multiple agents dynamically interacting in multiple ways, following local rules and oblivious to any higher-level instructions. But it wouldn't truly be considered *emergent* until those local interactions resulted in some kind of discernible macrobehavior.

(pp. 18–19)

This is a good picture of what we ought to expect from a large number of mechanistic entities interacting *locally* with one another and the environment according to fixed laws. *We claim that the fact of higher-order patternedness in nature, patterns that are stable despite perturbations, and despite replacement of their constituents, calls for a paradigm shift in our perceptions of (much of) the world.* The patterns that appear (such as the "intelligence" to locate the cemetery and trash piles in optimal locations) is a typical example of the exponential growth in degrees of freedom of a system due to context-sensitive constraints on its components.

Consider another aspect of our ant colonies. If an ant brain has approximately 250,000 neurons and a human brain has approximately 10,000 million, then a colony of 40,000 ants has, collectively, the same-size brain as a human. If all that matters is the parts and the laws governing their local interactions, then the ant colony should be as intelligent as a human. The theory of complex dynamic systems explains the difference in terms of interconnectivity. The neurons of the colony are in 40,000 nearly isolated packages, while the human brain is massively interconnected, allowing for the emergence of many levels of downward constraint, and consequently for many more degrees of freedom in its operations.

One final consideration: Johnson reports the puzzle of how ant colonies can grow more stable over time given the fact that their populations change from year to year. "It would not be wrong to say that understanding emergence begins with unraveling this puzzle" (p. 82). Juarrero points out that it is a *general* feature of complex adaptive systems that their behavior becomes more stable over time. Their ontogenic landscapes begin with flatter topography and develop deeper basins and higher ridges over time: "complex systems don't wander out of a deep basin of attraction."[77] This, of course, is a *description* of a typical dynamic system; there are no physical walls *causing* the ants to do anything. It is, rather, an indication of where to look for causal explanations: not to efficient, mechanical causes solely inside the ever-replaceable ants themselves, but to interactions among the

---

[77] Juarrero, *Dynamics in Action*, 255.

component functional systems that *do* survive throughout the life span of the colony. When we shift our focus to the system components as processes, it is not surprising that they should develop over time.

As we have stressed, the shift from one paradigm in science to another is not based on arguments; it is rather a matter of showing the superior explanatory power of the new paradigm. Alasdair MacIntyre argues that the relations between two paradigms are asymmetrical, in that both the strengths and the weaknesses of the old paradigm can be understood from the point of view of the new, while the reverse is not the case.[78] From the systems perspective, one major failure of the reductionist paradigm is its inability to explain how many systems with quite different starting points move into very similar and relatively stable patterns. The reason for this is the atomist assumption that the atoms (ants) are not changed by their interactions with other ants and their environment. The successes of the reductionist paradigm are due to the fact that there is, in fact, a very large role for bottom–up causes even in the most complex dynamic systems.

5.4 The Irrelevance of Determinism

The picture we have presented is of a world in which many systems come into being, preserve themselves, and adapt to their environments as a result of a tri-level process. Lower-level entities or systems manifest or produce (mid-level) variation; higher-level structures select or constrain the variation. Recall that our original illustration of downward causation was Campbell's selection of optimally effective termite and ant jaws. Variation in the gene pool is constrained by the demands of the environment. A very important point to note here is that genetic variation results from a variety of causes, some deterministic and others genuinely random—that is, quantum-level events causing mutations. In the case of the behavior of Heisenberg's flies, it is not known whether their initial moves are generated deterministically or randomly.[79] So, in general, there are two parts to causal

---

[78] Alasdair MacIntyre, "Epistemological Crises, Dramatic Narrative, and the Philosophy of Science", *Monist*, 60/4 (1977), 453–72.

[79] Imagine that we could build fly-bots, some of whose initial behavioral options are selected randomly and others whose behavior is governed by a (deterministic) simulated-random-number generator. The behavioral outcomes would look exactly the same.

stories of this sort: first, how the variants are produced, and second, the basis upon which and the means by which the selection takes place. A fairly insignificant part of the story is whether the lower-level processes that produce the variants are deterministic or indeterministic.

The account of insect behavior (above) in terms of probability matrices further complicates the picture. The philosopher will want to know what the technical meaning of "probability" is in this account. The major options would be to interpret it in terms either of relative frequency or of "propensities". The relative frequency option is inapplicable, because an organism is never in exactly the same situation (internal states, environmental conditions, recent history of behavior) more than once.

A propensity is defined as "an irregular or non-necessitating causal disposition of an object or system to produce some result or effect... usually conceived of as essentially probabilistic in nature".[80] Karl Popper regarded the existence of propensities as a metaphysical hypothesis needed to interpret probability claims about single cases. If we give up on the notion that determinism and indeterminism are exhaustive categories, then perhaps strict *indeterminism* applies only at the quantum level (and in cases where macro-systems amplify quantum events); *determinism* applies largely in the realm of mechanical processes, and *propensity,* a genuinely distinct option, applies to much of organismic behavior.

Probability, in the ordinary sense of relative frequencies, comes into downward-causal accounts, as well. For example, in the ant colony the frequency of encountering other foragers is like the scientist's sampling of a population. If the forager population is high, it is *more likely* that a given ant will encounter more than three foragers per minute than if the population is low, but not assured. This sampling procedure, however, works reliably in large numbers of trials. So for various reasons the philosophical concern with the dichotomy deterministic/indeterministic may not be particularly relevant in describing dynamic systems. In fact, Robert Van Gulick writes: "Though it is a question whose answer requires more knowledge of physics than I possess, I believe it could be shown that all physical properties that

---

[80] David Sapire, "Propensity", in Audi (ed.), *Cambridge Dictionary of Philosophy,* 657.

enter into strict exceptionless laws are themselves nothing more than stable self-sustaining recurrent states of the quantum flux of an irreducibly probabilistic and statistical reality."[81]

5.5 Retrospect

We began this chapter (sec. 1.1) with a five-point summary of the atomist metaphysic that inspired modern physics:

1. The essential elements of reality are the atoms.
2. Atoms are unaffected by their interaction with other atoms or by the composites of which they are a part.
3. The atoms are the source of all motion and change.
4. Insofar as the atoms behave deterministically (the Epicureans countenanced spontaneous "swerves", but Laplace and his followers did not), they determine the behavior of all complex entities.
5. Complex entities are not, ultimately, causes in their own right.

We noted that in such a world view causal reductionism, the bottom-up determination of all events by the laws of physics, seems obviously true and even inevitable. We presented (in sec. 1.3) a brief introduction to the ways in which we now know that the atomist world view is inadequate or false. In the rest of this chapter we hope to have made good on counter-claims to each of these five points. This is not to deny that there is a great deal of bottom-up determinism in the world, but only to say that it is not the whole story.

In contrast, we have emphasized that:

1. The essential elements of dynamic systems are not "atoms" in any sense, but component *processes*.
2. The components of systems are affected (constrained) by their relationships within the whole.
3. Dynamic systems are often the source of their own changes.
4. Some components of systems behave deterministically, and others are affected by genuine quantum-level indeterminacy; but the system as a whole behaves according to propensities.
5. Some systems are causes in their own right.

---

[81] Van Gulick, "Who's in Charge Here?", 254.

6 Prospect: From Ant Colonies to Brains

Juarrero draws conclusions regarding human behavior from her work on complex dynamic systems. We shall report on this work in the following chapters, but before doing so, we need to appreciate the vast change in degree of complexity as we go from the simplest of such systems to the human brain, and finally to the brain in the body in its cultural milieu. Our goal in this chapter was merely to establish and defend the concept of downward causation; we have therefore looked at the simplest examples—our most complex being the ant colony. But it is important to note that the level of complexity involved here is comparable to that of the very simplest of multi-celled organisms—those without a nervous system. The cells making up these organisms, like the ants, are restricted to local communication via the diffusion of molecules. This means that both ant colonies and simple organisms lack the high degree of coupling of their components that produces the most interesting cases of emergence.

In the next chapter we pursue the story of self-organizing, autopoietic, and increasingly flexible and goal-directed systems as we go up the hierarchy of complexity in the animal world. The goal will be to end with the picture of an organism that is an *agent,* the cause of (some of) its own behavior. As Stephen Rose argues:

The ... lesson is that organisms are not passive responders to their environments. They actively choose to change them, and work to that end. The great metaphor of what Popper rightly called "passive" Darwinism, natural selection, implies that organisms are the mere playthings of fate, sandwiched as it were between their genetic endowment and an environment over which they have no control, which is constantly setting their genes and gene products challenges which they can either pass or fail. Organisms, however, are far from passive: they—not just we humans, but all other living forms as well—are active players in their own futures.[82]

The variables that lead to increases in the capacity for self-causation include modifiability of parts (i.e., context-sensitive constraints on components), neural complexity, behavioral flexibility, and increasing ability to acquire information. In systems terms, this involves functional specialization of components and a high level of flexible coupling of those components.

---

[82] Steven Rose, *Life Lines: Life Beyond the Gene* (Oxford: Oxford University Press, 1997), 140–41.

As we move from rudimentary animal behavior toward humans, we see a vast increase in brain size, tighter coupling (number of axons, dendrites, synapses), structural complexification, recurrent neural interconnections, and complex functional networks that are hypothesized to be the source of consciousness. In subsequent chapters we address language, formal reasoning, morally responsible action, and free will.

3

From Mindless to Intelligent Action

1 From Machines to Organisms

Given the critique developed in the preceding chapter of simplistic accounts of causal processes in even relatively simple systems such as autocatalytic reactions, what explanation of human and animal behavior, richer and more plausible than either vitalism or reductive materialism, might capture our imaginations? What sort of images should attend the concept of an *organism*? The concept of an organism necessarily involves the concept of dynamic networks. That is, organismic action is generated out of larger dynamic patterns that bind smaller processing units into interactive patterns involving action—feedback—evaluation—action exchanges with the environment. These larger dynamic patterns have their own rules and causal powers (i.e., they have emergent functional properties) that are not present at the level of the smaller constituents. As a consequence of binding small constituents into larger interactive networks, the larger dynamic patterns have top-down (or whole—part) influence on the activity of the constituents. Thus, while constituent (micro-level) causal forces are necessary, they are not sufficient explanations of the ongoing behavior of organisms as they interact with the environment. For example, in the case of the jaw structure of the worker termite, successful interaction of the whole organism with the environment selects from among random mutations of DNA as these mutations contribute to a more or less useful jaw structure. This selection is top-down—from wider physical systems (including the environment), to the microstructure of DNA. Similarly, the processes of learning (in sea slugs, rabbits, rats, monkeys, or human beings) allows the causal properties of the larger patterns of information exchange inherent in action—feedback—evaluation—action loops to continually remodel the microstructure of the brain, causing new patterns of behavior to emerge. These newly remodeled neural networks incorporate rules of environmental interaction (emergent properties) that marshal (in a top-down manner) the participation of the various constituents.

In this chapter we first trace the increasingly complex behavior of organisms as we go up the biological hierarchy (sec. 2). One of the theses of this book is that it is foolhardy to attempt to understand human cognition without tracing its development from more rudimentary forms of interaction between organism and environment. In laying out the data, we shall describe several revealing points along a spectrum of forms of action, modulation, and selection, highlighting greater amounts of information available about the environment, more complex evaluative systems, and increasing behavioral flexibility, all resulting in enhanced levels of self-direction.

There are certain characteristics of the behavior of organisms that need to be kept in mind when considering the nature of action, from that of the simplest organisms to the most complex of human activities. One important feature of living organisms is that they are *always already active*; activity has no real beginning or ending points. In this sense, all behavior of organisms is emitted rather than caused by events in the environment.[1] Therefore, the interesting questions about behavior are not so much what initiates activity but what shapes and guides various forms of behavior.

Second, all activity, even of the most rudimentary sort, is *goal-directed*, and aimed toward solutions to problems created by interactions between internal states and environmental circumstances. Whether we consider a single-celled organism moving about to find nutrients in its fluid environment, a bee moving about a flower garden, a monkey foraging in the jungle, or a human commuting to work, activity is primarily about solving problems of one sort or another. What varies is the complexity of environmental analysis and the flexibility of behavioral responses available to organisms as these are made possible by a more complex nervous system.

---

[1] Martin Heisenberg makes this point cogently with respect to the flying behavior of the fruit fly (drosophila), discussed in Ch. 2. sec. 5.3.

Finally, a feature of even the most rudimentary biological activity is *action under evaluation*.[2] In most cases, this does not refer to conscious evaluation. Rather, it refers merely to a system that is able to modulate and correct ongoing behavioral routines when feedback from the environment indicates a mismatch between the outcome of current behavior and the goal. We shall see that action under evaluation is a characteristic of activity at both micro- and macro-levels of behavioral organization.

In Chapter 5 we shall extend this analysis to the level of human cognition. Whatever else may be involved, conscious, deliberate, human action is a form of goal-directed activity involving the most complex analysis of environmental conditions, the largest number of response options, and the widest spatio-temporal scope for the evaluation of action possibilities and their consequences. Reductionist instincts look for some causal micro-event at every stage. But the lesson to be learned is that all organisms are in constant, dynamic problem-solving interchanges with the environment. Therefore, behavior is not caused by internal processes alone, but is subject to modulation, including top-down modulation from environmental circumstances.

Figure 2.3 (p. 69) is Donald MacKay's activity loop; it illustrates the points made here about the nature of action. The fact that organisms are *always active* is suggested by the fact that the loop from receptors through effectors to the field of action and back to receptors is closed and continuous. The concept of *goal-directedness* is made clear by the indication of a goal state (I_g). Finally, the attribute of *action under evaluation* is represented by the existence of a comparator (C) that determines if the goal is being reached and makes appropriate adjustments in the organization of ongoing behavior (O). All organismic activity can be characterized in this manner. This schematic of an action−feedback−evaluation−action loop (or simply, action loop) graphically represents our claim that actions are to be attributed to the organism as a whole engaged with its environment. This is in contrast to the reductionist and Cartesian materialist account that attributes action to an interior part of the organism and ignores the dynamic interplay of bottom-up and top-down causal factors.

Our survey of levels of action in section 2 (below) will show that these three properties of behavior ("voluntariness", goal-directedness, and

---

[2] We follow Donald MacKay, who defines agency as "activity under evaluation". See Donald M. MacKay, *Behind the Eye*, The Gifford Lectures, ed. Valerie MacKay (Oxford: Blackwell, 1991), 45.

action under evaluation) go all the way down to the simplest levels of the biological ladder.

However, the nature of ongoing behavior–environment interactions changes significantly as the nervous system becomes more complex. Mac-Kay notes that Figure 2.3 well represents a simple feedback system such as a thermostat, whose goal state is set by something outside the system itself. The simplest organisms have their goal states set by evolution. Complex organisms are able to be the programmers of their own goals due to nested hierarchies of feedback and evaluation. In section 3, therefore, we consider the functional architecture that accounts, in abstract terms, for the increasing abilities of organisms to be the causes of their own behavior, increasingly autonomous from both biological determinism and the environment.

In section 4 we consider the neural architecture that makes such meta-representation and self-evaluation possible, ending (in sec. 5) with consideration of the contribution that consciousness makes to organisms' capacities for action.

What we see throughout is that there are two critical changes: (1) changes in the adaptability and flexibility of the interrelationships between environmental feedback and behavioral responses, and (2) changes in the levels and forms of evaluation of actions. Thus, we shall see that intelligent human action is distinguished by a wider range of flexibility in modulating behavior with respect to environmental contexts and new forms of behavioral evaluation, including the ability to evaluate goals themselves (as will be discussed in Ch. 6). These attributes of human action are made possible by an increasingly complex brain that allows for enhanced cognitive capacities such as the ability to organize behavior over longer epochs of time, an episodic memory to provide more detailed information about past events, symbolic representation (which we pursue at the end of this chapter and in Ch. 4), and consciousness.

2 Levels of Action and Adaptability

A physicalist account of human life, combined with the recognition that mental capacities have emerged over time as part of the evolutionary process, implies that we should be able to find a phylogenetic progression of mental capacities and their downward effects on the physical organism.

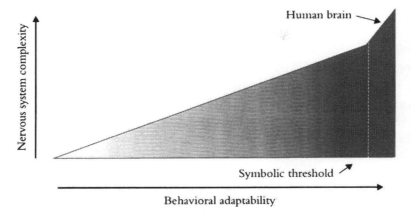

Figure 3.1. Graphic representation of the progressive increase in the appropriate-ness of the use of mentalist terms (shading within the figure) in characterizing the behavior of organisms related to increasing nervous system complexity (vertical axis) and behavioral adaptability (horizontal axis). The one discontinuous point is (maybe) the crossing of a symbolic threshold in humankind allowing for language.

That is, what we humans experience as thinking, planning, deciding, and acting for reasons must have roots in similar but simpler forms of mental activity in lower (or less complex) organisms. If we can appreciate the expanding role of the mental in shaping behavior as we move up levels of complexity within animal species, then the causal role of the mental in human life begins to appear less mysterious.

Although helpful in dissolving mysteries, studying animals creates a problem in applying abstract concepts derived from an understanding of human nature (concepts such as *reasons, beliefs, decision, consciousness*) to lower animals. The problem is that one cannot decide precisely where, in the continuum of increasingly complex species, such terms apply and where they do not. In fact, appreciation of our evolutionary continuity with animals suggests that these questions can seldom be answered "yes" or "no" with respect to any particular behavior in lower animals. The human quality under consideration will typically have some richer or poorer (thicker or thinner, saturated or pale) meaning when applied to organisms at various levels of the phylogenetic hierarchy of nervous system complexity.

Figure 3.1 is a simple visual model that suggests the distribution of mental characteristics along a continuum, without clear boundaries or sudden transitions. The presence of the mental dimension is indicated by the increased density of shading. Complexity of the nervous systems of various species is represented on the vertical axis. Thus, this figure is a graphic representation of the idea that mental characteristics emerge with the increasing complexity of the nervous system, and, most importantly, that there are no clear lines separating the presence and absence of most mental properties.

However, an exception to the continuity of the emergence of mental capacities is represented by one line (i.e, one discrete transition point) at the human end of the scale. This is what Terrence Deacon has described as a "symbolic threshold" in both human evolution and child development.[3] However, Deacon also suggests that, while there is a symbolic threshold, symbolic ability is nested in prior iconic and indexical systems clearly present in lower, less complex animals (see our Ch. 4).

We shall roughly classify behavior into three levels: (1) reflexive action (i.e., responses that interact with environmental feedback, but according to fixed forms), (2) unreflective adaptability (i.e., behaviors that are modified in form by remembered environmental feedback), and (3) reflective adaptability (i.e. behaviors that are modulated off-line by reflection using images or symbols). In fact, however, these categories merely reflect important milestones along a continuum of behavioral complexity as represented in Figure 3.1.

It is important to remember that all of these levels of activity continue to exist in humans and must be considered in understanding human behavior. However, in human behavior there are more elaborate processes of top-down influence that can modify or override even the most basic and fixed behavioral programs. For example, coughing may be a simple reflex reaction to obstruction of the airways, but concert-goers have learned to restrain coughing until the end of the piece. So, when humans cough between pieces, there is an added level of conscious permission that complicates analysis of the behavior.

2.1 Reflexive Action

In this category we will consider several types of behavior: (1) responses of the simplest organisms (protozoa), (2) fixed complex reactivity (wasps and flies), and (3) human homeostatic, autonomic, and reflexive responses.

---

[3] Terrence W. Deacon, *The Symbolic Species: The Co-evolution of Language and the Brain* (New York: Norton, 1997), 79–92.

2.1.1. Responses of Single-Celled Organisms   Among the simplest of behaviors is that of single-celled organisms such as protozoa. These organisms have a singular form of behavior, called chemotaxis, that involves swimming either toward higher concentrations of nutrients or swimming away from higher concentrations of toxins. Thus, the chemical receptors are the sensory mechanism, and swimming (or in the case of amoebae, oozing) toward or away from chemical concentrations comprises the limited response repertoire. The goal (I_g) that regulates behavior is attainment of nutrients and avoidance of toxins. Thus, there is a limited amount of information available, a small set of goals, and few options for behavior. Nevertheless, protozoa manifest "voluntariness" (their behavior is emitted, not elicited),[4] goal-directedness (finding nutrients and avoiding toxins), and action under evaluation (modifying the direction of swimming based on environmental feedback).

Homeostatic activity in more complex organisms works in a similar manner to maintain normal internal stability by means of responses that automatically compensate for environmental changes. This form of activity can be characterized as physiologically rudimentary, immediate, direct, and fixed in the form of stimulus–response interaction. These forms of activity are obligatory responses to the environment. A dog panting when its body temperature exceeds a certain limit is similar in principle to a single-celled organism swimming in one direction or another to avoid toxins.

2.1.2. Fixed Complex Activity   Insects are capable of more complex forms of activity. These organisms have sensorimotor systems sufficiently complex to allow them to respond to larger patterns of stimuli and to integrate small elements of activity into larger patterns of behavior extending over longer periods of time. Though more complex, most of these behaviors are relatively fixed in form for a particular insect species. Adaptability of these forms of activity occurs primarily through genetic variation and selection (although rudimentary forms of learning have been demonstrated in many insects). Moment-to-moment behavior is nevertheless modulated on the basis of immediate feedback.

---

⁴ We place "voluntariness" in scare-quotes. Although the term is used in this context we reserve the term in its ordinary meaning for human actions in which one's reasons for acting are subject to evaluation. See Ch. 6, sec. 2.

A fine example of this form of activity is found in the *Sphex ichneumoneous*, a type of wasp that is now the beloved insect of the philosophical literature on free will. One complex and stereotypic behavioral pattern of the *Sphex* is described by Woolridge:

> When the time comes for egg laying, the wasp *Sphex* builds a burrow for the purpose and seeks out a cricket which she stings in such a way as to paralyze but not kill it. She drags the cricket into the burrow, lays her eggs alongside, closes the burrow, then flies away, never to return. In due course, the eggs hatch and the wasp grubs feed off the paralyzed cricket, which has not decayed, having been kept in the wasp equivalent of deep freeze. To the human mind, such an elaborately organized and seemingly purposeful routine conveys a convincing flavor of logic and thoughtfulness—until more details are examined. For example, the wasp's routine is to bring the paralyzed cricket to the burrow, leave it on the threshold, go inside to see that all is well, emerge, and then drag the cricket in. If the cricket is moved a few inches away while the wasp is inside making her preliminary inspection, the wasp, on emerging from the burrow, will bring the cricket back to the threshold, but not inside, and will then repeat the preparatory procedure of entering the burrow to see that everything is all right. If again the cricket is removed a few inches while the wasp is inside, once again she will move the cricket up to the threshold and re-enter the burrow for a final check. The wasp never thinks of pulling the cricket straight in. On one occasion this procedure was repeated forty times, always with the same result.[5]

Philosophers have made much (we believe too much) of this description of the behavior of the *Sphex*. For example, Daniel Dennett comments: "The poor wasp is unmasked; she is not a free agent, but rather at the mercy of brute physical causation, driven inexorably into her states and activities by features of the environment outside her control."[6] Similarly, Howard Robinson writes: "The trouble with the Sphex is that the ritual in question is 'hard-wired' into its system, giving it no flexibility. Such unresponsiveness to the environment is incompatible with intelligence."[7]

---

[5] D. Woolridge, *Mechanical Man: The Physical Basis of Intelligent Life* (New York: McGraw-Hill, 1968), 82.

[6] Daniel C. Dennett, *Elbow Room: The Varieties of Free Will Worth Wanting* (Cambridge, Mass.: MIT Press, 1984). Dennett notes that one of the most powerful undercurrents in the free will literature is fear that all of our behavior is like this—"sphexish". Our goal in later chapters will be to show how we can be sure it is not.

[7] Howard Robinson, Introduction, in *idem* (ed.), *Objections to Physicalism* (Oxford: Clarendon Press, 1993), 5.

It is clear that this behavior of the *Sphex* is the expression of a genetically predetermined pattern. However, the alteration in this sequence triggered by moving the position of the cricket suggests goal-directedness and action under evaluation even in such a fixed-form behavioral pattern. What is missing in the *Sphex* is a way to keep track of its previous behavior—that is, a memory of having already entered the burrow to check it out. Thus, evaluation and reorganization of behavior cannot take account of previous behavior; the best option for accomplishing the goal is to reset to a previous point in the egg-laying sequence. While information available is limited (i.e., no short-term memory) and behavioral options are limited, still the *Sphex* is clearly a goal-directed organism involved in dynamic action–feedback–evaluation–action loops. It is inaccurate to consider the behavior of the *Sphex* as simply mechanical. In our view, it is also inappropriate to project limitations in the behavior of the *Sphex* onto other organisms that have a short-term memory (as well as other capacities for evaluating and modulating behavior), as if *Sphex*ish behavior represented some inescapable limitation of physiological systems.

What one tends to believe about insect behavior from Woolridge's description of the egg-laying behavior of the *Sphex* takes on a different flavor when considered in light of Martin Heisenberg's description of the behavior of fruit flies (presented in Ch. 2, sec. 5.3). Based on his experiments, Heisenberg concluded that the behavior of the fly is "voluntary" (i.e., the changes in direction of flight are spontaneous and endogenous in origin) and can be characterized as a means of "trying out" behavior.

The concept of a fly "trying out" behaviors is considerably different from the presumed implications of Woolridge's description of the behavior of the *Sphex*. Although insects may have genetically determined patterns of behaviors (such as egg laying in the *Sphex*), and a limited range of behaviors to try out, behavior is nevertheless flexible, variable, and responsive to the environment—at least more so than the impression given by the *Sphex* example. Certainly the *Sphex* is not a free agent, but equally certainly the *Sphex* is not, as Dennett says, "at the mercy of brute physical causation".

What is most lacking in the *Sphex* (and the fly) is an escape from dominance by immediate environmental feedback by means of an episodic record of its own immediately preceding behavior. We shall see that a short-term memory, as well as other means of representing and manipulating information, expands behavioral flexibility.

2.1.3. Human Reflexive Responses   What aspects of human behavior are *Sphex*ish in having stereotypic, fixed forms? The problem with recognizing these behaviors in humans is that, though hard-wired, they are typically co-opted into larger patterns of purposive behavior. For example, walking involves a relatively fixed sequential pattern of reflexive multi-muscle responses. Under the vast majority of circumstances, the activity of walking itself proceeds in a fixed, hard-wired sequence that is *Sphex*ish. However, the context, timing, and direction of walking are determined by higher and more complex levels of the nervous system. More importantly, attention to walking allows us to make temporary intentional modifications and variations of our gait such as skipping. As we mentioned earlier, concert listeners can voluntarily suppress the reflexive behavior of coughing until an intermission.

*Sphex*ish behavioral programs continue to operate in humans, and under most circumstances are executed in their stereotypic forms. However, in more complex organisms such as human beings, these fixed-form automatic behaviors can be modified intentionally in a top-down manner (feigning a limp), or caught up in a larger conscious, intentional process (walking outside to pick up the newspaper).

2.2 Unreflective Adaptable Action

The previous section illustrated action under evaluation in two very different species: simple organisms such as protozoa and more complex organisms such as insects. With increased neural complexity has come more complex behaviors (such as the egg laying of the wasp) that are subject to modification by natural selection. We have pointed out that it is mistaken to consider these behaviors as purely mechanical. Rather, all actions of organisms are adaptive and responsive to evaluation of feedback from the environment. The behavior of insects is clearly goal-directed and characterized by trying out behaviors, evaluating the consequences, and making necessary adjustments in ongoing activity. However, among the cognitive abilities that are missing in flies and wasps are (1) a form of short-term memory that would allow the organism to keep track of its own recent behaviors and to use this information to modulate ongoing activity, and (2) forms of procedural learning that would allow the accumulation of experience to modify instinctive behaviors and create entirely new forms of responding.[8] It is primarily complex memory (short and long term) that leads to the more adaptive action of organisms with the behavioral capacities of laboratory rats and pigeons.

Thus, in the category of *unreflective adaptable action* we place the sorts of activity of which more complex, "programmable" organisms are capable. At this level of phylogenetic advance, action—feedback—evaluation—action systems are capable of substantial modification through learning, resulting in new forms of automatic, habitual action. There is greater individual-organism modification and selection of behavioral programs, as opposed to species-wide selection shaped by evolution.

Unreflective adaptable actions (as we classify them) have three primary sources. Goal-related problems can be solved initially by either *imitation* or some form of *trial-and-error* activity. When the results of new behaviors are positively or negatively reinforced by feedback from the environment, learning of new habitual behavioral sequences occurs. In human beings, a third form of unreflective action derives from previous off-line reflection that has been put into action and become habitual (resulting in *automaticity*). Thus, we shall refer to rudimentary learning and imitation as *pre-reflective* adaptable action, while at least some habits in humans represent *post-reflective* adaptable action.

2.2.1. Pre-reflective Adaptations—Learning by Trial and Error   Rats learn to run mazes in order to solve the problem of finding food. Their initial behavior involves goal seeking, but otherwise random exploration of the maze. As the rat learns that food is to be found consistently in a certain place in the maze, and learns the most direct path to the food, the animal's behavior changes from trial-and-error exploration to a rapid run directly to the location of the food. This form of behavioral adaptation is serviced by neural systems (which have been reasonably well described by neuroscience research) in which the reward following a successful pattern of behavior causes particular brain systems (such as the dopamine system of the brain stem and forebrain) to become active in order to reinforce (i.e., make more likely to recur) the specific neural pattern involved in the preceding behavior. This

---

[8] Insects are able to learn very simple new information, such as the location of food, but are not able to learn complex new behavioral responses or procedures.

is a particularly important instance of the effect of top–down environmental feedback in reshaping the animal's organizing system (see Fig. 2.3).

There are important differences between the rat's maze running and the activity of the *Sphex*. One difference is captured by the concept of open versus closed instincts. The behavior of the *Sphex* occurs in service of a closed instinct, in that there is one and only one form of behavior that counts as satisfying the instinct. Thus, the behavioral sequence of the *Sphex* does not adjust to the simple fact of the cricket being repeatedly moved. Rats have open instincts (also called drives). That is, the demands of the instinct can be satisfied by a wide range of behaviors that have the appropriate end–product. Learning in the rat links open instincts to specific behaviors in a flexible and adaptable manner. Thus, the organism has increased openness and flexibility in goal–directed problem solving.

Another difference is that those behavioral variations that are most successful for the particular rat are retained for use in future similar situations. New complex patterns of behavior become established on the basis of the specific environmental feedback that the particular organism receives. Actions that are most successful in solving the biological problems of each particular rat in its particular environmental context are remembered for use in similar situations in the future. Thus, action under evaluation for the rat involves a wider range of behavioral flexibility that enables it to engage in exploration and trial-and-error problem solving, along with memory of the results of previous behavior.

Maze running by a rat is considered *unreflective*, because it comes about by the adaptable processes of trial and error and reinforcement. It does not necessarily require the rat to have available and to manipulate a mental representation of the maze, the food, and potential alternative actions. Once learned, the co–occurrence of a drive state and an environmental context results in an automatic execution of the response without prior manipulation of mental representations. However, the behavior is not *Sphex*ish in that, if interrupted, the rat can make a quick adaptation and resume activity at its previous point, or if the situation changes (the experimenter introduces changes in the successful maze path), the animal will try out alternative paths.

Research has demonstrated that rats "know" the location of the food in the maze and, if the path is blocked, will search for the most direct new route to that location. Furthermore, when searching a maze with eight radial arms and food randomly placed at the end of only one arm of the maze, rats maintain a record (a neural representation) of the arms of the maze that have already been searched on this particular trial. Describing maze running as an example of unreflective action does not imply that the rat does not have some form of mental representations, only that this well-studied form of rat behavior does not necessitate *manipulation* of mental representations prior to behavior.[9]

2.2.2. Pre-reflective Adaptations—Learning by Imitation Recent neuro-science research has suggested another method by which unreflective actions can become established in the behavioral repertoire of an animal or human. It has been discovered that mirror neural activity occurs in the motor system of one animal while watching the activity of another. Thus, when one monkey watches another monkey press a lever, it creates the same neural activity in the brain of the observer that would occur if the observer pressed the lever.[10] Therefore, there exist neural processes in the motor systems of the brain that are automatically engaged by watching the activity of another organism. This neural activation would increase the likelihood of imitation of the particular action. This allows new behaviors to be established by merely watching the actions of others. Such behavior is unreflective, in that engaging in the behavior does not require any prior manipulation of mental representations.

2.2.3. Pre-reflective Adaptability in Humans Detecting similar pre-reflective actions in humans is difficult. We can easily bring into attention and modify any particular behavior, even those behaviors that were originally learned entirely through processes of either imitation or trial-and-error learning, and that typically proceed entirely outside conscious reflection. Yet, the fact that a behavior can become the subject of reflection should not distract us from understanding its fundamentally unreflective character.

A readily understood example of unreflective human action is a golf swing or a tennis stroke. Neither of these actions could ever be considered *Sphex*ish. Most novice golfers feel that there is nothing less biologically

---

[9] See sec. 2.3.1 below on the distinction between presentations and emulations.

[10] G. Rizzolatti and L. Craighero, "The Mirror-Neuron System", *Annual Review of Neuroscience*, 27 (2000), 169–92; G. Rizzolatti, L. Fadiga, V. Gallese, and L. Fogassi, "Premotor Cortex and the Recognition of Motor Actions", *Cognitive Brain Research*, 3 (1996), 131–41.

natural than a golf swing. What is more, for all the talk that is wasted by golf and tennis instructors, it is questionable whether reflection (promoted by verbal instructions) makes a significant contribution to learning. By and large, these athletic performances are learned by a combination of imitation and trial and error. The best instructors show the correct stroke or swing (to elicit an imitative response in the student), and then allow the student many trial-and-error attempts with continual feedback (positive and negative reinforcement) from the instructor. The unreflective nature of these actions is made clear by the fact that, during a game of tennis or golf, it is considered a fatal mistake for the stroke to become the subject of reflection (i.e., subject to top-down conscious control). A devious ploy is to encourage your opponent in a tennis or golf match to become reflectively conscious of the stroke by complimenting him or her on some specific component of the back swing or follow through.

2.2.4. Post-reflective Adaptations—Automaticity   An extensive literature indicates that a very large portion of daily human complex behavior is automatic and unreflective. While most behaviors are considered willful and intentional by the agent, in many cases research shows otherwise. For some investigators the research question is not: Are some behaviors automatic?, but rather, Is any behavior deliberate? We usually do not consider our behavior to be automatic largely because most of our automatic, unreflective actions have been a part of some prior reflection. However, at the moment of execution, the behavior is initiated and continues to completion entirely automatically. For example, learning to drive a car involves a certain amount of explicit reflection, teaching, and continual conscious monitoring of actions. However, once one has become an experienced driver, handling the car and following the rules of driving become so automatic that one can carry on a conversation with a passenger, listen to a radio talk show, talk on a cellular telephone, compose a letter in one's mind, or daydream while driving.

R. F. Baumeister and K. L. Sommer have estimated that consciousness plays a causal role in as little as 5 per cent of our daily behavior, implying that 95 per cent of daily behavior is automatic. This estimate comes from research in what these investigators term "ego depletion". For example, they demonstrated that suppressing thoughts about white bears (an activity demanding conscious mental resources) diminishes one's ability to be persistent in solving unsolvable puzzles, both of which are actions demanding conscious mental resources.[11] However, suppressing such thoughts would have no effect on driving a car (when the processes of driving have become habitual). The point made by these experiments is that the capacity for conscious control of behavior is a very limited resource, which can be apportioned to only a very small part of our ongoing activity. Therefore, the rest of our complex daily activity must proceed automatically, outside conscious control.

J. A. Bargh and T. L. Chartrand suggest three important domains of activity in which automaticity plays the critical role. First is the automatic effect of perception on action. Research has shown that merely perceiving the actions of others increases the likelihood of performing the same acts.[12] As we have already seen, a likely neurophysiological basis for this form of observation-induced tendency for imitation has recently been suggested by demonstration of the existence of mirror neurons in the motor systems of the brain.

A second important form of automaticity suggested by Bargh and Chartrand is automatic goal pursuit. Behavioral goals are elicited automatically in situations on the basis of previous experiences in similar situations. A simple example can be seen in what happens when a student enters a classroom. The goal of finding a place to sit is automatically activated. Although the student may be aware of looking for a seat, the process of deciding that the immediate goal is to find a seat is, in most cases, never a conscious decision. The goal was automatically activated by entering the classroom.

Finally, Bargh and Chartrand argue that subjective emotions and evaluations are also automatic. There is a learned (but nevertheless unconscious and automatic) link between our perceptions of the environment and our emotional evaluative responses. In Chapter 1 (sec. 3.2) we described Antonio Damasio's account of "somatic markers" and their critical role in the unconscious regulation of behavior. Somatic markers are another term for the unconscious (or pre-conscious) emotional and evaluative responses that are automatically elicited as we interact with our environment either physically or within our internal, off-line mental processes.

[11] R. F. Baumeister and K. L. Sommer, "Consciousness, Free Choice, and Automaticity", in R. S. Wyer, Jr. (ed.), *Advances in Social Cognition*, vol. X (Mahwah, NJ: Erlbaum, 1997), 75–81.

[12] J. A. Bargh and T. L. Chartrand, "The Unbearable Automaticity of Being", *American Psychologist*, 54 (1999), 462–79.

The automatic behaviors described in this section are considered *post-reflective* because in the case of human beings, at least, the specific form of many of the behaviors that are automatically elicited are the product of deliberate, intentional behaviors, or conscious evaluations that took place in a previous situation. In our seat-finding example of automatic goal pursuit, early experiences of a child at school would have involved a much more conscious process of deciding (or being told) that finding a place to sit was what needs to be done when entering a classroom. Later in life, this goal is automatically activated. Thus, though there is no current reflection involved regarding the goal, reflection played a critical part in the history of the instantiation of the automaticity.

2.3 Reflective Adaptive Action

The previous section on non-reflective adaptive action emphasized the increased behavioral adaptability that is available when an organism is capable of memory and learning. Adaptability and modification of action have moved, more significantly, from the species level to that of individual organisms. Memory and learning have also expanded the time scale of individual adaptability in that these capacities are both retrospective, preserving information from the past, and prospective, in creating expectancy for what is likely to be the case given past experiences preserved through learning.

What is not yet well developed in the organisms described so far is the ability to represent and manipulate information entirely within the nervous system. This represents a form of mental/neural trying-out of potential behaviors. Thus, by *reflective adaptive action* we mean those forms of behavior that are mediated by the off-line elicitation and manipulation of some form of neural/mental representation of the situation and possibilities for action. In order to understand the nature of this form of action, we need first to consider the nature and forms of representation.

2.3.1. The Nature of Representation

There is no widely agreed-upon account of representation. This should not surprise us when we think of the vast number of ways in which we use the term "representation". For present purposes we shall employ a distinction among kinds of representation that is based on the semiology (theory of signs) developed by the American pragmatist philosopher Charles Sanders Peirce (1839–1914). Peirce distinguished three kinds of signs: icons, indices, and symbols. Icons

serve as signs in virtue of their resemblance to what they signify; indices serve in virtue of an association such as causal connection or temporal
succession; and symbols are purely conventional. In what follows we shall
speak of three sorts of *representation*, based on Peirce's three sorts of signs.

The use of iconic and indexical representation is prevalent in the animal
world. The mental process in understanding an icon is simply that the
cognitive system does not make a distinction between the representation
and that which is being represented. A fly fisherman's elk-hair imitation of
a caddis fly is (it is hoped) an iconic representation of a real caddis fly to a
lurking trout.

Indices represent predictable co-occurrences of icons and must be learned
through association and contiguity. To a hunting lion, the various movements of a herd of antelope would index their state of alertness. The
alerting calls used by various species of monkey are indices of the presence
of certain forms of threat. Infant monkeys must learn associations between
certain calls and specific forms of danger and danger-avoiding behaviors.
Thus, both icons and indices have some form of direct connection with
the aspects of the physical environment that are being represented. In
the discussion that follows, non-symbolic reflective action involves the
manipulation of icons and indices.

Symbols (primarily linguistic symbols) have meaning and referential value
due to their ability to link together collections of icons or indices, and also
to their semantic relatedness to other symbols. Thus, symbolic reflection
has the added power of representing abstract properties, processes, and
influences. That is, symbols can represent classes of properties, objects, or
events. Symbols can represent concepts that are not themselves perceptible,
such as the idea of tomorrow or of Paris (even if you've never been
there), the existence of a subatomic particle, the characteristic of honesty,
the institution of marriage, or the property of being morally good. Thus,
symbols allow reflection regarding an indefinitely wide spatial and temporal
conceptual range.

Following Peirce, Terrence Deacon argues that icons, indices, and symbols are related to each other in a hierarchical manner. Indices are learned
associations between icons. For a monkey to know the meaning of an
alerting call is for it to have a strong learned association between an iconic
representation of the particular call and an iconic representation of the threat
of a leopard, for example. Thus, indices remain stable due to continuing

co-occurrence of icons. Symbols are built upon the recognition of relation-ships among indices. A new representational token (a symbol) stands for the *relational pattern* within an assemblage of indices. Thus, indices are built upon relationships among icons, and symbols upon relationships among indices.[13]

However, another useful distinction has been made by Rick Grush. Grush provides the following analogy. He is playing chess with a friend, although not in the same location; the moves are described over the telephone. Grush has a chess board that he uses to keep track of the "official" game board, but also a second board on which he tries out moves in order to assess their possible consequences and countermoves. Grush argues that the first board should be thought of as a "presentation", and only the second should be thought of as a "representation". He says:

A presentation is used to provide information about some other, probably external in some sense, state of affairs. It can be used in this way because the presentation is typically causally or informationally linked to the target in some way. The representation's use is quite different: it is used as a counterfactual presentation. It is, in very rough terms, a model of the target which is used off-line to try out possible actions, so that their likely consequences can be assessed without having to actually try those actions or suffer those consequences. Second, and this is implicit in the first point, the ability to use an entity as an off-line stand-in depends crucially on its not being causally linked to, and its not necessarily carrying information about, the entity it represents.[14]

We believe that Grush's distinction is quite important, but do not wish to follow his terminological recommendations. We take both chess boards to be representations, but recognize another set of distinctions within the category of representation, which we shall call "presentations" and "emu-lations", respectively. This distinction cuts across the distinctions among icons, indices, and symbols. Thus, it is one thing to have a mental image (iconic presentation) of a stack of blocks, and another to be able to manip-ulate that image in space (iconic emulation). It is one thing to know the meaning of "cat" and "mat", and another to be able to try out "The cat is on the mat" and "The mat is on the cat". Thus, icons, indices, and symbols can be used as *presentations* to understand, interpret, and act in relation to what is present in the field of action; alternatively, they can be used

[13] Deacon, *Symbolic Species*, ch. 3.
[14] Rick Grush, "The Architecture of Representation", in W. Bechtel *et al.* (eds.), *Philosophy and the Neurosciences: A Reader* (Oxford: Blackwell, 2001), 349–68, at p. 351.

in *emulations*, as in off-line imagination of potential actions and the likely consequences of such actions.

Yet another distinction is between what we might call a "representation-in-use" and a "representation-in-itself". We take representation-in-use as the basic category. However, due to the fact that there are systematic practices for the production of representations-in-use (e.g., artistic conventions), the term "representation" is often applied to an item (e.g., a painting) even when it is not in use.

Earlier (Ch. 1, sec. 3.5) we endorsed Donald MacKay's definition of a mental/neural representation as "a conditional readiness to reckon". Similarly, William Bechtel defines a representation as "an information-bearing state or event which stands in for what it represents and enables the system in which it operates to utilize this information in coordinating its behavior".[15] Distinguishing between representations-in-use and representations-in-themselves, then, we can say that Joan's twin sister Jane is not a representation-in-itself of Joan. Terrence Deacon points out, however, that one object becomes a representation (in our sense of representation-in-use) when the user fails to distinguish the two objects. Thus, if I fail to distinguish Jean from Joan when Jean appears, then I am in a state of readiness to reckon with Joan. In short, an icon is a representation-in-use, which represents for the user any other item from which the user is unable to distinguish it.

In what follows, we shall consider reflective action in two categories: non-symbolic (i.e., reflection or emulation involving iconic and indexical representations) and symbolic (i.e., reflection involving linguistic symbols). The topic of symbolic representation—that is, the relation of language to the world—is complicated enough to defer to the next chapter. We shall argue in Chapter 7 that the infinite recombinatorial possibilities of symbolic language and the extent to which symbolic representations can float free of immediate referents (i.e., in imagination and emulation) are important sources of human freedom.

2.3.2. Non-symbolic Reflective Action Smoky the cattle-horse was in a corral with a herd of cattle. Hay was spread in an adjacent corral. Although the gate was open between the two corrals, the cattle stood at the dividing

---

[15] William Bechtel, "Representations: From Neural Systems to Cognitive Systems", in *idem et al.* (eds.), *Philosophy and the Neurosciences*, 332–48, at p. 347.

fence and bawled for the food. Eventually, Smoky rounded them up and drove them through the gate. Smoky's behavior may be a very rudimentary example of reflective action, in that Smoky may have had to have in mind some representation of the cattle, the fence, the gate, and the possibility of herding the cattle through the gate in order to execute this behavior. While the process of herding-cattle-through-gates may have been taught Smoky in the process of his learning to be a cattle-horse, the immediate problem and its solution would seem to require some form of representation, and thus some very rudimentary reflection, yet there is no way to know for sure.

Similar forms of rudimentary representational reflection may be involved in certain forms of hunting and predatory behavior in animals. For example, for lions the process of hunting appears to involve a variety of mental "calculations", including the direction of the wind, the position of the prey, the current positioning of other members of the pride, the distance to the prey, and the choice of likely targets within a herd of antelope or zebra. All of this must result in a decision regarding the direction and timing of the charge, sometimes with the objective of driving the herd toward other pride members. Again, though many elements of the hunting behavior may be either *Sphex*ish or learned through imitation and trial and error, for the particular hunt to be successful, off-line calculations and emulations would seem to be necessary, involving representations of a variety of immediate environmental parameters.

A more obvious example, and a less rudimentary form of non-symbolic reflective action, can be found in the oft-cited studies of "insight" in chimpanzees by *Gestalt* psychologist Wolfgang Köhler.[16] One scenario described by Köhler involved a chimpanzee named Sultan, who was typically able to use long sticks to reach bananas placed outside his cage. At one point Sultan was given two poles, neither of which was long enough to reach the bananas. Sultan tried to reach the bananas with each pole successively, but found neither pole long enough. He became frustrated and sat in the corner of his cage. Suddenly he went back to the poles, immediately put one inside the other to create a longer pole, and retrieved the bananas. Here the reflective aspect of action is more obvious. Sultan had clearly solved the problem by some form of representational reflection (employment of an emulation) prior to execution of the correct solution. Representations

---

[16] Wolfgang Köhler, *The Mentality of Apes* (London: Routledge & Kegan Paul, 1956).

of the poles, the bananas, and potential actions were mentally manipulated in a manner so as eventually to discover a successful solution.

A number of properties contribute to such non-symbolic reflective action. First, a neural/mental representation is necessary, not just of a goal state, but also of relationships between relevant environmental elements. Second, there must be an ability for mental manipulation of the representations (emulations), in order to imagine the form of a solution. This mental activity may be as complex as imaginative trial and error (as seemed to be the case for Sultan), or as rudimentary as integrating immediately present sensory representations and indices (as in the case of Smoky the cattle-horse).

2.3.3. Symbolic Reflective Action   The power of even the most rudimentary symbols in mediating action is illustrated by a simple experiment done with chimpanzees. S. Boysen and G. Bernston set up a problem that chimps could not solve.[17] Two piles of candy were presented, one larger than the other. One of two chimps was allowed to choose between the piles of candy. However, the pile chosen was always given to the other chimp. The chimpanzee that was allowed to choose always chose the large pile, and thus always received the smaller one (resulting in considerable displays of frustration). The chimp could not learn to choose the lesser amount of candy in order to receive the more desirable reward. Human children over the age of two years generally have no trouble solving this problem.

This problem could be solved by chimpanzees if they were first taught an association between Arabic numbers and differing quantities. Once this association was thoroughly learned, the chimpanzee was given the original problem, but now with Arabic numbers designating the piles of candy. Chimps were now able to learn to choose the Arabic number associated with a smaller quantity in order to obtain the larger quantity. Introducing the indirectness of the association of quantities with numerals reduced the power of the stimulus (a large pile of candy), allowing the chimp to choose the opposite of what it really wanted. Commenting on this experiment Deacon concludes, "the indirectness of indexical or symbolic reference helps to reduce the power of the stimulus (icon) to drive behavior.

---

[17] S. Boysen and G. Bernston, "Responses to Quantity: Perceptual versus Cognitive Mechanisms in Chimpanzees (Pan troglodytes)", *Journal of Experimental Psychology and Animal Behavior Processes*, 21 (1995), 82–6.

Ascending the representational hierarchy progressively frees responses from stimulus–driven immediacy, thus creating space for the generation and consideration of alternatives."[18] While the learned association between Arabic numbers and quantities probably did not meet the criteria for a symbol (and therefore constituted an index), it was nevertheless the case that providing the referential intermediary allowed a form of behavioral flexibility not otherwise possible.

As described above, the distinction between a symbol and other types of representation is that a symbol involves recognition of a pattern of relationships among other representations. This can be a pattern among indices or a pattern of other symbols. Thus, the meaning of a symbol is not directly related to the environment, but is related to relationships among other representations. Language is a symbolic representational system involving mappings of relationships among words (symbols) that are shared among particular groups of people. The critical aspect is not the relationships between the words and the external environment, but the mapping of relationships among words, and the degree to which these are shared within a larger group.

Because symbols do not directly refer to things in the world, but indirectly refer to them by virtue of referring to other symbols, they are implicitly combinatorial entities whose referential powers are derived by virtue of occupying determinate positions in an organized system of other symbols... Symbolic reference emerges from a ground of nonsymbolic referential processes only because the indexical relationships between symbols are organized so as to form a logically closed group of mappings from symbol to symbol.[19]

One of the points of contention in the research on language in chimpanzees is the degree to which the animal has crossed a symbolic threshold. Can it be shown, for example, that the chimpanzees in the candy experiment described above treated the Arabic numbers as symbols, or were they merely indices? Can they be shown to understand the logical relationships between symbols, not just the association between the Arabic numeral icon and other environmental icons? The symbolic insight that nearly every human child achieves, and is difficult (if not impossible) for a chimpanzee, is the shift from looking for indexical relationships in aspects of the sensory

---

[18] Deacon, *Symbolic Species*, 415.   [19] Ibid. 99.

environment to looking for *patterns* among indices and symbols—that is, how new symbol tokens fit into the pattern of symbols already known. This change in basic cognitive approach is considered by Deacon to be the "symbolic threshold".

Crossing the symbolic threshold allows for symbolic reflective action. We have already seen in the candy experiment with chimpanzees that a symbol (or perhaps an index in this case) allowed the chimpanzees to distance themselves from the immediacy of the stimulus environment (the sight of a large pile of candy) and to master the ability to choose that which they did not want in order to gain what they ultimately wanted. This illustrates one of the important aspects of symbolic reflection—it allows one to overcome intense impulses for immediate personal reward or protection in service of larger or less immediate aims.

Another benefit of reflective action that is provided by symbolic reference is the ability to represent the mind of another individual. Deacon argues that there is no possibility of understanding the mind of another individual through indexical reference. Indexical associations can tell us about the expected behavior of another. Mirror neurons also provide indexical information with respect to the intentions of the specific actions of others. However, the construction of the likely mental process of another individual (a "theory of mind") must be symbolic, in that it involves holding in mind multiple related indices. While empathy (shared emotions) can be created iconically (the contagion of laughing or crying) or indexically (an alarm call in a monkey colony), symbolic reference amplifies empathy through the process of knowing symbolically the likely experiences of another. Empathy enhanced by a symbolically constructed theory of mind accounts for the power of narrative to evoke profound emotions. Indeed, Deacon suggests that "the ability to let our emotions be activated by the virtual experiences constructed with the aid of symbols probably makes us the only species in which there can be a genuine conflict of simultaneous emotional states".[20]

A critical aspect of symbolic reflection for understanding the nature of action is its capacity to allow us to construct hypothetical mental scenarios of possible alternative future behaviors. Many different scenarios of potential action and the likely consequences of such actions can be represented symbolically for reflection, allowing behavior to be organized over the

---

[20] Ibid. 431.

long term in relationship to distant goals. Given the symbolic capacity for a theory of mind mentioned above, symbolic reference can also be used to represent the potential dynamics of social relationships, allowing one to consider the impact of the various behavioral options being considered on the networks of social relationships that are involved. "Symbolic analysis is the basis for a remarkable new level of self-determination that human beings alone have stumbled upon. The ability to use virtual reference to build up elaborate internal models of possible futures, and to hold these complex visions in mind with the force of the mnemonic glue of symbolic inference and descriptive shorthand, gives us unprecedented capacity to generate independent adaptive behaviors."[21] We pursue these issues throughout the remainder of this volume.

3   Adaptive Action Loops and Nested Hierarchies

We began this chapter with the idea that organisms are goal-directed and constantly involved in action under evaluation. We represented this understanding of the behavior of organisms using Donald MacKay's simple diagram of the minimal architecture of an agent (see Fig. 2.3 p. 69). We then described phenomenologically the increasingly flexible forms of adaptive action available to organisms as one moves up phylogenetic levels of complexity.

MacKay accounts for increasing degrees of flexibility in behavior as the outcome of higher-order supervisory systems capable of evaluating lower-order processes. Thus, MacKay expands his functional architecture of an agent to suggest overlays of more and more complex and abstract forms of modulation. He begins by suggesting that action loops are modulated by supervisory systems that function to set the goals of local action loops. Figure 3.2 incorporates the concept of a supervisory system (SS).

MacKay makes clear, however, that this "supervisor" is not some sort of "homunculus", or even a centralized place where, in Daniel Dennett's terms, "it all comes together". Rather, a supervisory system is a larger action loop within which the original loop in nested. This creates a higher-order system that imposes constraints on the original system. Figure 3.3 is the same diagram, but with the SS elaborated into its constituent parts.

---

[21] Deacon, *Symbolic Species*, 434.

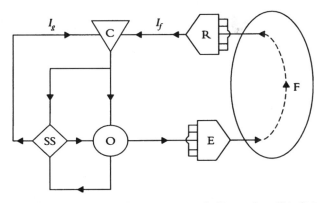

Figure 3.2. The simplest model of an active, goal-directed, and information-using (evaluative) system *that sets its own goals*. With respect to Fig. 2.3, a supervisory system (SS) has been added that can dynamically use system information to reset goals (I_g). *Source*: MacKay, *Behind the Eye* (Oxford: Blackwell, 1991), 51.

In Figure 3.3 we see that the functional architecture of a supervisory system is a meta-comparator (MC) and meta-organizer (MO)—that is, the same sort of architecture that comprises the original action loop, involving action, feedback, evaluation, and modified action. As MacKay states, "[w]e have drawn the meta-organizing system with a meta-evaluative procedure to take stock of how things are going. It adjusts and reselects the current goal in the light of its evaluation of the success of ongoing agency, and it also keeps up to date the organizing system to match the state of the world indicated by the feedforward from the receptor system."[22]

MacKay points out that it is reasonable to consider increasingly more complex levels of nesting of such modulatory feedback loops which we represent as in Figure 3.4. The supervisory system (SS) of Figure 3.4 would, by extension, involve a meta-meta-comparator and a meta-meta-organizer. Only the limits of imagination constrain the possibilities for nesting, particularly given the incredibly complex network that is the human brain, and the equally complex layers of cognitive scaffolding developed in human cultures. MacKay does not speculate as to what might be the various forms of comparisons and evaluations in the higher-level loops, but it is reasonable to presume that they would involve more complex memories, information distributed over longer epochs of time,

[22] MacKay, *Behind the Eye*, 141.

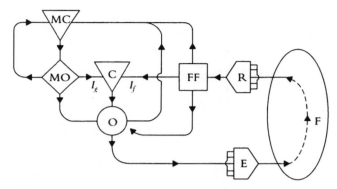

Figure 3.3. The same model of a simple system that sets its own goals (as in Fig. 3.2), but with the supervisory system specified here as a meta-comparator (MC) and a meta-organizer (MO) that dynamically uses system information to reset goals (I_g). FF refers to sensory feed forward. *Source*: MacKay, *Behind the Eye* (Oxford: Blackwell, 1991), 141.

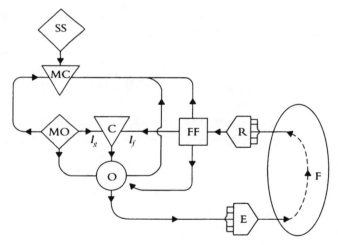

Figure 3.4. The same model of a simple system that sets its own goals (as in Fig. 3.3), but with a higher-level supervisory system specified that sets the goals for the meta-comparator. Adapted from MacKay, *Behind the Eye* (Oxford: Blackwell, 1991), 141.

and (at least in humans) more abstract forms of representation involving symbolic systems.

The following is an illustration of what meta- and meta-meta-level supervisory systems add to agency. Earlier we described the experiment in which chimpanzees had to solve the problem of getting the larger pile of candy by choosing the smaller one. Our emphasis there was on the value of symbolic representation in freeing the chimpanzee from the power of the immediate stimulus of the candy. This experiment also highlights a second ability that humans develop early on and that animals lack. What the chimpanzees in the first phase of the experiment were not able to do was to make their own behavior, their own cognitive strategy, the object of their attention. This ability to represent to oneself aspects of one's own cognitive processes in order to evaluate them is what is called in cognitive science "meta-cognition" and what we shall call self-transcendence. Thus, what the chimpanzee seems to lack are important, very high-level supervisory systems, as represented in Figure 3.4 above.

As Daniel Dennett points out, the truly explosive advance in the escape from crude biological determinism comes when the capacity for pattern recognition is turned in upon itself. The creature which is not only sensitive to patterns in its environment, but also sensitive to patterns in its own reactions to the environment, has taken a major step.[23] Dennett's term for this is the ability to "go meta"—that is, one represents one's representations, reacts to one's reactions. "The power to iterate one's powers in this way, to apply whatever tricks one has to one's existing tricks, is a well-recognized breakthrough in many domains: a cascade of processes leading from stupid to sophisticated activity."[24] This is but one instance of the phenomenon, recognized by Alicia Juarrero, whereby higher-order systems constrain the behavior of their constituents, but the imposition of *context-sensitive* constraints greatly increases the degrees of freedom of the system itself (see Ch. 2, sec. 4). We shall see another example in the creation of symbolic language (in Ch. 4).

4 Brains that "Go Meta"

The phylogenetic increase in the breadth and scope of flexibility in action that we have described (including the self-transcendent property of "going meta") was made possible by a progressive increase in the size and complexity of the brain. While increases in total brain size (versus

[23] Dennett, *Elbow Room*, 29; referring to D. R. Hofstadter, "Can Creativity Be Mechanized?", *Scientific American*, 247 (Sept. 1982), 18–34.
[24] Dennett, *Elbow Room*, 29.

body size) explain part of the expansion in the flexibility and adaptability of action, an increase in the relative size of the cerebral cortex was most important (particularly among mammals). Particularly critical to flexibility of action was an increase in the relative size of the areas of the cerebral cortex that are *not* directly involved in sensory and motor processing. There are three such cortical areas, called "tertiary association cortex": (1) the area of overlap between the occipital, parietal, and temporal lobes; (2) the inferior temporal cortex; and (3) the prefrontal cortex.

Expansion of the prefrontal cortex among mammals is remarkable. This area is only 3.5 per cent of the total cerebral cortex in a cat, 12.5 per cent in a dog, 11.5 per cent in a macaque, and 17 per cent in a chimpanzee. In the human brain, the prefrontal cortex enlarged to occupy 29 percent of the total cerebral cortex.[25] The "wiring diagram" of the prefrontal cortex is characterized by extensive two-way (or "reentrant") interactions with all of the motor, sensory, and affective areas of the cortex. In human development, the prefrontal cortex is slow to reach maturity, not being completely myelinated until sometime in the third decade of life.[26] Thus, it is likely that many of the differences in adaptability between different species of mammal, as well as the maturation of human behavioral regulation from infancy to adulthood, are related to expansion and development of the prefrontal cortex.

Studies of the role of the prefrontal cortex in cognitive functioning strongly suggest their important role in the development of human agency and adaptability. Joaquín Fuster summarizes the following four specific roles of the prefrontal cortex in the modulation of behavior:[27]

1. *Temporal integration of behavior.* The prefrontal cortex allows for the coordination of behavior across time with respect to biological and cognitive goals. It thus allows for actions to be organized over longer temporal epochs and for choice between alternatives. The ability of the prefrontal cortex to organize behavior over time has led some to suggest that the prefrontal cortex serves as a "central executive".

2. *Working memory.* Working memory refers to information held in mind for the short term in order to solve current problems. It appears

---

[25] Joaquín M. Fuster, "Frontal Lobe and Cognitive Development", *Journal of Neurocytology*, 31 (2002), 374–6.
[26] Ibid. 376.   [27] Ibid.

that at least part of the neurophysiology of working memory involves reciprocal interactions between neurons in prefrontal areas and neurons in the sensory/perceptual and motor brain areas that serve to keep specific neural circuits active over time. This maintenance of neural activity creates a focus of attention on internal representations of information for a sufficient span of time to allow for delayed responses (temporal integration) and manipulation of information (working memory).[28]

3. *Preparatory set*: Prefrontal neurons also have a role in preparing an animal for action. Reverberatory interactions are instantiated between prefrontal neurons and neural circuits in motor areas, which prepare the animal for anticipated action.

4. *Inhibitory control*: In order for a behavioral structure to be maintained over time, there must be suppression of external inputs or internal impulses that would distract from the current behavioral process. Unrelated sensory information, perceptual images, affective responses, or motor tendencies must all be suppressed.[29] The medial and orbital parts of the prefrontal cortex serve this inhibitory role. Damage to these brain areas in humans leads to impulsive, irritable, and hyperactive behavior.

Thus, in the most general terms, the prefrontal cortex allows for adaptability over time, incorporating both a retrospective aspect (memory) and a prospective aspect (preparedness for action and events, and anticipation of outcomes) into the control of behavior. In addition, the prefrontal cortex sits atop the nested hierarchy of behavioral evaluation and modulation described in the previous section.

Both the role of the prefrontal cortex in modulating behavior over time and the concept of nested hierarchies of control are nicely illustrated by recent research using functional magnetic resonance imaging (fMRI) by E. Koechlin, C. Ody, and F. Kouneiher.[30] In a single experiment, these investigators demonstrated the role in behavioral regulation of three areas within the lateral frontal lobe: (1) a posterior frontal area (called "the premotor cortex"), which is involved in selecting *specific motor actions*; (2) an area just in front of this area (called "the caudal lateral prefrontal

---

[28] Ibid.

[29] This is another instance of the phenomenon of context-sensitive constraints creating more degrees of freedom for the system as a whole.

[30] E. Koechlin, C. Ody, and F. Kouneiher, "The Architecture of Cognitive Control in Human Prefrontal Cortex", *Science*, 302 (2003), 1181–5.

cortex"), which holds information about the *immediate context* of current stimuli; and (3) an area even more anterior (called "the rostral lateral prefrontal cortex"), which keeps track of information about the *general episode of behavior* (maintaining immediate and past information relevant to the current behavioral episode). Koechlin and colleagues were able to demonstrate, using fMRI, that each area became progressively active as the task demands increased from sensory to contextual, to episodic control. The results demonstrated that these areas operate as a nested hierarchy of behavioral control.

The cascade of behavioral modulation demonstrated in this research, and graphically illustrated in Figure 3.5, can be understood in the following example.[31] When the phone rings, you usually answer it. This is "sensory control", and refers to situations in which the appropriate response is directly signaled by the stimulus. However, if you are in a different context, such as at a friend's home, you typically will not answer the phone. This is what is meant by "contextual control" in the model—the nature of the

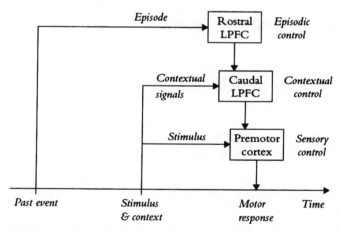

Figure 3.5. A graphic representation of the implications of the results of the study by Koechlin, Ody, and Kouneiher. Three levels of behavioral control (stimulus, contextual, and episodic) were found to activate three progressively more anterior frontal-lobe areas (premotor cortex, caudal lateral prefrontal cortex [LPFC], and rostral LPFC), forming a nested hierarchy of behavioral control loops. *Source*: Reprinted with permission from Etienne Koechlin et al., 'Architecture of Cognitive Control' *Science* 302 (2003): 1181–5, Copyright 2003 AAAS.

---

[31] This example is adapted from an illustration used in a description of this research written by Laura Helmuth, "Brain Model Puts Most Sophisticated Regions Front and Center", *Science*, 302 (2003), 1133.

stimulus–response contingency is conditioned by the context. Finally, if the friend asks you to answer the phone while he is in the shower, you would go ahead and answer the phone, at least for this period of time (this episode). Thus, "episodic control" refers to the fact that different contextual and response contingencies may be in operation during different periods of time.

It was clear from this experiment that the influences in this frontal lobe control hierarchy are top-down. Using statistical path analysis to detect which structures influenced other structures, it was demonstrated that the episodic information (processed in the rostral LPFC) has top-down influence on the area processing contextual information (the caudal LPFC). This contextual processing area, in turn, had top-down influence on stimulus–response selections (occurring in the premotor cortex). These investigators suspect that there is most likely an even higher-level processor in the most extreme anterior end of the frontal lobe (called frontopolar cortex) that is involved in cognitive branching and shifting between sub-episodes of behavior, with top-down influence on the episodic control area (rostral LPFC). In essence, the outcome of this experiment illustrates a nested hierarchy of influence on behavioral regulation within the frontal cortex, as well as the role of the prefrontal cortex in organizing goal-directed behavior with respect to changing immediate and long-term context.

The similarity between this experimental description of a nested control hierarchy in the frontal lobes (Fig. 3.5) and MacKay's and our diagrams suggesting meta- and meta-meta-levels of control of action loops is remarkable. A direct sensorimotor control loop (Sensory control in Fig. 3.5) is controlled by a meta-level feedback loop (Contextual control), which is in turn under the control of a meta-meta-level supervisory system (Episodic control). The point is not that Koechlin and colleagues have found the anatomical locations that correspond to MacKay's diagrams, since MacKay did not intend his diagrams to represent anything other than minimal *functional* architecture. Rather, this research makes clear that the sort of hierarchical control systems suggested by MacKay can actually be found in the brain, that the system operates in a nested and top-down manner, and that the highest level in Koechlin's experiment involves very long-term implications modulated by the comprehension of verbal instructions.

5 Consciousness and Adaptability

In the background of much of what has been discussed thus far regarding flexibility, adaptability, and agency have been questions about human consciousness. Our subjective experience is that conscious thought and decision are the primary forms of human adaptability and agency. But what is consciousness? What role does it play in modulating behavior? How is consciousness physically embodied? To what degree are various species conscious? These are complex questions about which many volumes have been written. In what follows we will very briefly describe some theories and neuropsychological studies of consciousness as they relate to the concepts of action loops, causes-in-process, and behavioral flexibility.

5.1 Disturbances of Consciousness

The role of consciousness in behavioral flexibility and adaptability can be readily understood by consideration of the neuropsychology (disabilities and residual abilities) of individuals with disturbances of consciousness due to certain forms of brain damage. Different disorders illustrate different properties of consciousness.

Much has been written in philosophy of mind about the phenomenon of "blind sight".[32] This phenomenon occurs in persons with damage to the visual cortex on one side of the brain, who consequently lose the ability to "see" anything on the opposite side of the visual world (i.e., loss of conscious visual perception). "Blind sight" refers to the ability of some of these individuals to reach out and intercept a target that is moving within the area of blindness, which they nevertheless report that they cannot see. Some would suggest that this proves that phenomenal awareness is unnecessary for action. The correct interpretation is that phenomenal awareness is unnecessary for some primitive forms of action (intercepting a moving target), but necessary for other forms of action. Thus, when the target moves from the area of blindness into the area of visual perception and awareness, the person can recognize specifically what the moving object is. For example, is it a fly or a wasp—a Frisbee or a football? Phenomenal awareness of stimulus meaning allows

---

[32] L. Weiskrantz, E. K. Warrington, *et al.*, "Visual Capacity in the Hemianopic Field following a Restricted Occipital Ablation", *Brain: A Journal of Neurology*, 97/4 (1974), 709–28.

the person to consider different possibilities for action with respect to the flying object based on conscious perception of the nature of the object, and to name or describe the object verbally. Thus, phenomenal awareness opens the possibilities for a wider and more flexible range of adaptive actions.

More recent studies of individuals with cortical blindness have documented new forms of blind sight. It has been shown using functional brain imaging that the brains of such individuals respond correctly to, and the person is to some degree aware of, the emotional expression of a face even when they are not consciously aware of seeing a face.[33] Again, this shows both what can be known outside consciousness (sensing the emotional impact of a facial expression) and what additional information is available with conscious perception (knowing that a face has been presented, being able to know various thing about the particular face, etc.).

The contribution of consciousness to behavior is also apparent in the contrast between individuals with anosognosia versus individuals with other forms of agnosia (agnosia means "absence of knowledge of"). "Anosognosia" is the clinical term used to identify a disorder (usually from damage to the right parietal lobe) that involves *adamant denial* of disability, often accompanied by paralysis of the opposite side of the body. Somehow the body representation of these individuals cannot be updated in such a way as to provide information to conscious awareness regarding their unilateral paralysis. Thus, they are not able to adjust their behavior to take the paralysis into account. In contrast, other forms of agnosia, such as the inability to recognize faces, create deficits regarding which the patient is acutely aware, and this awareness allows the patient to adjust his or her behavior to accommodate the deficit.

One extreme case of the impact of awareness in learning to compensate for agnosia was described by the famous Russian neuropsychologist A. R. Luria.[34] Luria reproduced (with his own accompanying commentary) portions of the painstakingly written 3,000-page diary of a Russian soldier called Zasetsky, who had suffered a brain injury during World War II. The injury left him with very severe deficits in visual perception (agnosia) and a very limited working memory. He had great difficulty reading

---

[33] B. de Gelder, J. Vroomen, *et al.*, "Non-Conscious Recognition of Affect in the Absence of Striate Cortex", *Neuroreport*, 10/18 (1999), 3759–63.

[34] A. R. Luria, *The Man with the Shattered World* (New York: Basic Books, 1972).

and writing, because he both struggled to recognize letters and could not hold the letters in mind long enough to read words or sentences. What is remarkable about Zasetsky's story is his acute consciousness of his limitations, and his persistence over a 20-year period in learning to overcome his deficits sufficiently to write his extensive diary. Zasetsky's conscious awareness of his deficiencies allowed him to marshal adaptive strategies that are not brought to bear by persons with anosognosia, due to inability consciously to recognize their disability. Since conscious awareness is necessary for such complex forms of behavioral flexibility it cannot be epiphenomenal.

Finally, the fractioning of the content of consciousness created by severing of the connections between the right and left cerebral hemispheres (resulting in individuals with a "split brain") is also revealing of the nature of consciousness.[35] The surgical procedure (done for the relief of otherwise intractable epilepsy) severs all neural connections between the cerebral cortices, including the 200 million axons of the corpus callosum. The result of this procedure (repeatedly demonstrated in a variety of experiments) is that sensory information, cognitive processing, and motor control within each hemisphere are isolated from processing in the other hemisphere. For example, information occurring only in the left side of the patient's visual world will be seen only by the right hemisphere and, therefore, can be responded to only by the patient's left hand (controlled by the right hemisphere, which is privy to the visual information). What has been suggested is that the split-brain patient now has split consciousness. Each hemisphere knows and processes different information without the benefit of sharing information from the opposite hemisphere. There are now two separate domains of consciousness, at least at the level of higher-order information and behavioral control. However, the continued unity of the lower brain (not split by this surgery) means that the lower-level evaluative and regulative systems of the person remain integrated, such that the person maintains a unitary sense of self.

There are two primary concepts of consciousness: consciousness as a state (awake, asleep, in a coma) and consciousness as awareness (the content of consciousness). Thus, while the brain stem regulates states of

[35] Roger W. Sperry, "Hemisphere Deconnection and Unity in Conscious Awareness", *American Psychologist*, 23/10 (1968), 723–33; *idem*, "A Modified Concept of Consciousness", *Psychological Review*, 76/6 (1969), 532–6.

consciousness, the cerebral cortex (dissociated in split-brain individuals) is the organ of consciousness with respect to what information currently occupies awareness. The state of being conscious was not affected by any of the disorders of consciousness we have described. In every one of these cases it was some aspect of the *content* of conscious awareness that was affected by the brain disorder. It is consciousness as awareness (the information within current awareness and its consequence for behavioral adaptability) that is most critical for an understanding of human agency and free will, and this is the focus of our concern throughout this book.

5.2 Models of Consciousness

The term "consciousness", even when applied specifically to awareness, covers several forms of animal and human functioning. Merlin Donald suggests that there are three forms of consciousness awareness.[36] *Level 1 awareness* involves sensory binding and selective attention such as to achieve perceptual unity. With this level of awareness, action loops would be modulated by formed images, rather than by disconnected sensory properties. The sensory binding of level 1 awareness occurs as the brain's sensory cortices interact with the thalamus, and may be dependent upon the establishment of frequency coherence in the electrical activity among various brain areas. *Level 2 awareness* involves short-term or working memory. A working memory allows larger amounts of information to be bound, related, and held from seconds to minutes. This, in turn, permits more active mental processing, modulation of action based on more temporally extensive information, and greater autonomy from immediate environmental influences. We have seen in the work of Fuster (in sec. 4) that recurrent interactions between the frontal lobes and the posterior sensory cortex are critical for this active form of mental processing in working memory.[37] This second form of awareness also includes body awareness and a stable model of the environment. When body awareness and body-in-the-environment are coupled with information from a historical memory, a rudimentary self-system emerges. Finally, *level 3 awareness* involves even longer-term awareness and governance, and even more

---

[36] Merlin Donald, *A Mind So Rare: The Evolution of Human Consciousness* (New York: Norton and Co., 2001).

[37] Joaquín M. Fuster, "Prefrontal Neurons in Networks of Executive Memory", *Brain Research Bulletin*, 42 (2000), 331–6.

intense voluntary control of action. Here the evaluation and modulation of action can occur with respect to a very long time frame (minutes to hours or even days), enhanced by symbolic processes and enculturated criteria for the evaluation of behavioral outcomes (i.e., values).[38]

Philosopher Thomas Metzinger provides an account of consciousness and the sense of self that is expressed in terms of representational systems.[39] Metzinger argues that consciousness is embodied in currently activated "world models". Consciousness can be broken down into four increasingly rich variants, each adding additional characteristics and constraints to the world model. These increasingly rich forms of consciousness emerge as one moves up the phylogenetic scale of brain complexity. Human consciousness is an amalgam of all four levels.

First, there is *minimal consciousness*, which involves merely a representational state constituted by a model of the immediate physical world within a window representing presence (or "now"). Second, Metzinger proposes *differential consciousness*, in which the world model is meaningfully and hierarchically segregated and there is a temporal (sequential) structure. In differential consciousness, the mental map now provides information about a dynamic and segmented scene. *Subjective consciousness* begins to approach that which characterizes human consciousness. Here the world model includes a self-model, allowing for a consciously experienced first-person perspective. The world map is now centered continuously on this self-representation. Finally, there is *cognitive subjective consciousness*. What is added here is the ability to elicit various world models (including a representation of the self) and process them *off-line*. "These systems would be able to engage in the activation of globally available representational structures *independently of current external input*."[40] Thus, this sort of conscious system could "engage in future planning, enjoy explicit, episodic memories, or start genuinely cognitive processes like the mental formation of concepts".[41] What is more, at this level of consciousness, cognitive systems would be able to "represent themselves as representational systems... They would be thinkers of thoughts."[42] Thus, Metzinger describes consciousness as an activated model of the world, in which the

---

[38] Donald, *A Mind So Rare*, 178–204.
[39] Thomas Metzinger, *Being No One: The Self-Model Theory of Subjectivity* (Cambridge, Mass.: MIT Press, 2003).
[40] Ibid. 561; italics original.   [41] Ibid.   [42] Ibid.

dynamic complexity of the model allows for emergence of richer forms of consciousness.

Metzinger's theory of consciousness can be fitted into our framework, in which the fundamental basis of agency is the modulation of action loops, simply by presuming that the organism is modeling (or mapping) the world in terms of immediate past, current, and potential future action—feedback—evaluation—action loops. More complex world models can be understood as the information available to meta- and meta-meta-comparators and organizers in MacKay's information-flow diagrams. Particularly critical for a notion of the highest forms of mental causation is Metzinger's suggestion that the most sophisticated form of consciousness (cognitive subjective consciousness) allows for off-line elicitation and manipulation of world models involving implications for action—that is, the ability to emulate action loops.

5.3 A Plausible Neuroscience of Consciousness

Gerald Edelman and Giulio Tononi present a neurobiologically plausible model of consciousness anchored in neuroanatomy, neurophysiology, and clinical neurology.[43] With respect to a phenomenological description of consciousness, they suggest a two-part model that is roughly consistent with both the three-level typology developed by Merlin Donald and the four-level theory of Metzinger. Edelman and Tononi speak of *primary consciousness,* which is evident in the ability of animals to "construct a mental scene", but with limited semantic or symbolic content, versus *higher-order consciousness* that is "accompanied by a sense of self and the ability in the waking state explicitly to construct past and future scenes. It requires, at minimum, a semantic capacity and, in its most developed form, a linguistic capacity."[44] Both forms of consciousness include body awareness and some degree of reference in space. For Edelman and Tononi, the fundamental characteristics of consciousness are *unity* (i.e., it is experienced at any moment as an undivided whole); *informativeness* (i.e., one conscious state is experienced out of billions of possibilities); and *privateness* (i.e., the experience is accessible only to the conscious agent,

---

[43] Gerald M. Edelman and Giulio Tononi, *A Universe of Consciousness: How Matter Becomes Imagination* (New York: Basic Books, 2000).
[44] Ibid. 103.

although reflections of the conscious state are available both in observations of brain physiology and in the behavior and verbal descriptions of the agent).

What is most noteworthy about Edelman and Tononi's theory is their specification of the most likely neurophysiological basis of conscious awareness. They argue that a state of consciousness and its content (whether primary or higher-order) is a temporary and dynamically changing process within the cerebral cortex that is characterized by a high degree of functional interconnectedness among widespread areas. This functional interconnectedness is created by rapid, two-way recurrent (or reentrant) neural interactions. They call such a state of widespread functional integration a "dynamic core". A dynamic core is a complex, highly differentiated neural state that, from moment to moment, includes different subsets of neurons or neural groups. It is the specific neural groupings involved, and the functional relations among the groupings, that define the nature and content of consciousness at any particular moment.

According to Edelman and Tononi, dynamic cores (and thus consciousness) are characteristic of the mental life of all animals to the degree that the cerebral cortex has sufficiently rich recurrent connections. As they express it, consciousness becomes possible by a

transcendent leap from simple nervous systems, in which signals are exchanged in a relatively insulated manner within separate neural subsystems, to complex nervous systems based on reentrant dynamics, in which an enormous number of signals are rapidly integrated within a single neural process constituting the dynamic core. Such integration leads to the construction of a scene relating signals from many different modalities with memory based on an entire evolutionary history and an individual's experience—it is a remembered present. This scene integrates and generates an extraordinary amount of information within less than a second.[45]

The higher-order consciousness that is characteristic of humans comes into play when symbolic representations and language are incorporated into dynamic cores, including the ability to represent the self as an abstract entity, and to use symbols to note time (past, present, and future). Since language

---

[45] Edelman and Tononi, *A Universe of Consciousness*, 211.

and other symbolic systems are learned, higher-order consciousness is a developmental achievement dependent on social interactions and social scaffolding.

In describing the anatomy of the cortex, Edelman and Tononi point out that the cerebral cortex is unusual compared to the rest of the brain in having a high degree of two-way reentrant interconnections. Most of the intercellular interconnections in other parts of the brain are essentially one-way; or if there are feedback paths, they are indirect and multi-cellular paths. However, the interconnections within the cerebral cortex, as well as the loops between the thalamus and the cortex, are reentrant pathways—that is, there are immediate and direct return connections.

The neurophysiology of consciousness involves the formation of dynamic cores by establishing networks of temporary functional linkages that are marked by spatially differentiated, coherent, high-frequency brain waves (i.e., EEG signals indicative of patterns of nerve cell responding). Thus, conscious awareness is incompatible with the pervasive (i.e., undifferentiated) very slow, high-amplitude EEG patterns of non-dreaming sleep and coma. The activity that forms a dynamic core would be something like Donald Hebb's notion of a cell assembly and a reverberating circuit.[46]

A dynamic core is a functionally interactive subset of the neurons of the cortex, and thus, not all of the cerebral cortex is admitted into a dynamic core at any moment. Sensitivity of a dynamic core to the current context is created by inputs to the core from sensory and memory systems that are not directly involved in the core. Similarly, direct motor output is influenced by the current functional state of the core, without these motor structures necessarily being directly included in the recurrently interactive patterns. Dynamic cores are also influenced by, and exert influences on, subcortical brain systems, including the basal ganglia (motor regulation), cerebellum (complex learned behavioral sequences), hippocampus (memory), amygdala (negative emotions), and hypothalamus (vegetative, autonomic, and

[46] Donald O. Hebb, *The Organization of Behavior: A Neuropsychological Theory* (New York: Wiley, 1949).

hormonal regulation). However, these brain areas do not become directly involved in the dynamic core that embodies consciousness, because they do not have the reentrant form of reciprocal connections that are characteristic of interneuronal cortical connections. Finally, other important inputs to a dynamic core are contributed by the evaluative systems of the locus coeruleus (norepinephrine), the raphé nucleus (serotonin), and the ventral tegmental area (dopamine) that signal aspects of the significance of information—but again, these structures cannot directly participate in a dynamic core.

Edelman and Tononi's Dynamic Core Hypothesis gives a reasonable account of the relationship between conscious control of behavior and automaticity. In the early learning of difficult tasks or behaviors, the performance must be incorporated in and regulated by the dynamic core (i.e., by consciousness). However, once the performance is well learned (automated), it can go forward efficiently, based on the activity of a smaller subgroup of cortical neurons (and subcortical connections), which do not have to be incorporated into the current dynamic core. For example, during normal adult speech, the basic lexical and syntactic aspects of language processing can go on in the background, while the dynamic core embodies the ideas that one is attempting to express.

The Dynamic Core Hypothesis is consistent with what one would expect if the brain were an extremely rich version of a complex dynamic system. The massively recurrently connected cerebral cortex is beautifully suited for emergence of the properties described by complex dynamic systems analysis.[47] Thus, the dynamic core that embodies a particular moment of consciousness can be described as a point in a very high-dimensional abstract state space of potential patterns of neural activity. When re-expressed in terms of the probabilities of various neural patterns (points within this high-dimensional neural space), the tendencies for the occurrence of particular dynamic cores at any moment can be represented by the kind of topological maps used in complex dynamic systems analysis, with the probabilities of occurrence of the most likely forms of the dynamic core representing attractor areas within the dynamic system topology.

---

[47] Alicia Juarrero, *Dynamics in Action: Intentional Behavior as a Complex System* (Cambridge, Mass.: MIT Press, 1999).

5.4 Consciousness and Mental Efficacy

The models of consciousness described here help to sort out the variety of phenomena that have been the referent of the term "consciousness". The Dynamic Core Hypothesis of Edelman and Tononi provides a very plausible neurophysiological model that is well supported by the research literature and by clinical observations. This model both suggests how phenomenal consciousness might be embodied and enlightens us regarding many of the broader cognitive implications of a state of consciousness. Observations of neurological patients with various disturbances of consciousness make it clear that disruption of consciousness has major implications for both thought and behavior. The presence or absence of phenomenal awareness is consistently linked to the presence or absence of higher forms of behavioral flexibility, adaptability, and agency. All of this suggests that consciousness opens persons up to wider behavioral options. Within consciousness, behavioral alternatives are explicitly available to awareness, allowing for modulation of real or simulated action loops with respect to a wide variety of information and memories, all bound together in the temporary work space that is a dynamic core. Agency, flexibility, adaptability, and purposiveness are maximally expanded within conscious awareness.

6 Retrospect and Prospect

The focus of this chapter has been the ways in which increasingly complex organisms are increasingly the causes of their own actions—self-causes, in Juarrero's terms (see Ch. 2, sec. 4). Future chapters will consider what needs to be added to our animal perceptions, judgments, and innate goals to account for specifically human reasonable, responsible, and moral action. In Chapter 4 we explore further the development of symbolic representation. We consider the charge that purely physical entities lack the capacity for language that is *intentional*, that is *about* something in the world. We also consider the contribution that full-fledged symbolic language makes to human capacities for self-direction.

Philosophers distinguish between acting *according to* reason and acting *for* a reason. Clearly, higher animals act according to reason. Chapter 5 addresses the question of what needs to be added to animal rationality to enable humans to act for a reason. Another label for this topic is the "problem of mental causation": how do reasons figure in the causal processes involved in human action?

In Chapter 6 we take up the question of moral responsibility. There we report on Alasdair MacIntyre's account of rational action, and detail the cognitive abilities and neural equipment needed to evaluate one's own behavior in light of moral norms. We end in Chapter 7 with the question of whether and where free will enters the picture.

4

How Can Neural Nets Mean?

1 The Mystery of Meaning

Terrence Deacon tells of walking past the Boston Aquarium one evening and hearing a gravelly voice yell, "Hey! Hey! Get outa there!", "Hey! Hey you!" He tracked the voice to a large pool in front of the aquarium, where four harbor seals were on display. He says: "Incredulous, I traced the source of the command to a large seal reclining vertically in the water; with his head extended back and up, his mouth slightly open, rotating slowly. A seal was talking, not to me, but to the air, and incidentally to anyone within earshot."[1] "Hoover" had been an orphan, raised by a fisherman. Deacon guesses that somehow Hoover had learned to mimic the fisherman's shouts when the seal had gotten into the day's catch. One purpose of this chapter is to consider what makes for the difference between a meaningful human utterance and an audibly indistinguishable vocalization by an animal such as Hoover. Our answer will employ, once again, Alicia Juarrero's concept of context-sensitive constraints in dynamical systems. A second purpose is to prepare the way for an account in the following chapter of specifically human capacities for reasoning and self-determination.

We have been presupposing all along that a physicalist can talk about (and use!) meaningful language. However, the essential character of language and thought is their "intentionality", their being *about* something. Some philosophers argue that only minds, understood as immaterial entities, can possibly be the source of thought and language, because nothing physical can stand in this relation to objects in the world. J. P. Moreland and Scott B. Rae put the argument this way:

---

[1] Terrence W. Deacon, *The Symbolic Species: The Co-evolution of Language and the Brain* (New York: Norton, 1997), 226.

Some (perhaps all) mental states—thoughts, beliefs—have intentionality. No physical state has intentionality. Therefore, (at least) those mental states with intentionality are not physical... Consider the following points about intentionality:

1. When we represent a mental state to ourselves (e.g., an act of thinking about something), there are no sense data associated with it; this is not so with physical states and their relations.

2. Intentionality is completely unrestricted with regard to the kind of object it can hold as a term, but physical relations only obtain for a narrow range of objects (e.g., magnetic fields only attract certain things).

3. To grasp a mental act, one must engage in a reflexive act of self-awareness (e.g., to grasp one's awareness of a tree, one must be aware of an awareness), but no such reflexivity is required to grasp a physical relation.

4. For ordinary physical relations (e.g., x is to the left of y), x and y are identifiable objects irrespective of whether or not they have entered into that relation (ordinary physical relations are external); this is not so for intentional contents (e.g., one and the same belief cannot be about a frog and later about a house—the belief is what it is, at least partly, in virtue of what the belief is *of*).

5. For ordinary relations each of the participants must exist before the relation obtains (x and y must exist before one can be on top of the other); but intentionality can be of nonexistent things (e.g., one can think of Zeus).[2]

So, the reasoning goes, if humans were (purely) physical organisms, their utterances could not be about things in the world—they could not be any different from the noises made by Hoover. Thus, showing how *physical* organisms with suitable neural equipment and social arrangements can use genuine symbolic language is an essential ingredient in our argument for a *nonreductive* view of human nature.

It is not only dualists, however, who raise the challenge of accounting for meaning. It is ironic that Deacon, who has himself written one of the most significant books on the biology of human language, expresses perplexity. Noting that the nature of word meaning has challenged thinkers since antiquity, he says:

Thousands of years and thousands of texts later, we still do not fully understand the basis of the relationship that invests words with their meanings and referential capacity. To be blunt, we do not really understand one of our most commonplace

---

experiences. We know how to use a word to mean something and to refer to something. We know how to coin new words and to assign new meanings to them. We know how to create codes and artificial languages. Yet we do not know how we know how to do this, nor what we are doing when we do. Or rather, we know on the surface, but we do not know what mental processes underlie these activities, much less what neural processes are involved.[3]

Considering the problems of intentionality and reference as they have been formulated according to the modern "idea theory" of meaning,[4] he notes the difficulties in defining ideas—candidates have included mental images, something like dictionary definitions, checklists of features, and others. "But how such mental objects pick out external physical objects, or whether they do, remains a thorny philosophical problem."[5]

In the foregoing, three interrelated issues have been raised: intentionality, reference, and meaning. The technical philosophical term "intentionality" stands for the ability to direct one's mind toward an object or state of affairs. Intentions in this technical sense include beliefs, desires, perceptions, memories, emotions (if they have objects—e.g., fear of dogs but not free-floating anxiety), and intentions in the ordinary sense of the word. Notice that this technical use in philosophy is at odds with usage in cognitive science. Cognitive scientists use "intention" in the ordinary sense, as associated with purposes in action, and use "attention" to refer to the ability to direct one's mind toward an object.

Intentionality is in the first instance a property of mental states ("original" intentionality), and can be applied derivatively to linguistic items such as sentences and books. The terms "reference" and "meaning" are in the first instance terms that apply to language. The German mathematician and logician Gottlob Frege (1848–1925) set out to clarify the meaning of "meaning". He distinguished between sense (*Sinn* in German) and reference (*Bedeutung*). For example, the two phrases "the Morning Star" and "the Evening Star" do not have the same sense, despite the fact that both phrases refer to the same object, namely Venus.[6] Frege's term "sense" comes closest to our ordinary meaning (sense) of "meaning". However, many modern theorists have attempted to understand sense in terms of

---

[3] Deacon, *Symbolic Species*, 51.   [4] We describe this theory in sec. 4 below.
[5] Deacon, *Symbolic Species*, 61.
[6] Gottlob Frege, "Über Sinn und Bedeutung" (1892), trans. M. Black as "On Sense and Meaning", in B. McGuinness (ed.), *Collected Papers on Mathematics, Logic and Philosophy* (Oxford: Blackwell, 1984).

reference, the relation whereby words (or whole sentences) are thought to "hook on to" the world. (We survey some of these modern theories of meaning in sec. 4 below.) As noted above (by Deacon), there remains "the thorny philosophical problem" of how mental objects (or words) "pick out external physical objects". In what follows we shall consider the interrelations among *reference*, *meaning*, and *intentionality*, as well as the relations of all three of these to the concept of *representation* introduced in Chapter 3.

Our approach to this nest of problems will take a form similar to that employed in the previous chapter. As with our approach to autonomous action, we shall attempt to construct a plausible account by looking, first, at the most basic ingredients of intentionality and reference, along with the most rudimentary biological equipment needed to support these capacities. Then we shall ask what needs to be added—both conceptually and in terms of enhanced neural equipment—in order to understand the full-fledged human phenomenon of genuine symbolic language.

We shall see that the "mysteries" involved in language use disappear when we consider meaning not as the product of inner mental acts, but as a result of engagement in adaptive action–feedback loops in the world—especially in the social world.[7] This is yet another rejection of the image of the mental as "inward"—yet another step away from Cartesian materialism.

In what follows, then, we first (in sec. 2) turn our attention to the nature of language itself. Here we shall employ Deacon's distinctions between genuine symbolic language and other kinds of signs (icons and indices) used by animals. We follow Donald MacKay and Fred Dretske in explaining how these natural signs acquire reference as they are *used* by purposive organisms.

In section 3 we consider two issues. First, what is the difference between genuine symbolic language and the icons and indices used by animals?

---

[7] One historical precedent for our position is Giambattista Vico (1668–1744). According to Arnold H. Modell, Vico was the first in two millennia to recognize that meaning is *embodied* in our total affective interest in the world. His work also foreshadowed that of George Lakoff and Mark Johnson (described below) in emphasizing the role of metaphors derived from bodily experience. Vico stated: "It is noteworthy that in all languages the greater part of the expressions relating to inanimate things are formed by *metaphors from the human body and its parts and from the human senses and passions*." See Modell, *Imagination and the Meaningful Brain* (Cambridge, Mass.: MIT Press, 2003), 15–16, quoting Vico (1774); Modell's italics.

Adapting Juarrero, we claim that a language emerges from a set of indices when context-sensitive (syntactical and semantic) constraints are imposed. Second, we consider what it is about human brains that makes this sort of language use possible while it is nearly impossible for animals.

In section 4 we return to the philosophical issues of intentionality and reference, and argue that the problems disappear when we understand meaning in a Wittgensteinian manner as a function of the activities of embodied agents in the social world. This is a move consistent with our insistence throughout this volume that a mental event must be understood as a *contextualized* brain event.

2 Representation and Intentionality

The concept of *intentionality* originated in the Middle Ages, but was given special prominence by the German philosopher Franz Brentano (1838–1917). Mental states are taken to possess "original" intentionality, and sentences and books, maps, pictures, and other representations in a derived way. Brentano took the capacity for (original) intentionality to be *characteristic* of the mental, and thus his thinking stands behind that of theorists such as Moreland and Rae, who believe that physical states are intrinsically different from mental states, and that physicalists therefore cannot account for the intentionality of brain states. In defense of physicalism, then, we shall have to address the question of how physical phenomena of a certain sort—neural states and processes—can be intentional. Recall that we understand a mental state to be a *contextualized* brain state. Without attention to its context in the organism's interaction with the world, its intentionality is indeed inconceivable—as inconceivable as the intentionality of a digestive state! We hope to show, by focusing on the causal nexus of which the intentional state is a part, that there is nothing mysterious about the intentionality of neural states and that (*pace* Brentano *et al.*) the intentionality of animal nervous systems is easier to understand than that of human consciousness and language.

2.1 A Hierarchy of Representations

In Chapter 3 (sec. 2.3.1) we introduced Charles Sanders Peirce's distinction among three kinds of signs, and applied it to types of representation.

Icons serve as representations in virtue of their resemblance to what they signify; indices serve in virtue of an association such as causal or temporal succession; and symbols are purely conventional. We distinguished there between a representation-in-use and a representation-in-itself, and claimed that representation-in-use is the basic category, since representation-in-itself is possible only on the basis of a system of conventions—conventional *uses*. As John Heil says, the point of making photographs is typically representational, but even when it is not, the result might seem obviously to be the production of a representational entity. However, he says, the matter is more complicated:

A photograph, I think, like the fossil impression of a fern in an ancient rock, a tree's rings, and the water level in my neighbor's birdbath is indeed informative or potentially informative. The features of such things covary nonaccidentally with the features of objects or states of affairs concerning which they might be said to afford information. Because of these informational characteristics, such things might come to function as representations. Their *being* representations, however, is a matter of their being *deployed* as representations, their having a role in a system that exploits their representational character.[8]

So in this section we shall explore the ways in which things *become* representations in virtue of how they are being used.

The use of icons and indices is prevalent in the animal world. However, it is a bit odd to speak of an animal *using* an icon, since the representative value of an icon comes from the organism's *inability* to distinguish what it perceives from other similar entities. It makes somewhat more sense to speak of an index being used by an organism to indicate something about some other aspect of the present environment. Nevertheless, we shall see that it is how sensory information links to action—feedback—evaluation—action loops that constitutes its function as an iconic or indexical representation.

In order to understand the nature of Peirce's categories from the standpoint of the nervous system, it will be helpful to consider Donald MacKay's ideas about the nature of perception. MacKay understands the *aboutness* of perception as the elicitation of a "conditional readiness to reckon" with the object being perceived. MacKay writes:

---

[8] John Heil, *The Nature of True Minds* (Cambridge: Cambridge University Press, 1992), 231.

I am suggesting that we look for the physical correlates of perceiving not in the receptive area of the brain, but rather in the organizing system which prepares and maintains the "conditional readiness" of the organism for the state of affairs giving rise to the received signals. On this basis to perceive something … is to respond by internal adaptation to it (setting up conditional readiness to avoid it, grasp it, describe it, etc. in case of need).[9]

To see what MacKay means by this, we need to refer again to his diagram of the minimal functional elements of an agent (Fig. 2.3, p. 69). This diagram shows the sensory receptors feeding information from the environment to a system labeled the comparator, whose judgment of a match or mismatch with the agent's goals is fed to the organizing system. The important point that MacKay is making in the quotation above is that representations are stored not, for instance, in parts of the brain that produce visual images, but rather in brain systems whose function is to initiate *action*.

MacKay proposes a comparable understanding of beliefs, which are "represented implicitly by the conditional readinesses that result from, and are left over after, the episode of [sensory] updating".[10] For MacKay, as for Heil, it is deployment with respect to action (or potential action) in the environment that constitutes the representational aspect of sensory information.

If the intentionality of perception is based upon the elicitation of a "conditional readiness to reckon" with the object (let us call this a CRR), then an iconic representation is the elicitation of readiness based upon mere similarity. Our example of an icon in Chapter 3 was a fisherman's lure, which (the fisherman hopes) will play the same role in eliciting the trout's feeding behavior as a real fly, due to the fish being unable to tell the difference. Therefore, an imitation caddis fly tied to the end of a fisherman's line, if it is an effective imitation of the real thing, is responded to iconically by a lurking trout insofar as the same CRR is elicited in its nervous system as that elicited by a real caddis fly. The CRR is presumed to be elicited, and to constitute an iconic representation, whether or not the trout (for other reasons) emits a specific physical response to the lure (i.e., approach and eating).

---

[9] Donald M. MacKay, *Behind the Eye*, The Gifford Lectures, ed. Valerie MacKay (Oxford: Blackwell, 1991), 73.

[10] Ibid. 112.

The representational nature of the CRR in this fishy illustration is indicated by additional attributes. First, if the artificial lure sets up a fly CRR in the nervous system of the trout, then the representation is *mistaken*—it is not a caddis fly, but only looks like a caddis fly—but the trout does not discriminate the difference. Also, the fact that this is a representational event in the fish (rather than a genetically hard-wired automatic response) is indicated by the fact that a trout that has been hooked once and has either escaped or been released may learn various cues to differentiate the artificial fly from a real fly (fly-like things with hooks are differentiated from the real thing). This learned discrimination means that the artificial fly will elicit a different CRR from that elicited by the real thing (i.e., an avoidance response rather than eating). Finally, the form of the CRR, and/or whether the CRR becomes the basis for expressed behavior, is contextually dependent. Unless the trout has been feeding on caddis flies in the recent past, it is not as apt either to perceive the lure on the basis of a CRR that includes eating or to initiate eating based on the possibilities inherent in the CRR.

We can use this same illustration to understand a primitive version of indexical representations—perceptions that gain through associative learning additional representational value as an index of other phenomena. Fly fishermen understand that older, wiser trout are typically "leader shy". That is, they have learned to use the presence of the leader line lying on the water near the fly as an index that what might otherwise be perceived as an attractive-looking fly worthy of eating is instead a harmful stimulus to be avoided. Sensing a leader on the water becomes an index eliciting a different perception of the lure (physically represented by a different CRR) than that produced by the sensory experience of the fly not accompanied by a leader. Obviously, this perceptual ability of older, wiser trout has been gained by associative learning from having been hooked at least once in the past.

MacKay is arguing that the aboutness of perceptions (i.e., their intentionality) is physically represented in the elicitation of implications for potential actions—the deployment of sensory information to set up potentialities for relevant action–feedback loops. While such representations become extensively elaborated in the cognitive systems of higher animals and humans, CRRs (as representations-in-use) are a fundamental aspect of the physical basis of intentionality in perception that we share with lower organisms such a trophy-sized brown trout.

We shall take up symbolic reference in section 3, showing how it builds on iconic and indexical representations. But first we consider a compatible philosophical account of the intentional character of neural events.

2.2 From Indices to Intentionality

In this subsection we follow the work of Fred Dretske. Dretske has argued that we find the source of intentionality in indexical (or what he calls "natural") representation.[11]

One way in which intentionality has regularly been understood to relate to representation is via *mis*representation. Brentano took the essence of intentionality to be the capacity of the mind to intend (believe in, think about, imagine, wish for) the nonexistent. Ruth Garrett Millikan says: "In recent years it has become generally accepted that he [Brentano] was right in this sense: the core of any theory of representation must contain an explanation of how misrepresentation can occur."[12] Dretske's goal is to show how neurocognitive events can be understood as intentional, despite the fact that they are physical events. He does so precisely by showing how they can acquire the capacity for misrepresentation. For a neural state to count as a misrepresentation, it is necessary to consider the *function* it plays in the organism's behavior.[13]

First Dretske describes three types of representational systems. Type I systems are purely conventional. His example is using coins or pieces of popcorn to represent basketball players' positions. In this case the relation of signifier to signified is established by the user's intent. Type II representational systems are hybrids of conventions and natural signs (indices); humans use natural signs for conventional purposes. For example, there is a (natural) causal relation between increased heat in the environment and the volume that a given amount of alcohol or mercury fills when

---

[11] Fred Dretske, *Explaining Behavior: Reasons in a World of Causes* (Cambridge, Mass.: MIT Press, 1988), ch. 3.

[12] Ruth Garrett Millikan, "Pushmi-Pullyu Representations", in James E. Tomberlin (ed.), *Philosophical Perspectives, 9: AI, Connectionism and Philosophical Psychology* (Atascadero, Calif.: Ridgeview Publishing Co., 1995), 185–200, at p. 186.

[13] For a complementary account see Millikan. She says: "I have argued that misrepresentation is best understood by embedding the theory of intentionality within a theory of function that allows us to understand, more generally, what malfunction is. For this we use a generalization of the biological notion of function as, putting things very crudely, the survival value of a reproduced type of entity" (ibid.). See also Ruth Garrett Millikan, *Language, Thought and Other Biological Categories* (Cambridge, Mass.: MIT Press, 1984).

enclosed in a glass tube. We devise a conventional system of marking lines and numbers on such tubes, and they become indicators of temperature.

Dretske points out that the natural signs used in Type II systems typically indicate a great many things. For example, an electrically operated fuel gauge indicates not only the amount of gas in the tank, but also the amount of current flowing in the wires connecting the gauge to the tank and the amount of torque on the armature to which the pointer is affixed. "Given the way these gauges operate, they cannot indicate (i.e., have their behavior depend on) the amount of fuel in the tank without indicating (exhibiting at least the same degree of dependency on) these related conditions."[14] However, this device *represents* the fuel level, because we assign it this *function* (rather than delivering any other sort of information). So what the gauge represents is partly conventional and partly a matter of what it is physically capable of doing. As Dretske points out: "You can't assign a rectal thermometer the job of indicating the Dow–Jones Industrial Average"![15]

Dretske's point in considering Type II systems is in order to understand how there can be systems that are purely natural (Type III). His consideration of Type II systems was to remind us of the way we use causal regularities to provide a specific sort of information *about* a specific condition in the world. This is how a physical entity or event can acquire *intentionality*. Type III systems of representation are those in which the sign exhibits intentionality because of the *function* it serves in an animal's behavior.

Consider this extremely simple example. There is a type of anaerobic marine bacterium with internal magnets (magnetosomes) that allow it to align itself parallel to the Earth's magnetic field. This is a natural causal relationship. As with the fuel gauge, the bacterium's magnetosome *might* be used for a variety of purposes. Perhaps a sailor with a microscope could use it for a compass. In such a case we would have another example of a Type II system; as with the examples of mechanical devices, the human agent would then have *assigned* a function to the magnetosome, thereby using its causal capacity to tell him something about the world.

However, the bacterium's magnetosome already serves a function for the organism itself: it aligns it with the Earth's magnetic field, which in turn causes it to swim away from deadly oxygen-rich water. Here it is not human convention but evolution that has assigned the magnetosome

---

[14] Dretske, *Explaining Behavior*, 59.   [15] Ibid. 60.

its function, which is to tell the bacterium the whereabouts of a safe environment.

Because the magnetic system has a function, it can fail to perform appropriately, and hence provide misinformation. For example, in the southern hemisphere it would "tell" the bacterium to swim in the wrong direction. Misrepresentation depends on two things: the way the world is and the way in which the world is being represented. The latter, Dretske emphasizes, is determined by the representative function of the system.

[A]s long as there remains [an] indeterminacy of function, there is no clear sense in which misrepresentation occurs. Without a determinate function, one can, as it were, always exonerate [a representational system] of error, and thus eliminate the occurrence of misrepresentation, by changing what it is *supposed* to be indicating, by changing what it is its *function* to indicate.[16]

So if it were up to us to assign a function to the bacterium's magnetosome, we could decide to call it a "suicide director" in the southern hemisphere, and it would work remarkably well. In Type III systems it is evolution, rather than human ingenuity, that assigns functions to potential representative systems. Note that the sort of reassignment of functions that leads regularly to the death of the organism is just exactly what evolution cannot do!

In Type II systems it is clear what the function is because we have decided it ourselves. In Type III systems the function is something that needs to be discovered. Here, Dretske says, the functional indeterminacy is eliminated by the way the system itself uses the information. This depends on internal indicators being harnessed to a control mechanism: "Only by *using* an indicator in the production of movements whose successful outcome depends on *what is being indicated* can this functional indeterminacy be overcome."[17] This is exactly MacKay's point in describing a neural representation as a conditional readiness to reckon. Dretske concludes:

The elements of a representational system, then, have a content or a meaning, a content or meaning defined by what it is their function to indicate ... These meanings display many of the intentional properties of genuine thought and belief. If, then, there are systems of Type III, and these are located in the heads of

---

[16] Ibid. 69.   [17] Dretske, *Explaining Behavior*, 70.

some animals, then there is, in the heads of some animals (1) something that is *about* various parts of this world...; (2) something capable of representing and, just as important, *misrepresenting* those parts of the world it is about; and (3) something that has, thereby a *content* or *meaning* (not itself in the head, of course) that is individuated in something like the way we individuate thoughts and beliefs.[18]

Despite his emphasis on the role of function in constituting intentionality, Dretske is not a functionalist. He says: "It is important, incidentally, to understand that this approach to thought and belief, the approach that conceives of them as forms of internal representation, is not a version of functionalism—at least not if this widely held theory is understood, as it often is, as a theory that identifies mental properties with functional properties."[19] Dretske's demurral is based on the fact that functional properties are usually understood to have to do with the way that something *in fact* behaves, with its syndrome of typical causes and effects. Dretske's account of intentional properties is more complex. He insists that for a state of the organism to exhibit intentionality, the state must not only provide information, but its *purpose* must be to provide information. There needs to be a teleological element,[20] which, in the case of animal perception, is provided by the role assigned to the receptors by evolution.[21]

In sum, a causal connection produces a state in an organism. This state bears information for the organism if the organism uses it to guide its behavior. Only because of its enmeshment in the action and purposes of the organism can such a state also constitute misinformation—for example, if the same state of the organism is produced in some unusual manner (say, a leaf or a fisherman's fly producing an indistinguishable state of readiness to bite in the fish).

So our account of what we may call natural intentionality—in contrast to the full-blown intentionality of human mental processes and language,

---

[18] Dretske, *Explaining Behavior*, 77.

[19] Fred Dretske, "Fred Dretske", in Samuel Guttenplan (ed.), *A Companion to the Philosophy of Mind* (Oxford: Blackwell, 1994), 259–64, at p. 261.

[20] However, this is merely goal-directed rather than goal-intended.

[21] We would distinguish our own position from functionalism as follows. Functionalism is an attempt to *define* mental states (in some sense, to define them away). We are simply saying that one will not *understand* the nature of intentional states if one does not consider, among other things, the role such states play in behavior. We would, in fact, be reluctant to attempt to define a mental or intentional state. Definitions call for distinct categories, while the biological phenomena we are attempting to understand always fall along gradients.

which depend on the conventions of symbolic language—is as follows: A state of an organism (perceptual or merely neural) possesses (natural) intentionality if it is causally connected to some other entity, event, or state of affairs (in the world or elsewhere in the organism) such that it provides information about that other state of affairs. Such a causal connection provides information insofar as it is used for the organism's purposes in such a way that the content of the representation is relevant to the success or failure of the behavior in question.

We believe that our attention to the role of function or action in constituting intentional states is salutary. One of the reasons for philosophers' puzzlement over intentionality seems to be the tendency since Augustine's day—strongly reinforced by Descartes—to view the mind as *inside* the person and as (largely) *passive*. If one is shut up alone all day in a stove-heated room,[22] then it might indeed seem mysterious how one's thinking could be *about* something far away. We emphasize throughout this volume that the mental cannot be understood except as it is involved in adaptive action–feedback loops in the world.

3 The Leap to Symbolic Language

As noted above, some thinkers see the ability of minds to manifest intentionality as unproblematic, but take physical things having intentionality to be (perhaps) inconceivable. William Hasker puts it bluntly: "We still have no idea how the 'aboutness' is to be incorporated into a materialistic worldview."[23]

We take the seriousness of the two problems to be the reverse. Following Dretske, we believe that it is clear enough how physical states or events (e.g., the position of a bacterium's magnetosome and the fish's conditional readiness to bite) can be intentional in the technical philosophical sense (not in the sense that the fish has an intention). In contrast, as Deacon points out, the capacity for human (symbolic) language to refer to things in the world is much more difficult to explain—and Deacon ought to know, having written a 500-page book on the subject!

---

[22] Cf. René Descartes, *Discourse on Method*, ch. 2.
[23] William Hasker, *The Emergent Self* (Ithaca, NY, and London: Cornell University Press, 1999), 32.

In this section we shall summarize a small part of Deacon's work. Deacon shows how symbolic reference is built hierarchically from iconic and indexical reference. To explicate his account, we employ Juarrero's concept of context-sensitive constraints. In section 3.3 we report on the brain modifications that make symbolic language relatively easy for humans, while it is nearly impossible for animals, including here neuroscientific research on the role of the prefrontal cortex in language use and in other higher cognitive functions. Critical here for symbolic reference is evidence for nested levels of top-down causation (behavioral control and evaluation). However, the prefrontal cortex is only a role-player in larger whole-brain networks that evaluate and modulate action. In section 3.4 we present an account of syntax and semantics as realized neurobiologically in the topography of self-organized regions in neural space.

3.1 From Indices to Symbols

Deacon says that his work on the biology of language was stimulated by a child at his son's school who asked why animals do not have their own simplified languages. Given the high level of intelligence of some species, Deacon concluded that there must be something about genuine symbolic language for which animal brains are *pre-maladapted*. The centerpiece of his neurobiological account is a description of the radical re-engineering of the entire brain that must have taken place hand in hand with the development of human language.

Deacon's account of the difference between animal vocalizations and human language employs our now familiar distinction among icons, indices, and symbols. All *natural* animal communication is indexical. An example that some have taken to be "proto-language" is the alarm calls of vervet monkeys. These have different calls to warn troop members of the presence of different predators—eagles, leopards, and snakes. In response to the "eagle" call, the monkeys race out of trees; to the "leopard" call, they climb into the trees; and to the "snake" call, they rise up and look around them.[24]

Deacon argues that such calls fail the test of genuine language because, while they do communicate, there is no *intention* to convey information.

---

[24] Deacon, *Symbolic Species*, 54–6; referring to Robert Seyforth *et al.*, "Monkey Responses to Three Different Alarm Calls: Evidence of Predator Classification and Semantic Communication", *Science*, 210 (1980), 801–3.

Consider another of Deacon's examples. Suppose a parrot is rewarded for saying "wanna cracker" by being given crackers. It will then say "wanna cracker" when it wants a cracker, but this is a mere indexical relationship—a link established by the temporal association between the two events, the utterance and the feeding. If the parrot had been rewarded with crackers for saying "wanna worm" it would say this instead in order to get a cracker. The utterance has no meaning for the parrot. Similarly, evolutionary history has established a set of associations between the sighting of a predator and the vocalization, and between hearing the vocalization and appropriate evasive action.

These are indexical relationships built on iconic relationships. The first step is to recognize (or fail to distinguish) *this* appearance (of, say, a leopard) from prior appearances, so that it produces the same behavioral response—a cry. On the part of the troop members, *this* cry is not distinguished from prior instances, and therefore elicits the same conditional readiness to reckon in the present situation as in past total situations of cry-plus-sighting-of-leopard.

Two features of the monkeys' signaling behavior help us to see what is distinctive of human language. The calls are involuntary and contagious. Deacon says:

When one vervet monkey produces an alarm call, others in the troop both escape and echo the call again and again, and all will join in until the general excitement is gone. This redundancy provides a minimum of new predator information for any troop members subsequent to the first presentation (though it may indicate that danger is still present). It also certainly has more to do with communicating and recruiting arousal than predator information, as is analogously the case with laughter and humor. Knowing that another saw a predator does not appear to inhibit the vervet's tendency to call and knowing that another also got a joke does not apparently inhibit a person's tendency to laugh—indeed, both may be potentiated by this knowledge.[25]

John Searle's theory of "speech acts" provides the resources for explaining the difference between an animal call and human language. In order to utter a warning, one needs not only to utter the appropriate words, followed by the appropriate effect. One has to utter the words with the intention that those words be *taken* by the hearer *as* a warning. So an important

---

[25] Deacon, *Symbolic Species*, 58–9.

requirement for language is a theory of mind, which allows speakers to take account of what the hearer does or does not know. This is just what the contagious and continuous repetition of the alarm call shows to be absent in the vervet's form of communication.[26]

Although there is no animal language in the wild, there are several instances of chimpanzees being trained to use symbols. Sue Savage-Rumbaugh and Duane Rumbaugh trained two chimps, Sherman and Austin, to use a rudimentary symbol system that began with four lexigrams on a keyboard representing four food or drink items and two "verb" lexigrams glossed as "please machine give", for requesting solid foods, and "please machine pour", for requesting liquids. Teaching indexical relationships to chimps is relatively easy. The difficulty was in training them to chain the lexigram pairs in a simple verb–noun sentence. The experimenters solved the latter problem by means of a vast number of trials in which *inappropriate* strings of lexicons were extinguished through lack of reward. Eventually the chimps learned to use one of the four correct sentences to ask, using the appropriate verb, for the food or drink they wanted. To test whether the chimps had caught on to the system *as a symbolic system*, they introduced new lexigrams for liquids and solids to see whether the chimps would know how to use them without further training. Indeed, they had learned the implicit categories of *liquid* and *solid*, and the syntactic rule for pairing each with the appropriate verb.[27]

Higher animals learn indexical relations between words and objects rather easily. So the question is why this *very simple* symbolic system was so difficult for Sherman and Austin. Deacon's account sheds a great deal of light on the nature of symbolic reference. To summarize his account, we shall use English glosses in place of the chimps' lexigrams. Thus, they were able to do something analogous to associating "banana" with bananas, "bread" with bread, "water" with water, and "juice" with juice. The

---

[26] John R. Searle, *Speech Acts: An Essay in the Philosophy of Language* (Cambridge: Cambridge University Press, 1969). Similarly, the parrot's "wanna cracker" fails the test of a genuine request. McClendon and Smith list as one of the requirements for a "felicitous" request that "the speaker's intention in issuing this sentence is to use the language's convention for requesting … and the speaker intends the hearer to understand (by her use) that she is so using it". See James Wm. McClendon, Jr. and James M. Smith, *Convictions: Defusing Religious Relativism* (Valley Forge, Pa.: Trinity Press International, 1994), 57.

[27] Deacon, *Symbolic Species*, ch. 3; cf. Duane Rumbaugh (ed.), *Language Learning by a Chimpanzee: The Lana Project* (New York: Academic Press, 1977); and E. Sue Savage-Rumbaugh, *Ape Language: From Conditioned Response to Symbol* (New York: Columbia University Press, 1986).

outcome of the training was, first, that they could correctly use analogues of the sentences (1) Please machine give banana, (2) Please machine give bread, (3) Please machine pour water, and (4) Please machine pour juice. After they had caught on to the system and were trained to associate, say, "raisin" with raisins and "milk" with milk, they could correctly devise analogues of the sentences (5) Please machine give raisin, and (6) Please machine pour milk.

What must have happened when they caught on to the system, and why was it so difficult? Deacon says that they had learned not only a set of associations between lexigrams and objects or events, but also a set of logical relationships between the lexigrams—relations of inclusion or exclusion. "They had discovered that the relationship that a lexigram has to an object *is a function of* the relationship it has to other lexigrams, not just a function of the correlated appearance of both lexigram and object. This is the essence of a symbolic relationship."[28]

This shift is difficult to make, because it involves an *unlearning* task. In order to see this, it will help to have before us a second example of Sherman's and Austin's linguistic competence. Savage-Rumbaugh and her colleagues taught Sherman, Austin, and a third chimp, Lana (who had not learned the previous symbolic system) to sort a given set of food items into one pan and a set of tools into another. Then they were given new food items and new tools, and all three placed them in the appropriate pan. Next the chimps were required to associate each of the previously distinguished food items and tools with lexigrams glossed as "food" and "tool" respectively. Deacon says:

Although all three chimps learned this task in a similar way, taking many hundreds of trials to make the transference [from individual lexigrams for each to the lexigrams for "food" and "tool"], Sherman and Austin later spontaneously recoded this information in a way that Lana did not. This was demonstrated when, as in the prior task, novel food and novel tool items were introduced. Sherman and Austin found this to be a trivial addition and easily guessed without any additional learning which lexigram was appropriate. Lana not only failed to extend her categorization to the new items, [but] the novelty and errors appeared to produce a kind of counterevidence that caused her to abandon her prior training in a subsequent test. Though on the surface this task resembles the sorting task, these conflicting results demonstrate

---

[28] Deacon, *Symbolic Species*, 86.

that there is a critical difference that undermined the rote learning strategy learned by Lana and favored the symbolic recoding used by Sherman and Austin.[29]

To illustrate, let us suppose that the chimps had first learned associations such as "screwdriver"–screwdriver, "hammer"–hammer, "bread"–bread, and "banana"–banana. Then they were taught "food"–banana; "food"–bread; "tool"–hammer; and "tool"–screwdriver. Learning this new set of indexical associations will at first be simply confusing, and prior learning of "banana", "hammer", and so on will interfere. Before symbolic insight can take place, they need to learn the whole new set of pairings (with "tool" versus "food") by rote. At some point, though, they perceived an implicit pattern—the similarity among the food items was perceived to correspond with the fact that each food item was associated linguistically with the "food" lexigram. A relationship among food items was seen to relate to a corresponding relationship among a set of sentences. They perceived an analogy between shared stimulus features and shared semantic features that allowed for a quick association of new food items with previously learned semantic regularities.

Deacon says:

In summary, then, symbols cannot be understood as an unstructured collection of tokens that map to a collection of referents because symbols don't just represent things in the world, they also represent each other. Because symbols do not directly refer to things in the world, but indirectly refer to them by virtue of referring to other symbols, they are implicitly combinatorial entities whose referential powers are derived by virtue of other symbols.[30]

3.2 Creation of Symbolic Systems via Context-Sensitive Constraints

What Deacon means in saying that symbols are implicitly combinatorial entities is better expressed in the terms of dynamical systems and the role of top-down context-sensitive constraints (see Ch. 2, sec. 4). Context-sensitive constraints are those that establish divergence from independence—that is, they are operative when what happened before affects the probabilities of what happens now.[31] Language provides a wealth of

---

[29] Deacon, *Symbolic Species*, 90–1.   [30] Ibid. 99.
[31] Alicia Juarrero, *Dynamics in Action: Intentional Behavior as a Complex System* (Cambridge, Mass.: MIT Press, 1999), 137.

examples. In a sentence, the occurrence of the first word alters the probabilities regarding the next word. For example, beginning a sentence with "the" dramatically increases the probability that the next word will be a noun and dramatically decreases the probability of a verb. Syntax (grammar) imposes (or, better, *is* a set of) context-sensitive constraints. In the language of dynamic systems theory, syntax creates dynamical attractors. Semantics is also a set of context-sensitive constraints. A sentence beginning with "The boy ran to the ... " constrains what can follow not only in terms of parts of speech but also in terms of meaning. One can run to the store, but not to the moon. So the chimpanzees described above had to learn not only the syntactical constraints of grammar but also the semantic constraints based on recognition of the similarities among beverages and among food items.

In short, the difference in learning to use a symbolic system, rather than merely a set of indices, is coming to embody context-sensitive constraints. It is layers upon layers of such constraints that give human language its expressive power. Alicia Juarrero says:

When the appearance of a *q* increases the likelihood of *u*, the two have become related, not just by an external conjunction, but systematically: the pair are now what grammarians call an *i*-tuplet with *q* and *u* as components. Similarly, as relations among *i*-tuplets are constrained, words become possible; additional contextual constraints (on top of the contextual constraints that create words) make sentences possible. Systems, systems of systems, and so on can be assembled. By making the appearance of letters in an alphabet interdependent, contextual constraints thus allow complex linguistic structures to emerge.[32]

This is one of the clearest examples of the way in which constraints at the lower level exponentially increase degrees of freedom at a higher level. With 26 letters we can form all of the words in the dictionary. With those words we could theoretically form an infinite number of sentences.

Our emphasis in this chapter is on the layers of constraint that are provided by the *use* of language in the social world—in J. L. Austin's terms, in speech acts; in Ludwig Wittgenstein's terms, in language games and forms of life. This provides yet another level of constraint. For example, a particular set of social conventions make a use for the otherwise meaningless yet grammatical sentence "I bid three hearts".

---

[32] Juarrero, *Dynamics in Action*, 137–8.

One of many advantages of thinking of linguistics in dynamic terms is that, in contrast to linguistics based on formal rules, it is possible to explain not only the regularities of linguistic behavior, but also its flexibility. That is, an attractor is a probability space with vague outlines. Given the right (poetic) context, we *could* find a use for and understand "The boy ran to the moon". Reader–response critics have made a living examining ways in which authors violate our expectations by using highly improbable, but nonetheless meaningful, combinations of words.[33]

3.3 *The Biology of Symbolic Reference*

What is it about our brains that allows us so readily to achieve symbolic insight, while it is so difficult for chimpanzees? What allows us to unlearn or transcend mere indexical token–object associations in order to understand the logical and complex patterns of token–token relationships inherent in symbolic systems?

3.3.1. Brain Regions and Reorganization   The usual response to questions about the unique aspects of the human brain with respect to language is to point to the specific functions of two areas in the left cerebral hemisphere—Broca's area and Wernicke's area—and to the general dominance of the left hemisphere in language processing.[34] This model of the language functions of the brain arises from observations of adults with brain damage. When the left inferior frontal area (Broca's area) is damaged by a stroke or traumatic injury, the predominant symptoms are dysfluency in the expression of language (often labeled "telegraphic speech" due to the slow, halting, word-at-a-time language output) and agrammatism (referring to the relative simplicity of syntactic structures in spoken language and some detectable difficulty in the comprehension of syntax). When the left superior temporal lobe is damaged (which includes Wernicke's area), the problems lie more in the realm of language comprehension. These individuals have a problem linking the auditory signal, clearly understood to be words, with the meanings of the words. This is often accompanied by a reduction in the number of content words in language expression,

---

[33] See, e.g., Stanley Fish, *Is There a Text in this Class?: The Authority of Interpretive Communities* (Cambridge, Mass.: Harvard University Press, 1980).

[34] B. Kolb and I. Q. Whishaw, *Fundamentals of Human Neuropsychology*, 4th edn. (New York: W. H. Freeman and Co., 1996), 387–414.

with the patient substituting either fillers (e.g., "you know", "that thing") or neologisms (nonwords that sound like they should be words) for words the patient cannot find. These observations of individuals with focal brain damage have led to the classic model of language that focuses on the function of two brain modules: Broca's area serving language expression and syntax, and Wernicke's area serving word comprehension and semantics. Typically (but not always) these two areas are found in the left hemisphere. The right hemisphere plays a less specific role, undergirding language with the appreciation of the meaning carried by prosody (vocal inflection) and the establishment of broader semantic fields for understanding that extend beyond the meaning of individual words and sentences.

A number of observations suggest that this model does not entirely capture all of the critical neurobiology of language processing. First, younger children do not experience the same outcomes of focal damage to these two brain areas, or to one particular hemisphere. More of the brain (including both hemispheres) is involved in language processing during early childhood. Second, there appears to be a variety of forms of lateralization and modular specialization, in that focal brain damage in adults does not always create this pattern of language-processing deficits. Third, modern functional brain imaging suggests that many other brain areas are involved in most forms of language processing, such as the prefrontal cortex, the supplementary motor cortex, the anterior cingulate gyrus, the basal ganglia, and parts of the cerebellum. Thus, the human propensity for language cannot be explained adequately by the development of two distinctive left hemisphere brain modules, as implied by the classic model of language and brain.

Deacon argues convincingly that the development of Broca's and Wernicke's areas and the left lateralization of language are secondary by-products of more fundamental evolutionary changes in the human brain.[35] These changes have served to redistribute the proportion of cortex available for various functions, and to re-engineer the pattern of connectedness both within the cortex and from the cortex to lower brain structures. The lack of this broad cortical redesign prevents natural and efficient development of even simple language. Mastery of the vocal skills of speech is impossible (due to difference in larynx structure), and the "symbolic threshold" can

---

[35] Deacon, *Symbolic Species*, 316–18.

only be crossed minimally via intensive, explicit training for even the most intelligent apes.

According to Deacon, the critical difference in humans is the relatively smaller size of the cortical areas devoted to sensorimotor processing and, consequently, the relatively large areas available to higher-order associative processing. Particularly critical are the absolute and relative sizes of the prefrontal cortex of humans. While other brain structures are roughly the same size as those found in the brain of a chimpanzee, the prefrontal cortex is six times larger in human beings than in chimpanzees. This increase in the size of the prefrontal cortex has a major impact on the way in which the brain becomes connected during prenatal and infant development. Since the human genome does not contain sufficient information to predetermine the hyper-complex wiring of the brain, most of the specific pattern of interconnections results from a process (often referred to as "neural Darwinism"[36]) in which an exuberant overproduction of axons growing in many directions is followed by a process of elimination of axons or axon branches that are not able to form viable functional connections. One of the factors determining success in developing viable connections between one brain area and another is how many axons originally attempt to connect. If they are few relative to the number of axons arriving from other brain areas, then what few axons arrive are likely to be eliminated in the competition for priority in connection. However, if many axons arrive, these connections will predominate over connections from other areas. Thus, a very large prefrontal cortex means not only that more complex processing can go on within the very large neuronal network of this area of cortex, but also that the prefrontal cortex will be much more likely to be successful in forming connections to other cortical and subcortical brain areas. Thus, another unique feature of the human brain is the degree to which cortical axons, particularly from the prefrontal cortex, connect with nuclei of the basal ganglia, limbic system, cerebellum, midbrain, brain stem, and spinal cord, as well as with other areas of the cerebral cortex. This increase in the size of the prefrontal cortex and the predominance of its connections to lower brain areas has major implications for the two critical human abilities that allow for the

---

[36] See Gerald M. Edelman, *Neural Darwinism: The Theory of Neuronal Group Selection* (New York: Basic Books, 1987).

development of language: skilled control of vocalization and symbolic learning.

With respect to the vocal abilities of humans, the critical aspect of brain organization is increased frontal lobe connections to the nuclei of the midbrain, brain stem, and spinal cord that are involved in vocalization. In apes and other mammals, vocalizations are controlled by nuclei in the midbrain that orchestrate stereotyped patterns that are linked to, and thus are expressions of, arousal and emotion. These patterns are orchestrated through lower brain nuclei (brain stem and spinal cord) that specifically control the larynx, mouth, tongue, and respiration. In humans, axons from the prefrontal cortex not only directly connect to the midbrain area that contains the programs for orchestrating species-specific vocal expression, but also connect directly to the various nuclei that control the face, mouth, tongue, larynx, and respiration. Thus, in humans, stereotypic and emotive patterns can be inhibited (e.g., suppressing for the moment the tendency to laugh or cry), and more precise patterns of skilled control over vocalization can be imposed, in a top-down manner, by the prefrontal cortex. It is primarily because of the lack of extensive direct cortical connections between the prefrontal cortex and the vocal control apparatus of the lower brain that chimpanzees cannot talk, even though they are capable, as we have seen, of learning indexical and very simple symbolic relationships.

The development of skilled vocal mechanisms allowed humans to express a wide range of phonemes upon which a large vocal word lexicon could be built. However, as we have already seen, language is much more than word–object indexical relationships. Symbolic reference demands large patterns of word–word associative networks in which the meaning of words is derived from their connections to other words, even more than to their association with objects in the external sensorimotor world. Crossing what Deacon calls the "symbolic threshold" and entering cognitively into the world of symbolic reference demands a new form of associative learning. The expanded network of connections from the prefrontal cortex to other cortical and subcortical processing areas allows for the construction of these expanded word–word symbolic networks. Thus, since symbols are not tokens but large networks of associations, the neural substrate of a symbol most likely resides not in one part of the brain, but is widely distributed across the brain. To the degree that meaning includes the potentials for action in the world (a conditional readiness to reckon), these networks would include brain areas involved in organization of action. These mnemonic networks are made possible by the widespread interconnectedness of the prefrontal cortex.

3.3.2. Language, the Prefrontal Cortex, and Top-Down Causation   The functions of the prefrontal cortex create the bias toward symbolic reference and allow humans to become "lightning calculators of reference".[37] The prefrontal cortex is generally considered to be critical for tasks involving attention, response suppression, and context sensitivity, as well as the maintenance of recent memory and manipulation of information within working memory. It also allows for the ability to inhibit one response tendency, shift to an alternative, and generate various alternatives for action. Individuals with damage to the prefrontal cortex have deficiencies in divergent thinking, behavioral spontaneity, strategy formation, associative learning, and abiding by rules and instructions in tasks.[38]

With respect to language, the prefrontal cortex "helps inhibit the tendency to act on simple correlative stimulus relationships and guides our sampling of alternative, higher-order sequential or hierarchical associations".[39] Because of its role in inferential abilities, the prefrontal cortex is important in constructing the widely distributed mnemonic networks of word–word relationships that constitute symbolic reference.

These functions of the prefrontal cortex are illustrated nicely in the experiments by Koechlin and colleagues (described earlier, Ch. 3, sec. 4), which demonstrate a nested hierarchy of direct sensory, contextual, and episodic task control within the frontal cortex. Based on verbal instructions from the experimenter, the participants were shown to have activated the levels of the hierarchy of task control within the frontal cortex that were sufficient to meet the demands of the task.

Thus, the prefrontal cortex is a critical structure in higher cognitive functions in animals, and particularly in humans. The greater relative size of the prefrontal cortex in human beings allows richer interactions and increased top-down regulation of information processing, which is particularly important for symbolic processing and language.

Another important aspect of the prefrontal cortex with respect to language, as well as other human cognitive capacities, is its very slow

---

[37] Deacon, *Symbolic Species*, 302.   [38] Kolb and Whishaw, *Fundamentals*, 305–31.
[39] Deacon, *Symbolic Species*, 265.

development in humans compared to chimpanzees. Whereas the pre-frontal cortex of a chimpanzee reaches full development within the first two years of life, the frontal cortex of a human is still developing at the end of the second decade of life.[40] Regarding the impact of this difference in the rate of development on human cognitive capacities (par-ticularly when combined with a stronger basic social instinct), O'Reilly comments:

The fact that monkeys also show some degree of abstract representation in [prefrontal cortex] raises the perennial question of what exactly is different between us and them. The critical difference may be that people have a basic social instinct for sharing experiences and knowledge with each other that is largely absent in even our closest primate relatives. Thus, the qualitative difference comes not from the hardware (which is still quantitatively better) but from the motivations that drive us to spend so much time learning and communicating what we have learned to others. This account dovetails nicely with [computational] modeling work, which found that the abstract [prefrontal cortex] representations took a long time to develop and required integrating knowledge across multiple different but related tasks. Furthermore, the development of the [prefrontal cortex] is the most protracted of any brain area, not fully maturing until adolescence. Thus, the full glory of human intelligence requires the extensive, culturally supported developmental learning process that takes place over the first decades of life.[41]

Despite the cognitive power contributed by neural processes within the prefrontal cortex of the brain, it would be wrong to presume that the prefrontal cortex is where "it all comes together", or that this area contains a brain module that works autonomously to regulate all other brain processing. Rather, the prefrontal cortex is a major node in large distributed brain networks that are working (either on-line or off-line) in the modulation of ongoing action in the world. Terms such as "mental", "intelligent", and "symbolic" are all labels for products of the entire person (or animal) as that person (or animal) interacts with a complex environment, most particularly the social environment.

[40] J. N. Giedd, "Structural Magnetic Resonance Imaging of the Adolescent Brain", *Annals of the New York Academy of Science*, 1021 (2004), 105–9; J. M. Fuster, "Frontal Lobe and Cognitive Development", *Journal of Neurocytology*, 31/3–5 (2002), 373–85.
[41] Randall C. O'Reilly, "Biologically Based Computational Models of High-Level Cognition", *Science*, 314/5796 (6 Oct. 2006), 93.

3.4 Semantic Networks, Neural Nets, and Ontogenic Landscapes

How, then, are we to understand the neural realization of the capacity for symbolic language? If we are correct in attributing symbolic language to context-sensitive constraints, then the answer must require an understanding of contextual constraints on the neural activities that embody language use.

We have considered the structural features of the brain that are necessary for the acquisition of language. First, there is simply the vast number of neurons in the human brain, the density of their interconnections, and, especially, the recurrent connections that enable reentrant feedback loops. Second, there is the reorganization of the human brain that gives priority to a high degree of connectivity between the prefrontal cortex and other regions. Third, there is the organization of the cortex itself in such a way as to enable a nested hierarchy of top-down controls, as we have already seen in the case of the prefrontal cortex.

We can easily imagine that semantic relations (such as the close association between "grandmother" and "grandfather", and the distant association between "grandmother" and "frog") are realized by means of neural networks that overlap or not, and higher-order classifications (such as "family members") realized by larger webs of such networks.

Patterns of functional connections between regions specifically subserving language and those serving narrative memory, emotions, sensations, and motor activity are the basis for the rich connotations of some words. Alwyn Scott gives a plausible account of the interactions activated when one hears the word "grandmother":

Presumably an image of grandma may come to mind, and that would appear to involve the optic lobes. But other parts of the memory relating to voice would have originated, presumably, in the temporal lobes. These recollections are connected to others related to things she said and did, the way her house smelled on Thanksgiving Day, the colors of her kitchen, and so on. Because the memory of your grandmother is no doubt imbued with emotional overtones, those cells, whose locations are not known, would also need to be activated. And finally there is the not inconsequential linguistic task of matching the word "grandmother" to one elderly or even long-deceased human female who happened to be the mother of one of your parents.[42]

---

[42] Alwyn Scott, *Stairway to the Mind: The Controversial New Science of Consciousness* (New York: Springer Verlag, 1995), 78.

This is, in Scott's terms (following Donald Hebb[43]), the activation of a particular cell assembly, or in Gerald Edelman and Giulio Tononi's terms, the activation of a specific form of dynamic core (see Ch. 3, sec. 5.3).

Recent attempts at computer simulations of neural networks have suggested theories about the sorts of neural changes that are involved in learning language. Computer networks with interconnected layers of units have been able to learn to recognize words. This requires an input layer (e.g., one that receives information about configuration of words) and an output layer (e.g., one that produces sounds). In between there are one or more layers of units with each unit linked to a large number of both input and output units by means of connections that can vary in strength. Juarrero says:

Both artificial and biological neural networks share an interesting feature. Both are *coarse coded*; that is, each unit receives input from many other units. Moreover, some of the connections to a given unit may be excitatory, others inhibitory. The artificial network as a whole computes all the inputs to all the units and settles into a state that best satisfies the overall set of constraints. The first-order context-sensitive constraint that a particular connection represents is therefore "soft" or "weak": the overall input from the rest of the network can override it. Each layer in a connectionist network in fact integrates information from lower layers by "detecting higher order combinations of activities among the units to which they are connected."... As a result there is no one-to-one mapping between input and output. Instead, the overall output consists of a blend of the various outputs from the individual units. A significant by-product of this apparent sloppiness is that as a result, neural networks acquire the ability to generalize.[44]

The key to learning is "backward error propagation."[45] That is, the network starts with random assignment of connection weights. Each time the net produces an incorrect answer, a small change (proportional to the error) is made in the connection weights to see if it moves the system closer to the desired output. This is repeated until the system has learned the desired responses; it can take hours, days, or even weeks.[46]

---

[43] Donald O. Hebb, *The Organization of Behavior: A Neuropsychological Theory* (New York: Wiley, 1949).

[44] Juarrero, *Dynamics in Action*, 164.   [45] Ibid. 165.

[46] Paul M. Churchland, *The Engine of Reason, the Seat of the Soul: A Philosophical Journey into the Brain* (Cambridge, Mass.: MIT Press, 1995), 44–5. Churchland provides a detailed and very readable account of research on artificial neural networks.

Because the output is a blending of the inner layer's responses to all of the input, the system must be understood in dynamic terms. The gradual reorganization of the internal weights is the creation of attractors. Insofar as brains self-organize in similar fashion, it is reasonable to describe language learning as the development of attractors. Or, given the complex relations among multiple attractors, a better description is the development of an ontogenic (probability) *landscape* of basins (attractors) and ridges (repellers).

Semantics, says Juarrero, is embodied in such a landscape. Categories are basins of attraction for words representing similar items. As already mentioned, it is the coarse-coding strategy of neural networks that allows them to form general categories. Constrained pathways through the landscape embody syntax.

There is a variety of ways in which this dynamical approach to linguistics explains linguistic phenomena. We mention three. First, as George Lakoff and Mark Johnson argue, the more typical formal-syntax-and-semantics paradigm never actually manages to account for meaning (see sec. 4.2 below). In contrast, Juarrero's ontogenic landscape has semantics built in. Second, it is biologically realistic, in that each such system, whether artificial or biological, will be unique—each self-organizes differently in response to accidental details of its history and its interaction with the environment. Juarrero says that the constraints that govern such a system's behavior "run through both the environment and time, as well as through the system's internal dynamics"[47]—a point we emphasize below (sec. 4). Third, it explains what Deacon noted in the chimpanzees: the development of symbolic language happens suddenly, not gradually. Juarrero speculates that the sudden grasp of symbols is a "catastrophic reorganization"[48] of phase space, a simpler example of which would be a phase transition in an autocatalytic process.

4 The Meaning of Meaning

We turn now to philosophical puzzles about language. We began this chapter by acknowledging the claim of many thinkers that the relation between language and the world is mysterious (and in the eyes of some,

---

[47] Juarrero, *Dynamics in Action*, 173.   [48] Ibid.

particularly mysterious for the physicalist). We believe that four factors contribute to this sense of mystery. One is the attempt to give a single, grand theory of meaning; we claim that many of the theories provided by philosophers through the ages provide partial insights, yet none alone is sufficient. A second, related factor is the attempt to understand symbolic language without understanding its difference from, but dependence upon, icons and indices. Deacon notes that trying to understand symbolic reference without appreciating the constitutive role of lower forms of reference is like kicking away the ladder after climbing up to the symbolic realm and then imagining that there never was a ladder in the first place.[49] A third factor is the attempt to understand language on the model of formal systems.

The most important factor, as emphasized above, is the tendency to look for the source of meaning "in the head", whether this be in a substantial *mind*, or in a *brain* cut off from its attached body's engagement in action in the social world. This is clearly a holdover from Augustinian and Cartesian emphases on the mental as inner and from the dualists' supposition that meaning is generated by internal mental acts.

In this section we survey some of the history of theories of meaning. Then we turn to two resources for conceiving meaning as a product of *action in the environment*. One is the philosophical work of Ludwig Wittgenstein. The other is the work in linguistics of George Lakoff and Mark Johnson. Finally, we shall examine the compatibility of accounts from Deacon and Juarrero, Wittgenstein and Lakoff and Johnson.

4.1 Modern Theories of Meaning

The oldest of the modern theories of meaning is the idea theory. A classic expression was John Locke's: "The uses, then, of words is to be sensible marks of ideas; and the ideas they stand for are their proper and immediate signification."[50] The conception of language that lies behind this theory goes at least as far back as Augustine—language is the communication of thought; thought is a succession of ideas in consciousness, which are immediately accessible to the thinker. Communication is successful when one's utterance arouses the same ideas in the hearer's mind. This theory

---

[49] Deacon, *Symbolic Species*, 453.
[50] John Locke, *Essay Concerning Human Understanding*, bk. iii, ch. 2, sec. 1.

has been criticized on the grounds that it is simply false that all meaningful expressions are regularly associated with ideas. William Alston says:

Consider a sentence taken at random, "Increases in the standard of living have not been offset by corresponding increases in the income of clerical personnel." Ask yourself whether there was a distinguishable idea in your mind corresponding to each of the meaningful linguistic units of the sentence, "increases," "in," "the," "standard," etc.[51]

If one were to reply that this piecemeal way of associating words with ideas is wrongheaded, and that the sentence as a whole gets its meaning from the idea that increases-in-the-standard-of-living-have-not-been-offset-by-corresponding-increases-in-the-income-of-clerical-personnel, then it is not clear that the theory tells us anything useful. What is it to have this idea beyond the entertaining of this sentence?

Finally, explaining meaning in terms of ideas is surely an attempt to explain the obscure by means of the more obscure, since it is not at all clear what it is to have an idea. Difficulties in pinning down the idea of an idea have led in more recent theories to consideration of the relation of language to the world. That is, for Locke and others, words were taken to represent ideas, and ideas in turn represented things in the world. If ideas are too obscure to be of use, then they might best be left out of account, and meaning be accounted for simply in terms of language's relation to the world.

Frege's distinction between sense and reference should have shown that meaning cannot simply be equated with reference. Also, there are countless words that have no referent, such as "unicorn" and "such".[52] Yet, the language—world relation *does* seem to be crucial for meaning. So various theorists have set out to define meaning in terms of whole sentences. Some have held that a sentence refers to the *fact* or state of affairs that makes it true or false; others that its meaning is a function of whatever experiences could empirically confirm of disconfirm it. Still others have argued that all true sentences have the same referent, either the world as a whole or *Truth*, conceived as a single abstract entity. Donald Davidson has proposed a "truth-conditional" theory of meaning according to which the meaning

---

[51] William P. Alston, "Meaning", in Paul Edwards, (ed.), *The Encyclopedia of Philosophy* (New York: Macmillan Publishing Co., 1967), v. 233–41, at p. 235.

[52] We follow philosophers' conventions in using quotation marks to designate (rather than use) a word. Concepts are italicized. Thus, the term "unicorn", the concept *unicorn*.

of an utterance is determined by the conditions that must be met if it is to be true.[53] The meaning of every significant part, then, is accounted for on the basis of the role it plays in determining truth conditions.

As straightforward as referential theories may seem, we suggest that they do not serve the purpose for which they were intended, in that they do *not* actually address the relation between words and world. For example, the meaning of "Snow is white" is said to be determined by the conditions that must be met if it is to be true. What are those conditions? Presumably, snow's being white. How are we to get beyond merely rearranging the words? By finding some of the stuff and pointing at it? But, of course, without a verbal explanation, no one would understand the meaning of the gesture.

Lakoff and Johnson argue that modern philosophy of language took an entirely wrong turn after Frege. Frege took the *senses* of words and sentences to be abstract entities something like Platonic forms. This approach is unappealing to most current theorists, but most analytic philosophers and many cognitive scientists have adopted Frege's supposition that natural languages can be modeled by formal systems. This has led to the development of the "formal-syntax-and-semantics" paradigm, according to which all meaning and thought is disembodied and formal, sentences are well-formed formulas, and transformation of sentences proceeds by means of logical rules. The difficulty is that reference and syntactic rules have to bear all the weight of meaning.

Lakoff and Johnson believe that this approach to language makes the representation-to-reality problem insuperable. Representations have been shrunk to the minimum—bare symbolic representations with no properties other than being distinct from one another. "This symbol-system realism maximizes the chasm between mind and world, since the abstract entity of the symbol shares nothing with anything in the world."[54] We would say that it is an attempt, via syntactic rules, to create a symbol system that does not trade in icons and indices. If human language in fact worked this way, then we would no more know the meanings of words than computers know the meanings of the symbols they manipulate.

---

[53] Donald Davidson, *Inquiries into Truth and Interpretation* (Oxford: Oxford University Press, 1984).

[54] George Lakoff and Mark Johnson, *Philosophy in the Flesh: The Embodied Mind and Its Challenge to Western Thought* (New York: Basic Books, 1999), 95.

Our own critiques of reference-based theories are implicit in the previous section.

4.2 Concepts as Embodied Metaphors

In section 3.1 we followed Deacon's account of the development of the capacity to use abstract categories of what we might call a very rudimentary level: "tool", "food", "drink". In the philosophical tradition there is a long-standing distinction between categories pertaining to sensible objects and those pertaining to abstract entities. The latter have been taken as a (or *the*) mark of human rationality. For example, Thomas Aquinas attributed the latter to the specifically human rational soul, which he distinguished from the animal soul.[55]

Juarrero describes the formation of abstract concepts in terms of the development of broader basins of attraction in semantic space. Our emphasis here is on how this process (as well as the development of narrower concepts) depends on our embodied experience. Here we turn to the work of linguist George Lakoff and philosopher Mark Johnson on the *metaphorical* basis of philosophical concepts, and on the *neural* basis of metaphors.[56]

Lakoff and Johnson distinguish between primary and complex metaphors. An instance of a primary metaphor is *Knowing Is Seeing*.[57] Primary metaphors can be combined with others and with common-sense knowledge to construct complex metaphors. Drawing on the work of a number of cognitive scientists, linguists, and neuroscientists, Lakoff and Johnson offer a plausible hypothesis about the formation of primary metaphors. These metaphors are acquired automatically and unconsciously during childhood. For young children, subjective experiences and judgments are regularly conflated with sensorimotor experiences. For example, the subjective experience of affection is typically correlated with the sensory experience of warmth; the experience of coming to know something is regularly associated with seeing, as in "Let's see what is in the box". During the period of conflation, associations are automatically built up between the two domains: affection and warmth, knowing and seeing.

Later on, children are able to differentiate the domains, but the associations persist because they are realized neurobiologically. Each cluster of

---

[55] Thomas Aquinas, *Summa Theologica*, 1a, 75–9.
[56] Lakoff and Johnson, *Philosophy in the Flesh*.
[57] The convention of capitalization is their indication that they are referring to a metaphor.

memories is realized by means of the formation of a neural network.[58] Simultaneous activation of two neural networks results in permanent neural connections such that future activation of one network automatically activates the other. Once learned, primary metaphors are recognized automatically, without recourse to a multi-stage process of interpretation. In addition, primary metaphors provide a skeletal structure for further inference by allowing activation to spread between the neural networks associated in the metaphoric relationship.

Lakoff and Johnson present 25 examples of primary metaphors, along with the sensorimotor experiences hypothesized to give rise to them. For example, Affection Is Warmth derives from the primary experience of feeling warm while being held affectionately; the metaphor Categories Are Containers derives from the frequent observation that things that go together tend to be in the same bounded region; the metaphor Causes Are Physical Forces derives from the experience of achieving results by exerting forces on physical objects.[59]

Primary metaphors are like atoms, in that they can be combined with commonplace knowledge to create complex metaphors. To see how this works, consider Descartes's development of the Knowing Is Seeing metaphor. Descartes conceived of the mind according to the metaphor of Mind As A Container. More precisely, he conceived of it as an inner theater with a stage upon which metaphorical objects (ideas) are illuminated by an inner light (the "Natural Light of Reason"), and are observed by a metaphorical spectator. Mental vision is termed intuition. Mental attention is visual focusing. Descartes's peculiar (and false) conclusion that ideas he could conceive clearly and distinctly were therefore immune to doubt follows from the structure of the complex metaphor. In the source domain of actual seeing, we are in fact unable to doubt what we clearly and distinctly perceive.[60]

Lakoff and Johnson argue that, embodied creatures that we are, it stands to reason that our primary conceptual resources should come from our

---

[58] The early basis for this understanding is found in the work of Donald Hebb. See, e.g., Hebb, *Organization of Behavior*. Arnold Modell notes that such networks are likely to be intrinsically multi-modal, involving visual, auditory, and kinaesthetic elements. See *Imagination and the Meaningful Brain*, 32.

[59] Lakoff and Johnson, *Philosophy in the Flesh*, ch. 4.

[60] Ibid. ch. 19.

sensorimotor experiences. The brain tends *not* to develop neural structures that it does not need. Thus, if it is possible to reason by employing structures developed for coping with sensorimotor experiences, then it is likely that we do so.[61] The import of this hypothesis is that much of our thinking is unconsciously structured by inference based on the source domains of our metaphorically based concepts.

The notion that the neural representation of at least primary concepts is sensorimotor is what MacKay had in mind in suggesting the idea that perception is the establishment of conditional readiness to reckon with what is being perceived. For an infant to recognize its mother is for the sensorimotor memories of interactions with her to be primed, including the thus far conflated experiences of affection and warmth. When later these ideas are differentiated, they are nevertheless forever linked in the sensorimotor and emotional-evaluative memories elicited by either concept. Similarly, the experimental demonstration of mirror neurons (described in Ch. 3, sec. 2.2.2) in the motor system of monkeys demonstrates that the perception of the intentional actions of another monkey is represented by activity in the motor areas of the brain that would occur if the monkey were to perform the same actions itself. Perceptions and understandings are embodied in the elicitation of basic sensorimotor and emotional-evaluative memories. Primary metaphors are the consistent linkage through co-occurrence of two or more domains of sensorimotor experience.

Raymond Gibbs has a similar view of the relationship between language meaning and bodily experience. He argues that "patterns of linguistic structure and behavior are not arbitrary, or due to conventions or purely linguistic generalizations, but are motivated by recurring patterns of embodied experience ... which are metaphorically extended".[62] Thus, memories of embodied experience influence how people process speech and word meanings. "In fact," he argues, "language understanding within real-world communication contexts may be best described as a kind of embodied simulation, rather than the activation of pre-existing, disembodied, symbolic knowledge."[63]

---

[61] Lakoff and Johnson, *Philosophy in the Flesh*, 39.
[62] Raymond W. Gibbs, *Embodiment and Cognitive Science* (Cambridge: Cambridge University Press, 2006), 12.
[63] Ibid.

We conclude, then, that while the vast systems of neural connections that encode semantic networks are indeed "in the head", the meaning of symbolic language is essentially dependent on remembered, observed, and potential action in the world.

4.3 Wittgensteinian Language Games

Ludwig Wittgenstein may well turn out to have been the most important philosopher of the twentieth century. Two complementary foci of his work are an attempt to provide an account of the relation of language to the world and a critique of theories of the mental as *inner* actions. Fergus Kerr aptly sums up his contribution to the understanding of language in the title of a section of his book: "The Hermit in the Head Goes Shopping."[64] In Chapter 1 we mentioned Wittgenstein's objections to the Augustinian idea that learning language is simply a matter of the immaterial ego learning to attach labels to objects (see Ch. 1, sec. 3.3). Attempts to teach language to chimps show the difficulties at even the most rudimentary level. If one points to a banana and says "yellow", the chimp has no way of knowing that it is the color being defined, since it has no concept of color.

Wittgenstein often made his points about language by means of imagined (highly simplified) languages or "language games". For example:

Now think of the following use of language: I send someone shopping. I give him a slip marked "five red apples". He takes the slip to the shopkeeper, who opens the drawer marked "apples"; then he looks up the word "red" in a table and finds a colour sample opposite it; then he says the series of cardinal numbers—I assume that he knows them by heart—up to the word "five" and for each number he takes an apple of the same colour as the sample out of the drawer.———It is in this and similar ways that one operates with words.[65]

This shows, says Kerr, that in the simplest situation one can imagine, meaning is interwoven with other activities. The linking of objects with words goes along with already being able to do a great deal more.

Within the very first paragraph of the *Investigations*, then, [Wittgenstein] moves meanings out of the infant Augustine's head to retrieve them in a mundane transaction in the village store. From the outset he reminds us of the obvious:

---

[64] Fergus Kerr, *Theology after Wittgenstein*, 2nd edn. (London: SPCK, 1997).
[65] Ludwig Wittgenstein, *Philosophical Investigations*, ed. G. E. M. Anscombe and R. Rhees, trans. G. E. M. Anscombe (Oxford: Blackwell, 1953), §1.

the locus of meanings is not the epistemological solitude of the individual consciousness but the practical exchanges that constitute the public world which we inhabit together.[66]

So knowing the meaning of a word or phrase is a matter of knowing what to do with it, of knowing how to make plays with it in a language game. It is essential to recognize that language games are not purely verbal; they involve interaction with both people and things. For example, to know the meaning of the word "chair" is to be able to recognize one when one sees it, but also to know what to *do* with a chair. "It is part of the grammar of the word 'chair' that *this* [sitting] is what we call 'to sit in a chair.' "[67] Wittgenstein's account of language is compatible with our insistence, throughout this volume, that the mental can be understood only when we take seriously its social character and its role in action; language is to be understood in the first instance in light of its role in adaptive action—feedback loops within the physical and social environments.

As mentioned above, a central goal of Wittgenstein's work was to exorcise the Cartesian view that the meaning of language is based on inner mental acts. The example of selling apples is a caricature, but its point is that no inner operations were needed. The shopkeeper followed rules for matching items to the shopping list, and the rules governed *actions*, not mental events.

It is important to note that Wittgenstein was not denying the existence of inner accompaniments to behavior. So, for instance, it may be the case that one has a mental image of a chair when one reads the word "chair"; the shopkeeper might have been thinking to himself: "Now get the color chart." Wittgenstein's point is that these mental events cannot be *constitutive* of the meaning of language; if so, language would be impossible to learn. The criteria for understanding have to be public.

On Wittgenstein's account there neither can nor need be a grand theory of meaning, except to say that to find the meaning, look for the use. And language is used in too many different ways to catalogue. The answer to the question of how language "hooks onto" the world is to be found in

---

[66] Kerr, *Theology after Wittgenstein*, 57–8.
[67] Ludwig Wittgenstein, *The Blue and Brown Books*, ed. R. Rhees (New York: Harper & Row, 1958), 24.

the activities we engage in, and in the socially established patterns and rules that shape our speech.

4.4 Language in Action

The account of language that we have offered above, largely indebted to Peirce's semiology, Deacon's study of linguistic abilities in animals, and Juarrero's dynamical approach to cognitive processes, is surprisingly congruent with Wittgenstein's, based largely on the invention of greatly simplified language games.[68] The goal of this section is to tie our accounts of language learning and of the neural prerequisites for language more closely to Wittgenstein's rather enigmatic discussion of language at the beginning of his *Investigations*. In section 4.5 we note the complementarity between Wittgenstein's work and that of Lakoff and Johnson. Finally, in section 5 we shall ask whether any mysteries about reference or meaning remain.

We mentioned in Chapter 1 that Wittgenstein begins his *Philosophical Investigations* with a paragraph from Augustine's *Confessions* in order to criticize a still common theory of language.

When they (my elders) named some object, and accordingly moved towards something, I saw this and I grasped that the thing was called by the sound they uttered when they meant to point it out. Their intention was shown by their bodily movements, as it were the natural language of all peoples: the expression of the face, the play of the eyes, the movement of other parts of the body, and the tone of voice which expresses our state of mind in seeking, having, rejecting, or avoiding something. Thus, as I heard words repeatedly used in their proper places in various sentences, I gradually learnt to understand what objects they signified; and after I had trained my mouth to form these signs, I used them to express my own desires.[69]

Wittgenstein is critical of the supposition expressed in this passage that *naming* is the essence of language. We note that the passage also expresses the view that children come into the world already having the *idea* of language, and only need to be taught the words. Current advocates of such a theory include the "language of thought" theorists—those who

---

[68] We believe that Deacon came to his conclusions independently of Wittgenstein, both because there are no references to Wittgenstein in Deacon's book and because many other things Deacon says about language, which we note below, are so thoroughly un-Wittgensteinian.

[69] Wittgenstein, *Investigations*, §1.1 The quotation is from *Confessions*, I, 8. Subsequent references to *Investigations* are given parenthetically in the text.

believe that humans' ability to learn language must result from their already possessing "Mentalese", an unarticulated, internal language allowing them to formulate beliefs and intentions.[70] Helen Keller's account of first catching on to language is instructive. She recalls having desires and intentions, and learning to express some of them by means of crude signs: "A shake of the head meant 'No' and a nod, 'Yes,' a pull meant 'Come' and a push 'Go.' "[71] Of course this is *a description of her intentions in language* that she could provide only long afterwards—after catching on to the very idea of language, which only occurred several years later. Her teacher, Anne Sullivan, set out to teach her language by shaping her hands into patterns of finger spelling. She first learned to imitate the letters (iconically) and then to associate the patterns of letters with objects.

When I finally succeeded in making the letters correctly I was flushed with childish pleasure and pride. Running downstairs to my mother I held up my hand and made the letters for doll. I did not know that I was spelling a word or even that words existed; I was simply making my fingers go in monkey-like imitation. In the days that followed I learned to spell in this uncomprehending way a great many words.[72]

Several weeks later, she says, "somehow the mystery of language was revealed to me. I knew then that 'w-a-t-e-r' meant the wonderful cool something that was flowing over my hand. That living word awakened my soul, gave it light, hope, joy, set it free."[73] At this point, Helen had learned to play the "name game". Recall that Juarrero's account of what is happening neurobiologically in crossing the symbolic threshold is a catastrophic reorganization of phase space. She also mentions Keller's account of the suddenness of the change.

   Wittgenstein and Keller agree that this is only the beginning of the process. There follows in Wittgenstein's text the passage we quoted in section 4.3 above: "I give him a slip marked 'five red apples'." Given that this example immediately follows Wittgenstein's criticism of Augustine for not distinguishing different *kinds* of words, we take it that the primary purpose here is to illustrate how differently the words "five" and "red"

---

[70] See, e.g., Jerry Fodor, *The Language of Thought* (New York: Thomas Y. Crowell, 1975).
[71] Helen Keller, *The Story of My Life* (New York: Penguin, 1988), 7.   [72] Ibid. 17.
[73] Ibid. 18.

function than does the noun "apples". Wittgenstein's imaginary interlocu-tor responds: "But how does he know where and how he is to look up the word 'red' and what he is to do with the word 'five'?" Wittgenstein replies: "Well, I assume that he *acts* as I have described. Explanations come to an end somewhere."

As we noted above, this bit of a language game exhibits symbolic reference, in that the shopkeeper must recognize the categories of *color* and *number* (even if he has no words for the categories).

Wittgenstein then asks us to imagine a language for which Augustine's description *is* correct:

The language is meant to serve for communication between a builder A and an assistant B. A is building with building-stones: there are blocks, pillars, slabs and beams. B has to pass the stones, and that in the order in which A needs them. For this purpose they use a language consisting of the words "block", "pillar", "slab", "beam". A calls them out;—B brings the stone which he has learnt to bring at such-and-such a call.——Conceive this as a complete primitive language. (§2)

Several pages later Wittgenstein says:

We could imagine that the language of §2 was the *whole* language of A and B; even the whole language of a tribe. The children are brought up to perform *these* actions, to use *these* words as they do so, and to react in *this* way to the words of others.

An important part of the training will consist in the teacher's pointing to the objects, directing the child's attention to them, and at the same time uttering a word; for instance, the word "slab" as he points to that shape .... This ostensive teaching of words can be said to establish an association between the word and the thing. (§6)

Wittgenstein's further description of how this language game is learned involves both iconic and indexical associations:

In instruction in the language the following process will occur: the learner *names* the objects; that is, he utters the word when the teacher points to the stone [creating indexical reference of word to object].—And there will be this still simpler exercise: the pupil repeats the words after the teacher [creating word icons]——both of these being processes resembling language. (§7)

However, he says, naming is not yet language, it is "mere preparation for language" (§49). While Wittgenstein said earlier that we were to *imagine* this as a complete language, we take his view to be that this use of words does not in fact constitute language—it merely resembles language. In our terms, there is no symbolic reference involved. Next, however, Wittgenstein proposes an expansion of the language game, which we believe would transform it into genuine language.

Besides the four words "block", "pillar", etc., let it contain a series of words used as the shopkeeper in (1) used the numerals (it can be the series of letters of the alphabet); further, let there be two words, which may as well be "there" and "this" (because this roughly indicates their purpose), that are used in connexion with a pointing gesture; and finally a number of colour samples. A gives an order like: "d—slab—there". At the same time he shews the assistant a colour sample, and when he says "there" he points to a place on the building site. From the stock of slabs B takes one for each letter of the alphabet up to "d", of the same colour as the sample, and brings them to the place indicated by A.—On other occasions A gives the order "this—there". At "this" he points to a building stone. And so on. (§8).

Wittgenstein's point is that different *kinds* of words function differently, and that their functions depend on actions performed along with their use. Again his example illustrates the role of higher-order classifications, which make syntax possible: "d—slab—there" is syntactically correct, while "c—d—there" is not. Note the close tie between action and syntax. It is not simply that the latter string violates arbitrary abstract rules, it is that there is nothing for which one could *use* it. Wittgenstein's "And so on" is important. Symbolic systems with syntax must be learned as a closed system, but once learned, given more than the most rudimentary syntax, can be extended to new situations.

Several pages later, he returns to his criticism of the notion that (true) language can be learned by ostensive definition.

In languages (2) and (8) there was no such thing as asking something's name. This, with its correlate, ostensive definition, is, we might say, a language-game on its own. That is really to say: we are brought up, trained, to ask: "What is that called?"—upon which the name is given. (§27)

In our terms, participation in social practices is required in order to catch on to the very idea that words signify things. As Wittgenstein says, "the ostensive definition explains the use—the meaning—of the word when the overall role of the word in language is clear" (§30).

Sue Savage-Rumbaugh's work in teaching language to chimpanzees nicely parallels Wittgenstein's understanding of the nature of language itself. It was relatively easy to get the animals to use language for specific "speech acts" such as requesting food. The use of such "speech acts" required sensitivity to context—they never attempted to request food when there was no one there to give it.[74] The hardest task was teaching chimpanzees to communicate with one another. Before they would do so, she had to devise a situation in which one chimpanzee knew that the other did *not* know something.[75] Even so, they would not communicate the information unless it was necessary in order to *do* something.[76] So language learning for apes as well as for humans requires a social context and something to do with the language. Language, even for chimpanzees, is intelligible only within a context of action.

4.5 Metaphors and Philosophical Therapy

Wittgenstein's name does not appear in the index of Lakoff and Johnson's *Philosophy in the Flesh*, yet upon reading it we were immediately struck by the value of each to the other. First, the value of Lakoff and Johnson for understanding and extending Wittgenstein's work: Wittgenstein is often read as a relativist. This is because of his claims that justification depends on language games, and language games in turn depend on forms of life. The appearance of relativism comes from the fact that we tend to imagine forms of life to be arbitrary and highly variable. Wittgenstein tried to point away from this conclusion by suggesting that forms of life and language arise out of shared bodily experiences. Unfortunately, his most prominent illustration is linguistic expressions of pain "going proxy" for pain behavior. Pain and its expression are universal enough, but it is difficult to imagine much of the rest of our language functioning on analogy to "ouch, that hurts!"

Yet there is something right about his insight that forms of life and language games are *not* arbitrary. Lakoff and Johnson provide resources for showing how the non-arbitrariness of language games derives from the commonalities we share in virtue of our embodied selfhood. Compare Wittgenstein's notion of the *grammar* of our concepts with Lakoff and Johnson's notion of *metaphorical implication*. In "The Blue Book" Wittgenstein

---

[74] Savage-Rumbaugh, *Ape Language*, 72–5.   [75] Ibid. 132–4.   [76] Ibid. 149.

asks us to consider as an example the question "What is time?" We ask for a definition, he says, in order to clear up the *grammar* of a word.

[T]he puzzlement about the grammar of the word "time" arises from what one might call apparent contradictions in that grammar.

It was such a "contradiction" which puzzled St. Augustine when he argued: How is it possible that one should measure time? For the past can't be measured, as it has gone by; and the future can't be measured because it has not yet come. And the present can't be measured because it has no extension.[77]

In other words, the puzzlement arises from attempting to imagine how to apply measurement techniques such as we would use for the length of an object "to a distance on a travelling band".[78] Here, precisely, is an instance of the metaphor of Moving Time described by Lakoff and Johnson.

To illustrate the extent to which metaphors provide cross-cultural language games, consider Lakoff and Johnson's example of concepts of *self* in the West and in Japan. The metaphoric system we use for describing our inner lives is based on a fundamental distinction between what they call the Subject and one or more Selves. The Subject is the locus of consciousness, reason, and will. The Selves consist of everything else about us, and can be metaphorically construed as persons, objects, or locations.[79] They hypothesize that the Subject–Self opposition arises from a variety of common experiences, such as ways in which we attempt and sometimes fail to control our bodies, and cases where conscious values conflict with our behavior.[80] The metaphors that arise from these experiences are cross-cultural. For example, there is the Essential Self metaphor such that there is a real self hidden inside an outer self, as in "You've never seen what he's really like on the inside". In Japan one would say "He rarely puts out [his] real self," or "He always wears a mask in public."[81] They conclude that "the multifarious notions of subject and self are far from arbitrary".[82]

So Lakoff and Johnson's account of the rootedness of the metaphorical entailments or *grammar* of our concepts in bodily experience provides rich resources for supporting and elaborating Wittgenstein's insights into the non-arbitrary nature of language games.

---

[77] Wittgenstein, *Blue and Brown Books*, 26.   [78] Ibid.
[79] Lakoff and Johnson, *Philosophy in the Flesh*, 267.
[80] Ibid. 266.   [81] Ibid. 286–7.   [82] Ibid. 268.

It is particularly interesting for our purposes that the central example of cross-cultural agreement in metaphorization that Lakoff and Johnson present has to do with the hiddenness of the self, since this was a manner of thinking in philosophy that Wittgenstein was at pains to criticize. Wittgenstein expresses his view succinctly in *Philosophical Investigations*: "If one sees the behavior of a living thing, one sees its soul."[83] Kerr summarizes:

In hundreds of such remarks Wittgenstein brings out the power of the picture of the hidden thoughts behind the facade of my face, and the invisible soul inside the carapace of my body .... Again and again ... we return to the paradigm of the material object, deny its materiality, visibility and so on, and think that we have found our true selves.[84]

So what Wittgenstein offers to Lakoff and Johnson—or, we should rather say, to philosophers influenced by Lakoff and Johnson—is his notion of philosophical therapy. Lakoff and Johnson point out that philosophical puzzles arise from uncritical assumptions based on metaphors. But if metaphorical inference is as deeply rooted and inevitable as they say it is, then their prescription for avoiding philosophical puzzles is about as helpful as a former American First Lady's prescription for avoiding drugs: "Just say no." In contrast, Wittgenstein recognized how seductive metaphorical thinking is, and worked for most of his life at developing therapeutic techniques to help confused students escape it.

In sum, Wittgenstein and Lakoff and Johnson agree that ordinary language is largely fixed by embodied life in the physical world, and that this ordinary language is entirely in order. Problems arise when philosophers use pictures (for Wittgenstein) or metaphors (for Lakoff and Johnson) to construct general philosophical theories. Then their thinking gets into "cramps". Wittgenstein shows us by a painstaking process where and how pictures/metaphors mislead us, and trains us not to say the misleading things we are tempted to say. More important for present purposes is that Lakoff and Johnson's emphasis on *universal* sources for abstract concepts in embodied experience forecloses a likely objection to Wittgenstein's social account of language by providing an argument against radical cultural relativity of meaning.

---

[83] Wittgenstein, *Philosophical Investigations*, §357.
[84] Kerr, *Theology after Wittgenstein*, 100.

4.6 Mysteries Solved?

Our claim, following Wittgenstein, is that the supposed mysteries about how language gets its meaning and reference dissolve when one focuses not on inner mental acts but rather on social activities and conventional uses. In a number of instances in the *Investigations* Wittgenstein seeks to exorcise the view that establishing an association between the word and the object requires some inner experience. It is common to suppose that the connection depends on a picture of the object coming before the child's mind when he hears the word. But Wittgenstein asks:

...if this does happen—is it the purpose of the word?—Yes, it *may* be the purpose.—I can imagine such a use of words (of series of sounds). (Uttering a word is like striking a note on the keyboard of the imagination.) But in the language of §2 it is *not* the purpose of the word to evoke images....

...Don't you understand the call "Slab!" if you act upon it is such-and-such a way? (§6)

We believe that the nagging worry that this cannot be all there is to understanding the meaning of a word is a result of Cartesian pictures of the mind as enclosed within the body. Note the role of inner processes in Deacon's descriptions of the mysteries of language:

we do not really understand one of our most commonplace experiences. We know how to use a word to mean something and to refer to something. We know how to coin new words and to assign new meanings to them. We know how to create codes and artificial languages. Yet we do not know how we know how to do this, nor what we are doing when we do. Or rather, we know on the surface, but we do not know what mental processes underlie these activities, much less what neural processes are involved.[85]

Considering the modern idea theory of meaning, Deacon notes the difficulties in defining ideas—candidates include mental images, something like a dictionary definition, checklists of features, and so on. "But how such mental objects pick out external physical objects, or whether they do, remains a thorny philosophical problem."[86] "What endows those otherwise inanimate things [sounds, configurations of ink on paper] with the capacity to refer to other things is an interpretive process, a critical part of which (though not all) occurs 'in the head'."[87]

---

[85] Deacon, *Symbolic Species*, 51.   [86] Ibid. 61.   [87] Ibid. 62–3.

We have seen that the philosophical question of what is language is a difficult one, and have followed Deacon's account in terms of the construction of the symbolic by means of hierarchical relations among icons and indices. Thus, meaning cannot be understood in terms of either sense or reference alone. Sense is a product not of an inner mental act, but rather of *communally shared* semantic networks. The development of a symbolic system depends on temporally prior indexical reference, but the derivation of symbolic reference is indirect, and is dependent upon the ability to use words to refer to other words as well as to indexical relationships between words and objects. Once in place, it is primarily the interrelations among symbols rather than reference that endows words with meaning. Inner processes such as mental images may be an important accompaniment of our language use, but, being inaccessible to others, they cannot be the source of the meaning of language. So the meaning of language depends on use. The use of language, as the difficulties in teaching chimpanzees to communicate with one another illustrates, depends on shared activity.

So when we understand the practices and conventions regarding the use of a language game, there is no further source of meaning "in the head". The scientific question of what is necessary biologically to be able to form and use language is complex, but not mysterious.

5 Retrospect and Prospect

In this chapter we have addressed three issues: (1) What *is* language (as opposed to an animal cry)? We used Juarrero's account of context-sensitive constraints in creating a symbolic system out of icons and indices. (2) What is it about human brains that makes it possible for us to cross this symbolic threshold? Our answer involved a neural structure with enough levels of nested hierarchical control systems to embody the "system upon system" of contextual constraints that created human language. Finally, (3) there was the question with which we began: how does (genuine symbolic) language "hook onto" the world? Our answer was to suggest that this problem would not have arisen in the first place apart from a Cartesian preoccupation with inner mental acts. Language hooks *onto the world* as we use it in our socially constructed (i.e., contextually constrained) embodied activities *in the world*.

In the next chapter we turn to another problem, thought by some to involve as much mystery as language. This is "the problem of mental causation": What causal work does the mental *qua* mental do, over and above the work of the brain? To dissolve it, we shall employ the concept of downward causation, defended in Chapter 2, and shall argue that, as in the case of language, the appearance of mystery comes from locating the mental exclusively in the head.

5

How Does Reason Get its Grip on the Brain?

1 What's the Problem?

The purpose of this chapter is to address what is known in the philosophical literature as "the problem of mental causation". This problem is usually stated as follows: if mental events are, in some sense, brain events, and if we assume that every brain event has a sufficient physical cause, then what is the causal role of the mental *per se*? Fred Dretske puts it this way:

> The project is to see how reasons—our beliefs, desires, purposes, and plans—operate in a world of causes, and to exhibit the role of reasons in the *causal* explanation of human behavior. In a broader sense, the project is to understand the relationship between the psychological and the biological—between, on the one hand, the *reasons* people have for moving their bodies and, on the other, the *causes* of their bodies' consequent movements.[1]

We are intentionally vague in saying that we shall "address" the problem, because we believe that there are actually a number of questions subsumed under this heading. We shall address six of these here, but conclude that *the* problem as it is most often formulated in philosophy of mind is insoluble, due specifically to the *way* it is formulated. The six questions that matter for the nonreductive physicalist are the following:

1. Why are mental processes *in general* not reducible to neurobiological processes?
2. Why does consciousness matter; why could we not be zombies instead? That is, why could there not be organisms that behave exactly as we do, but without being conscious at all?

[1] Fred Dretske, *Explaining Behavior: Reasons in a World of Causes* (Cambridge, Mass.: MIT Press, 1988), p. x.

3. What role do beliefs play in causing or redirecting behavior?
4. What role do reasons play in causing or redirecting behavior (Dretske's question)?
5. How, in neurobiological terms, can we understand the role of principles of reason in human thought and behavior?
6. How it can be that efficacious mental events fail to violate the causal closure of the physical sciences?

This set of problems has been difficult to address for a variety of reasons. First, given the extent to which reductionism in general has been built into the modern world view, it is difficult to argue (successfully) that *anything* is irreducible. Second, the discussion of neurobiological reductionism is complicated immensely by the fact that we do not fully understand consciousness itself. Third, the literature on what we might call "higher" mental processes—primarily those dependent on symbolic language—is largely bewitched by Cartesian accounts of the mental as "inner".

Our approach in this chapter will be twofold. One is to take the question of the reducibility of the mental to be an instance of the broader question of why properties of a higher-level system are generally not reducible to those of the lower level. This will provide an opportunity to pull together our emphases on the role of downward causation in complex systems, on mental events as characterized primarily in terms of neural processes embedded in broader causal and semantic systems, and on the role of sentience, consciousness, and symbolic language in providing for increasingly more flexible and effective modulation of behavior.

We approach the first question (in sec. 2) by means of an analogy. We show that the (supervenient) property of being a bearer of information is not reducible to the physical state that realizes it because of its embeddedness in a broader context. Mental states are essentially contextualized and, *a fortiori*, a mental property should not be expected to reduce to the brain processes that realize it. We address the question of the effectiveness of consciousness in section 3. Here the emphasis is on the informativeness of consciousness, so our argument against the reducibility of information to neural processes applies here, as well. In section 4 we address the causal role of beliefs, elaborating on Fred Dretske's account of beliefs as structuring causes of behavior. Section 5 focuses on a variety of features that provide for specifically human rational capacities, such as self-transcendence (the ability to evaluate our own evaluations), the ability to run off-line simulations of behavior and predict their outcome, and the cultural resources that Andy Clark refers to as "external scaffolding". In section 6 we address the question of how principles of reason come, in neurobiological terms, to be causally efficacious. In brief, we argue that downward causation from the cultural environment restructures the brain in such a way that its causal processes realize or subserve rational mental processes.

If our answers to all of these questions are adequate, we shall have addressed what we take to be the most significant issues that go under the heading of "the problem of mental causation". In fact, if we are right in emphasizing throughout this volume the action-relevance of sentience, cognition, reason, and language, then must not the *problem* of mental causation be an illusion? Nonetheless, many philosophers have concluded that this problem is insoluble.[2] So, section 7 attempts to show that the appearance of insolubility is due to the inadequate manner in which the problem is now most commonly formulated in the philosophy of mind. In particular, the problem involves a "bewitching" picture of the relation between the mental and the physical.

2 Why Mental Phenomena Cannot be Reduced

The goal of this entire chapter is, essentially, to answer the question of why mental processes are not reducible to the neurobiological level. As already mentioned, mental properties, properly understood, are *higher-level* properties relative to neural events and structures. They are contextualized brain events, co-constituted by their role in action–feedback–evaluation–action loops in the environment. "Mental causation" is an instance of downward causation, as understood in Chapter 2.

Discussions of reductionism in philosophy of mind are bedeviled by the fact that our understanding of consciousness, although advancing, is still in its infancy. Thus, it will be helpful to consider a simpler but analogous

---

[2] See, e.g., Jaegwon Kim, "The Myth of Nonreductive Materialism", in Richard Warren and Tadeusz Szubka (eds.), *The Mind–Body Problem* (Oxford: Blackwell, 1994), 242–60; and *idem, Physicalism, or Something Near Enough* (Princeton: Princeton University Press, 2005).

problem, that of information. While full-blown human consciousness does more than provide information, it does at least that. We begin our argument for the nonreducibility of mental events by considering the nonreducibility of the property of being a bearer of information. The context dependence (and thus the irreducibility) of information, we argue, is analogous to the context dependence (and thus irreducibility) of mental events. In so arguing, we criticize typical definitions of the concept of supervenience and distinguish our position from functionalism.

2.1 An Informative Analogy

A reasonable analogy to the (supposed) supervenience of mental states on physical events is the supervenience of the property of being a *representation* or an *information-bearer* on the physical property, state, or event that realizes it.[3] This analogy is a way of using the concept of *supervenience* that we believe is most illuminating—one that pays attention to the role of a broader *context* to which the supervenient property relates.

Consider the metal coil in a thermostat that serves to measure the temperature of the room. Its contraction and expansion open and close an electrical circuit, and this in turn switches the heat on or off. It has the capacity to inform the system that the room is either too cool or warm enough, relative to where the thermostat is set. Its information-bearing capacity is dependent not only on its physical composition, shape, and so forth, but also on the larger system of which it is a part. When the coil is in a state (S_1) that opens the circuit, it carries the information "warm enough" $(T+)$; when it is in a state (S_2) that closes the circuit, it carries the information "too cool" $(T-)$. So we can say that the information-bearing properties of the circuit, $T+$ and $T-$, *supervene* on the physical states S_1 and S_2 respectively. Notice, though, that taken out of the context of the rest of the thermostat, the heating system, and the room whose temperature it is meant to regulate, the coil no longer serves its purpose, and its supervenient informational properties disappear.

We call the supervenient informational properties *higher-level* properties, then, because they pertain to the coil only under the conditions of its being properly connected to a broader (and more complex) causal system (see

---

[3] Note that this is "information" in the ordinary sense, not in the sense of the mathematical theory developed by Claude Shannon and others.

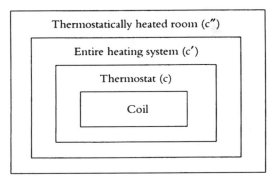

Figure 5.1. A nested set of increasingly complex systems in which the thermostat's coil is involved.

Ch. 2, secs. 2.2.3 and 3.2.1). There are actually several layers of increasingly complex systems, which we may represent as in Figure 5.1.

Are the supervenient properties $T+$ and $T-$ reducible to the physical properties that realize them? The reductionist answer is to say yes: all of the causal work is being done at the physical level, and, in fact, the laws of physics determine the expansion and contraction of the length of the coil and thus determine whether the system turns on or off. Notice, though, that there are multiple levels of explanation in which we may be interested. If we want to know only how the thermostat works, the reductive answer is just the one we want. But we can ask, further, why does the heat come on at, say, 65 degrees? Then we have to answer in terms of a broader system which includes the sliding device for setting the temperature, its position, and the calibration of the device as a whole. Furthermore, we can ask why the thermometer is set at 65 degrees rather than some other temperature. The answer would then have to include something about the room that is being heated and the reason it is being heated—say, to promote the growth of plants in a greenhouse.

So $T+$ supervenes on S_1 (and $T-$ on S_2) *only under condition c''*. Stated another way, S_1 *constitutes* or *realizes* $T+$ under c'' (see Fig. 5.2). It is only in the context of the goal of keeping the plants growing that "too cool" and "warm enough" have any meaning. In c' we could only have a lesser form of information—"below the set point" or "above the set point". In c the information would only be "sufficient to close the circuit" or "insufficient to close the circuit". Outside c, the length of the coil means nothing at all.

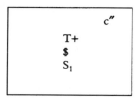

Figure 5.2. The room's being warm enough (T+) supervenes on the state of the thermostat's coil (S_1) only under the condition (c ") that the room needs to be 65 degrees or more to make the plants grow.

2.2 A Phylogenetic Progression

To begin to see the *causal relevance* of supervenient (informational, representational, mental) properties, consider an extremely simple organic system—a Venus flytrap. These plants have hairy leaf structures that fold shut when insects land on them and stay closed while the plant absorbs the nutrients from the insect. The plant needs a system such that it (ordinarily) closes when there is food present but stays open until then; otherwise, the chances of it catching food are too small. It is the bending of the hairs on the leaf that signals the presence of an object, and in its natural environment the objects landing on the hairs are often enough insects. In such a context the information "food here" supervenes on a state of having its leaf hairs bent, and a message that food is absent supervenes on non-bent hairs. In this context, a typical causal sequence would look as in Figure 5.3.

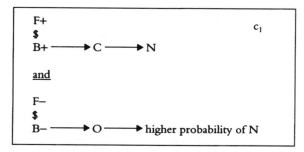

Figure 5.3. Under ordinary conditions (c_1) when the Venus flytrap's leaf hairs are bent (B+), this is indicative that food is present—that is, the information that food is present (F+) supervenes on B+—and so B+ causing the leaf to close (C) leads to the plant absorbing nutrients (N). The leaf remaining open (O) in the absence of bent hairs ordinarily indicates no food present and increases the probability of capturing food later when it *is* there.

Now we change the plant's environment. Say we take it to a classroom where there are many small children, but no insects. In this context (c_2), B+ will still cause C and B− will still result in O, but the supervenient informational properties F+ and F− are gone.[4] And *the longer-term effects of B+ and B− will be different*. In both cases, they fail to lead to the plant getting nutrients (−N).[5]

So the supervenient properties are causally relevant, and it is because of their embeddedness in a *broader* causal context. The informational properties (when they obtain) are *contextualized* physical states of the leaf hairs. The informational properties are not reducible to the physical properties B+ and B− because they pertain to the *relation* of B+ and B− to the entire plant in its proper environment with its food-seeking goals.

No one would count the ability of the Venus flytrap to respond to the presence of an insect as mental, but it falls at the extreme end of a continuum whose opposite end is human reasoning abilities (see Fig. 3.1). We take mental properties to supervene on brain events in the same sense as the information about a likely food source supervenes on the flytrap's bent leaf hairs. As we go up the phylogenetic ladder, we find increasingly sophisticated capacities for representing states of the organism itself and of its environment in ways that are relevant for the outcome of the organism's behavior. If the simpler representative capacities of the flytrap are not reducible to plant biology, *a fortiori*, we should not expect more sophisticated representational (mental) capacities to be reducible to brain states.

In the animal world, consider a simple case of classical conditioning. The sound of a bell and a puff of meat powder are paired until a dog

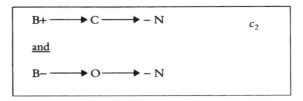

Figure 5.4. A representation of the plant in a setting where bending leaf hairs (B+ and B−) is no longer indicative of the presence of food.

[4] Note, this is c_2 *as opposed to* c_1, whereas in the example of the thermostat, c' and c'' are *broader* systems that incorporate c.

[5] Note the similarity here to Dretske's account of natural representation. There is information involved here only if there is some purpose for which the organism uses it *and* if there is the possibility of misinformation (see Ch. 4, sec. 2.2 above).

is conditioned to salivate on hearing the bell alone. We assume that the dog's hearing the bell (B) is realized by a series of brain events, including a network of neurons firing in its auditory cortex (b), and the taste of meat (M) by another set of neuron firings (m). The simultaneous firing of the two neural networks b and m results in a neural connection (n) either developing or being strengthened between the two networks so that stimulation of one cell network automatically spreads to the other.[6] This explains how the sound of the bell alone becomes a cause of salivation. We can picture the causal relationships at the beginning of the conditioning process as in Figure 5.5.

After conditioning, the causal relations are as in Figure 5.6.

Now, we are assuming that the dog's conscious awareness of the bell (B) supervenes on the neural processes (b), and M on m, but these are not the relations with which we shall be concerned here. Our interest is in the new (or newly strengthened) *connection* (n) between b and m. For simplicity's sake, let us make the contrary-to-fact assumption that there is a single neuron connecting cell assemblies b and m. This neuron has the

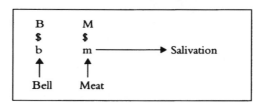

Figure 5.5. At the beginning of the conditioning process, hearing the bell (B) supervenes on a neural assembly (b), tasting meat (M) supervenes on a second neural assembly (m), which causes salivation, but there is no causal connection between b and m.

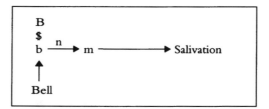

Figure 5.6. After conditioning, a neural connection (n) has formed between b and m such that b causes m, which in turn causes salivation.

---

[6] In fact, this would be a network of connections, with all of the implications of a dynamical system.

base property C of being that connection. Once the connection is in place, however, it is *a bearer of information* about the dog's (past) environment—the information that bell ringing and meat powder occur together. There is now a new supervenient property, R, the property of being a *representation* of the relationship between bells and meat. R supervenes on C, the property of being the connection between b and m. In Figure 5.7 the line between b and m represents our new neuron, n, with C and R representing its properties.

If the existence of the neural connection is considered apart from its role in a broader causal system (the dog's history with bells and meat powder), it is just another neuron—its information-bearing character disappears. The information is dependent on the existence of C but also on the *circumstances* under which it was formed. The formation of C is an instance of downward causation. In this case, the auditory assembly b would have been multiply connected to regions throughout the brain. The simultaneous pairing of b with m resulted in the *selection* of this particular connection for reinforcement. From that point on, the brain is restructured so that the ringing of the bell triggers a new effect, salivation.

As in the other cases of supervening informational properties, R may play a causal role over and above that played by the neural connection itself. If we look only at a single instance of the bell being rung and the dog salivating, we can see no causal relevance of R. The picture looks as in Figure 5.8. It does *not* work as in Figure 5.9.

While R is relevant for explaining why the connection C is there, it is not relevant for explaining how b causes salivation now that it is in place.

If we consider the future, however, there is still a (minimal) causal role for R. For example, if the experimenters want to extinguish the dog's response, they can tamper with the neuron only by means of

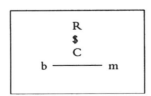

Figure 5.7. R is a property supervening on the neural connection between the assemblies b and m that *represents* the fact about the dog's environment that bells and meat powder occur together.

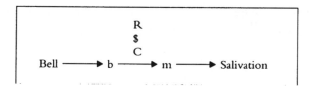

Figure 5.8. The causal path from the bell ringing to salivation after conditioning.

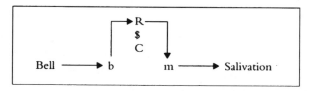

Figure 5.9. This is the sort of causal path that some philosophers of mind seem to believe to be necessary in order to argue for the relevance of mental events or properties.

its representational relationship to the environment. It is because of R that the repeated sounding of a bell (rather than any other stimulus), without associated meat powder, will weaken or eliminate the connection. So we might say that the supervenient representational property is the "handle" (a dynamic parameter control knob) that allows the environment to have a selective causal impact on a particular neuronal connection.

We can see this more clearly in a slightly more complex example. In the example so far, the causal relevance of R is minimal, because there is nothing for the dog *to do with* R. So suppose that our dog is now in a cage with meat outside. The latch to the cage door is controlled electronically. The dog discovers that while a bell is sounding the cage door is unlocked. Now we have a (much more complex) neural connection, n, which has the base property of being the connection (C) between the neural realization of hearing the bell (b) and the motor instructions for pushing the cage door (m). R is the supervenient property of C's *representing* a fact about bells and doors in the dog's environment.

Notice that R supervenes on C only under the condition that the door is unlatched while the bell sounds; it is co-determined by C and this fact about the world. The experimenter can change the situation so that the door no longer opens when the bell sounds, and in this case n no longer possesses the property R, even though (or because of the fact that) C has *not* changed.[7] In this case, R clearly makes a difference not to the dog's immediate behavior (it will still for a time push the door when the bell sounds), but it *will* make a difference to the longer causal chain resulting in its getting or not getting the meat.

So R has no downward efficacy on n (and it is not even clear what this might mean). But R is not eliminable from the causal account. R is a functional property, not a neural property, and it comes and goes depending on the experimenter's changing the circumstances. Behavior caused by C will succeed in some cases and fail in others. C is necessary and sufficient for some of n's causal roles, but not sufficient for all of them.

We suggest the following as morals of these little stories:

1. The representational property is constituted by *contextualized* brain events.
2. We call R a higher-level property because it involves the brain processes in relation to a broader, more complex system: the brain in the body in its environment and with a history.
3. R is supervenient on the neural processes (in the sense we define in sec. 2.3 below) because it can vary without a change in the base property (i.e., due to changed circumstances).
4. The causal relevance of R is a function of the way it serves to relate the neural property to a broader causal system. It is in virtue of R (its informational, representational content) that C is able to play the causal role that it does.
5. It is in virtue of R that agents in the environment have access to C.

Extrapolating from these conclusions regarding the causal role of supervenient representational properties, we make the following analogous suggestions concerning the causal role of mental processes and their properties:

1. Mental properties are *contextualized* brain events.
2. Mental properties are higher-level properties because they involve the brain processes in relation to a broader, more complex system: the brain in the body in its environment and with a longer causal history.

---

[7] Again, recall Dretske's argument that natural representation requires that there be the possibility for misinformation.

3. Mental properties are supervenient on brain events because their nature and significance can vary without a change in the base property (i.e., due to a change in their relationship to environmental circumstances). For example, a true belief may become a false belief if the world changes.

4. The causal relevance of supervenient mental properties is a function of the way they serve to relate the neural base property to a broader causal system. It is in virtue of their informational, representational, semantic content that the base properties are able to play the causal role in the world that they do.

5. It is in virtue of the mental properties that agents in the environment *and subjects themselves* have access to the neural basis.

We pursue the contextualization of brain events below (sec. 2.4). An important caveat is in order here. We describe informativeness as supervening on physical structures, and *for present purposes* we are describing mental properties as supervenient as well. It is important to note that this is an extreme oversimplification. In Chapter 2 (sec. 3.3) we described Terrence Deacon's account of three levels of emergence. In his account, a supervenient property is first-order emergent. Second-order emergence involves history, because it depends on symmetry breaking. The simplest sort of learning (conditioning) is an example. In Alicia Juarrero's terms, conditioning changes the probability matrix for spreading neural activation.[8] So we need to say that the information embodied in such a neural connection is something like "second-order supervenient" on the neural processes. This suggests that any events, states, properties that are classed as mental must be at least third-order emergent (supervenient) on the neural processes that realize them. If we consider the levels of hierarchical ordering requisite for the apprehension of symbolic language, we need to consider several more levels of emergence/supervenience. Thus, a verbalizable belief or intention supervenes on a set of neural events in a much more complicated manner than does the informational character of the bent hairs of the leaves of a Venus flytrap.

---

[8] Expressed in the terminology of dynamical systems, elicitation of a brain/behavior pattern (m) by a bell (b) is the elicitation of a particular probability matrix or topography with m as its main attractor. Thus, the probability topography is an expression of C, and is the historical product of self-organization based on interactions with the environment (i.e., the outcome of previous action loops).

2.3 Redefining Supervenience

We have been using the term "supervenience" in this section, but have judged it best to *show* its usefulness for this discussion before engaging in arguments about how best to define it. We noted above (Ch. 1, sec. 2) that R. M. Hare is credited with introducing "supervenience" as a technical term in philosophy to relate evaluative judgments (including ethical judgments) to descriptive judgments. We quote him again:

First, let us take that characteristic of "good" which has been called its super-venience. Suppose that we say, "St. Francis was a good man." It is logically impossible to say this and to maintain at the same time that there might have been another man *placed in precisely the same circumstances* as St. Francis, and who behaved in them in exactly the same way, but who differed from St. Francis in this respect only, that he was not a good man.[9]

The concept of supervenience is now widely used in philosophy of mind,[10] but there is no agreement on its proper definition. All that is agreed is that the supervenience relation is asymmetrical; supervenient properties are understood to be "multiply realizable". This is a term from computer science—different configurations of hardware (vacuum tubes versus circuits) can realize, constitute, the same machine considered at the functional level. So if S supervenes on B (a Base property), then something's being B entails its being S, but its being S does not entail its being B. For example, goodness is multiply realizable; there are many life patterns different from St Francis's that also constitute one a good person. Thus, from the statement "R. M. Hare was a good man" we cannot infer that he lived as St Francis did.

This has led many to define supervenience simply as an asymmetrical relation of property covariation: no difference in S properties without a difference in B properties.[11] One sort of dissent from this popular approach

---

[9] R. M. Hare, *The Language of Morals* (Oxford: Oxford University Press, 1966, originally published in 1952), 145; italics added.

[10] See, e.g., Jaegwon Kim, *Supervenience and Mind: Selected Philosophical Essays* (Cambridge: Cambridge University Press, 1993); John Heil, *The Nature of True Minds* (Cambridge: Cambridge University Press, 1992); and David J. Chalmers, *The Conscious Mind: In Search of a Fundamental Theory* (New York: Oxford University Press, 1996).

[11] It is now common to distinguish three types of supervenience relations: weak, strong, and global. Kim has defined these as follows, where A and B are two nonempty families of properties:

A *weakly supervenes* on B if and only if necessarily for any property F in A, if an object x has F, then there exists a property G in B such that x has G, and if any y has G it has F.

is to note that it leaves out of account Hare's original insight that one is a moral person *in virtue of* having the descriptive properties one has. Terrence E. Horgan writes:

The concept of supervenience, as a relation between properties, is essentially this: Properties of type A are supervenient on properties of type B if and only if two objects cannot differ with respect to their A-properties without also differing with respect to their B-properties. Properties that allegedly are supervenient on others are often called consequential properties, especially in ethics; the idea is that if something instantiates a moral property, then it does so *in virtue of*, i.e., as a (non-causal) *consequence of*, instantiating some lower-level property on which the moral property supervenes.[12]

Notice that there are two distinguishable notions of supervenience in this passage. The first sentence captures the notion of property covariation, but the second emphasizes a connection between the two kinds of properties. We wish to emphasize another factor represented in Hare's work. The qualification "placed in precisely the same circumstances" (which we have italicized) is an important one. St Francis's behavior (e.g., giving away all his possessions) would be evaluated quite differently were he in different circumstances (e.g., married and with children to support). If this is the case, then the standard definitions of supervenience are not only in need of qualification but are entirely wrongheaded. Thus, we propose the following as a more adequate characterization of supervenience:

Property S supervenes on base property B if and only if x's instantiating S is *in virtue of* x's instantiating B *under circumstance c*.

The aspects of supervenience that we emphasize here are not ignored entirely in the literature. Several other authors consider the *in-virtue-of* relation. For example, Daniel Bonevac says that strong supervenience "does not capture the 'because' or 'in virtue of' that people have in mind when they think of dependence. A physicalist thinks that the mental

---

A *strongly supervenes* on B just in case, necessarily, for each x and each property F in A, if x has F, then there is a property G in B such that x has G, and *necessarily* if any y has G, it has F.

A *globally supervenes* on B just in case worlds that are indiscernible with respect to B ("B-indiscernible", for short) are also A-indiscernible.

See Jaegwon Kim, "Concepts of Supervenience", *Philosophy and Phenomenological Research*, vol 45, no 2 (Dec. 1984), 153–76, at pp. 163, 165, and 168.

[12] Terence E. Horgan, "Supervenience", in Robert Audi (ed.), *The Cambridge Dictionary of Philosophy* (Cambridge: Cambridge University Press, 1995), 778–9.

depends on the physical in the sense that something has the mental state it does because or in virtue of its physical state."[13] Brian McLaughlin says:

We could stipulate that we have supervenience of S-respects on B-respects when and only when there could be no difference of sort S without some further difference of sort B that *makes it the case* that there is the difference of sort S in question. The strengthened idea is that for S-respects to supervene on B-respects, S-differences must hold *in virtue* of B-differences. "In virtue of" implies "because of". Thus, supervenience so understood would require an explanatory relationship: for S-differences to supervene on B-differences, S-differences must be explainable by B-differences.[14]

A number of authors call attention to the sorts of factors that we mean to highlight by making the supervenience relation relative to context or circumstances. Externalists in philosophy of mind argue that relevant features of the way the world is are crucial for determining what intentional state supervenes on a given brain state. Another illustration from a different sphere is Thomas Grimes's example of the economic properties of currency.[15] To put his example in our terms, the property of being, say, a US penny supervenes on its being a copper disk with Lincoln's head stamped on one side, and so forth, only under the causal circumstances of its having been made at a US mint, and under a vast number of other, more complex circumstances having to do with the federal government, its powers, and its economic practices. All of this results in the currency being usable to *do* things that one could not otherwise do.

Berent Enç claims that there is a *species* of supervenient properties that have causal efficacy that does not get fully accounted for by the causal role played by the micro base properties. "The properties I have in mind", he says,

are locally supervenient properties of an individual that are associated with certain globally supervenient properties. These globally supervenient properties will have their base restricted to a region outside the individual in which properties causally interact with the properties of the individual in question. I do not know how to

---

[13] Daniel Bonevac, "Reduction in the Mind of God", in Elias E. Savellos and Ümit D. Yalçin (eds.), *Supervenience: New Essays* (Cambridge: Cambridge University Press, 1995), 124–39, at p. 131.

[14] Brian McLaughlin, "Varieties of Supervenience", in Savellos and Yalçin (eds.), *Supervenience*, 16–59, at p. 18; For consistency of representation, we substituted S for A in McLaughlin's text, e.g., "S-respects" for "A-respects".

[15] Thomas R. Grimes, "The Tweedledum and Tweedledee of Supervenience", in Savellos and Yalçin (eds.), *Supervenience*, 110–23.

give a general formula that captures all of these globally supervenient properties. But some examples will illustrate the idea...

1. Properties that are defined "causally," for example, being a skin condition that is caused by excessive exposure to sun rays, that is, being a sunburn...
2. Properties that are defined in terms of what distal properties they have, for example, fitness in biology...
3. Properties that are defined in terms of what would have caused them under a set of specifiable conditions, like being a representation of some state of affairs.[16]

In our terminology, the property of being a sunburn supervenes on a micro-condition of the skin cells *under the circumstance* of its having been brought about by overexposure to the sun. Fitness supervenes on any particular configuration of biological characteristics only within certain environmental circumstances. The relevant context in both cases is a causal one: what caused the burn and the future effect of the property on the organism's reproductive success.

Paul Teller makes similar points:

Let us restrict attention to properties that reduce in the sense of having a physical realization, as in the cases of being a calculator, having a certain temperature, and being a piece of money. Whether or not an object counts as having properties such as these will depend, not only on the physical properties of that object, but on various circumstances of the context. Intensions of relevant language users constitute a plausible candidate for relevant circumstances. In at least many cases, dependence on context arises because the property constitutes a functional property, where the relevant functional system (calculational practices, heat transfer, monetary systems) are much larger than the property-bearing object in question. These examples raise the question of whether many and perhaps all mental properties depend ineliminably on relations to things outside the organisms that have the mental properties.[17]

These minority voices with their various examples support our claim that we need a concept of supervenience that (1) recognizes hierarchies of systems in which (2) properties of higher-level systems are co-constituted

---

[16] Berent Enç, "Nonreducible Supervenient Causation", in Savellos and Yalçin (eds.), *Supervenience*, 169–80, at p. 175.

[17] Paul Teller, "Reduction", in Audi (ed.), *Cambridge Dictionary of Philosophy*, 679–80, at p. 680.

(a) by properties, events, states of affairs pertaining to a lower-level system as well as (b) by the involvement of that lower-level event or state of affairs in the higher-level (broader, more complex) causal or semiotic system. It is in this sense, we propose, that even the most rudimentary forms of sentience and cognition supervene on neural processes.

In short, the point of this section is to argue for the nonreducibility of informational or representational states to their physical realizers on the grounds that the informational property exists only because of an appropriate *relationship* of the physical state to a broader context—in particular, there being something to represent and there being something to *do* with the representation. Analogously, we claim, mental events can best be understood in terms of their relations to states of affairs in the environment (or in the organism itself) that are relevant for redirecting the organism's behavior. Mental events are not reducible to brain events, because mental events are largely constituted by relations to actions in the environment. In this respect, mental events are constituted in action loops in which brain processes are interlocked with environmental context, with the history of the outcome of previous action loops playing a primary causal role.

2.4 *The Contextualization of Brain Events*

Our argument so far has involved recognition of a progression from the simplest organisms' abilities to represent states of themselves and of the environment to our own mental capacities (we emphasized in Ch. 3, sec. 2, the gradual nature of the transitions). In the previous section we argued that supervenient representational or informational properties are not reducible to their subvenient realizers because they are co-constituted by their involvement in broader causal systems. We suggested that mental events will be similarly irreducible. To a great extent the apparent insolubility of the problem of mental causation is due to a residual Cartesian view of mind. as interior and effectively disembodied. Here we gather together considerations pointing to an alternative view of mind as *embodied* (see Ch. 1, sec. 3.1) and *embedded*—that is, contextualized in action—feedback—evaluation—action loops in the environment. Mental events and properties are contextualized brain events and properties. Our reasons for this emphasis fall into three categories: phylogenetic, neurobiological, and conceptual.

2.4.1. Mind on the Hoof: From Animals on Up Following Andy Clark and others, we have claimed that human brains are best understood in terms of their original function in lower organisms as organs for controlling bodily action, for initiating moves in real-world situations. We pointed out (in Ch. 3) that it is necessary to view all organisms as characterized by three important properties:

1. All organisms are continuously active. Behavior is emitted by the organism; it is generally not triggered by external stimuli. Thus, behavior is always (or nearly always) "voluntary", rather than elicited in a passive organism by a particular stimulus.

2. Most behavior of organisms is goal-directed. Behavior is tried out in order to meet some internal goal (whether this goal is represented simply or in a complex manner in particular organisms). Even protozoa have the goals of finding nutrients and avoiding toxic substances. They emit swimming behavior in order to try out directions of movement to determine if they will result in more nutrients or less toxicity. In more complex organisms capable of associative learning, there exist both pure desires (based on biological needs) and derived desires that are acquired due to some association with pure desires.[18]

3. All organisms have the ability to evaluate the outcome of behavior and modify their ongoing behavior in relationship to evaluations. As we can already appreciate in the behavior of protozoa (as well as insects, laboratory rats, monkeys, and human beings), behavior is a constantly recurring loop of emitting behaviors, evaluating the behaviors based on a comparison of sensory feedback and internal criteria for desired outcomes, and adjusting ongoing behavior based on the evaluation of feedback.

We refer again to MacKay's now familiar diagram (Fig. 2. p. 69) used to represent the minimal functional architecture of an agent, which captures these aspects of the behavior of organisms.[19] This diagram represents the fact that behavior is always a process of continuous loops of action–feedback–evaluation–action. Behavior has no beginning or end, and is not typically triggered by external stimuli. Rather, feedback from the

---

[18] Dretske, *Explaining Behavior*, 111.
[19] Donald M. MacKay, *Behind the Eye*, The Gifford Lectures, ed. Valerie MacKay (Oxford: Blackwell, 1991), 43.

field of action is used for constant monitoring of the success of the current goal-directed behavior of the organism, allowing for necessary adjustments in behavior. This view reorients one's notion of causation in the behavior of organisms. Causation is not triggering of action in an otherwise inert organism; it is not necessary to find the cause that set a particular behavior in motion. Rather, causes are the processes whereby a continuously active organism evaluates and modulates its action. The roots of mental causation appear in early forms of modulation of ongoing goal-related behaviors that are based on information about the organism itself and its environment, along with many forms of evaluation (genetic and learned), and on the application of skills gained from previous experiences.

Extensive work by Clark shows that complex forms of mental functioning in humans can best be understood by presupposing that our cognitive faculties are built along the same lines. His evidence comes largely from noting the kinds of strategies that do and do not work in attempting to model animal and human cognition. The strategy that does *not* work is the Cartesian model of mind as mirror.

Clark argues for a fairly direct sensorimotor understanding of representations.[20] He believes that mental processing does not necessarily involve manipulation of abstract representations by a centralized information processor. In the world of robotics, a collection of low-level sensorimotor networks can do sophisticated tasks without the necessity of creating and processing high-level representations. These local networks are intelligent, in allowing for rapid pattern completion. Action of a large number of local networks can be coordinated by passing a minimal amount of information among networks. Thus, Clark emphasizes the importance of distributed, low-level, sensorimotor representations, resulting in the "ad hoc messiness" of the organization of brain systems that subserve many cognitive skills.[21]

Sensorimotor contingencies are also essential in higher-level reasoning and planning. For example, Clark makes a distinction between pragmatic and epistemic action. Pragmatic action is undertaken to alter the world to achieve some goal. "Epistemological action, in contrast, is action whose primary purpose is to alter the nature of our own mental tasks." In our

[20] Andy Clark, *Being There: Putting Brain, Body, and World Together Again* (Cambridge, Mass.: MIT Press, 1997), 47–51.
[21] More recently Alva Noë has argued at book length for dependence of our perceptual capacities on action. See his *Action in Perception* (Cambridge, Mass.: MIT Press, 2004).

terms, it is an action that reconfigures or self-organizes the cognitive system. Here we still act on the world, "but the changes are driven by our own computational and information-processing needs". A simple example is the way we order and reorder the tiles when planning moves in a Scrabble game so that the new patterns we see will prompt our own on-line neural resources.[22]

2.4.2. Action and Cognition: The Same Neurobiology   There is a growing body of evidence from neuroscience for intimate ties between cognition and action. We have already mentioned that the experimental demonstration of "mirror neurons" (neurons in the premotor cortex that discharge both when doing a particular action and when viewing another individual doing the same action) provides direct evidence for the participation of motor systems in at least some forms of perception.[23] Exploration of the functional characteristics of the nervous system shows close ties between sensory capacities and motor capacities. For this reason, current theories in cognitive science emphasize the role of action in perception.[24] These are often referred to as "skill theories", in which current perception is the activation of neural records of previous active exploration.[25]

We have noted MacKay's claim that perception can be understood as the elicitation of a conditional readiness to reckon with the current elements of the sensory world.[26] Perception generates a matching response in the form of the activation in memory of the sensorimotor record of previous actions with respect to this stimulus pattern. This activated sensorimotor record provides predictive information about ways one might interact with what is currently being sensed. Thus, one is conditionally ready to reckon with what is being perceived. For example, to perceive an object lying on the desk as a pen is for the nervous system to activate a neural network that consists of learned potentialities for actions involving pens.

---

[22] Clark, *Being There*, 64.

[23] G. Rizzolatti, L. Fadiga, V. Gallese, and L. Fogassi, "Premotor Cortex and the Recognition of Motor Actions", *Cognitive Brain Research*, 3 (1996), 131–41.

[24] Raymond W. Gibbs, *Embodiment and Cognitive Science* (Cambridge: Cambridge University Press, 2006).

[25] J. K. O'Regan and A. Noë, "A Sensorimotor Account of Vision and Visual Consciousness", *Behavior and Brain Science*, 25 (2001), 5.

[26] MacKay, *Behind the Eye*, 109–13; cf. our Ch. 2, sec. 3.4.

Finally, we have mentioned the work of George Lakoff and Mark Johnson, who argue that most of our conceptual resources come from metaphorical extension of concepts derived directly from sensorimotor experiences. Raymond Gibbs, as also described earlier, is in agreement with Lakoff and Johnson in understanding language meaning as derived from recurring bodily experiences that are metaphorically extended (see our Ch. 4, sec. 4.2).

The tight coupling between perception and action is also reflected in recent neuroscience research and theory. Joaquín Fuster has developed an account of the function of the human cerebral cortex that emphasizes the multi-level recurrent interactions between the perceptual and motor areas of the cerebral cortex.[27] Fuster considers the prefrontal cortex to be the summit of the perception–action cycle (what we have called nested action loops). There are two parallel hierarchies that form the perception–action cycle. However, the perceptual side and the motor side are linked at every level by dense, two-way recurrent neural connections. The consequence of this anatomical configuration is that action is always under immediate perceptual feedback, and perception is always strongly influenced by action consequences. In addition, it can be seen that lower levels are nested within higher-level loops (as in the hierarchy of action loops in MacKay's diagrams, such as Fig. 2.3). Figure 5.10, taken from Fuster's recent book, indicates the two-way perceptual–motor interactions at every level, converging at the polymodal association and prefrontal cortices.[28]

The important cognitive capacities allowed by the prefrontal cortex (e.g., temporal integration of behavior, working memory, and attention) are due to its position atop this highly interactive perception–action hierarchy. As Fuster argues, the anatomical characteristic that makes the frontal lobes so important to these high-level mental capacities is the massively recurrent network of interactions with both the perceptual and the motor sides. Most of the higher-level properties of the prefrontal cortex have been shown (in Fuster's various experiments) to disappear when recurrent interactivity is temporarily interrupted through cooling of various areas of the cortex.

---

[27] Joaquín M. Fuster, *Cortex and Mind: Unifying Cognition* (Oxford: Oxford University Press, 2003).
[28] Ibid. 109.

SENSORY   MOTOR
HIERARCHY   HIERARCHY

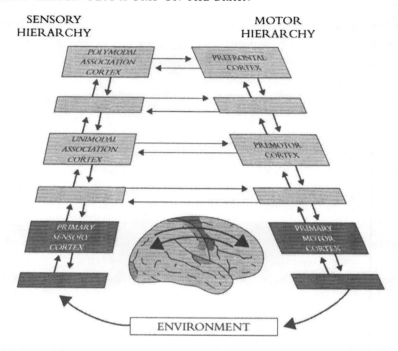

Figure 5.10. Illustration of the hierarchy of perceptual–motor control loops, culminating at the highest level with interactions between the polymodal association cortex (posterior cortex) and the prefrontal cortex (anterior cortex). *Source*: Joaquín M. Fuster, *Cortex and Mind: Unifying Cognition* (Oxford: OUP, 2002) Figure 4.7, 109. Reproduced by permission of Oxford University Press, Inc.

2.4.3. Conceptual Considerations   Finally, we present a thumbnail sketch of an argument to the effect that most basic mental operations need to be understood conceptually as action-relevant.

In Chapter 4 we reported on Fred Dretske's account of the dependence of representation on function. We argued there that the basic concept of a representation has to be a representation-in-use; that is, in line with Dretske's account of the role of function in making sense of natural representations, we need to understand conventional representations as derivative of representations-in-use. We shall consider beliefs further below, but it is worth noting here that MacKay considers a belief to be a conditional readiness to reckon with what is not immediately present in the sensory environment.[29] For example, if one believed that there was a dangerous

---

[29] MacKay, *Behind the Eye*, 112.

animal in one's front yard, the consequence would be to have activated a readiness to reckon with the animal if one were to decide to go outside. One's map of the field of potential actions has been altered by activation of new potentialities for the actions that would be required should one go out. This new map of potentials for action-in-the-world is the representation of the belief.

So these are moves from cognitive neuroscience tending in the direction of some form of what is known in philosophy of mind as the externalist thesis: that one's propositional attitudes (beliefs, desires, intentions, etc.) cannot be characterized without reference to features of the environment. Our addition is to emphasize their relation not merely to the way things are in the world, but to the causes in the world that produce them and the actions that they might prepare one to engage in. This is clear in cases of perception and memory, in which the perception (or memory) can only be a perception (or memory) of x if its causal etiology somehow involves x. It is also clear in cases of the intention to do y, where the intention could not be that intention without the possibility that it be involved in causing one so to act.

Finally, in the preceding chapter we considered the problem of intentionality (in the technical philosophical sense). Our central thesis was that language hooks onto the world as we use it in our socially constructed embodied activities in the world. Thus, the meaningfulness and reference of all of the mental events that involve language are essentially dependent upon interactions with the world.

Does this amount to a satisfactory argument for the embeddedness of mental life *in general* in action loops? Probably not, given the odd grab bag of "entities" that our Cartesian heritage includes as mental. Here is Richard Rorty's list: "Pains, moods, images, and sentences which 'flash before the mind,' dreams, hallucinations, beliefs, attitudes, desires, and intentions."[30] Our goal does not require such an argument, however; all we need to show is that much of the mental life of humans is in fact co-constituted by the involvement of the relevant neural and bodily systems in action—feedback loops in order to make our argument for its nonreducibility. Note that in the process of addressing the nature of mental life we have subtly shifted the "problem of mental causation". If we are right about the inherent

---

[30] Richard Rorty, *Philosophy and the Mirror of Nature* (Princeton: Princeton University Press, 1979), 17.

action-relevance of (much of) mental life, then the problem of mental causation *must be* illusory.

2.5 Excursus: Why Not Functionalism?

While we have been noting the empirical evidence for the action-relevance of much of conscious organisms' mental lives, we do not wish to make the functionalist move here of *defining* mental events in terms of their typical causes and effects; rather, we claim that without attending to their role in action, it will not be possible to explain why they are *not* reducible to brain events.

Functionalism, a successor to behaviorism, has been an influential move in philosophy of mind. This is the thesis that a mental state is to be *defined* in terms of a triplet of causal connections: what stimulation typically causes it, how it interacts causally with other mental states, and what effect it typically has on behavior. What makes an inner state *mental,* on this view, is not an intrinsic property of the state, but rather its relations to sensory stimulation, to other inner states, and to behavior. The advantage of functionalism, as with behaviorism, is that it frees one from having to attempt to deal with inaccessible "inner" states of the person—in fact, consciousness becomes irrelevant.

There are a variety of problems with functionalism, one of which is its leading to counter-intuitive conclusions such as that speakers of different languages could never have the same mental states. For example, if English speakers say "Ouch!" when stuck with a pin and Spanish speakers say "Ay!", then, by definition, what they are feeling is not the same sensation. And of course, it leaves out of account the obvious fact that what we ordinarily mean by "pain" is *pain!*[31]

Thus, we claim that while the functionalists were right to call our attention to the role of causes and effects in constituting mental states the states they are, functionalism goes too far by ignoring altogether the qualitative aspects of conscious states. The counter-intuitive results are a consequence of *defining* mental states functionally (i.e., saying that a mental state can be understood as *nothing but* that which plays such a role), rather than merely recognizing the essential functional *aspects* of mental events.

---

[31] This is not to say that all experienced pain is qualitatively the same, only to deny that the qualitative feel can simply be left out of the account altogether.

3 Couldn't We Be Zombies?

A second facet of the problem of mental causation is the question of the role of consciousness. The question is sometimes raised in this form: could there be organisms that do all of the things that conscious organisms do, but without the consciousness?[32] This question is based on our ability to distinguish between the qualitative aspects of our conscious awareness (philosophers' qualia) and the information that it imparts. Güven Güzeldere has helpfully pointed out that there are two influential "pretheoretical characterizations" that shape the way in which problems regarding consciousness are defined. One is the *causal characterization*, which takes the causal role that consciousness plays in the general economy of our mental lives as basic. The other is the *phenomenal characterization*, which "takes as fundamental the way our mental lives seem (or 'feel', for lack of a better term) to us—that is, the phenomenal qualities that we typically associate with our perceptions, pains, tickles, and other mental states".[33]

Güzeldere claims that these two characterizations are equally attractive, but as we have been at pains to argue, an evolutionary account of mind strongly favors a causal account as basic. Critics, though, will argue that by focusing on the informational/action aspects we have simply evaded the hard problem of explaining the causal relevance of qualia *per se*. In addressing it, we make two moves. One is to distinguish between realistic issues and those that belong to a category of philosophical worries that are based on highly contrary-to-fact speculations. The second is to argue that nothing of importance is lost if it turns out that *some* aspects of phenomenal consciousness *are* epiphenomenal.

So how realistic is the worry about zombies? We can motivate the question in two ways. One is by comparing ourselves to simple organisms that operate on the basis of information, but without any consciousness at all. Consider a light-sensitive bacterium that swims toward light and

---

[32] Daniel C. Dennett says: "According to common agreement among philosophers, a zombie is or would be a human being who exhibits perfectly natural, alert, loquacious, vivacious behavior but is in fact not conscious at all.... The whole point ... is that you can't tell a zombie from a normal person by examining external behavior.... [So] *some of your best friends may be zombies.*" See *Consciousness Explained* (Boston: Little, Brown, and Co., 1991), 73.

[33] Güven Güzeldere, "The Many Faces of Consciousness: A Field Guide", in Ned Block, Owen Flanagan, and Güven Güzeldere (eds.), *The Nature of Consciousness: Philosophical Debates* (Cambridge, Mass.: MIT Press, 1997), 1–67, at p. 11.

thereby moves toward more nutrient-rich surface water. The bacterium is not conscious of the light, but nonetheless acts on the basis of information provided by its sensor. What difference is there between an unconscious bacterium that is hard-wired to swim toward a light source and an imaginary bacterium that can "see" the light but is still hard-wired to move in its direction? In such a case we could conclude that the "mental" or experiential element is epiphenomenal—it does no causal work.

A second way to motivate the question is by considering the extent to which humans *do* operate without conscious awareness. We previously discussed the phenomenon of blind sight (Ch. 3, sec. 5.1).[34] Certain victims of damage to the visual cortex are either completely blind or have blind spots in their visual fields. Nonetheless, they are receiving information about their environments. If they are asked to say where a moving object is, they will reply that they do not know; but if told to guess or to reach for the object, they do much better than would be expected by chance. So is *our* visual experience epiphenomenal? We have also attended (in Ch. 3) to the high degree of automaticity in human behavior. Not without reason do we often accuse ourselves of operating on "auto-pilot", but we get where we meant to go. We have also already described Antonio Damasio's work on "somatic markers"—feelings about whether or not to perform an action—that sum up a person's unconscious evaluations of similar experiences in the past (Ch. 1, sec. 3.2).

For a more striking case of performance on the basis of unconscious cognitive processes, consider the following experiment regarding procedural knowledge done by D. C. Berry and D. E. Broadbent (as described by John Anderson):

Berry and Broadbent ... asked subjects to try to control the output of a hypothetical sugar factory (which was simulated by a computer program) by manipulating the size of the workforce. Subjects would see the month's output ... and then choose the next month's workforce. [The rule relating workforce and output was a complex mathematical formula] ... Oxford undergraduates were given sixty trials at trying to control the output of the sugar factory. Over the sixty trials, they got quite good at controlling the output of the sugar factory. However, they were unable to state what the rule was and claimed they made their responses

---

[34] See Lawrence Weiskrantz, *Blindsight: A Case Study and Implications* (Oxford: Oxford University Press, 1986).

on the basis of "some sort of intuition" or because it "felt right." Thus, subjects were able to acquire implicit knowledge of how to operate such a factory without corresponding explicit knowledge.[35]

This experiment illustrates several aspects of cognitive processing. First, the behavior of these university students in interacting with the sugar factory program is a very complex form of mental activity, even though the students had no *conscious* awareness of the basis for their increasingly accurate responses. While the process of engaging in the task and making decisions was conscious, the process of making the multivariate calculations was unavailable to consciousness. Second, the students were conscious of knowing something, and of being able to "feel" the difference between a more or less accurate response—an example of Damasio's somatic markers. So it is not unreasonable to ask, if we can do so much on the basis of unconscious processes, what does consciousness add?

As we have argued, the primary causal role of consciousness is to provide information relevant to an organism's action. Consciousness provides flexibility in modulating one's behavior that is not available to more primitive organisms. It allows for the prioritization of needs and drives. An earthworm is hard-wired to withdraw when it is touched, and has no need for pain sensors. More complex organisms have pain sensors that *dispose* them to avoid harmful stimuli while not determining a withdrawal. For example, an animal may tolerate a degree of pain in order to satisfy a powerful feeling of hunger or to continue a fight with a rival. However, consciousness would allow the individual to risk pain, hunger, or violence for a distantly perceived goal that may be an abstract ideal. We shall argue below that in the sugar-factory experiment conscious awareness of the algorithm governing the output would dramatically enhance the subjects' performance when faced with any change in the program.

The critic will again (rightly) be noting that we are not addressing the question: could there not be people who *have* all of this (valuable, action-relevant) information but no qualia? For a first response, consider again the case of blind sight. These patients have information about the visual world, but a very significant difference is that they do not know

[35] D. C. Berry and D. E. Broadbent, "On the Relationship between Task Performance and Associated Verbalizable Knowledge", *Quarterly Journal of Experimental Psychology*, 35A (1984), 209–31; as described in John R. Anderson, *Cognitive Psychology and Its Implications* (New York: Worth Publishers, 2000), 236–7.

that they have it. So one of the functions of consciousness is to provide what we might call second-order knowledge. A conscious organism not only knows things about its environment, but it also knows that it knows. The important observation for our purposes here is that patients with this condition undertake action (e.g., reaching for the object) only when pressured to do so. The conscious perception of objects can lead to action that would not otherwise occur. So we can see that consciousness provides a level of knowledge (knowledge *that* one knows something), and this in turn has immense consequences for successful activity in the environment.

The critic might now rephrase the question: What about someone who *also* has all of this second-order information but no qualitative awareness?[36] Notice, though, that this proposal is incoherent. A person with sight knows that she is seeing something and also knows that she knows because she is conscious of seeing it. If a zombie were to possess the second-order *belief* that she is conscious, then this is not information but *misinformation*.

"Well, it may be the case that *our* knowledge that we have first-order sensory knowledge comes from conscious awareness, but imagine a case where all of that same information comes by means of a different route."

The fact that such arguments turn to more and more fanciful possibilities raises an issue of philosophical method. The philosopher says: "I can conceive of such a thing as a zombie, and if you cannot explain why it is not possible, then you cannot explain why consciousness is necessary for human behavior, and therefore consciousness is epiphenomenal." The cognitive neuroscientist responds by pointing to some of the facts about neurobiology. For example, we argued above (Ch. 3, sec. 5.4) that the neural processes that give rise to the qualitative aspects of experience are tied into wide interactive networks that inescapably include implications for further thought and action. The philosopher replies, "No, I don't want to know why it doesn't work that way but why it *couldn't*." At this point we detect again the ghost of Descartes: I can *conceive* of existing without my body.[37]

One final note. The zombie thought experiments are used for a variety of purposes in the philosophical literature: critiques of functionalism,

---

[36] See Dennett, *Consciousness Explained*, ch. 11, for a discussion of this possibility.

[37] For an explanation of our rejection of arguments based on wildly contrary-to-fact examples, and on philosophical intuitions in general, see Nancey Murphy, "Nonreductive Physicalism", in Joel B. Green (ed.), *In Search of the Soul: Four Views* (Downers Grove, Ill.: InterVarsity, 2005), 65–8.

critiques of materialism, and so forth. Our interest here is the general problem of mental causation, but this is in the context of working out an anti-reductionist account of mental life. The anti-reductionist does not need to be committed to saying that *all* qualia play a causal role in an organism's behavior, only to saying that some do, and being able to explain how. The "qualities of qualia" that provide no information may indeed be epiphenomenal. For example, it does matter that red and green look different to us, but it may not matter causally that they look different in just the way they do.

4 Beliefs as Structuring Causes

The purpose of this section is to begin to address Dretske's question of how our beliefs, desires, and plans operate in a world of causes. Here we pick up the thread of our argument for the causal relevance of supervenient representational or informational properties, and our claim that the mental supervenes on the physical in much the same way. We shall first report here on Dretske's own contributions, and then in subsequent sections turn to further resources for understanding the causal role of mental events.

We have already reported on Dretske's work on natural representations (Ch. 4, sec. 2.2), showing that a natural representation cannot *be* a representation at all if it has no purpose, and that what it is a representation *of* depends on an appropriate causal etiology from the referent to the representation. Such representations have content or meaning, which is defined by what it is their function to indicate. If there are such representations located in the heads of some animals, Dretske says, then there is:

something that is *about* various parts of the world, even those parts of the world with which the animal has never been in direct perceptual contact; (2) something capable of representing and, just as important, *misrepresenting* those parts of the world it is about; and (3) something that has, thereby, a *content* or *meaning* (not itself in the head, of course) that is individuated in something like the way we individuate thoughts and beliefs.[38]

Animals' beliefs can be thought of as structuring causes (see our Ch. 2, sec. 2.2.2) of their behavior. Learning is a process that reorganizes control

---

[38] Dretske, *Explaining Behavior*, 77.

circuits so as to incorporate indicators into the chain of command, and it does so *because* these indicators indicate what they do.[39] For example, consider our dog that has learned to open the cage door when a bell sounds. The explanation of the existence of the neural connection between hearing the bell and pushing the door depends on the fact that it indicates something about the world regarding the bell and the door latch.

Dretske's account of (full-fledged) beliefs, desires, and intentions is consistent with this account of representations. Just as the meaning of the dog's neural connection is a relational rather than an intrinsic property of the neurons, so too the meaning or content of beliefs and intentions derive from their relations. "[The neural realizers of beliefs], intentions, and desires may be in the head, but ... the content of the belief, intention, and desire is surely not there."[40] This is consistent with our general account of the mental as supervenient on the neural in the sense of being co-constituted by the neural connection's involvement in a broader causal or semiotic system.

Dretske argues that learning structures the nervous system in a way that provides the reason why, for this organism, stimulus A causes behavior X. Further, learning explains how stimulus B can come to predict the likelihood of A and thus also trigger behavior X. Learning is the explanation of why behavior X is known by the animal as an effective behavior in the context A. Thus, an animal can be said to act (behavior X) for the *reason* of the learned *belief* that this behavior in the context of A (or in the context of B, which predicts A) will have an outcome relevant to current needs or goals. In Dretske's formulation, mental causation is rooted in this sort of acting for *reasons* on the basis of *beliefs*, and he argues cogently that animals do this to the degree that associative learning reshapes the nervous system, amounting to new "structural causes" of behavior.

Andy Clark makes a point similar to Dretske's regarding the role of memory in structuring behavior. One of the fundamental properties of even simple nervous systems is rapid pattern completion in the face of incomplete information.[41] The demands of rapid ongoing behavior typically do not allow organisms either to await expected further information, or to sample the entire sensory environment. Based on a minimal amount of information sampled, the brain fills in the remainder in order to make a rapid response. This process of pattern completion is based on memory records of previous

---

[39] Dretske, *Explaining Behavior*, 99.   [40] Ibid. 129.   [41] Clark, *Being There*, 59–62.

experience. Extrapolation based on incomplete information is one of the important rudiments of mental activity.

What we know from cognitive psychology about the nature of memories is that they are held in associative networks, which become activated by current external or internal context. What is more, there is some process, typically called "spreading activation", by which wider networks of more or less distantly associated memories become pre-activated in ways that guide the directions of future behavior (or, subjectively in the case of humans, further thought). Thus, the structuring causes of behavior involve not only what is contributed by learning to immediate responses, but also contributions from complex networks of learned associations, which can prime future thought and behavior in ways related to previous experiences.

5 From Animal Beliefs to Human Reasoning

Dretske notes that much more needs to be said about the "enormously rich interplay of beliefs, desires, and behavior in cognitively and cona-tively developed animals such as humans".[42] To address the question of specifically human, linguistically mediated reasoning, we presuppose not only the resources from Dretske, nicely tying together our account of supervenient mental states as *contextualized* brain states, the role of *top-down causation* (from the environment) in structuring and restructuring neural networks, and the role of such restructuring as the creation of structuring *causes* of behavior, but also our account of symbolic language (Ch. 4). Further resources we need to bring to bear are: (1) the top-down effect of higher-level cognitive supervisory systems; (2) the ability to run off-line simulations—the internalization, for certain specified purposes, of action loops involving cultural and cognitive resources; (3) what Clark describes as the "external scaffolding" on which we off-load cognitive processes; and (4) Alicia Juarrero's account of the role of intentions in guiding (rather than triggering) action.

5.1 Meta-Level Self-Supervision

A crucially important ingredient in human rationality is the development of higher-order supervisory systems capable of evaluating lower-order

---

[42] Dretske, *Explaining Behavior*, 137.

cognitive processes. We reported (in Ch. 3, sec. 3) on Donald MacKay's expansion of his functional architecture of an agent to suggest overlays of more complex and abstract forms of modulation. He suggests that action loops are modulated by supervisory systems that function to set the goals of local action loops.

Our example of the kind of self-supervision of which animals are *not* capable was the chimpanzees who were not able to modify their candy-pile choosing in order to get what they wanted. They were not able to make their own behavior, their own cognitive strategy, the object of their attention. This ability to represent to oneself aspects of one's own cognitive processes in order to be able to evaluate them is what we call meta-representation or self-transcendence.

We also reported on the research by Koechlin, Ody, and Kouneiher that demonstrated a nested hierarchy of functions within the prefrontal cortex, as well as top-down influences of this hierarchy. This begins to sketch the neural architecture that allows humans to prioritize desires and goals, to evaluate conflicting beliefs and reasons, and so forth. All of this will be important in our accounts of formal reasoning (sec. 6, this chapter) and moral responsibility in the next chapter.

5.2 Off-Line Simulations

A second factor that needs to be considered in order to understand the difference between human and (most) animal cognition is the capacity for off-line simulations of action loops (i.e., running imaginary mental scenarios). The emphasis we have placed throughout this volume, and especially in the previous subsections, on mind being resident in action loops (and as we shall see below in external scaffolding) pushes much of what we call "mind" toward more peripheral, sensorimotor aspects of the nervous system (and even out into the environment). While this view is helpful at the outset in understanding the causal role of mental events, a complete account needs to take into account more internalized and complex forms of mental processing. Nonetheless, we argue, these more complex forms can be understood as elaborations of action loops.

We ended our account (in Ch. 3) of the increasingly complex cognitive capacities that allow for increasing flexibility in pursuit of goals. This is due in part to the capacity of some higher animals to run behavioral scenarios off-line (emulations of behavior in the imagination) in order to predict the likely outcome of behavior (section 2.3.2). For example, Köhler's ape was apparently able to "try out" the attaching of two short poles to achieve the goal of reaching bananas outside his cage before the sudden appearance of the behavior. When combined with the ability to use language, off-line scenarios become a form of inner problem solving using self-talk.

5.3 External Scaffolding and Symbolic Language

To understand how reason gets its grip on the brain, we must consider a form of representation and memory that is *not* located in the brain or the body. Clark argues for the importance of "external scaffolding" in the emergence of higher mental processing.[43] "Scaffolding" refers to all of the ways in which an organism relies on external supports for augmenting mental processing. Animals engage in this scaffolding process, but it is particularly critical in human cognition. Such devices range from simple aids to memory, such as writing down an appointment, through the use of pencil and paper to represent spatial and arithmetical problems, to calculators and computers. He writes: "We use intelligence to structure our environment so that we can succeed with less intelligence. Our brains make the world smart so that we can be dumb in peace! ... It is the human brain plus these chunks of external scaffolding that finally constitutes the smart, rational inference engine we call mind."[44]

Human culture involves a vast array of artifacts that scaffold cognitive processing, the most remarkable of which is language. E. Hutchins and B. Hazelhurst performed an experiment with a simulated neural network that illustrates both the emergence of more and more useful symbols and the contribution of symbol systems to group problem solving.[45] The simulation involved a group of "citizens", each a connectionist neural network. Input to each citizen involved both information about events themselves, and symbols from other citizens representing these events. The task was to predict the tides based on the phases of the moon. The simulation also involved sequential generations of groups of citizens, who did not inherit the knowledge of the previous generation, but did inherit the current meanings of the symbols. There were two outcomes of this simulation that

---

[43] Clark, *Being There*, 179–92.   [44] Ibid. 180.
[45] E. Hutchins and B. Hazelhurst, "Learning in the Cultural Process", in C. Langton *et al.* (eds.), *Artificial Life II* (Reading, Mass.: Addison-Wesley, 1991); reported by Clark, *Being There*, 189–90.

are important in considering the relationship of language to the problem of mental causation: (1) there was a gradual evolution of better and better symbols, and (2) the improved symbols allowed later generations to learn environmental regularities involved in the task that earlier generations could not learn. Thus, the emergence of better symbols allowed for the emergence of better group problem solving.

This illustration fits with Clark's emphasis on the social scaffolding of cognition. Linguistic symbols pre-structured individual learning and group problem solving so as to allow later generations to accomplish a task that could not be mastered by previous generations. Language thus provides scaffolding for both internal and external problem solving. Language provides "structuring causes" (to use Dretske's terminology) for forms of problem solving not possible without the use of language tools. Language is, in Clark's words, "a computational transformer that allows a pattern-completing brain to tackle otherwise intractable classes of cognitive problems".[46]

Some of the contributions of language to cognition specifically described by Clark are:

1. off-loading of memory into the socially maintained language environment;
2. use of labels as perceptually simple cues regarding a complex environment;
3. coordination of action of individuals and groups via internal self-talk, dialog, or in written plans, schedules, and so forth.[47]

Terrence Deacon has also provided an important analysis of the role of language in the emergence of human thought (which will be especially important for our consideration of moral responsibility in Ch. 6).[48] These contributions include:

1. *Distancing of action from the demands of immediate motivations and needs*: Language facilitates behavior involving delayed need-gratification by augmenting the ability to consider alternative actions through entertaining various symbolic "what if" scenarios.

---

[46] Clark, *Being There*, 194.   [47] Ibid. 200—1.
[48] Terrence W. Deacon, *The Symbolic Species: The Co-evolution of Language and the Brain* (New York: Norton, 1997), 411—32.

2. *The ability to form a self-concept*: The symbolized self can become the object of evaluation.[49] Clark also describes the importance of language in allowing for second-order cognition (or meta-cognition) in the form of self-representation and self-evaluation.

3. *Expanded empathy*: We can enter into the experiences of others through emotional engagement created by stories. Such empathy also allows for the development of a theory of mind—the ability to model and predict the mental life of other individuals.

4. *A virtual common mind among groups of people*: Common semantics, metaphors, and stories create cultural groups with similar world views.

5. *Ethics*: Language encodes communal values for judging between "what if" scenarios.

It has been supposed at least since the writings of Augustine in the fifth century that humans come equipped with the ability to think their own inner thoughts, and that expression of the thoughts in language or action comes later and is optional. In the account given here, "inner" thinking is dependent on, parasitic upon, socially constructed scaffolding for mapping action–feedback loops—the most important of which is symbolic language. The development of language vastly increases humans' capacities for trying out solutions to problems, and especially the resources for *evaluating* our own inner, off-line problem solving (sec. 5.2).

5.4 *The Dynamics of Intentional Action*

Again we find that Alicia Juarrero's work, employing the language of dynamical systems theory, helps to synthesize and sharpen points we have attempted to make. In section 2 and in this section we argue that mental acts in general should *not* be thought of as events that set an organism in motion. Rather, organisms are always already active. They come into the world with preset propensities for action and preset criteria for evaluating their actions in light of goals. Experience constantly restructures these propensities. Language provides a semantic space enabling representations of the world, the self, and a set of possible actions. It greatly enhances humans' abilities to evaluate possible courses of action, and to perform second- and third-order evaluations of behavior, consequences,

---

[49] See our report on Metzinger's account of consciousness in sec. 4 above.

goals, and cognitive strategies. The social context in which we participate constrains possibilities for actions, but also creates new possibilities for social practices.

Juarrero describes intentional action as the product of top–down (self-causal) control. The problem, she says, is to explain how intentions as *meaningful* flow into actions. In general, intentions are not just triggers of actions but operate as contextual constraints that provide behavior with continuous ongoing control, modifying in real time the probability distribution of behavioral alternatives.[50] Behavioral propensities at birth are embodied in the dynamics of the agent's biological organization. Factors as disparate as gravity, classroom instruction, and religious education constantly restructure the person's dynamical landscape (p. 176). The integration of conscious, meaningful information with the affective system entrains both, leading to an evaluative level of organization (p. 178).

A person's general state of mind is a high–level distributed organization; its attractors represent available act types. Feedback between external circumstances and internal dynamics can drive neural dynamics far enough from equilibrium so that one attractor becomes an intention, reorganizing the landscape. After this one needs to consider only a subset of possible alternatives—all prior probabilities have changed. For example, deciding to greet someone is constituted by a few behavioral possibilities becoming much more probable (waving, saying "hello"), while others (e.g., turning away) drop to zero (pp. 179–80). Feedback circuits monitor the effectiveness of a proximate intention—a mismatch causing a shift in the dynamical landscape of future possibilities for action (p. 188). The description of an action is necessarily narrative in form; one does this now because one first set out to do that and to get from here to there … (p. 8).

Being an action depends on the behavior having been an alternative within the agent's semantically self-organized contrast space; for example, one cannot form the intention to write a check if there is no such social practice or if one is unaware of the practice (pp. 182–3). One also needs to be minimally aware of the action's consequences (p. 185).

In short, "proximate intentions are dynamical attractors that function as top–down control operators entraining other subsystems, including (in the

---

[50] Alicia Juarrero, *Dynamics in Action: Intentional Behavior as a Complex System* (Cambridge, Mass.: MIT Press, 1999), 8. Parenthetical references in this section are to this text.

case of behavior) motor control. These second-order contextual constraints restrict some of the motor subsystems' potential as these become entrained to the intention's organization" (p. 192).

This account of how the semantic content (meaning) of a propositional attitude becomes embodied in action will be essential for our accounts of moral responsibility and free will in the following chapters.

6 Formal Reasoning

We have recognized several important issues that properly fall under the heading of "the problem of mental causation". In section 2 we addressed the general question of why mental events are not reducible to brain events, and argued that it is because of their intrinsic enmeshment in the organism's interactions with the world. In section 3 we addressed the problem of qualia; we argued that consciousness (almost always) makes a difference to an organism's behavior because, at a minimum, it provides second-order information to the organism *about* the information it is receiving. In section 4 we provided an account of the causal role of beliefs as structuring causes of organisms' behavior. In the preceding section we considered a few of the ingredients that go into specifically human rationality and behavior.

We turn in this section to one further question, regarding the capacity for formal reasoning. If mental events and processes are realized by (supervene upon) brain processes, how can it be the case that mental processes obey the dictates of reason rather than (merely) being determined by the laws of neurobiology? Colin McGinn asks: "How, for example, does *modus ponens* get its grip on the causal transitions between mental states?"[51] We rephrase his question as follows: "How does *modus ponens* get its grip on the causal transitions between *brain* events?"

Many take the problem of mental causation to be intrinsically insoluble because of the traditional understanding that acting for a reason is necessarily to be *contrasted* with being caused to act. Notice, though, that much of the technological scaffolding upon which our higher cognitive processes depend (e.g., a computational device) is *designed* so that its causal processes

---

[51] Colin McGinn, "Consciousness and Content", in Block *et al.* (eds.), *Nature of Consciousness*, 255–307, at p. 305.

realize rational transitions. A calculator, for example, is built so that its deterministic internal processes produce *true* answers.

Our account of the restructuring of neural networks via feedback from the environment explains how we "design" our children's and our own brains so that their causal processes realize rational processes. The simplest examples are in cases of rote learning. Let us suppose, for simplicity, that a child begins to learn multiplication tables by memory. The teacher asks, "What is five times five?" The child tries out a series of answers. When the child gives a wrong answer, negative feedback from the environment (the teacher) will cause neural changes that make it less likely that the same answer will be given in the future. Positive feedback (via relatively well-understood processes involving neurotransmitters) will make the repeated activation of that pathway more likely. Thus, feedback from the environment acts (top-down) to select from among a vast number of neural connections the one that results in the production of a correct answer. At the end of this process it no longer makes sense to ask, Did the child give that answer because of physical *causes* in its brain, or because it is the *correct* answer? Clearly it is both: causation and rationality cannot be set in opposition in the normal case.

This process can be represented using MacKay's diagram in Figure 2.3. Here O, the organizing system emits a series of answers in response to R, hearing the question. E represents the child's verbalizing of the answers; F is the classroom. The teacher's response is received by the student (R) and transmitted to the comparator, which evaluates the teacher's response as positive or negative. If negative, O emits a different response. This positive and negative reinforcement alters O, changing the probabilities of future responses to the question.

One might well raise the question at this point: What is the difference between a 7-year-old hearing "What's five times five?" and replying "twenty-five" and a parrot trained by means of rewards to respond in the same way? Briefly, the central difference is that numbers, for the 7-year-old, are already tied into a fairly rich semantic network, realized via interconnected cell assemblies in the brain, such that "five" is known to fall under the category of *number*, that numbers form a series, and so forth. Furthermore, it will have been associated with motor activities, such as counting beads into jars, and with visual patterns such as the dots on dominoes. The transition from rote learning to higher forms of learning and reasoning depends on the complexification of semantic networks—for example, catching onto the meaning of "times" and "divided by", and their relation to one another. Most important, though, is the development of higher-order processes that involve pattern recognition, cognitive operations involving patterns of patterns, and, finally, evaluation of such higher-order operations. These are processes of self-organization or "going meta" that depend on the symbolic scaffolding that cultures have developed over the centuries.

So let us see if we can elaborate on our (not very realistic) account of rote learning to provide not only for the environmental shaping of the brain, but for the reshaping of an individual's own neural pathways by means of one's own mental operations. Learning arithmetic is not merely rote learning but learning both skills and evaluation procedures that ultimately allow for internal correction of mental operations. In the case of rote memorizing of multiplication tables, the O in MacKay's diagram would represent the production of answers, at first, by random spreading of neural activation. But in the case of learning *how* to multiply, O represents a system that involves a skill or operation that produces answers. Feedback from the environment corrects wrong answers *and at the same time* trains and tunes the organizing system itself. Once this system has been trained, it can take the place of the teacher, selectively reinforcing right answers and thus the neural connections that subserve them. So the brain becomes a self-modifying system, modifying its own neural structure in response to norms incorporated into its operations. The organizing system is trained by the environment, and it in turn has downward causal efficacy in governing lower-level cognitive processes and thus the neural structures that subserve them. But here we are still to some extent begging the question of mental causation because of the assumption that the norms according to which the organizing system operates are imposed by rational agents in the environment.

Let us return to Colin McGinn's (rephrased) question of how *modus ponens* gets its grip on the causal transitions between brain states. It is beyond the scope of this chapter to give a respectable cognitive-science account of how logic is learned, but MacKay's approach to cognition puts the emphasis first on the empirical rather than the a priori, and we shall follow his lead. Some sets of sentences or statements work in the world, in the field of action. Sets of sentences such as the following receive positive feedback from the environment: (1) If it is raining, the streets will be wet. (2) It is raining. (3) The streets will be wet. Other sets, such as the following, result in negative feedback: (1) If it is raining, the streets will be wet. (2) It is not raining. (3) The streets will not be wet. A goal, such as keeping one's feet dry, is either met or frustrated.

Daniel Dennett emphasizes the advances made possible by turning our pattern-recognition capacities to monitoring themselves (see Ch. 3, sec. 4). To know what *modus ponens* means is to have acquired (with the aid of cultural resources—scaffolding) the ability to recognize a particular *pattern* among sentences. We now need a more complex figure (Fig. 3.2, p. 129) to represent the process. Here a supervisory system has been added. Rather than correcting O sentence by sentence, SS gives O general instructions to act only on sets of sentences that fit the pattern ($(p \rightarrow q)$ & p) $\rightarrow$ q; that is, if p implies q, and p, then q. This diagram suggests that second-order cognitive operations are still influenced by feedback from F, only the feedback is indirect. For example, if SS instructs O to operate with the pattern $((p \rightarrow q) \& - p) \rightarrow -q$ there will be massive failures to achieve goal states, and as a result SS will be required to readjust O.

An illustration will help to pull together our account of the causal role of symbolic reasoning. We have now listed seven factors that we take to be involved in understanding the role of reason in human action: (1) the character of mental events as *contextualized* brain events, (2) the role of top-down causation from the environment in structuring neural networks, and (3) the role of such self-organized neural structures as structuring *causes* of behavior. In this section we emphasized (4) external scaffolding, (5) off-line simulations, (6) the top-down effect of higher-level cognitive supervisory systems, and (7) symbolic language. In section 3 we used the example from Berry and Broadbent of students learning to control the output of a hypothetical sugar factory without having conscious access to the cognitive-neural processes that produce the answers. This illustrates points 1–3; feedback from the environment makes structural changes in the subjects' neural systems, resulting in increasingly effective performance.

The computer program that simulates the output of the factory is designed by means of a multivariate formula, which was unavailable to the subjects in the study. Consider, now, the different capacities for effective action if the subjects are given the formula—this is an example of Clark's external scaffolding, employing symbolic language. First, the long series of training exercises is not necessary. Subjects with knowledge of mathematics and access to a calculator can produce correct responses immediately; the process of calculation is an example of running an off-line simulation. Second, if something changes in the factory, it will be possible to correct for it immediately—one will be able to perform a meta-evaluation of one's own cognitive operations by means of a higher-level cognitive supervisory system.

Our conclusion is that there is no intrinsic conflict between having a brain that runs on causes, yet one whose causal processes *realize* rational mental operations. The key is to recognize how our brains become designed to implement rational processes. Neurobiological reductionism is only a threat if we fail to recognize the constant downward causal shaping and reshaping of the brain by means of the external scaffolding that has been gradually built up, over the centuries, and tested by its efficacy in furthering our action in the world.

7 The Enigma of Mental Causation

Jaegwon Kim has been most influential in sharpening the problem of mental causation, and he has convinced many philosophers that "nonreductive physicalism" is an oxymoron. Figure 5.11 shows the typical way in which the problem is set up.

The question, then, is about the causal role of M. Does it cause M*? If it does so, presumably it is because its realizer, P, causes P*. But if P is an adequate (physical) cause of P* (and therefore of M*), what causal

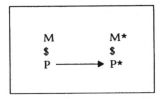

Figure 5.11. Here M and M* represent supervenient mental properties; P and P* represent physical properties; and the arrow represents a causal relation between P and P*.

work is left for M? If no such account can be given, then this amounts to epiphenomenalism—the mental *qua mental* does no causal work. If so, this represents the end of *nonreductive* physicalism.

Kim has concluded that no account can be given of M's causal role without giving up important philosophical commitments. One possibility, of course, is to give up physicalism and revert to some sort of dualism. Another is to say that M and P are both sufficient causes of P* (and M*), but this would amount to causal overdetermination, which Kim judges "absurd".[52] The third possibility is that there is some form of downward causation from M to P* (i.e., M and P together are the cause of P*). Kim rejects this possibility because it "breaches the causal closure of the physical domain". And

> ... to give up this principle is to acknowledge that there can in principle be no complete physical theory of physical phenomena, that theoretical physics, insofar as it aspires to be a complete theory, must cease to be pure physics and invoke irreducibly non-physical causal powers—vital principles, entelechies, psychic energies, elan vital, or whatnot.[53]

Thus, Kim opts for reductive physicalism, claiming that mental properties are causally efficacious only to the extent that they are reducible to physical properties. He believes that all are reducible except qualia, which are epiphenomenal.[54]

We agree that the problem of mental causation is insoluble *if it is set up in this manner.* That is, we believe that the *problem* of mental causation could not get off the ground without one or more of the following theses or assumptions:

1. Mental properties supervene on neural properties in the sense that they covary with the neural properties *regardless of context* (see our sec. 2.3).
2. The causal relevance of the mental can be addressed without considering the *longer-term effects* of the organism's *action* in its environment (sec. 2).
3. Mental properties are properties of events *in the brain*, rather than properties of the organism as a whole (Ch. 1, sec. 3.1).[55]

---

[52] Jaegwon Kim, "The Non-Reductivist's Troubles with Mental Causation", in John Heil and Alfred Mele (eds.), *Mental Causation* (Oxford: Clarendon Press, 1995), 189–210, at p. 208.

[53] Ibid. 209.   [54] Kim, *Physicalism*, ch. 1.

[55] It may be that formulating the problem in terms of mental properties is a large part of the problem. Richard Rorty warns against devising a sort of neo-dualism by hypostatizing a property (e.g.,

4. The causal role of the mental can be addressed adequately while pre-supposing the *qualitative* characterization of consciousness, as opposed to the informational characterization (sec. 3).

In fact, Kim holds versions of three of these four. (1) Kim is largely responsible, thanks to his precision and prolific writing, for the understanding of supervenience as property covariation regardless of context. (2) The two-event series in the diagrams he uses to set up the problem presume that the longer causal history of the organism's action need not be considered. (3) Kim speaks of the mental as inward, saying, for instance, that perception is "our sole window on the world"; that our capacity for intentionality and speech "depends on our being or having been, in appropriate cognitive relations with things *outside*".[56] So, Kim certainly qualifies, on our account, as a Cartesian materialist.

Kim's account of the reduction of the mental requires as a first step the functionalization of the mental: pain equals by definition that which is caused by tissue damage and results in typical pain behavior. Reduction, then, is merely to find the neural realizer that plays this intermediate causal role. Relations between qualia, such as there being a difference between red and green, can be functionalized and reduced; qualia themselves (the redness of red) cannot, and are therefore epiphenomenal. So, we would not categorically disagree with Kim on this last point that *some* qualia may be epiphenomenal; our diametric disagreements about everything else stem largely from his acceptance of points 1–3.

Another reason for opposite conclusions reached by Kim and ourselves has to do with world-view issues. Kim notes that the two intractable problems of mental causation and consciousness "seem deeply entrenched in the way we conceptualize the world and ourselves, and seem to arise from some of the fundamental assumptions that we hold about each". He asks: "Does this mean that there is some hidden flaw somewhere in our system of concepts and assumptions, and that we need to alter, in some basic way, our conceptual framework to rid ourselves of these problems?"[57]

---

painfulness) into a special sort of particular, a pain. Depiction of the problem as in Fig 5.11 subtly pushes one in this direction. One imagines that P is a neural event; M is presumably some quale hovering above it and doing nothing. In contrast, we take mental properties to involve essentially neural events' relations to broader contexts—their environmental causes, their representative relation to the environment, and so forth. See Rorty, *Philosophy and the Mirror of Nature*, 30.

[56] Kim, *Physicalism*, 9, 10; italics added.   [57] Ibid. 29–30.

In fact, Kim's world view is surprisingly close to that of the early modern atomists. Physicalism for him is "the thesis that bits of matter and their aggregates exhaust the content of the world". These bits behave "in accordance with physical law". According to the principle of the causal closure of the physical domain, "physics is causally and explanatorily *self-sufficient.*"[58]

Kim rejects the idea that a framework could be rejected just because it leads to intractable problems. He says that to "motivate the discarding of a framework, we need independent reasons—we should be able to show it to be deficient, incomplete, or flawed in some fundamental way, independently of the fact that it generates puzzles and problems that we are unable to deal with".[59] We hope to have shown on scientific grounds and on the basis of philosophical arguments independent of the problem of mental causation that the atomist–reductionist–determinist world view that Kim embraces is indeed *fundamentally* flawed.

8 Retrospect and Prospect

We have barely begun to treat here the relation between the psychological and the biological, the rational and the causal, but we hope to have steered the philosophical discussion in a more helpful (and realistic) direction. Following MacKay, Clark, Dretske, Juarrero, and others, we have pursued an account of mind and cognition that substitutes, in Clark's terms, a model of representation as control for the (2,500-year-old) model of mind as mirroring.[60] Dretske says: "The idea here is that the brain should not be seen primarily as a locus of inner *descriptions* of external states of affairs; rather it should be seen as a locus of inner *structures* that act as operators upon the world via their role in determining actions."[61]

In Chapter 6 we turn again to the role of reason in human affairs. We have addressed here the question of how brain processes come to

---

[58] Kim, *Physicalism*, 3, 7, 16.   [59] Ibid. 30.
[60] Clark, *Being There*, 47; cf. Rorty, *Philosophy and the Mirror of Nature*.
[61] Dretske, *Explaining Behavior*.

realize patterns of formal reasoning. Our concern in Chapter 6 will be with practical reasoning, and our goal will be to show how *moral* principles can come to play a causal role in human action. Of course, there is the long-standing assumption that one cannot be responsible for one's action if one was *caused* to perform it, so we end (in Chapter 7) with the vexing problem of free will.

6

Who's Responsible?

1 Retrospect and Prospect

We have, at last, reached a central issue with which this book is concerned—that of morally responsible action. The goal we have set for ourselves has two interrelated aspects. One is to show that moral responsibility is not *incompatible* with our essential nature as physical organisms. The second aspect is to examine what we know so far about the cognitive and neural prerequisites for morally responsible action. We have assembled most of the resources we need in the previous chapters. Thus, it may be good to remind the reader of what we (hope to) have accomplished so far before staking out the problems yet to be faced.

A central purpose of this book could be described as the final exorcism of Descartes's ghost from philosophy of mind, action theory, and ethics. Most contemporary scholars have rejected Descartes's concept of the mind. However, physicalist accounts of human nature face daunting objections, most of which are expressions in one way or another of the problem of causal reductionism. If humans are (purely) physical organisms, then how can it fail to be the case that all of their thoughts and behavior are determined by the laws of neurobiology?

This question is difficult to answer because it is raised against the background of three well-entrenched metaphysical assumptions: one peculiarly modern, one going back to the fifth century, and one all the way back to Aristotle. Causal reductionism is the crucial modern assumption, the assumption that the behavior of any entity or system is determined by the laws governing its parts. This modern assumption is now entangled with Aristotle's thesis that nothing can be the cause or mover of itself. Another assumption originated with Augustine—it is the notion that the real self is *inside* the body. For Augustine it was the homunculus within the roomy chambers of memory; for Descartes it was the ego within the mind/soul, which is itself "within" the body; for current "Cartesian materialists" it is the brain (or brain processes) within the body.[1] These three assumptions reinforce one another. The self is *inside* the body, and the body is governed (largely) by this special inner part—whether spiritual or physical.

In Chapter 1 we catalogued assorted versions of Cartesian materialism as signposts of the way not to be taken. This was to clear the way for an account of mental events and properties as attributes of the person as a whole, essentially engaged in action in the natural and social world. In Chapter 2 we tackled the causal reductionist assumption itself, arguing that higher-level entities become causal players in their own right.

In Chapter 3 we attempted to lay to rest the Cartesian view of bodies as mere machines. We did this by canvassing the increasing capacities of organisms for flexibility and self-direction, ending with the claim that higher organisms can be understood to act according to reason. The capacity to use representations plays a large role in providing flexibility in action; symbolic representation is one of the keys to understanding human rationality. In Chapter 4 we turned to the question of language, giving an account of the emergence of meaning in rudimentary forms and then in full-fledged symbolic language. That chapter had both descriptive and defensive goals. It has been objected that a physical system such as a brain is incapable of true reference and intentionality. We offered an account of meaning and reference based on action in the world rather than on inner intendings, and hope thereby to have dispelled the worry that physical organisms must be nothing but parrots.

The next step (in Ch. 5) was to investigate higher forms of specifically human rationality—what is it for humans to act *for reasons*? Critics of physicalist accounts of human nature claim that there is no way to reconcile physical causation and rationality. The philosophical tradition has long taken acting for a reason to be incompatible with being caused to act. Thus, the goal of that chapter was to tackle the problem of mental causation by showing how physical causes become harnessed in the service of reason. Or, put the other way around, we showed how beliefs and reasons become causal players in human life.

[1] See M. R. Bennett and P. M. S. Hacker, *Philosophical Foundations of Neuroscience* (Oxford: Blackwell, 2003).

This puts us in position to consider moral reasoning and moral responsibility. We shall employ with slight modification Alasdair MacIntyre's account of the prerequisites for morally responsible action. We summarize MacIntyre's position as follows: morally responsible action is action based on the evaluation of that which moves one to act in light of a concept of the good. Our modification takes into account the fact that humans, like all other organisms, are intrinsically and spontaneously active. A better formulation, then, is that one is morally responsible when one has the ability to evaluate, in light of some concept of the good, the factors that serve to shape and modify one's action.

In the following section we report on MacIntyre's conceptual analysis. In section 3 we ask what component cognitive abilities enable such evaluation and action, and comment on what is known so far about the neural processes that subserve these abilities. In section 4 we consider explanations for the inability we sometimes experience to turn our moral evaluations into actions. We end with the suggestion that the explorations of morally responsible action in this chapter provide the basis for *reinterpreting* some aspects of the problem of free will.

2 A MacIntyrean Account of Moral Responsibility

Western conceptions of action still bear the marks of their origin in Greek philosophy, with its dualism and overvaluation of the "higher faculties" of the intellect. Augustine's conception of the tripartite soul has lingered in philosophy of action in the form of the distinction of mental processes into the categories of thought, feeling, and will. A central problem for action theory is to answer the question of what distinguishes an action from a mere bodily doing. Such accounts have tended to invoke the notion of an act of will. That is, the hallmark of an action is its being preceded or accompanied by a special act of will, a "volition".

Although the problematic notion of an act of will has been abandoned by current approaches to a theory of action, we still perceive vestiges of the Augustinian and Cartesian theory of the mind as mover of the body, even when mental states of belief and desire are understood as brain states. In contrast, our investigation of levels of action in Chapter 3 has shown remarkable continuity between conscious intelligent action and a rich assortment of bodily processes without mental components. Bodies are inherently active, and only later come to have their activities shaped by mental processes.

MacIntyre's understanding of action is thoroughly physicalist and thoroughly non-Cartesian in that (1) he attributes actions and judgments to the entire physical organism (not to inner mental acts *or* to brain processes) in its environment, both natural and social; and (2) he sets his account of human reasoning and morality within the biological world, recognizing the continuities with other animals against which the distinctives of human rationality can best be illuminated. This is in contrast to those of us who, he says, are "forgetful of our bodies and of how our thinking is the thinking of one species of animal".[2]

The central goal of his book *Dependent Rational Animals* is to attend to a feature of human life that has been conspicuously absent in nearly all Western accounts of the moral life: the extent of vulnerability and dependence on others that is consequent upon our nature as both animals and practical reasoners. He states his thesis as follows:

It will be a central thesis of this book that the virtues that we need, if we are to develop from our initial animal condition into that of independent rational agents, and the virtues that we need, if we are to confront and respond to vulnerability and disability both in ourselves and in others, belong to one and the same set of virtues, the distinctive virtues of dependent rational animals, whose dependence, rationality and animality have to be understood in relationship to each other.[3]

MacIntyre begins his account with the rational capacities of higher animals such as dolphins. As biological organisms, both dolphins and humans aim at goods intrinsic to their species. Many of these goods are shared by both: food, reproduction, satisfaction of curiosity, play. Also for both, survival depends on social knowledge that can only be acquired during progress through a range of relationships from the initial dependence of infants on parents to full membership in adult groups.

As with humans, in order to distinguish dolphin actions from mere sequences of bodily movements, it is necessary to identify dolphin goals.[4] MacIntyre argues that if we can indeed ascribe goals to dolphins, then it

---

[2] Alasdair MacIntyre, *Dependent Rational Animals: Why Human Beings Need the Virtues* (Chicago: Open Court, 1999), 5.

[3] Ibid. 5.

[4] In the case of dolphins and human infants, of course, this is goal-directed action in contrast to full-fledged human intentions.

is natural also to ascribe to them reasons for doing much of what they do. Neither humans nor dolphins need to be able to *state* a belief that *x* will bring about *y* and *y* is the good I am aiming to achieve. Thus, "an agent may possess the relevant beliefs and the actions of that agent may exhibit the relevant goal-directedness without the agent giving utterance to any statement of his or her reasons for so acting."[5]

So MacIntyre understands actions, both human and in higher animals, to originate in the biological needs and drives of the species—the goods at which such a form of life must aim if it is to flourish. Humans have the capacity to expand their range of goals, but the whole system of valuation could not get off the ground if we were not innately goal-directed, and if our goal-directed behavior at its simplest were not already subject to evaluation. MacIntyre says that denial of reasons for action shared with dolphins and chimpanzees "would render the transition to specifically human rationality unintelligible".[6]

What constitutes the difference, then, between animal and human rationality? MacIntyre follows Thomas Aquinas in arguing that the ability to act voluntarily and for a reason depends on the capacity to evaluate one's own reasons. The capacity to evaluate one's reasons depends in turn on language, and, MacIntyre emphasizes, not only on possession of abstract concepts but also on a high level of syntactical competence. This sort of meta-level judgment requires language with the resources necessary for constructing sentences that contain as constituents a representation of the first-order judgment.[7] That is, mature human rationality develops when children attain the ability to consider why they are doing what they are doing, and then to raise the question of whether there might be better reasons for acting differently. This requires the linguistic capacity to be able to say something like the following: "I wanted to smoke to impress my friends, but I decided that wasn't a good enough reason."

Children become independent *moral* reasoners when they can switch from acting to please parents or peers to acting on the basis of some abstract concept of the good; not just what seems good to me now, but what is good *per se*.[8] MacIntyre says: "In so evaluating my desires I stand back from them.

---

[5] MacIntyre, *Dependent Rational Animals*, 24. This is a contentious point, but we shall not go into his arguments here.

[6] Ibid. 56.   [7] Ibid. 53–4.   [8] Ibid. 71–2, 84.

I put some distance between them and myself *qua* practical reasoner, just because I invite the question both from myself and from others, of whether it is in fact good for me to act on this particular desire here and now."[9]

MacIntyre considers the social and political conditions without which children will be unable to attain this level of practical reasoning. He emphasizes (1) parents and other caretakers who instruct children in the craft of moral reasoning, but then give them enough independence to evaluate what they have been taught; (2) friendships and other forms of collegiality that help one to recognize errors in moral reasoning; and (3) forms of local political community in which the requisite virtues can be developed and sustained. Our interest here will be to examine more closely the cognitive abilities that make morally responsible action possible and to tie these abilities as closely as possible to their neural prerequisites.

3 Cognitive Prerequisites for Moral Responsibility

Our summary of MacIntyre's account of the capacity for moral responsibility is "the ability to evaluate that which moves one to act in light of a concept of the good." Note that his concern here is not to present a criterion by which particular actions can be judged as morally responsible, but rather to ask the philosophical question of what are the essential requirements for anyone's attaining the capacity to act in a fully mature, rational, responsible, and moral manner.[10] Here is how MacIntyre ties together the capacities that comprise practical reasoning:

as a practical reasoner I have to be able to imagine different possible futures *for me*, to imagine myself moving forward from the starting point of the present in different directions. For different or alternative futures present me with different and alternative sets of goods to be achieved, with different possible modes of flourishing. And it is important that I should be able to envisage both nearer and more distant futures and to attach probabilities, even if only in a rough and ready way, to the future results of acting in one way rather than another. For this both knowledge and imagination are necessary.[11]

---

[9] Ibid. 69.

[10] We recognize that for practical purposes weaker criteria apply: e.g., much behavior is based on previous reflections of our own or of others.

[11] MacIntyre, *Dependent Rational Animals*, 74–5.

We can draw from this overview a list of requisite cognitive capacities:

1. A symbolic sense of self ("different possible futures *for me*").
2. A sense of the narrative unity of life ("to imagine myself moving forward from ... the present"; "nearer and more distant futures").
3. The ability to run behavioral scenarios ("imagination") and predict the outcome ("knowledge"; "attach probabilities ... to the future results").
4. The ability to evaluate predicted outcomes in light of goals.
5. The ability to evaluate the goals themselves ("alternative sets of goods ... different possible modes of flourishing") in light of abstract concepts.
6. The ability to act in light of 1−5.

We shall consider more specific cognitive and affective abilities that comprise each of these six capacities and note, insofar as possible, their neural prerequisites. Note that these capacities *presuppose* that the organism/person has the ability to be the cause of its own actions. In Chapter 2 we noted how odd it is that we place humans in the hierarchy of complex systems and worry that their behavior is all determined bottom-up by biology (or physics), or top-down by the environment, or by some combination, yet without considering that significant causal factors might originate with the agent. Alicia Juarrero diagnosed this strange omission as a holdover from Aristotle: the dogma that nothing can be the cause or mover of itself. Our position is that complex organisms are in fact self-causes, self-movers.

3.1 A Symbolic Sense of Self

The term "self" is used in a variety of ways in psychology and philosophy. What is at issue here is not the question of what it means to *have* or *be* a self. Rather, the issue is that of having a self-*concept*.[12] This concept arises early in life, but becomes more complex through maturation.[13]

---

[12] See Bennett and Hacker, *Philosophical Foundations of Neuroscience*: "As we shall show, the 'self' or the 'I' (thus conceived) is a fiction generated by conceptual confusions. There is indeed such a thing as self-consciousness in the philosophical sense of the term, but it is not consciousness of a 'self'. It is a distinctively human capacity for reflexive thought and knowledge, wholly dependent upon possession of language" (p. 324).

[13] Charles Taylor traces the development of Western conceptions of the self from ancient philosophy to the present. See *Sources of the Self: The Making of Modern Identity* (Cambridge, Mass.: Harvard University Press, 1989).

Michael Lewis distinguishes between implicit and explicit self-awareness. The former he refers to as the biological "machinery of self", the latter as "the idea of me". The machinery of self is shared with other organisms: the distinction of self from non-self and conservation of self over time. Conservation is exhibited in very rudimentary form even in very simple organisms in their ability to habituate to stimuli.[14] Patricia Churchland views the awareness of self as a function of the self-representational capacities of the brain, and lists some of the brain systems known to be involved—for example, representation of the internal milieu of the viscera via pathways to the brain stem and hypothalamus, and autobiographical events via the medial temporal lobes.[15]

As described earlier (Ch. 3, sec. 5.2), Thomas Metzinger describes self-awareness as a form of consciousness that involves a model of the self (the *phenomenal self model*) embedded within, but differentiated from, the organism's model of the external world.[16] Intentionality is formed by a relational "vector" between the self model and various aspects of the model of the external world. Or, to view it the other way around, the world is modeled with reference to the self model. Metzinger calls this *subjective consciousness*. The further emergence of the "idea of me" Metzinger calls *cognitive subjective consciousness*. This has two important attributes: (1) the ability to activate and manipulate world models (including the self) off-line (via imagination); and (2) the consequent ability to model the self as the possessor and manipulator of models—as a "thinker of thoughts".[17]

Lewis describes two stages in the origination of the idea of me, of explicit self-consciousness. The first is physical self-recognition, which generally appears around 18 months of age. It is tested by putting a spot on the child's nose to see if the child reacts to it in a mirror. Chimpanzees also have this ability. A more advanced form of self-awareness appears during the third year of life and is measured by the ability to engage in pretend play and by the use of personal pronouns. This capacity is closely linked

[14] Michael Lewis, "The Emergence of Consciousness and Its Role in Human Development", in Joseph LeDoux, Jacek Debiec, and Henry Moss (eds.), *The Self: From Soul to Brain*, Annals of the New York Academy of Sciences, 1001 (New York: New York Academy of Sciences, 2003), 104–33.

[15] Patricia S. Churchland, "Self-Representation in Nervous Systems", *Science*, 296 (Apr. 2002), 308–10.

[16] Thomas Metzinger, *Being No One: The Self-Model Theory of Subjectivity* (Cambridge, Mass.: MIT Press, 2003).

[17] Ibid. 205.

to the development of a theory of mind—that is, the ability to attribute thoughts and feelings to others.[18]

Leslie Brothers reports on research showing that we come well equipped neurobiologically to develop and use what she calls the *person* concept. The perception of a person is a higher-order perception of bodies, a perception that endows them with mental life. In normally developing children this perception becomes automatic.[19] The variety of brain disorders that result in *loss* of the ability to perceive persons (e.g., damage to regions of the temporal lobes, or the right hemisphere in general, or the right parietal lobe in particular) suggests that the capacity is encoded in widespread regions of the brain.[20]

Brothers hypothesizes that our ancestors began with a brain system specialized for perceiving and responding to bodies and their gestures, and that slight modifications of the system have enabled us to generate the concepts of *person* and *mind*. For example, we have remarkable abilities to recognize faces, and we have neurons that specialize in detecting bodily motions such as hand movements and direction of gaze that indicate other actors' intentions.[21] Understanding of the intentions of others is reinforced by being able to attribute outcomes either to oneself or to others. Recent brain-imaging studies have found agent-specific responses to action outcomes ("me" versus "not me") that are arranged in a systematic spatial pattern along the cingulate cortex.[22] However, Brothers notes that there is another dimension to the concept of *person*, which is the ability to locate ourselves in social networks of morals, reasons, and status.[23]

Terrence Deacon emphasizes the essential role of language in the development of this *symbolic* self-concept:

Consciousness of self in this way implicitly includes consciousness of other selves, and other consciousnesses can only be represented through the virtual reference created by symbols. The self that is the source of one's experience of intentionality, the self that is judged by itself as well as by others for its moral choices, the self

---

[18] Lewis, "Emergence of Consciousness".

[19] Leslie A. Brothers, *Friday's Footprint: How Society Shapes the Human Mind* (New York: Oxford University Press, 1997), 4.

[20] Ibid. 9–10.   [21] Ibid. ch. 3.

[22] D. Tomlin *et al.*, "Agent-Specific Responses in the Cingulate Cortex during Economic Exchanges", *Science*, 312 (2006), 1047–50.

[23] Brothers, *Friday's Footprint*, 4.

that worries about its impending departure from the world, this self is a symbolic self.[24]

Thus, it is no accident that use of personal pronouns serves as a *measure* of the possession of a self-concept and that the appearance of personal pronoun use correlates with development of a theory of mind. M. R. Bennett and P. M. S. Hacker point out that to have concepts is to know how to use words. "The idea of me" is thus dependent on the ability to use the words "I" and "me". These words cannot be used correctly without acquisition of a *system* of words including second- and third-person pronouns, which depends on the ability to distinguish other people from inanimate objects.[25]

Brothers argues that while our brains have the capacity to generate the concepts of *person* and *social order*, they must take their specific form from exposure to a particular culture. This culture is transmitted largely in the form of narratives. The relationship between individuals and the social order is the essence of narrative, and our conversations are largely made up of such narratives.[26]

3.2 The Narrative Unity of Life

Another prerequisite for both practical reasoning and moral responsibility is a narrative understanding of the history of one's life and recognition that the narrative will continue into the future with many alternative possibilities for the nature of that continuance. Understanding of the narrative unity of our lives depends on the existence of a long-term memory for events from our pasts that is accessible to consciousness. This sort of memory is called episodic memory (memory of previous life episodes) or autobiographical memory (memory of one's own autobiography). Episodic memory is our recall of the events of our past that are marked in our recollection by specifics of time and place.[27]

---

[24] Terrence W. Deacon, *The Symbolic Self: The Co-evolution of Language and the Brain* (New York: Norton, (1997), 452.

[25] Bennett and Hacker, *Philosophical Foundations of Neuroscience*, 348.

[26] Brothers, *Friday's Footprint*, 80–1.

[27] Larry R. Squire, *Memory and Brain* (Oxford: Oxford University Press, 1987), 169–74. Squire differentiates general semantic memory and episodic memory. This differentiation, proposed originally by Endel Tulving, is controversial in the research literature. However, it is not critical to our argument whether episodic memory is different from semantic memory so long as persons can be shown to have memory for life events, a point which is uncontroversial.

Episodic memory appears to develop during early childhood, not being fully developed until after the third year of life.[28] That other forms of memory are fully functional prior to this is attested by the vast amount of procedural and semantic learning that takes place during these early childhood years. The term "infantile amnesia" refers to our inability to remember events (episodes) from our very early childhood, although we are typically able to remember significant events from later childhood.[29]

It is not clear whether episodic memory is something we share with higher animals. Apes clearly have memories of previous events. However, whether in apes these memories are truly episodic, autobiographical memories is uncertain. For example, chimpanzees are very good at remembering where they saw a trainer hide a desirable stash of food and can return without error to the spot after many hours or days. However, whether the memory is of the nature of "I-remember-the-trainer-hiding-food-there-yesterday" (an episodic memory) or "I-know-food-is-hidden-there" (non-episodic) is not yet known. There are a few anecdotal reports of expressions of an episodic memory in the more language-competent chimpanzees. Nevertheless, the existence or capacity of an episodic memory in subhuman primates has not been established.

Two points suggest that human episodic memory is apt to be of greater scope and complexity than that which might exist in the non-human. First, the capacity of human language to preserve historical detail provides an economy for memory. To be able not only to preserve an experience as a specific, historical sensory memory, but to add to it a memory of verbally encoded labels (such as "on my wedding day" or "at my 21st birthday party" or "my first day on the job") adds important dimensions of autobiographical coding to memory storage. Language can form temporally coded linkages in the network of semantically remembered information, which would endow humans with a richer autobiographical memory.

Second, certain aspects of autobiographical memory may be more developed in humans due to the remarkably expanded size and complexity

[28] P. A. Ornstein, B. N. Gordon, and L. E. Baker-Ward, "Children's Memory for Salient Events: Implications for Testimony", in M. L. Howe, C. J. Brainerd, and V. F. Reyna (eds.), *Development of Long Term Retention* (New York: Springer Verlag, 1992), 135–58.

[29] J. Perner and T. Ruffman, "Episodic Memory and Autonoetic Consciousness: Developmental Evidence and a Theory of Childhood Amnesia", *Journal of Experimental Child Psychology*, 59 (1995), 516–48.

of frontal lobes in humans relative to even the highest non-human primates. Frontal lobes are important for what Joaquín Fuster has referred to as the temporal organization of behavior.[30] Behaviors that are complex and require sequences of purposive behavior extending over long periods of time rely on frontal lobe function. Based in part on the remarkable development of frontal neocortex, humans have the capacity to remember the previous steps in, and current status of, very complex plans that have extended over considerable periods of time; that is, we have episodic memories for the events that constitute progress thus far in carrying forward a complex plan.

As symbolic language enhances mature humans' episodic memory, so too it creates the capacity to imagine stretches of time beyond the present moment and imaginatively to place oneself in that future. This capacity is dependent on having a concept of *time*. George Lakoff and Mark Johnson trace the various ways in which literal descriptions of space and motion serve metaphorically to structure our concept of time. There is the Time Orientation metaphor, with an observer at the present who is facing toward the future with the past behind. The Moving Time metaphor involves a stationary observer with an indefinitely long series of objects moving past. The Flowing Time metaphor associates time with a flowing substance such as water in a river.[31] The capacity to imagine and describe a "stretch of time" extending "backwards" to long before the beginning of our own episodic memories allows us to place our stories in the context of longer histories, of family, nation, and now even of cosmic history. More important for present purposes is the fact that it allows us to consider the distant future consequences of our current actions.

Given this capacity to remember our own past and to place it in a longer temporal framework, it is difficult to imagine life without autobiographical memory. However, there are cases in the neuropsychological literature that suggest the consequences of a deficient episodic memory. The classic example of loss of the ability to form new episodic memories (called "anterograde amnesia") is the case of H. M.[32] Due to bilateral damage

---

[30] Joaquín Fuster, *The Prefrontal Cortex: Anatomy, Physiology, and Neuropsychology of the Frontal Lobe* (New York: Raven Press, 1980).

[31] George Lakoff and Mark Johnson, *Philosophy in the Flesh: The Embodied Mind and Its Challenge to Western Thought* (New York: Basic Books, 1999), ch. 10.

[32] B. Milner, S. Corkin, and H. L. Teuber, "Further Analysis of the Hippocampal Amnesic Syndrome: 14-Year Follow-up Study of H. M.", *Neuropsychologia*, 6 (1968), 215–34.

to important structures in the temporal lobe of the brain, H. M. lost the ability to form new episodic memories accessible to consciousness. If you met H. M. and carried on a short conversation with him, then walked out of the room for a few minutes and returned, H. M. would express no knowledge of the previous meeting. Any new information that passes out of his immediate memory (also called "short-term" or "working" memory) is lost forever to conscious recall. Thus, H. M. is trapped within a narrow window of the memories of immediately preceding events, a window no wider than the amount of information he can keep consciously in mind at one time. Episodic memories formed prior to the onset of H. M.'s brain pathology were still well remembered, but all events that occurred during the intervening years continue to be permanently lost.

A somewhat similar story can be told of patient N. A., who received an accidental injury to a brain structure slightly different in location, but within the same system as in the case of H. M. Like H. M., N. A. appears normal on first encounter, yet his episodic memory difficulties are considerable. "His memory impairment is best understood as a difficulty in retaining the events of each passing hour and day ... He loses track of his possessions, forgets what he has done, and forgets whom he has visited."[33]

The consequences for interpersonal relationships of such memory impairment are well described by Squire with regard to N. A. "He has no close friends. His socializing is limited by his difficulty in keeping a topic of conversation in mind and in carrying over the substance of social contacts from one occasion to another ... He says that watching television is difficult, because he forgets the story content during commercial breaks."[34] In an expression that reflects the pathos of a person without memory of a recent past, Milner quotes H. M. as saying, "Every day is alone in itself, whatever enjoyment I've had, and whatever sorrow I've had ... Right now, I'm wondering. Have I done or said anything amiss? You see, at this moment everything looks clear to me, but what happened just before? That's what worries me. It's like waking from a dream; I just don't remember."[35]

Thus, these two tragic cases illustrate that important aspects of personhood are deeply affected by a loss of conscious access to memories of

---

[33] Squire, *Memory and Brain*, 178.   [34] Ibid.

[35] B. Milner, "Memory and the Temporal Regions of the Brain", in K. H. Pribram and D. E. Broadbent (eds.), *Biology of Memory* (New York: Academic Press, 1970), 37.

our not-too-distant past (i.e., an inability to form new episodic memories). While intact episodic memory of events prior to their brain injuries has preserved some feeling for the narrative unity of their lives, they are persistently disoriented with respect to their current context. Since they are unable to form new episodic memories, neither H. M. nor N. A. (nor other patients like them) would be able to utilize information from recent events in either prudential or moral reasoning. They have also lost any idea of a current life trajectory. Life is now always like "waking from a dream". Neither individuals with anterograde amnesia nor children with infantile amnesia would be held morally responsible for acting on the basis of past events that they could not remember.[36]

3.3 Running Behavioral Scenarios

The third cognitive component needed for moral responsibility is the capacity to imagine different possible courses of action and predict their likely outcomes. We have argued throughout that mental capacities in general are best understood in terms of their role in guiding action. At the most basic level of representations of potential action, we characterized perception (following Donald MacKay) as a *conditional readiness to reckon* with what is perceived, and a belief as a conditional readiness to reckon with something that is not immediately present. Thus, perceptions and beliefs are cognitive associative networks involving potential-action scenarios.

In Chapter 3 we speculated that higher animals have the capacity to run off-line emulations of potential behaviors. The chimpanzee Sultan, who solved the problem of how to reach bananas outside his cage by attaching two sticks end to end, did so without trial and error. He was apparently able to manipulate representations of the sticks imaginatively, and thus to imagine the outcome of such potential actions. Rick Grush's distinction between representations and emulations (Ch. 3, sec. 2.3.1) highlights the value of being able to *manipulate* internal representations in order to plan action.

---

[36] This section is taken, with some modification, from the section on episodic memory in Warren S. Brown, "Cognitive Contributions to Soul", in Warren S. Brown, Nancey Murphy, and H. Newton Malony (eds.), *Whatever Happened to the Soul?: Scientific and Theological Portraits of Human Nature* (Minneapolis: Fortress Press, 1998), 113–16.

In Chapter 3 (sec. 5.2) we discussed the neurobiologically plausible account of consciousness and sense of the self presented by Thomas Metzinger.[37] Metzinger's theory of consciousness is based on the idea that complex organisms operate out of models of the external world in which consciousness is constituted by the currently activated world model. The most complex form of consciousness that Metzinger outlines is *cognitive subjective consciousness*. What is important about this highest form of consciousness is the ability to elicit and process various world models off-line. Such off-line processing means for Metzinger that organisms (presumably humans) can "engage in the activation of globally available representational structures *independently of current external input*".[38] That is, cognitive subjective consciousness allows the individual to model potentialities for action in the world off-line. In this manner one can "engage in future planning, enjoy explicit, episodic memories, or start genuinely cognitive processes like the mental formation of concepts".[39] Thus, the ability to run an off-line simulation is also critical to Metzinger's account.

In Chapter 5 we noted Andy Clark's concept of external scaffolding—external devices we can manipulate in order to increase our capacity to predict consequences of action. Symbolic language is one of the most important sorts of external scaffolding for mental operations. The limitless possibilities for combining linguistic elements in new ways enhances humans' abilities to construct scenarios for possible future actions. Terrence Deacon notes that the increasingly indirect linkages between symbolic mental representations and their grounds of reference free our imaginations to roam over possibilities of which we have had no previous experience.

Symbolic analysis is the basis for a remarkable new level of self-determination that human beings alone have stumbled upon. The ability to use virtual reference to build up elaborate internal models of possible futures, and to hold these complex visions in mind with the force of the mnemonic glue of symbolic inference and descriptive shorthands, gives us unprecedented capacity to generate independent adaptive behaviors. Remarkable abstraction from indexically bound experiences is further enhanced by the ability of symbolic reference to pick out tiny fragments of real world processes and arrange them as buoys to chart an inferential course that predicts physical and social outcomes.[40]

---

[37] Metzinger, *Being No One.*   [38] Ibid. 205; italics added.   [39] Ibid.
[40] Deacon, *Symbolic Species*, 434.

These symbolically mediated models "exhibit complicated nonlinearity and recursive structures as well as nearly infinite flexibility and capacity for novelty due to their combinatorial nature".[41]

So the typical adult is capable of imagining an immense number of possible actions and is often able to predict their consequences. MacIntyre notes, however, that this ability is not likely to develop in children if they are provided by their caretakers and teachers with too impoverished a view of future possibilities. Children need to be "educated in imagining alternative possibilities".[42] Educational failure in this regard can be of three types. One is the result of inculcating false beliefs about how far our lives are determined by uncontrollable circumstances. The second is by encouraging children to indulge in fantasies that blur the difference between realistic expectations and wishful thinking. The third sort is failure to question children's reasons for acting as they do and thus failure to alert them to the range of objects of desire and range of goals that constitute possible alternative reasons for action.[43]

Note that the capacity for running behavioral scenarios *for me* presupposes a sense of self (sec. 3.1) and a sense of the narrative unity of life (sec. 3.2).

3.4 Evaluation of Predicted Outcomes in the Light of Goals

We have already emphasized that animals act so as to attain goods specific to their species, and that the most sophisticated of animals apparently have the capacity to run behavioral scenarios, the outcome of which is to find means of attaining their goals.

Much human evaluation of predicted outcomes of behavior is done primarily at the emotional level. Michael Lewis reports on the development in children of "self-evaluative emotions"—shame, pride, guilt, and embarrassment. These emotions occur later in life than more basic emotions such as fear and joy (at $2\frac{1}{2}$ to 3 years of age) since they require a sense of self and the recognition of standards.[44] Robert H. Frank, reporting the work of Jerome Kagan on moral development in children, maintains that the desire to avoid negative emotions is the principal motive force behind moral behavior. He describes these emotions as anxiety,

---

[41] Ibid.   [42] MacIntyre, *Dependent Rational Animals*, 75.   [43] Ibid. 76.
[44] Lewis, "Emergence of Consciousness", 121–5.

empathy (with those in need or at risk), responsibility, fatigue/ennui, and uncertainty.[45]

Antonio Damasio's thesis regarding somatic markers (see Ch. 1, sec. 3.2) offers an account of the neural equipment necessary in order for this sort of emotional feedback to be effective in shaping behavior. His work shows that no matter what capacities one has for predicting, at an intellectual level, the outcomes of anticipated behavior, without these "gut reactions", behavior is capricious and not appropriately linked to the attainment of goals. Thus, the experience of the emotional responses of our bodies ("gut reactions") is important in translating moral reasoning into adequate practical behavior.

While the pursuit of goals would never get off the ground without both built-in and conditioned emotional motivators, the capacity for symbolic language clearly enhances human ability to predict and evaluate the probable outcomes of behavior. Consider the difference between imagined scenarios for reaching bananas outside the cage and various scenarios for investing one's money for retirement.

Sophisticated language allows not only for understanding a variety of abstract possibilities, but also for second-order evaluations of one's own evaluative processes. For example, suppose one has read about empirical research on the tendency to make irrational judgments in favor of immediate versus later rewards. If given a choice between $100 today and $120 in three days' time, most people choose $100 today, despite the fact that there is no way to make $20 in profit on the money in three days. Apparently both humans and animals are hard-wired to act on the principle that a bird in the hand is worth two in the bush. Frank notes that an awareness of this tendency allows us to devise "commitment devices" that set up ways to avoid such temptations.[46]

3.5 Evaluation of Goals in the Light of Abstract Concepts

We have already noted (in Ch. 3) that even quite simple organisms have the capacity to abandon the pursuit of one goal (e.g., getting a drink of water) in favor of a more salient goal (e.g., avoiding a predator). Animals

---

[45] Robert H. Frank, *Passions within Reason: The Strategic Role of the Emotions* (New York: W. W. Norton and Co., 1988), 152–3; referring to Jerome Kagan, *The Nature of the Child* (New York: Basic Books, 1984).

[46] Frank, *Passions within Reason*, 77–86; see also sec. 3.6 below.

also have the capacity to evaluate goals in light of the fact that their pursuit is turning out to be either unattainable or simply too costly—the sour grapes phenomenon that Aesop attributed to foxes.

Recall that our definition of morally responsible action (following Mac-Intyre) is action undertaken on the basis of evaluation of one's goals in light of a concept of the good. We shall come back to *moral responsibility* shortly, but there is another sense in which we speak of responsibility—for example, some children are "responsible" about getting their homework done, and others are not. Children become responsible in this sense when they attain the ability to evaluate that which shapes and reshapes their action. Such evaluation is what we shall call "self-transcendence".[47] Humans, like all other organisms, are intrinsically active, and their actions are directed by biological drives and emotions, by immediate desires and longer-term goals, and by social expectations. The forms their action takes are shaped by learning, by imagination, by judgments about what will be effective. *Responsible* action, as here understood, is that which is consequent upon the ability to represent to oneself what one is doing and why one is doing it. We reported above (sec. 3.3) on MacIntyre's account of the role that parents and teachers play in children's development of this ability by asking "Why are you doing that?" We reported as well on his recognition of the sophisticated syntax required before children are able to raise such questions for themselves (sec. 2).

Bennett and Hacker emphasize the role of language as well. One who has developed the sophisticated linguistic powers

to use proper names and pronouns, as well as psychological predicates and predicates of action, in both the first- and third-person cases and in the various tenses ... is a self-conscious creature, who has the ability to be transitively conscious of its own mental states and conditions, who can think and reflect on how things are with it, who can not only act but also become and be conscious of itself as so acting. And it will also have the ability to reflect on its own past, on its character traits and dispositions, on its preferences, motives and reasons for action.[48]

One can act for a motive without having the concept for denoting such a motive, but one cannot know that one is acting for such a motive.[49] *Moral* responsibility, then, depends on the capacity to use moral *concepts* to

---

[47] This is what Daniel Dennett calls "going meta"; see *Elbow Room: Varieties of Free Will Worth Wanting* (Cambridge, Mass.: MIT Press, 1984), 29.

[48] Bennett and Hacker, *Philosophical Foundations of Neuroscience*, 334.   [49] Ibid. 350.

describe (and *in so doing* to evaluate) one's own actions, character traits, dispositions, and so on. We devoted much of Chapter 5 to an attempt to dispel the worry that a physical (causal) system is incapable of acting for a reason.

3.6 An Example

It may be worthwhile at this point to put our account of the cognitive capacities that comprise moral reasoning together in an example. Consider the fight-or-flight response. This is pre-wired in humans, as in other animals, and the ability to recognize threatening behavior is apparently built up easily from preexisting perceptual capacities.[50] Thus, a typical series of events can be represented by means of the now familiar diagram from Donald MacKay representing a simple feedback system (Fig. 2.3). A likely series of events involves perception of the behavior of another person (R); evaluation of the behavior as threatening (C); selection of a response—fleeing, fighting, conciliation—by the organizing system (O); and effecting the response (E). Feedback from the field of operation (F) will provide differential reinforcements that actually change the configuration of the brain.

Jesuit priest and ethicist G. Simon Harak describes an event that exemplifies such conditioning:

When I was younger, I studied karate for a few years, going three times a week for practice. One day, two fellow students of theology and I decided to go to a movie. Fran was a former Marine sergeant. John was a bright and articulate student. After we had bought our tickets individually, we regrouped in the lobby. "Did you see that guy on the other side of the ticket booth?" Fran asked me. "Yeah," I replied. "He sure was crusin' for a bruisin', wasn't he?" "You know," Fran said, "the look on his face ... I was just waiting for him to try something," and he put his fist into his left palm. I started to say, "If he made a move on me, I would've ..." But John interrupted us by saying, "What guy?"

The facts are these: Fran and I saw this young man, and were ready even to fight with him. John, a bright and alert person, didn't even perceive him. Why? The key lies in our respective backgrounds. In our history, Fran and I shared a training in violence. It was, significantly, a *physical* training which *disposed* us to "take things in a certain way." Specifically, we were "looking for trouble." And

---

[50] Brothers, *Friday's Footprint*, ch. 3.

we found it. John, with no such training, didn't even perceive the "belligerent" young man.[51]

Now, MacIntyre's account of moral development involves self-transcendence—that is, becoming aware of and evaluating that which moves one to action. In Harak's case this evaluation happened as a result of the contrast between his and John's responses. He says: "I could see my deficiency precisely because of my association with John and others like him in another community."[52] The other community was the Jesuit Order, and, in due course, he realized that he needed to give up his practice of martial arts, and adopted a pacifist ethic.

This story fits MacIntyre's account of the emergence of moral responsibility. Harak became conscious of what moved him to action, and then evaluated it, first, in light of the norms of other community members, and finally, in light of an abstract conception of the good.

To represent this process in information-engineering terms, we need a more complex diagram, as in Figure 3.3 (p. 130). Notice that in Figure 2.3 (p. 69) I_g, the goal state of the system, is set by something outside the system—in the first instance it was set by natural selection. In Figure 3.3 the goal state itself is set by higher-level processes within the system. In the case of our pacifist, the meta-comparator places a higher value on nonviolent resolution of conflict than on survival. The meta-organizing system then adjusts the comparator's priorities accordingly. C's job will now be to evaluate threatening behavior not in terms of threats to survival, but in terms of threats to the peace of the community. A different repertoire of skills and norms will have to be developed in the organizing system. As this system develops, the feed-forward path (FF), which selects relevant features of sensory input, will be affected by a different form of action and by reactions from the environment. As Harak points out, virtuous behavior effects changes in the agent's perceptions.

Notice that in Figure 3.3 there is also feedback from the field of operation to the meta-comparator. This represents the fact that, in the case in question, the moral principle is subject to readjustment in light of the effects produced by acting in accordance with it. For example, it is often argued that pacifist responses increase others' aggression. The pacifist might re-evaluate his commitment to this principle if this turned out to be true.

---

[51] G. Simon Harak, *Virtuous Passions* (New York: Paulist Press, 1993), 34.　　[52] Ibid. 35.

So Figure 3.3 represents a system in which first the social environment and then an abstract moral concept exercise downward causal efficacy on an individual's behavior, and the change in behavior will have a downward effect in reshaping neural connections in such a way that the new behavior becomes habitual. Thus, we have a dynamic interplay between neurobiology and environment.

A worry arises, though, regarding the pacifist's moral responsibility: what if his acceptance of pacifism was *socially determined*, for example, because of a strong need for social conformity? Notice that if this worry occurs to Harak, it provokes another level of self-transcendence. That is, it engages once again his ability to make himself the object of his reflections and evaluations—a meta-meta-evaluation. This means that as soon as the suspicion of social determination arises for the agent, he is able to transcend that determination. In this case, he may invoke a higher-level evaluative principle to the effect that all genuine moral commitments must be accepted on the basis of autonomous rational examination, not on the authority of one's community. Representation of this second act of self-transcendence requires a more complex diagram in which a higher-level supervisory system has been added that evaluates the meta–comparator of Figure 3.3. In Figure 3.4 (p. 130), the supervisory system, SS, represents the cognitive capacity to evaluate, in light of a still more abstract goal, the whole complex of motives and principles that, up until then, have moved him to act.

There is no limit, other than lack of imagination, to the ability of the agent to transcend earlier conceptions. For example, our pacifist may take a course in philosophical ethics and become persuaded that Alasdair MacIntyre's tradition-based approach to ethics is better argued than his previous Kantian position. He then comes to see his bid for moral autonomy as both unrealistic and culturally determined. So a higher level of meta–ethical evaluation (SS') overturns his earlier ethical program, thereby changing the content of SS. In other words, *meta*-ethical reflection (SS') on the criteria for choosing a first-order ethical system (SS) is a new and higher form of cognitive evaluation.

4 Ability to Act

Our interest in this chapter is in the cognitive and neural prerequisites for morally responsible action. So far we have concentrated on the sort of cognitive processes that make an action morally responsible; but another question is, What is required to take these evaluations of possible future behaviors and turn them into *actions?* So in this section our question is, What are the necessary conditions for enacting our intentions? The first, obvious one is that one not be physically constrained in any way—bound and gagged or paralyzed.

Several topics we have raised earlier are relevant for addressing less obvious helps and hindrances to action. We reported on the chimpanzees that were not able to overcome the biological urge to take the large pile of candy even when they came to understand that their actions were not effective in attaining their goal. Humans sometimes suffer from comparable inabilities to deny immediate biological urges. We also reported on Phineas Gage, the railway worker with damage to his prefrontal cortex, and similar patients of Antonio Damasio, who were able to evaluate future courses of action as prudent (or foolish), socially acceptable (or not), moral (or immoral), but who lacked the subtle emotional pushes (or impediments) that normally provide the impetus (or restraint) that turns these evaluations into actions.

On the positive side, we have presented the hypothesis that our ability to get ourselves to do what we know we should do is dependent in part on self-talk. At some point in a child's development, it becomes possible to internalize the encouragement, imperatives, cautions, and prohibitions that she or he has heard from caretakers and provide for her or himself the same sorts of stimuli to act or refrain from acting.

However, we simply do not have the cognitive processing capacity to evaluate each action. Fortunately, in many cases after repeated actions it is no longer necessary to continue to evaluate a course of action and "tell ourselves" to do it. Our "mental butlers" take over the task, freeing up conscious resources to invest in novel evaluations and consequent activity. Thus, the moral nature of these behaviors has been conditioned by prior conscious decisions or moral reflection.

4.1 Weakness of Will as Temporal Discounting

A long-standing interest in the philosophical literature is the problem of *akrasia*—that is, weakness of will. Why do we so often choose to do things that we know we will regret later? Why do we opt for short-term pleasure at the cost of health and other long-term goals? We can express this problem in our MacIntyrean terms as follows. Moral responsibility depends on a second-order evaluation of an action—evaluation of the drives, desires, reasons, motives, that, apart from such evaluation, would issue in action. The cases to which we refer here are cases in which such an evaluation goes contrary to one's first-order needs or desires, yet one nonetheless acts on the basis of the lower-level motives rather than on the basis of the higher-level evaluation. Harry Frankfurt discusses this issue in terms of second-order desires—desires to have or not have one's own lower-order desires.[53] However, we follow John Searle in recognizing that our second-order evaluations are often based on desire-independent reasons, which come from our participation in social practices.[54]

George Ainslie in his recent book, *Breakdown of Will*, notes that little progress has been made on this problem since the Victorian era.

The paradoxes of how people knowingly choose things they'll regret don't need rehashing. Examples of self-defeating behaviors abound. Theories about how this could be are almost as plentiful, with every discipline that studies the problem represented by several. However, the proliferation of theories in psychology, philosophy, economics, and the other behavioral sciences is best understood as a sign that no one has gotten to the heart of the matter.[55]

Most contemporary cognitive-science accounts of self-defeating behavior fall into one of two categories, the cognitivist or the utilitarian. Cognitivists (in line with Socrates) believe that no one ever knowingly does wrong. For example, Roy Baumeister and Todd Heatherton state that "[m]isregulation occurs because [people] operate on the basis of false assumptions about themselves and about the world, because they try to control things that

---

[53] Harry Frankfurt, *The Importance of What We Care About* (Cambridge: Cambridge University Press, 1988); and *idem, Necessity, Volition, and Love* (Cambridge: Cambridge University Press, 1999).
[54] John R. Searle, *Rationality in Action* (Cambridge, Mass.: MIT Press, 2001).
[55] George Ainslie, *Breakdown of Will* (Cambridge: Cambridge University Press, 2001), 3.

cannot be directly controlled, or because they give priority to emotions while neglecting more important and fundamental problems".[56]

The utility theory postulates that

your options have to compete for your favor on the basis of some elementary motivational quality—call it "reward"—a common dimension along which all options that can be substituted for each other have to compete. Reward is supposed to operate on your choices the way natural selection operates on species: It keeps the successful candidates and drops the others. Utilitarian writers in fields from economics to abnormal psychology depict people as simply trying to maximize their satisfactions.[57]

Ainslie shows ways in which both of these approaches are inadequate, and develops his own account on the basis of quantitative motivational research. His particular interest comes from his work in the field of addiction, but his account sheds light on a broader range of self-defeating behaviors. The key to his model comes from empirical studies of "discounting"; that is, the tendency people (and animals) have to choose a small immediate reward over a greater reward in the future. There are cases in which this is the rational thing to do. For instance, if I am offered $100 today or $120 a year from now, it is rational to take the smaller amount if I have a pressing need for the money now, which I shall not have later, or if I calculate that I could invest the money and make more than $20 in a year's time. Yet most people would still choose the $100 today even if the amount offered in the future is "objectively" much more valuable. For example, Ainslie reports:

If I ask a roomful of people to imagine that they've won a contest and can choose between a certified check for $100 that they can cash immediately and a postdated certified check for $200 that they can't cash for three years, more than half of the people usually say they would rather have the $100 now. If I then ask what about $100 in six years versus $200 in nine years, virtually everyone picks the $200. But this is the same choice seen at six years' greater distance.[58]

A rational discounting of a reward should follow a curve such as the solid line in Figure 6.1. People's typical responses follow something like the dashed line, which represents the decreasing perceived value of a

[56] Roy F. Baumeister and Todd Heatherton, "Self-Regulation Failure: An Overview", *Psychological Inquiry*, 7 (1996), 1–5; quoted in Ainslie, *Breakdown of Will*, 14.
[57] Ainslie, *Breakdown of Will*, 15.   [58] Ibid. 33.

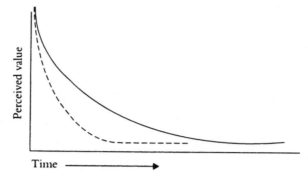

Figure 6.1. The rational amount of discounting of the value (vertical axis) of a reward as it is delayed in time (solid line) compared to the more precipitous discounting of the perceived value of a delayed reward (dashed line) that is typical of most human decision making.

reward offered in the future. In other words, the rational discount curve should be exponential, but the empirically established discount curve is hyperbolic. This overvaluation of an immediate reward means that as the time approaches to receive a reward, there is a similar hyperbolic curve representing the perceived value, as in Figure 6.2.

Ainslie provides several speculative accounts of why both humans and animals might have come to be biologically predisposed to discount the future in this way. When life is typically a struggle to survive (long enough to reproduce), it makes sense genetically to opt for the bird in

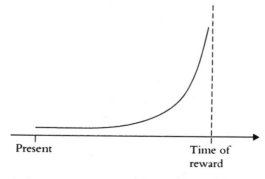

Figure 6.2. Hyperbolic increase in the perceived value of a reward as the time of its availability approaches.

the hand—one may well be dead before the two in the bushes can be caught.[59]

Ainslie's explanation for why people choose, for instance, to break a diet is that the reward of attaining one's preferred weight is a long time in the future, while the opportunity for the forbidden food is immediate. Even though the value of the ideal weight is intrinsically much higher than the pleasure of one pastry, the time factor reverses the priority. In Figure 6.3 the solid line represents the discounting of weight loss, and the dashed line the pastry. That is, despite its lower baseline value, the *immediate* prospect of the food causes its value to "spike" and rise above that of the long-term goal. So *akrasia* can be seen as a simple case of maximizing expected reward, given the way we *perceive* nearer rewards as greater than more distant ones.

Ainslie says that we can understand a great deal about the exercise of will if we think of ourselves as a temporal series of selves who have to bargain with one another. So, for example, this morning while one is hung over, the prospect of going off the wagon again this evening is relatively far off and vastly less appealing than it will be when the time comes. To prevent this evening's self from doing so, this morning's self might pour out all the liquor in the house. In general, knowing what the later self is likely to do, the current self can set up external constraints to foil the later.

Why is it the case that slipping off one's diet today makes it harder to stay on it tomorrow? Ainslie employs game theory to understand this familiar sort of phenomenon. Today's self may forgo the pastry if he has

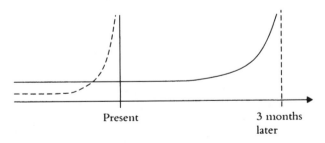

Present   3 months later

Figure 6.3. Precipitous rise in the perceived value of a lesser-valued but immediate reward (dashed line), compared to the perceived value of a higher-valued but delayed reward (solid line).

[59] Ainslie, *Breakdown of Will*, 45–7.

a reasonable expectation that it will result in weight loss in the long run. But if yesterday's self indulged, this weakens his reason to believe that future selves will collaborate and, consequently, the long-term reward seems less likely to materialize, even if he deprives himself today. So another strategy for increasing self-control is to recognize the effect of a single lapse as a self-fulfilling predictor of failure and to make the behavior in question a matter of principle. The longer one adheres to the principle, the greater stake one has in not violating it, and the greater confidence one has that the long-term reward will be forthcoming. Such principled action greatly increases motivation.

This is yet another example (as we suggested in sec. 3.4) of humans' capacity to "go meta". Consciousness of patterns in one's own motivational systems allows for higher-order evaluation of the patterns, running scenarios off-line, and setting up contingencies to cope with self-defeating patterns.

4.2 Weakness of Will as a Dynamical Process

Ainslie describes the fact of our tendency to opt for the bird in the hand, and evolutionary history can provide a likely historical account of how humans and other animals came to be this way. But what is happening neurobiologically when we make such choices? Again we turn to the work of Alicia Juarrero. In Chapter 2 we reported on her account of downward causation by means of context-sensitive constraints in complex dynamical systems, and in Chapter 4 on her use of this account to explain how both syntax and semantics are neurobiologically embodied. We also described (in Ch. 5) how her dynamical model explains how the meaning (semantic content) of an intention plays a causal role in making the intended behavior more likely to occur. In summary:

When I form a prior intention to A, my current, overall dynamics, including other cognitive, physiological, mechanical, conative, and similar attractors, reorganize in such a way as to stack the conditional probability of behavior A differently. The more dramatic the intention, the more radical the change in the landscape. Then by entraining motor control, the dynamics of a proximate intention sculpt an attractor that not only exhibits cognitive and evaluative traits; it now has "executive" or "pushing" ability as well. As a newly hewn valley straight ahead in my motor systems' conditional probability landscape, a proximate intention to

A "pushes" by dramatically increasing the likelihood that I will *A*, given present circumstances.[60]

Juarrero also addresses the question at issue here: how does it happen that our intentions are sometimes *not* enacted? The answer involves the shape of the agent's dynamical probability landscape. Self-organized systems' basins of attraction are intertwined. If the basin of attraction representing the intended act is shallow and there are other deeper attractors nearby, one of those other attractors may succeed in pulling behavior into its basin.

Juarrero's account also addresses Ainslie's recognition that falling off a diet today makes it less likely that one will stay on it tomorrow. The belief that one will succeed or fail is one of the factors that re-contours one's dynamical landscape.[61]

Self-organized systems tend to have shallower topographies at the beginning but to lock in features over time, creating deeper attractors and higher separatrices. This explains the fact that people's character becomes more set with age. An old dog learning a new trick requires a catastrophic transformation of neural dynamics.[62]

5 Reflections on Free Will

Our purpose in this chapter has been to defend the claim (against dualists and reductive materialists alike) that traditional ascriptions of moral responsibility are compatible with a physicalist account of human nature. Our argument has presupposed satisfactory answers (in Chs. 4 and 5 respectively) to two significant charges. One, derived from Brentano's distinction between the mental and the physical *on the basis of* the mind's essential intentionality, is that a *physical* organism by definition cannot use language meaningfully. The other, based on a Kantian opposition between reason and causation, is the objection that a physical being cannot act for a reason.

We structured the present chapter by means of MacIntyre's account of morally responsible action. We listed the elements taken, on his account, to comprise moral responsibility, and then described bit by bit the increasing abilities of animals, children, and adults to perform these cognitive

---

[60] Alicia Juarrero, *Dynamics in Action: Intentional Behavior as a Complex System* (Cambridge, Mass.: MIT Press, 1999), 208.

[61] Ibid. 207–8.   [62] Ibid. 232–3.

operations. We then sketched some of the empirical results and some theoretical models that help to explain why we sometimes do and sometimes do not manage to act on the basis of these evaluations.

Some readers will charge that we have neglected one of the most important conditions for moral responsibility: namely, free will. We noted (in the Introduction) that the most significant reason for wanting free will is to preserve traditional notions of moral responsibility and associated practices of social rewards and punishment. So it would be possible to end our book with the claim that, having made adequate sense of moral responsibility, we have shown arguments for free will to be beside the point.

Nonetheless, we believe that much of what we have written so far has implications for various aspects of the problem of free will. In the next chapter, then, we employ some of the work done in earlier chapters to take a fresh and perhaps clearer look at human action, in light of which at least some aspects of the tired old problem may become more tractable, if not disappear altogether.

7

Neurobiological Reductionism and Free Will

1 Prospect

There are two broad issues in considering free will, which we shall distinguish "prepositionally": there is freedom *from* (a wide variety of real or imagined) constraints, but also freedom *for* or *to*. The latter is variously described: to pursue the good, to act for reasons, for development of one's character, to pursue increasingly sophisticated understanding of the good.[1] We would add to this the capacity to *inhibit* one's propensities for action. These capacities closely match the cognitive capacities we listed in the previous chapter as prerequisites for morally responsible action. This should not be surprising, given the close connections between the problems of free will and moral responsibility.

Current literature on the free–will problem focuses largely on freedom *from*; that is, the major worry is (some form of) determinism. In this chapter we hope to do two things. One is to show that the preceding chapters have provided resources for dispelling the worry about one form of determinism. Then we raise questions about other aspects of the free–will problem as it is ordinarily formulated.

In section 2 of this chapter we shall report briefly on the status of the current philosophical debate regarding free will, and note other authors' judgments to the effect that it has reached a stalemate. We diagnose the stalemate as arising in large part from a narrow focus on the issue of determinism versus indeterminism.

[1] Cf. Alasdair MacIntyre, *After Virtue: A Study in Moral Theory*, 2nd edn. (Notre Dame, Ind.: University of Notre Dame Press, 1984), 219: "The virtues therefore are to be understood as those dispositions which will...furnish us with increasing self-knowledge and increasing knowledge of the good."

In section 3 we argue that the most pressing issue, instead, is reductionism: do agents in fact exercise downward control over their constituent parts (i.e., is reductionism false?)? Determinism/indeterminism at the neurobiological level is irrelevant, on our account, because downward causation amounts to selection among or constraint of lower-level causal processes, regardless of whether those lower-level possibilities are generated deterministically or randomly. In the next section we examine one of the most prominent accounts of free will, that of Robert Kane the "libertarian", and note the extent to which his position conforms to reductionist assumptions.[2] In section 5 we employ arguments regarding the nonlinearity of causation in complex systems and the teleological elements of human and animal behavior to question certain formulations of the free-will problem. In section 6 we examine Daniel Dennett's "compatibilist" position and conclude that, due to his reductionist approach, he is only able to argue for pseudo-responsibility and pseudo-free will.

In section 7 we briefly revisit the determinist issue, claiming to have defused the issue of neurobiological determinism and to have called into question the cogency of more general determinist theses.

In section 8 we raise the question of whether the moral reasoner we described in Chapter 6 (and for whose appearance the previous chapters laid groundwork) in fact meets the most important (and realistic) criteria for a person's possessing free will. We shall suggest that free will be seen as a holistic capacity of mature, self-reflective human organisms acting within a suitable social context.

2   The Stalled Debate

There is no such thing as *the* free-will problem. Over the centuries, philosophers and theologians have debated a number of problems that share a family resemblance. Ancient Greek dramatists explored the role of fate. In the early Christian era two problems arose. First, if God had predestined some humans to be saved (and by implication the others to be lost), as Augustine taught, is this reconcilable with anyone's freely choosing to

---

[2] This is an account of Kane's position in his very influential book *The Significance of Free Will* (Oxford: Oxford University Press, 1996). We are pleased that in his later writings he has endorsed conclusions very much closer to our own.

obey the will of God? The second problem (still hotly debated) is whether human freedom is reconcilable with divine foreknowledge. What these three have in common is that they are in one way or another opposing *some* concept of human freedom to *some* concept of determinism.

The major difficulty in addressing the contemporary free-will problem is the fact that the very meaning of "free will" is contested. In fact, even the preceding statement is contested: philosophers of the ordinary-language variety claim that we know quite well enough what we mean when we say that someone did something freely. It means that one was able to act as one chose, and was not, for instance, compelled to do it by having a gun to one's head.

For other philosophers, the question is not merely whether one is able to act as one chooses, but whether one is able to *choose* freely. But if all events are determined by prior causes, then must not human choices themselves be determined by prior causes? Thus, current philosophical literature is structured by the compatibilist–incompatibilist distinction: free will either is or is not compatible with determinism. The concept of determinism at play in current debates is often a general thesis such as the claim that every event or state of affairs must have a cause. There are two questions, then: Is the causal determinist thesis true? And if so, Is free will possible?

2.1 *Interminable Arguments*

Galen Strawson, in his article on free will in the new *Routledge Encyclopedia of Philosophy*, sees little chance of progress in settling this issue: "The principal positions in the traditional metaphysical debate are clear. No radically new option is likely to emerge after millennia of debate."[3] Similarly, Louis Pojman concludes a particularly lucid overview of the problem of determinism and free will with a confession of ignorance: "I do not know the answer to this enigma... [a] paradox which has, since the dawn of reflective thought, perplexed the very best minds."[4]

Strawson describes a cycle in free will/determinist debates. The motor that drives the cycle is the issue of moral responsibility: there are powerful arguments that seem to show that we cannot be morally responsible in

[3] Galen Strawson, "Free Will", in Edward Craig (ed.), *Routledge Encyclopedia of Philosophy* (London and New York: Routledge, 1998), iii. 743–53, at p. 749.

[4] Louis Pojman, "Freedom and Determinism: A Contemporary Discussion", *Zygon*, 22/4 (1987), 397–417, at p. 416.

the ultimate way we suppose, and these clash with powerful psychological reasons to believe that we *are* morally responsible. His account begins with the position most often in our day called *compatibilism*. Free will is taken to be compatible with determinism because in ordinary parlance, "free will" means being free from various forms of coercion or restraint.

However, the determinist objects that if all events are determined, then the distinction between actions for which one is and is not responsible (as in legal settings) must be invalid. An incompatibilist notion of free will is essential to make sense of the idea that we are genuinely morally responsible.

This step in the argument triggers what Strawson calls the pessimists' objection, the argument that *lack* of determinism cannot contribute to moral responsibility either. The pessimists therefore conclude that free will is not possible in the strong sense required for moral responsibility. And if this ultimate sort of responsibility is not possible, then punishment or reward can never be just.

Now, says Strawson:

the argument may cycle back to compatibilism. Pointing out that "ultimate" moral responsibility is obviously impossible, compatibilists may claim that we should rest content with the compatibilist account of things—since it is the best we can do. But this claim reactivates the incompatibilist objection, and the cycle continues.[5]

2.2 A Clutter of Terms

In speaking of terminology it is important to note first that while "the free-will problem" and "the problem of the freedom of the will" are used as conventional designations for the issues at hand, they are no longer descriptively appropriate. The terms arose in an earlier era in which the soul was taken to have a variety of faculties. Plato distinguished three: reason, spirit (*thumos*), and appetite. Some scholars credit Augustine with the invention of our traditional Western conception of the will.[6] It was necessary in his theology to explain how it could be the case that a person knows the right thing to do, yet not do it. Given the shift to physicalism, it would be better not to speak of "the will" at all and to describe the problem as the question of free agency or free choice. Nonetheless we

---

[5] Strawson, "Free Will", 749.
[6] Cf. Phillip Cary, *Augustine's Invention of the Inner Self* (Oxford: Oxford University Press, 2000).

shall use the standard terminology. In light of our emphasis on avoiding the Augustinian and Cartesian picture of interior actors, we would want to insist that the agent or chooser is the whole person, neither a self or soul nor some bit of neural tissue inside the brain.

As noted above, the current discussion focuses on the libertarian and compatibilist positions. However, these are not exact contraries, as can be indicated initially by the following chart. That is, compatibilists believe that determinism is true and that we have free will nonetheless. Hard determinists believe that determinism is true, that free will is incompatible with determinism, and so we do not have free will. Libertarians believe that free will is incompatible with determinism but reject (complete) determinism.

	Determinism	Indeterminism
Compatibilism	Compatibilists	– – – –
Incompatibilism	Hard determinists	Libertarians

The picture is complicated, though, by Strawson's pessimists, who believe that free will is also *in*compatible with *in*determinism. We therefore need two categories of incompatibilist theses: one regarding determinism and one regarding indeterminism. Let us designate these as incompatibilism–d and incompatibilism–i. So the chart of possible positions actually looks more like this.

	Determinism	Indeterminism
Compatibilism	Compatibilists	– – – –
Incompatibilism–d	Hard determinists	Libertarians
Incompatibilism–i	– – – –	Pessimists

There are a variety of related terms in the literature. The incompatibilist–libertarian's criterion for choosing freely is being able to have chosen differently (and thus acting differently) than one in fact did. Thus, another term for libertarian free will is "counterfactual free will". An older term in the literature is "liberty of indifference", meaning that one has motivational equilibrium. Older terms for compatibilist free will are "liberty of spontaneity" and "soft determinism", the latter being contrasted with "hard determinism".

We suspect that the reason for the stalemate in free-will debates is the focus on the issue of determinism versus indeterminism. In the next section we consider one form of determinism, neurobiological determinism, and argue that setting up the problem in this way is misguided, in that the real issue here is causal reductionism. In section 7 we remind the reader of our worries about the cogency and/or truth of more general determinist theses.

3   Defining the Determinist Threat

One problem with the compatibilist–libertarian debate is that the concept of determinism itself is too vague to be useful. One has to be more precise and ask what it is that is taken to determine human choices. We have set aside the ancient concept of fate, as well as the theological issues. In B. F. Skinner's day, social determinism was a pressing issue.[7] We have argued that dynamical systems exhibit a degree of autonomy from their environments. Juarrero says: "Because all self-organizing systems select the stimuli to which they respond, behavior constrained top-down is to that extent increasingly autonomous of forceful impacts from the environment. Self-organized systems act from their own point of view."[8]

In our own day the threat of biological determinism—genetic or neuro-biological—has displaced environmental determinism. Genetic determinism can be set aside for two reasons. First, instances of human behavior that are in any way candidates for free choice (unlike height, for instance) are never perfectly correlated with genes. That is, identical twins show similarities in political attitudes, temperament, sexual orientation, and so forth, but the imperfect correlation means that genes are only part of the story. In fact, same genes plus same environment (i.e., for identical twins raised together) do not produce perfect correlations. A second line of reasoning is based on the total quantity of information contained in the genome versus the total amount of information that would be needed to determine the synaptic connections in any particular individual's brain. The genes fall short of this capacity by a factor of ten billion.[9]

---

[7] However, reductionists in sociology and psychology regularly translated environmental determinism into neurobiological determinism by arguing that the environment cannot affect the person unless the person is aware of it, and so it is the neural representation of the environment that is actually the causal player in the person's behavior—bottom-up, after all.

[8] Alicia Juarrero, *Dynamics in Action: Intentional Behavior as a Complex System* (Cambridge, Mass.: MIT Press, 1999), 249.

[9] There are known to be about 30,000 genes in the human genome. The usual estimate for the number of neurons in the human brain is 100 billion. Although the number of synapses per neuron

3.1 Defusing the Threat of Neurobiological Determinism

In contrast to genetic determinism, we have taken the threat of neuro-biological determinism to be real and highly significant. However, this more specific focus actually misses the point in a subtle way. The issue is not whether the laws of neurobiology are themselves deterministic, but whether neurobiological *reductionism* is true. If we have made our case for the intelligibility of downward causation and its prevalence in shaping and reshaping the neural system, then the question of whether or not the laws of neurobiology are deterministic is actually not particularly relevant to the issue of free will. On our account of downward causation via selection or constraint, it makes no difference whether the laws of the bottom level are deterministic or not; higher-level selective processes can operate equally well on a range of possibilities that are produced (at the lower level) by either random *or deterministic* processes.

In contrast to the atomist–reductionist assumption of the modern world view, we have sketched a view of reality that recognizes the emergence, over the course of cosmic history, of new and more complex entities, *many of which possess new causal capacities.* (This is the rejection of atomist reductionism; see Ch. 2, secs. 1.2 and 1.3.) Some of these new capacities produce regular results, and thus their causal roles in the world can be modeled by deterministic laws. For example, the Hodgkin–Huxley laws that describe the transmission of nerve impulses are strict (deterministic) laws. If we give up the presupposition that the behavior of all higher-level entities must be deterministic, and simply look, we see that there are also complex systems (e.g., organisms) that depend on (largely determinate) lower-level systems but do not behave in regular (deterministic) ways—as we shall elaborate in the following subsection.

The widely accepted conclusion that the lowest level of the hierarchy of complex systems (the quantum level) is genuinely indeterministic should long ago have laid to rest the assumption of the determinism of higher levels based on the notion of (deterministic) bottom–up causation. There are a few cases in which the *indeterminism* of the quantum level works its way up to the macroscopic level. One example is when a single quantum

varies throughout the brain, a reasonable but rather conservative number per neuron would be 1,000. See E. R. Kandel, J. H. Schwartz, and T. M. Jessell, *Principles of Neural Science*, 3rd edn. (Norwalk, Conn.: Appleton & Lange, 1991), 121.

event is sufficient to account for a genetic mutation.[10] But in most cases, the indeterminacy at the bottom gives rise instead to deterministic systems at the next higher level. If we have to look to see whether and where indeterminacy works its way up the hierarchy, should we not also have to look to see whether and where determinism works its way up to higher levels?

As we pointed out above (Ch. 2, sec. 1.3.2), it may in fact be the case that the first and most basic example of downward causation is the phenomenon of decoherence in quantum physics; that is, the effect of interaction or measurement on an otherwise indeterminate state. So the basic "causal structure" of the universe, all the way from the bottom to the top may be a dynamic interplay of downward causation from large webs of structures that have evolved over time with bottom–up constraints provided by the original lower-level constituents. Science has attempted and often succeeded in capturing the laws governing lower levels by sealing off simple systems from interactions with their environments. But this may in fact have resulted in a false conception of the very nature of reality.

3.2 The Irrelevance of Indeterminism in Animal Behavior

The way biology works on a number of levels is by means of luxuriant overproduction of a range of possibilities followed by selection among the variants on the basis of criteria pertinent to a higher level of organization. This was, of course, first recognized as the mechanism of the evolutionary process. Mutations (at the genetic level) and cross-breeding (at the organismic level) produce a varied population of offspring. Factors at the ecological level do the selecting. Another example is the immune system, which works by producing a vast number of antibodies, but only the ones that work are produced in great numbers. Neural connections are

---

[10] See Robert J. Russell, "Special Providence and Genetic Mutation: A New Defense of Theistic Evolution", in idem, William R. Stoeger, and Francisco J. Ayala (eds.), Evolutionary and Molecular Biology: Scientific Perspectives on Divine Action (Vatican City State and Berkeley: Vatican Observatory and Center for Theology and the Natural Sciences, 1998), 191–224. Other examples are superconductivity and superfluidity, which are essentially quantum effects at the macro-level, and various devices (such as the human eye) that register a quantum-level event (e.g., the reception of a single photon) and thereby amplify its effects. See George F. R. Ellis, "Quantum Theory and the Macroscopic World," in Robert J. Russell et al. (eds.), Quantum Mechanics: Scientific Perspectives on Divine Action (Vatican City State and Berkeley: Vatican Observatory and Center for Theology and the Natural Sciences, 2001), 259–91, at pp. 260–1.

overproduced in infancy and selectively maintained or strengthened only as they are used.

There are two parts to causal stories of this sort: (1) how the variants are produced (this was a problem plaguing evolutionary theory until the development of genetics), and (2) the basis upon which and the means by which the selection takes place. A fairly insignificant part of the story is whether processes that produce the variants are deterministic or indeterministic. For example, genetic mutation occurs in some cases due to factors at the quantum level (indeterministically) and in others due to macro-level (deterministic) processes.

Animal behavior needs to be understood on the same model. The picture we are prone to have in mind is an organism whose "default position" is inactivity. When it acts, the question arises as to what caused it to act and whether the action was "up to it" or "not up to it"—that is, was the behavior stimulated by something in the environment or by something internal to the organism. If the latter, then we want to know, could it have done otherwise?

A more accurate picture is of an organism that is constantly active (to some degree or other). Thus, the question is not what initiated any part of the behavior, but rather, what the factors are that modify ongoing behavior. As we pointed out (in Ch. 3, sec. 2.1.2), the action of even very simple organisms is the result of the emission of a variety of behavioral components that are either continued or altered on the basis of feedback from the environment and evaluation in relation to the organism's goals.

For example, the flying movements of a fruit fly can best be modeled by sampling from a probability matrix. At a particular moment in behavior, the ongoing context has activated a matrix of behavioral probabilities. The highest probability behavior is apt to be expressed, but a lower probability might also occur, particularly if the matrix of probabilities is rather flat. The matrix is influenced by current appetites, drives, avoidances, and previous learning, but also by feedback from immediate past behavior. The behavior that is expressed next is the outcome of sampling from this matrix. Once a behavior is sampled and tried out (e.g., turning 20 degrees left), the outcome is immediately evaluated, and the probability matrix modified (or not). Thus, behavior is continuously sampled, tried, evaluated, and modified, based on probabilities that are themselves constantly modified by experience and learning.

We suggested above (Ch. 2, sec. 5.4) that there are two possible meanings for "probability" is in this account. The major options would be to interpret them in terms either of relative frequency or of "propensities". The relative frequency option is inapplicable because an organism is never in exactly the same situation (internal states, environmental conditions, recent history of behavior) more than once. A propensity is defined as "an irregular or non-necessitating causal disposition of an object or system to produce some result or effect ... usually conceived of as essentially probabilistic in nature".[11] Karl Popper regarded the existence of propensities as a metaphysical hypothesis needed to interpret probability claims about single cases.[12] If we give up on the notion that determinism and indeterminism are exhaustive categories, then perhaps strict *indeterminism* applies only at the quantum level (and in cases where macro–systems amplify quantum events); *determinism* applies largely to the realm of mechanical processes, and *propensity,* a genuinely distinct option, applies to much of organismic behavior. Juarrero interprets propensities in terms of dynamical attractors. She describes infants as coming into the world with a basic set of inherited propensities embodied in the dynamics of their biology, "the conditional probability distribution of the context-sensitive constraints that give the organism its identity".[13] But this landscape of attractors constantly changes in response to the infant's interaction with the environment.

The important point here, for present purposes, is that when top-down evaluation of emitted behaviors is the primary determinant of the larger course of the organism's activity, then it matters not whether the (bottom-up) production of behavioral variants is deterministic, indeterministic, or "probabilistic". Significant units of action are the "resultant" of three factors: (1) spontaneous emission of behavioral variants, (2) feedback, and (3) criteria for evaluation, both those built in by biology and those reshaped by action in the world. To put this in the language of structuring and triggering causes, the built-in goals are structuring causes; failure of an action to achieve a goal (a mismatch signal in MacKay's terms) triggers the emission of another behavioral possibility. In all but the most rudimentary organisms, the success or failure of an action changes the probability

[11] David Sapire, "Propensity", in Robert Audi (ed.), *The Cambridge Dictionary of Philosophy* (Cambridge: Cambridge University Press, 1995), 657.

[12] Karl R. Popper, *A World of Propensities* (Bristol: Thoemmes, 1990).

[13] Juarrero, *Dynamics in Action,* 176.

matrix according to which future behaviors will be emitted. This is a *downward* effect, from the system that is the whole organism acting in its environment, to the components of the nervous system that channel behavioral options.

If biological reductionism is false, and if most organisms are (to a degree) the causes of their own actions, and thereby top-down shapers of their own neural processes and structures, does this amount to free will? It would if "free will" meant nothing other than "not biologically determined". So we make the modest claim to have defused one possible element in the determinist's argument against free will. We turn now to ask whether our account of downward causation in organisms' behavior might shed light on any of the other debates in the current free-will literature.

4 Libertarian Reductionism

In this section we shall criticize the attempt to work indeterminism into an account of free will as being a direct result of the assumption of neurobiological reductionism. In section 4.1 we note the reductionist assumptions in Robert Kane's libertarian theory based on quantum indeterminacy. Our critique, however, will highlight valuable contributions, especially his claim that the essential meaning of free will is an agent's having *responsibility for his or her action*.

4.1 Robert Kane: Indeterminism in the Cartesian Theater

From Augustine through Descartes and beyond, the soul was understood to have a variety of faculties, one of which was the will. For an act to be free, it must be willed by the agent *and* the act of willing itself must not have a prior cause. Cartesian materialists substitute for a free *inward* act of will an undetermined event *in* the brain. Given the wide acceptance of indeterministic interpretations of quantum mechanics, an important move in recent free-will literature has been to attempt to use a quantum event to break the chain of causes in which the agent is assumed otherwise to be bound.

We are, in general, suspicious of such moves. First, it is a category mistake to identify a free choice with an indeterministic brain event. This is, in Donald MacKay's terms, an illegitimate mixture of the I story with the brain story. It is the agent as a whole to whom the ascription of freedom applies.[14] Second, in line with our argument throughout this volume, we object to the reductionist assumption that the person's behavior must be the product of the working of his or her micro-level parts. Finally, as we argue in this chapter, the recognition of top-down causation makes lower-level determinism and indeterminism (largely) irrelevant.

Despite these objections, much can be learned, we believe, from examining the most sophisticated and well-respected attempt to secure free will via quantum indeterminacy. We shall argue that Kane had in fact already supplied most of the ingredients necessary for a viable account of free will in his theory published in 1996.

Kane places his account squarely in the libertarian camp. He defines free will as the power of agents to be the ultimate creators or originators of their own ends and purposes.[15] That is, if causal chains of actions are traced back to their sources, they must come to an end in the willings of the agents. If those willings are caused by something else—heredity, environment, God—then the ultimacy would not lie with the agent.

Kane takes it for granted that making room for free will, so understood, depends on there being occasions when the atoms "swerve", and this must take place in the brain.[16] Desires are among the inputs to practical reasoning; the outputs of will are choices, decision, intentions. There must be an indeterminate step somewhere between input and output, and this step Kane takes to be quantum-indeterminate events in the brain. The centerpiece of his work is to show how quantum events can be worked into an account of the freedom of the agent (Kane is very critical of the mistake of simply equating indeterminacy with free will).

Despite our diametric opposition to the centerpiece of Kane's work, we find ourselves in agreement with much of what he says. The most helpful elements of Kane's writings, if pulled into a different constellation, provide most of what is needed for an account of free will in terms of downward causation. The fact that Kane does *not* make this further step, this *Gestalt* switch, illustrates the extent to which reductionism retains its grip on the imaginations of even the most sophisticated thinkers in the field. Here are some of the major elements in Kane's writings that we endorse.

---

[14] See Ch. 1, sec. 3.1 above.   [15] Kane, *Significance of Free Will*, 4.   [16] Ibid. 17.

1. Kane, along with many others, recognizes that a crucial issue in the consideration of free will is that of character development. In many cases, what is wanted in the way of free will is an account of action flowing from the actor's character and deepest motives. But if one's character is entirely determined by something or someone other than the agent, then, Kane says, one may have some freedom of action but not freedom of the will.[17] So an important question is how one can become responsible for one's own character development. Kane speaks helpfully here of the necessity of there being, at points in the actor's development, "self-forming actions".

2. Kane, along with Harry Frankfurt, recognizes the importance of *levels* of desires, motives, goals. A particular choice *is* the agent's choice if the agent endorses it as compatible with her larger (higher) motivational system. This motivational system Kane calls the "self-network".[18] In the language developed in our Chapter 5, we would say that a particular neural event constitutes a choice (a mental event) only within the broader context of prior goals, deliberation, and remembered outcomes of action. In addition, following Kane, the choice is the agent's choice (rather than a mental event that simply happens to her) when it fits into the context of her self-network.

3. The argument between libertarians and compatibilists has largely focused on the question of whether the ability to have done otherwise is an essential condition for free will. Kane notes that a second criterion fueling incompatibilist intuitions is what he calls the ultimate responsibility criterion.

The idea is this: to be ultimately responsible for an action, an agent must be responsible for anything that is a sufficient reason (condition, cause, or motive) for the occurrence of the action. If, for example, a choice issues from, and can be sufficiently explained by, an agent's character and motives (together with background conditions), then to be *ultimately* responsible for the choice, the agent must be at least in part responsible, by virtue of choices or actions voluntarily performed in the past, for having the character and motives he or she now has.[19]

Kane argues that the ultimate responsibility criterion, rather than the alternative possibilities criterion, is the essential one. We agree that responsibility

---

[17] Robert Kane, "Some Neglected Pathways in the Free Will Labyrinth", in *idem* (ed.), *The Oxford Handbook of Free Will* (Oxford: Oxford University Press, 2002), 406–37, at p. 414.
[18] Ibid. 423–4.   [19] Ibid. 407.

is conceptually the primary criterion for free will. We shall take issue only with Kane's use of "ultimate responsibility". We shall argue instead that an agent is never the sole cause of her own actions. Thus, the appropriate term is something like "primary responsibility". We come back to this in section 4.4.

Kane takes his account to be dependent upon further developments in brain science. The scenario that he hopes will be made more plausible by future research is this: when an agent faces a choice and there are conflicting motives on both sides, this puts the brain into a chaotic state—or in other terms, a state far from thermodynamic equilibrium—which in turn makes its processes (more) sensitive to quantum indeterminacies. Thus, the chaotic state serves as a possible route for the amplification of an indeterminate event at the quantum level.

The problem with such an account so far, as Galen Strawson has pointed out, is that an indeterminate event in the middle of a chain leading from desires to actions would seem to make it arbitrary rather than free. Kane's intention, then, is to show how an act whose causal pedigree contains an indeterminate event can still be (partially) a result of the actor's motives and character. Kane argues that while a quantum event may indeed be arbitrary, the choice that it triggers and the person's subsequent acting upon it are not arbitrary because it is in accord with *one of* the agent's prior motivational sets.[20] This, he argues, fulfills the widely accepted condition that an agent's reasons must play a role in the causal etiology of the action.[21]

4.2 Our Critique

The decision, as Kane describes it, is in accordance with (one of) the agent's motives, but, we argue, there needs to be more in order for the choice to be *hers*; it has to be *brought about by* her motives. Granted, the agent's motives in Kane's account play an *indirect* causal role: it is the conflict in motives that produces the chaotic state such that a macro-level transition can be caused by a quantum event.[22]

---

[20] Kane, *Significance of Free Will*, 130.   [21] Ibid. 136.

[22] Motivation is an abstract concept covering a variety of neurobiological functions, mostly related to the activity of limbic brain systems. "These concepts include homeostasis, setpoints and settling points, intervening variables, hydraulic drives, drive reduction, appetitive and consummatory behavior, opponent processes, hedonic reactions, incentive motivation, drive centers, dedicated drive neurons (and

We might say that there is in Kane's account a downward *interpreta-tion* of the quantum event in terms of the higher-level system of drives and goals, but not downward *causation* of the patterns of micro-level events by those higher-level goals. A second problem is that the oppor-tunity for self-forming actions on Kane's account appears only in cases where the agent is faced with conflicting motives. We address this in section 4.3 below.

Our point here is not to pursue a critique of Kane's work for its own sake, but rather to illustrate the grip of reductionist thinking even in what is perhaps the most brilliant and judicious theorizing to be found in the libertarian camp. However, there is an interesting progression away from reductionism in Kane's thought. In *The Significance of Free Will* (1996) he quotes almost in passing a line from Gordon Globus that describes top-down causation in the brain. This is in the context of spelling out the reasons for viewing the brain as involved in chaotic processes. He speaks of the influence of the whole net of neurons affecting each individual node and of each node in turn affecting the whole.[23] There seems to be no further development in this direction in "Some Neglected Pathways" (2002). We suspect that despite publication in the same year, Kane's "Free Will: New Directions" was actually written later. Here, in response to the work of Timothy O'Connor, he writes:

Indeed, I also believe that emergence of a certain kind (now recognized in self-organizing systems) is necessary for free will, even of the causal indeterminist kind that I defend. Once the brain reaches a certain level of complexity, so that there can be conflicts in the will of the kind required for [self-forming actions], the larger motivational system of the brain stirs up chaos and indeterminacy in a part of itself which is the realization of a specific deliberation. In other words, the whole motivational system realized as a comprehensive "self-network" in the brain has the capacity to influence specific parts of itself (processes within it) in novel ways once a certain level of complexity of the whole is attained. This is a kind of emergence of new *capacities* and indeed even a kind of "downwards causation" (novel causal influences of an emergent whole on its parts) such as are

drive neuropeptides and receptors), neural hierarchies, and new concepts from affective neuroscience such as allostasis, cognitive incentives, and reward 'liking' versus 'wanting'." See K. C. Berridge, "Motivation Concepts in Behavioral Neuroscience", *Physiology & Behavior*, 81/2 (2004), 179–209.

[23] Kane, *Significance of Free Will*, 130; referring to Gordon Globus, "Kane on Incompatibilism: An Exercise in Neurophilosophy", unpublished paper, 1995.

now recognized in a number of scientific contexts involving self-organizing and ecological systems.[24]

Our suggestion, then, is that recognition of the limitations of neurobiological reductionism and replacement with a recognition of the role of downward causation in cognitive and brain processes would allow all of these other valuable pieces of Kane's work to fall into a set of new relations. Kane postulates that presentation of a choice between two courses of action, each one desirable in its own way, moves certain relevant brain states far from equilibrium and sets up possibilities for chaotic processes. Let us grant this for the sake of argument. However, we would describe the process as follows. Our emphasis has been on self-transcendence—that is, on making one's plans, goals, motives, drives the object of second-order reflection. Donald MacKay offers an intriguing analogy. He describes what happens when a video camera is focused on its own monitor screen. If "we swing the camera to look at its own screen we find it is generating a pseudo picture. And if we zoom in to try to get more detail the whole thing goes haywire."[25] This is, in fact, a chaotic state, and it helps in imagining how intensely focused self-evaluation might result in radical changes in brain activity.

Kane suggests that in this chaotic state the system as a whole is moved in one of two directions by a random event that "breaks the tie" by definitively activating the neural network realizing one or the other of the agent's motivational sets. We suggest instead that the focusing on the problem moves the network far from equilibrium. (This may or may not involve a chaotic system and may or may not involve a definitive role for single quantum events.) In our scenario, the choice is determined not by the bottom-up action of one quantum event, but rather by selection of one of the possible options by means of a higher-order supervisory system.[26]

Kane emphasizes that self-forming choices are "value experiments", whose justification lies in the future.[27] In parallel, we emphasize that

---

[24] Robert Kane, "Free Will: New Directions for an Ancient Problem", in *idem* (ed.), *Free Will* (Oxford: Blackwell, 2002), 222–46, at pp. 241–2.

[25] Donald M. MacKay, *Behind the Eye*, The Gifford Lectures, ed. Valerie MacKay (Oxford: Blackwell, 1991), 10.

[26] Note that this is no homunculus in the brain. Rather, it is the whole person, in her environment, taking into account a broader range of factors than are involved in the lower-order system.

[27] Kane, "Some Neglected Pathways", 425.

such choices, for agents with sophisticated enough cognitive processes, result from running behavioral scenarios off-line and evaluating likely consequences in terms of the agent's previous experiences, goals, values, and moral conceptions. This is followed by enactment in the field of operation, which will supply ongoing feedback, changing synaptic weighting so as to enhance or inhibit the likelihood of the agent acting similarly in the future. In cases involving significant choices, this is the neural–cognitive–behavioral process of character formation.

Our picture is essentially different from Kane's in this regard: For Kane, an event at the bottom of the hierarchy of complex systems gets amplified by brain processes and moves the agent to follow one of the courses of action. Because it is in the context of the agent's prior deliberation, it is interpreted by the agent as *her* choosing that course of action. So long as it is consistent with or a reasonable extension of her self-network, "she will endorse that as *her* resolution of the conflict in her will, voluntarily and intentionally, not by accident or mistake."[28]

We object that it is still, on this account, the quantum event that is the primary cause of the agent's action, even though it may be endorsed as consistent with motives instantiated by higher-level (broader) neural networks. On our account, one of a variety of (lower-level) neural pathways for future action is selected on the basis of a higher-level supervisory system whose comparator recognizes a match with its goals and labels it "good to enact" rather than "bad to enact". So the difference is Kane's bottom–up causation, bit by bit, by means of random events having an effect over time on the agent's system of goals, versus our top–down selection of lower-level processes on the basis of goals shaped by previous actions in the world—especially by action within the social world, with the external scaffolding it provides in the way of symbolic representation, abstract concepts, and, especially, moral concepts.

4.3 The Ubiquity of Self-Forming Actions

We mentioned above that a defect in Kane's account is the restriction of self-forming actions to cases in which one faces a moral dilemma. We believe this is wrong, for two reasons. First, all complex organisms are constantly re-forming themselves. Almost every action has at least

---

[28] Ibid. 421.

minor effects on the organism's neural structures. This is the basis for the formation of habits—the "mental butlers" that relieve us of the requirement for conscious decisions about routine activities. Action results in feedback from the environment that promotes the development of somatic markers, which subtly guide future behavior. In a sense, these are all "self-forming actions", but we shall follow Kane (and Dennett—sec. 6) in retaining this term for actions that matter *morally*.

Kane's account of the narrow range of self-forming actions coheres with the narrow scope of much of modern ethical theory. James McClendon notes that many twentieth-century ethicists have restricted the scope of morality to decision making. The perfect expression is found in the claim of existentialist Jean–Paul Sartre that "true morality consists not in deciding this or that, but purely and merely in deciding. Decide, and you have acted morally, while not to decide is—bad faith."[29] McClendon traces this "decisionism" to a pervasive interiorization in Western self-understanding, particularly in Christian spirituality, that goes back to Augustine. Originally "decide" and its Latin cognate meant "to cut off"—to end a battle or a lawsuit by a decisive victory for one side. The emphasis on inwardness led to the application of the term to an interior "battle" in which the mind wavers until one "side" overcomes the other.[30] Unquestionably, McClendon says, "such inner struggle is a recurrent feature of human life. But in modern Christianity, the new exaltation of the will, together with the interiorization of the Christian life, made it seem that such struggles are not part but the whole of morality."[31] Despite its origin in Christian thought, decisionism was the core of modern ethics from the utilitarians and Kant to John Rawls.

More recently, under the influence of writers such as Alasdair MacIntyre, the focus of ethics has shifted to the development of character, understood as a continuous project situated in the context of social narrative.[32] We followed MacIntyre in locating the capacity for morality in exercising one's ability to evaluate that which moves one to act in light of a concept of the good. Thus, it is not so much deciding which way to resolve a dilemma that forms moral character as the second-order reflection on and evaluation of one's propensities, emotions, reasons, goals. This sort

---

[29] James Wm. McClendon, Jr., *Ethics: Systematic Theology, Volume 1*, 1st edn. (Nashville: Abingdon Press, 1986), 56–7.
[30] Ibid. 58.   [31] Ibid.   [32] See esp. MacIntyre, *After Virtue*.

of reflection does not depend on an interior "battle"; it is more likely to occur as a result of social interaction. The development of moral character involves the development of the *habit* of such self-reflection. Consequently, the scope of moral action includes not only actions undertaken on the basis of conscious decisions (let alone agonizing decisions), but also the much more frequent actions undertaken automatically in light of moral evaluations made in the past. What matters most, McClendon claims, is not deliberate decisions, if any, but "unreckoned generosity... uncalculating love... 'aimless' faithfulness".[33]

Our second critique of Kane's account of self-forming actions is related to the first, and applies equally to MacIntyre's definition of moral responsibility. Both authors seem to be assuming a picture of human nature in which inactivity is our "default" condition and action begins as the result of some inner event. MacIntyre speaks in terms of "that which moves one to act"; Kane focuses on the quantum event that becomes magnified into a decision. We have emphasized throughout that organisms' "default" condition is constant activity. So interesting questions about human actions will be questions not (usually) about what triggered a particular act but rather about the criteria for evaluating a variety of branching possibilities for an ongoing series of actions—in dynamical terms, the factors reshaping the ontogenic landscape representing the possibilities of future actions. This is another route that leads to the conclusion that character formation must be (primarily) a matter of the long-term accumulation of evaluations of one's own criteria for evaluation of action. If we are always already active, like other organisms, then the moral challenge, as both the parent and the spiritual director know, is to develop the habit of stopping long enough to reflect on what we are doing and why.

4.4 Ultimate versus Primary Responsibility

Despite the fact that Kane terms his primary criterion for free will "ultimate responsibility", he recognizes that self-forming actions never totally re-create the person's character. Thus, as is recognized in legal settings, one's responsibility for an act undertaken in line with one's character is always only partial:

---

[33] McClendon, *Ethics*, 59.

I think what motivates the need for incompatibilism is an interest in … a control related to our being to some degree the ultimate creators or originators of our own purposes or ends and hence ultimate "arbiters" of our own wills.[34]

We agree that humans are never entirely responsible for their own characters. We come into the world with some degree of initial biological (genetic) predetermination. As with other organisms, we are always already active due to this innate biological machinery. We try out various actions and modify our behavioral tendencies based on feedback. The maturation process is that of slowly developing higher-order evaluative systems that nest and modulate the systems that control our biological processes, and having built into our nervous system maps of how the world works. This action–feedback process involves increasing susceptibility to social influences. However, the childhood task is not only social adaptation, but also the development of autonomy. In biological terms, this involves development of capacities for intentionally directed action. In social relations, an important step is the development of a theory of mind, which allows one to distinguish one's own perceptions and desires from those of others and to predict the likely mental lives of others.

As we emphasized in Chapter 6 and in the previous subsection, the most important step, which separates (older) children from animals, is development of the ability to evaluate one's own actions and, especially, one's *reasons* for action. This begins with evaluation in light of conformity to parents and peers, but ultimately in terms of reasons, goals, and values that can be expressed only via symbolic language.

Graphically, we might represent human development as a trajectory in a two-dimensional space. One axis is from total biological determinism to total biological flexibility; the other is from complete social determinism to total social autonomy. At birth we are neither determined by society nor autonomous; we have to develop the capacity for social control *before* we can begin to establish our autonomy. Also, given the fact that our bodies tend to fail in old age, there is often a return toward biological determinism as well as loss of autonomy. Thus, a typical trajectory might be represented by the solid line in Figure 7.1.

The dashed line represents what some philosophers would see as the ideal trajectory. However, we emphasize that this process does not *and should not*

---

[34] Kane, "Some Neglected Pathways", 432.

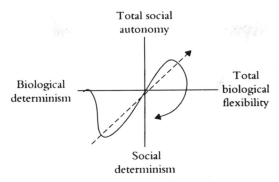

Figure 7.1. Trajectory of a human life (*solid line*) with respect to biological deter-minism–flexibility (horizontal axis) and social determinism–autonomy (vertical axis). The dashed line represents the idealized trajectory of some philosophers toward complete freedom from either biological or social determinism.

end with total flexibility and autonomy. Both biology and human culture have evolved to promote human flourishing. The ability to act contrary to both our biological nature and all social constraints can be predicted to lead (often enough) to disaster. Juarrero, noting that we are in part a product of "a complex dance" between our innate endowments and an already structured physical and social environment, says: "We are enmeshed in a fabric of time and space, which we unravel at our peril."[35]

For a somewhat whimsical depiction of the results of pursuing the goal of total autonomy, we return to our pacifist in Chapter 6. Let us return to the point at which he has been convinced by the teaching and example of the Jesuits to become a pacifist, but through an act of self-transcendence has come to suspect that his decision was determined by a need for social approval. The advocate of libertarian freedom might well raise the objection that surely something *caused* him to question the source of his pacifism, and if so, then again he is not free. To pursue this issue, *let us grant that there is a cause*, and let us further suppose that the causal factor is, in fact, his being given a book that convinces him of the ultimate importance of libertarian free will. Let us also suppose that this *causes* the emergence of a higher-level supervisory system that is *determined* to make freedom from biological and environmental determinism its highest priority. Detecting the influences of his community on the decision to become a pacifist, he immediately abandons his pacifism. But now he recognizes that he was caused to make this change by the book he was given, and so his highest-level supervisory system requires rejecting his rejection of pacifism. But acting contrarily to the authority of the book is equally to be influenced by the book, only in a negative way. So what next?

Kane, of course, also rejects such a notion of free will. So where does our disagreement lie, since his ultimate-responsibility criterion in fact requires only that the person have some responsibility for his own character-forming decisions? We quoted him above saying that the person "must have been responsible for choices or actions *voluntarily* performed in the past".[36] But "voluntarily" here means without proper cause, and thus the central point where Kane believes himself compelled to turn to indeterminism—in a linear chain of determined events, there must be an occasional chink. This brings us to our next topic: a critique of the linear picture of causation implicit in this demand.

5 Questioning the Regress Argument

Peter van Inwagen is credited with one of the sharpest arguments for incompatibilism. Stated briefly:

If determinism is true, then our acts are the consequences of the laws of nature and events in the remote past. But it is not up to us what went on before we were born; and neither is it up to us what the laws of nature are. Therefore, the consequences of these things (including our present acts) are not up to us.[37]

5.1 *The Nonlinearity of Human Responsibility*

Note both the linear model of causation presupposed in van Inwagen's argument as well as the dichotomous option: up to us or not up to us. Our Chapter 2 was devoted to an exploration of the many reasons for rejecting a linear model, especially one in which it is assumed that each event in the linear sequence is simply determined by the previous event along with a relevant law of nature, as in Figure 7.2.

---

[36] Kane, "Some Neglected Pathways", 407; italics added.
[37] Peter van Inwagen, *An Essay on Free Will* (Oxford: Clarendon Press, 1983), 16.

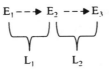

Figure 7.2. A linear model of causation in which each event (E₁, E₂...) is determined by a prior event along with a relevant law of nature (L₁, L₂...).

We first noted the role of boundary conditions in co-determining the effect of a given event. Pictorially this is easiest to represent by incorporating Fred Dretske's structuring causes into the picture. Many events occur because of the intersection of two streams of causal trajectories, as in Figure 7.3. The structuring causes that create conditions in organisms such that a given triggering cause is able to produce a given effect are in the first instance biological.

The next step in the defeat of simple linear models of causation is the recognition of the role of feedback. When an organism is triggered to act, its actions have consequences in the environment. Positive and negative consequences are fed back to the organism, often resulting in restructuring the organism itself. At this point we need to refer (one last time!) to Donald MacKay's diagram involving an organizing system, effectors, receptors, and a comparator (Fig. 2.3). Initially O is structured largely by genetics, with limited capacities to respond to triggering causes from the environment. Again, it does not matter whether the variety of responses is hard-wired or produced in some indeterministic or probabilistic manner. What is important is that positive or negative results in the field of operation result in the restructuring of O. At this level of complexity we have an organism restructured by experience, so it still seems appropriate to say that what it does is "*not* up to it", even if its responses were emitted by means of genuinely indeterministic processes—again we see the irrelevance of determinism versus indeterminism.

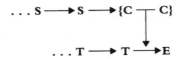

Figure 7.3. A series of structuring causes leading up to a condition such that a triggering cause is able to cause an effect.

We then considered systems capable of evaluation and modification of their own goals as a result of their actions. This is the beginning of a self-modifying system. From this point on, we have a system whose activity is in some minimal sense "up to it".

We added, then, the capacity for higher-order self-evaluation, the capacity to run behavioral scenarios off-line so that behavioral propensities could be restructured by imagined positive or negative feedback, and, finally and most importantly, the ability to evaluate behavior and one's own propensities in light of abstract symbols—to subject one's behavior to reason.

This process is vastly too complex to represent diagrammatically. The important point is that it is not a linear process, since the feedback from the environment *and from the person's own higher-order evaluative processes* is constantly restructuring the structuring causes themselves. We have to imagine countless iterations of such causal loops, the consequence of which is that the structural causes are to a greater and greater extent the consequences of prior actions and *evaluations* of the organism.

If we recognize (along with Kane) that the dichotomy "up to us, not up to us" is entirely unrealistic, then the important issue is that a (fuzzy but real) boundary is crossed at some point, so that some decisions and actions are to be attributed more to the agent than to the triggering cause together with structuring causes put in place by biology and the environment. In everyday life, in moral discourse, and in legal practices, we in fact judge whether people have acquired the capacity for responsibility, and by that we mean not total responsibility but rather that they bear the *primary* responsibility for their actions and decisions. Dynamic systems act from their own point of view, but based on history.

5.2 *From Mechanism to Teleology*

A second problem with the image of ourselves as having our decisions determined by a long series of causes reaching back to the beginning of the universe is failure to recognize that properly equipped organisms are teleologically directed entities. The modern scientific revolution began with the rejection of Aristotelian categories, among which were teleological explanations of natural phenomena. Thus, we have been set up by several centuries of history to view mechanistic causes as utterly different from teleological causes (if in fact there be any of the latter at all). We have argued, in contrast, that proper design of mechanisms endows them with the capacity to act teleologically. We saw this even in simple devices such as thermostats. Their ability to pursue goals is not in contrast to their obedience to mechanical causes, but is enabled by it.

Thermostats are not particularly interesting here, because their goals are set by their designers; nor are the simplest organisms, whose goals are fixed by inheritance. The really interesting cases appear in conscious organisms, and especially in humans, whose imaginations and symbolic abilities allow them to imagine future scenarios, evaluate them, and shape their behavior accordingly. Language allows us to build up elaborate models of possible futures, which, along with finely modulated and flexible descriptions of motives, provide "final causes" for behavior.[38]

6 Daniel Dennett's Compatibilist Reductionism

Daniel Dennett's recent *Freedom Evolves* has drawn a great deal of attention, but reviews by philosophers have expressed deep disappointment with the book, dismissing it as just another version of compatibilism.[39] There are striking parallels between Dennett's book and our work in this volume (some not accidental, since we have made use of his earlier work in *Elbow Room*). In this section we shall first spell out the most significant parallels between our account and Dennett's, and then point out some of the ways in which Dennett encourages his critics' conclusions that what he offers in the way of free will is *not* worth wanting. We then attempt to sort out the underlying reasons for Dennett's book appearing to be so much like ours and yet, we shall claim, utterly different in essence. In the process, we hope further to muddy the libertarian–compatibilist waters.

6.1 Striking Parallels

There are structural parallels between Dennett's treatment and ours. Both begin with a story of increasing flexibility and use of information, leading

---

[38] Both Juarrero and Alwyn Scott favor reinstating all of Aristotle's four causes. Scott (in personal communication, 16 Aug. 2004) identifies triggering causes as efficient, structuring causes and boundary conditions as formal causes. Juarrero describes an attractor as a rudimentary precursor of a final cause (*Dynamics in Action*, 127).

[39] Daniel C. Dennett, *Freedom Evolves* (New York: Viking, 2003).

to degrees of self-direction in the animal world. Both emphasize the role of language in human affairs, accounting for the development of selfhood, self-transcendence, moral responsibility, and, finally, free will.

Dennett examines the development in living organisms of what he calls "evitability". Determinists are often, essentially, fatalists—concluding that whatever happens happens *inevitably*. Dennett examines ways in which organisms are equipped to evade outcomes that go against their interests by using information to guide the increasingly flexible behavioral repertoires one finds as one goes up the ladder of complexity. The result is organisms such as ourselves who are "virtuoso avoiders, preventers, interferers, forestallers" of happenings that do not serve their interests.[40]

Dennett emphasizes the critical role of language. It is language that makes hominids into persons (p. 173). Language, when installed in the human brain, creates the capacity for morality (p. 260). The shift from the amoral unfreedom of an infant to moral agency is gradual and involves environmental scaffolding and bootstrapping (p. 273). It is our practice of asking children about the reasons for their behavior that turns them into selves (p. 273). Engaging in this social practice allows us to develop the capacity for examining our own reasons (p. 249). We develop the capacity "for monitoring not just the results of [our] action, but of [our] prior evaluations and formation of intentions as well" (p. 248). While Dennett rejects Kane's turn to indeterminism to secure free will, he does make use of Kane's concept of self-forming actions, and notes that such an evaluation of one's reasons is a prime example of a self-forming action (p. 251). We are more readily redesigned—by ourselves—than any other organism on the planet (p. 277).

In almost the same terms as MacIntyre, Dennett states that our capacity to engage in the practice of asking and giving reasons, when directed toward ourselves, "creates the special category of voluntary actions that sets us apart" (p. 251). Dennett rejects the notion that freedom is an all-or-nothing concept, and reminds us of the fact that we have usable, if not infallible, cultural resources for discriminating degrees of responsibility (p.291). One often *becomes* responsible by *taking* responsibility—this is another crucially important sort of self-forming action (p. 302). This parallels our emphasis on using one's capacity for self-transcendence in order to free oneself from

---

[40] Dennett, *Freedom Evolves*, 54. Parenthetical page references that follow refer to this text.

undue social pressure. There is no need for self-forming actions to be undetermined (p. 302); the incompatibilists' arguments commit a misstep by pushing the causal chain preceding a person's action too far back in time. "Events in the *distant* past were indeed not 'up to me,' but my choice now...is up to me because its 'parents'—some events in the *recent* past, such as the choices I have recently made—were up to me (because *their* 'parents' were up to me), and so on, not to infinity, but far enough back to give my *self* enough spread in space and time so that there is a *me* for my descriptions to be up to!" (pp. 135–6). Throughout the book Dennett argues against taking the self to be some small operator in the brain (e.g., p. 302). He states that this *I*, the larger, temporally extended self can control what goes on inside (p. 253).

Dennett's reviewers accuse him of having broken no new ground. Two critical reviewers are Galen Strawson and Jerry Fodor. Fodor says that Dennett's compatibilism, like other versions, turns out to be "a sort of Chinese lunch: there's the lurking sense that what you got isn't quite what you ordered, and half an hour later you're hungry again".[41] Fodor and Strawson both conclude that Dennett should bite the bullet and acknowledge that "radical freedom" (Strawson),[42] "metaphysical freedom", "freedom *tout court*" (Fodor) is impossible.

To a great extent these reviewers' reactions are simply a result of their accepting the libertarian–compatibilist dichotomy. Yet Dennett gives his detractors plenty of ammunition to argue that he has engaged in an exercise of "bait and switch".[43] Regarding intentionality, Dennett's claim is not that humans (and some animals) actually have beliefs, desires, intentions, but rather that we are pragmatically justified in employing the "intentional stance" (i.e., attributing to them beliefs, etc.). Since we cannot understand human behavior by means of an account of the calculations made by the myriad tiny robots in the brain, and because the ascription of beliefs, desires, intentions *does* permit us to predict behavior, we are justified in assuming the intentional stance with regard to our fellow humans. Fodor labels this an instrumentalist view of agency: "there's no more to a creature being an

[41] Jerry Fodor, "Why Would Mother Nature Bother?", *London Review of Books*, 6 Mar. 2003, 17–18, at p. 17.
[42] Galen Strawson, "Evolution Explains It All for You", *New York Times Book Review*, 2 Mar. 2003), 11.
[43] Fodor, "Why Would Mother Nature Bother?", 17.

agent than its behaving like an agent."[44] "I strongly suspect that, though it may be heuristically useful for predicting behavior, the kind of agency that instrumentalists can certify is useless for explaining it ... heuristic fictions don't cause anything."[45]

In Dennett's account of altruism he describes how "benselfishness" can emerge as a result of recognizing, first, the social pay-off of being perceived as a good person and, second, that the easiest way of being so perceived is actually to *be* a good person.[46] Thus, reviewer Adam Schulman rejects Dennett's claim to have explained morality: Dennett has given an account only of "pseudo-altruism", whereas morality requires doing what is right for its own sake, not merely for selfish reasons.[47]

6.2 The Deep Difference: Reductionism

Is it possible to make a case for moral responsibility and free will, or only for pseudo-responsibility and pseudo-freedom? We have been suggesting that the answer lies in the concept of downward causation. Dennett looks at all of the right ingredients for an account of free will, but his goal is to *interpret* them all as products of bottom-up causation. Dennett has rightly concluded that determinism versus indeterminism in science is not the critical issue (cf. p. 306), but he does not distinguish between the determinism/indeterminism issue and that of causal reductionism.

We claimed at the outset that an account of humans that does not reject Descartes's view of bodies as machines is bound to be reductionistic. Dennett explicitly describes a human as an organization of a "trillion robot teams"; we are each "*made of* mindless robots and nothing else" (p. 2). This mind-set is the root of the reviewers' (accurate) perceptions that Dennett can account only for the *appearance* of intentionality, altruism, responsibility, and freedom. To illustrate, consider Dennett's position on language. This is taken from his earlier *Elbow Room*, but relevant here because so much in his current account hinges on human language use.

Dennett argues that our brains only appear to be "semantic engines", that is, meaning manipulators. Rather, being physical machines, they can only be "syntactic engines", responding to the structural or formal properties

---

[44] Fodor, "Why Would Mother Nature Bother?", 17.   [45] Ibid. 18.
[46] Dennett, *Freedom Evolves*, ch. 7.
[47] Adam Schulman, "Why Be Good?", *Books in Review*, May 2003, 71–3.

of language.[48] Because meaning does not reside in the physical features of stimuli, no physical process could distill or respond to it.[49] However, Dennett argues, human capacities for meta-level pattern recognition allow for so much fine-tuning of our linguistic behavior that eventually "the overpowering 'illusion' is created that the system is actually directly responding to meanings".[50]

We take it that Dennett is making a point comparable to our Wittgensteinian rejection of understanding meaning as dependent solely on an inner "aha!" But lacking an alternative account of meaning in terms of language games and "grammar"—in terms of action in the social world—he concludes that there must be no meaning at all.

Dennett's position on language is an appropriate *entrée* for "diagnosing" his entire project, since he describes it as the first stable conclusion he reached in his philosophical career and as the foundation of everything he has done since then.[51] It is the source of his views of the nature of consciousness: "The appreciation of meanings—their discrimination and delectation—is central to our vision of consciousness, but this conviction that *I*, on the inside, deal directly with meanings turns out to be something rather like a benign 'user illusion'."[52] The denial of our ability to *understand* the meanings of words is also the foundation of his claim regarding the intentional stance. When he says that humans have beliefs, he means only that their behavior can be predicted by treating them as though they do. In this sense, "even lowly thermostats have beliefs."[53] Furthermore, if people act only *as though* they have beliefs, then it would seem to follow that they act only *as though* for a reason—for example, *as though* for the good of another person (pseudo-altruism)—and only *as though* taking responsibility for their actions.

We detect a profound irony here. Dennett is the inventor of the term "Cartesian materialism", which he uses to pillory the cognitive scientists and neuroscientists who expect there to be a place in the brain "where it all comes together", as in Descartes's mental theater.

---

[48] See Juarrero, *Dynamics in Action*, ch. 11, for a solution to this problem.

[49] Daniel C. Dennett, *Elbow Room: The Varieties of Free Will Worth Wanting* (Cambridge, Mass.: MIT Press, 1984), 28.

[50] Ibid. 30.

[51] Daniel C. Dennett, *Brainchildren: Essays on Designing Minds* (Cambridge, Mass.: MIT Press, 1998), 357.

[52] Ibid.   [53] Ibid. 327.

His rejection of a semantic account of language is specifically the result of his rejection of a neural substitute for the homunculus, who is the one on the "inside" who "gets the meaning". We have used "Cartesian materialism" more broadly to designate views of the mental that fail to take account of context: action–feedback–evaluation–action loops in the social environment. Thus, our account of the meaning of language depends not only on dynamical semantic networks *in* the brain, but especially on the *use* of language in the social world.

Our account of meaning depends on top-down causation at two levels. First, to understand a word *symbolically* is to have a hierarchically ordered semantic network such that higher-level categories (e.g., *food*) constrain the use of lower-level terms ("banana"). Because there is no exhaustive definition of food (as for many concepts), the system cannot simply be constructed bottom-up. The studies we reported on language learning in chimpanzees showed that while the first set of food items was learned by rote, the chimpanzees had, in Wittgenstein's terms, to learn "to go on", to extend the categories to incorporate new items. There did appear to be a point when the animal "got it".[54] This involved (as Dennett would grant) a higher-order recognition of patterns (edibles versus drinkables), but the ability to extend the categories was also dependent on both embodiment and interaction with the world—the downward influence of participation in language games. The category of food is determined not only biologically but also culturally.

So Dennett is right that higher-order pattern recognition is essential to language learning. He is also right that if knowing the meaning of a word could only be the result of better and better recognition of patterns among formal features of words and sentences, then it could never happen; machines can manipulate symbols but cannot understand them.[55] But knowing the meaning of language is a social achievement; it is the ability to use language appropriately in social interactions. It is also a result of the patterns of resemblance and causal and other connections that go into the use of icons and indices, respectively, as Deacon argues (see our Ch. 4, secs. 2–3).

---

[54] In Juarrero's terms, this is a catastrophic reconfiguration of the semantic and syntactical dynamic landscape; *Dynamics in Action*, 173.

[55] See Lakoff and Johnson's critique of the formal-semantics paradigm in linguistics, quoted in our Ch. 4, sec. 4.1.

We noted above that Dennett takes his position on language to be the source of his positions both on the intentional stance and on consciousness. We have argued that Dennett's account of language does not amount to (genuine) symbolic language. But we do not take the absence of symbolic language (as in higher animals and young children) as a reason for denying that they have (genuine) beliefs and other intentional states. Following Fred Dretske, we treated beliefs (in Ch. 5) as structuring causes of behavior. In this sense, human and animal beliefs are on a continuum with other sorts of information built into an organism's neural system (e.g., by genetics or classical conditioning).

Despite the continuities, however, an extremely important threshold is crossed when consciousness appears (see Ch. 3, sec. 5). Differentiating our position from Dennett's is complicated throughout by his stance on consciousness. We confess that we are unable to decide whether he denies the existence of consciousness or merely argues against misleading accounts of the nature of consciousness. Galen Strawson claims that "Dennett continues to deny the existence of consciousness, and continues to deny that he is denying it".[56] It may be significant in this regard that Dennett ends his *Consciousness Explained* with a section headed "Consciousness Explained, or Explained Away?"[57] Unfortunately, this brief section did not remove the question mark for us.

Our conclusion, then, is that Dennett's world view is largely Cartesian: his account of bodies is mechanistic; he works with a strictly bottom–up account of brain functions; he has an inadequate appreciation of the fact that the mind is essentially social and engaged in action. As noted above, Dennett remarks that "*I*, the larger, temporally and spatially extended self, can control, to some degree, what goes on inside",[58] but this does not seem to reflect his settled views of how organisms work, and especially does not take into account the downward causation from the social environment. So despite the parallels noted above, Dennett's book is, in the most important sense, as different from ours as could be. Our goal throughout has been to show where and why reductionism fails. Dennett's is *specifically* to provide a reductionist account of human phenomena, including "free will"; but the result is a very imaginative account of how

---

[56] Strawson, "Evolution Explains It All for You", 11.
[57] Daniel C. Dennett, *Consciousness Explained* (Boston: Little, Brown, and Co., 1991), 454–55.
[58] Dennett, *Freedom Evolves*, 253.

complex machines could *appear* to have language, beliefs, morality, and free will.

7 Determinism Revisited

One thesis of this chapter has been that contemporary free-will debates have stalled due to their focus on the issue of determinism. Determinism *would be* the crucial issue if the early modern atomist–reductionist picture were true. That is, if the causal capacities of complex entities were nothing but the combined causal effects of the entities' constituents, and if the most basic constituents operated according to deterministic laws, then it would indeed seem to be the case that humans could do nothing other than what their atoms, in aggregate, do. We would have what Stuart Goetz calls bottom-to-top determinism,[59] in contrast to our common-sense notion that macroscopic entities are causes in their own right.

We have argued that this picture is wrong on three counts. First, it is widely accepted that the "atoms" (in the philosophical sense) do not behave deterministically. Second, it is becoming more and more widely recognized that complex dynamical systems can exhibit new sorts of causal capacities not found at the level of their constituents. We have emphasized, among these, sentience, goal seeking, consciousness, acting for a reason, and self-evaluation. Third, we have argued that higher-level systems exert downward effects on their constituents via selection among possibilities generated randomly, probabilistically, or according to deterministic lower-level laws. Thus, we have judged the issue of bottom-to-top determinism to be (largely) irrelevant to the free will problem.

This, of course, is only one sort of determinist threat to free will; there is also the form of determinism that Goetz calls past-to-present determinism. However, we have already noted the difficulties in making sense of a general past-to-present determinist thesis (Ch. 2, sec. 1.3.4). If determinism is defined as the *general* thesis that every event has (or *must* have) a cause, then at this point in intellectual history it is a very debatable metaphysical claim, and there are a variety of reasons for thinking that the issue could never be settled in favor of determinism (apart, perhaps, from a theological perspective).

---

[59] Stuart Goetz, "Naturalism and Libertarian Agency", in William Lane Craig and J. P. Moreland (eds.), *Naturalism: A Critical Analysis* (London and New York: Routledge, 2000), 156–86, at pp. 167–8.

8 Constructing a Concept of Free Will

Our goal in this section is twofold. First, we have attempted to show that the critical issue in the debate is one's ability, as a whole person, to exercise downward control over one's own behavior, cognition, and neural processes, and in so doing to become a causal player in one's own right. But if animals do this as well as humans, and if animals are taken *not* to possess free will, then there is the further (conceptual) question of the conditions under which such downward control in fact constitutes free will. The longer history of free-will debates offers a variety of options for analyzing the concept. We shall examine several of these here and relate them to the cognitive capacities incorporated into our account of morally responsible action (in Ch. 6). The goal will be to show that most of these traditional requirements are satisfied by our morally responsible actor. A second purpose, though, is to provide something of a corrective to these traditional concepts themselves in light of (what we hope is) a neurobiologically realistic account of human cognition and behavior.

8.1 Alternative Conceptions

We shall consider here (1) free will conceived of as acting for a reason; (2) various versions of free will as autonomy, distinguished by what one is taken to require autonomy *from*; (3) Harry Frankfurt's "hierarchical mesh theory"; and (4) free will as dependent on "agent causation". We shall then raise the question of whether the conditions for morally responsible action are in fact the same as those for free will.

8.1.1. *Freedom as Acting for a Reason*   Immanuel Kant is largely responsible for the understanding of free will as acting for a reason. Kant identified the moral law with what reason demands, and further identified freedom with the conformity of the will to the moral law. Kant's sharp distinction between acting for a reason and being caused to act was based on his distinction between noumena (things in themselves) and phenomena (things as they appear to us). The concept of causation applies only in the phenomenal world. The self is noumenal, and thus immune from causal forces.

Even though Kant's noumenal–phenomenal distinction is no longer influential, there are still many thinkers who see reason and causation as irreconcilable. The point of Chapter 5 was to call this assumption into question, and to begin to spell out in neurobiological terms how "reason gets its grip on the brain"—that is, how reasons become causal players in human affairs.

Alasdair MacIntyre has argued that the absence of language is no reason to withhold the attribution of reasons to animals.[60] Nonetheless, there is a marked increase in freedom from biological and environmental demands that comes with symbolic language, and particularly with abstract concepts such as moral concepts.

It has been common throughout the Western tradition to contrast acting for a reason with acting under the influence of passion. This goes back at least to Plato, who postulated three aspects of the soul—the highest being reason, and the lowest being the passions or appetites. While it is true that overpowering emotion sometimes detracts from our freedom, there is increasing recognition that reason and emotion ordinarily work together. Daniel Dennett points our that apart from the "interests" attributable to organisms (survival, replication), there would be no reasons in the universe, only causes.

How could reason ever find a foothold in a material, mechanical universe? In the beginning there were no reasons; there were only causes. Nothing had a purpose, nothing had so much as a function; there was no teleology in the world at all. The explanation for this is simple: there was nothing that had interests. But after millennia there happened to emerge simple replicators, and while *they* had no inkling of their interests, and perhaps properly speaking had no interests, we, peering back from our Godlike vantage point at their early days, can nonarbitrarily assign them certain interests—generated by their defining "interest" in self-replication.[61]

Similarly, Austin Farrer wrote in his Gifford Lectures that without "subjective factors", nothing coming before the mind would have the least tendency to produce action. "Even mortal danger would leave us unmoved if we had no repulsion against death or bodily harm."[62]

Antonio Damasio's research on patients with damage to the medial portion of their frontal lobes provides the beginning of an understanding in biological terms of how emotional processes provide signals about aspects

---

[60] Alasdair MacIntyre, *Dependent Rational Animals: Why Human Beings Need the Virtues* (Chicago: Open Court, 1999), ch. 4.

[61] Dennett, *Elbow Room*, 21.

[62] Austin Farrer, *The Freedom of the Will* (London: Adam & Charles Black, 1958), 127.

of our knowledge of the world that are not directly available to conscious awareness, and thus, how emotions are necessary for making reasoned judgments about potential action (see Ch. 1, sec. 3.2 above). Thus, reasons would not move us were it not for interest, affections, passions, and emotions.

8.1.2. Free Will as Autonomy   The central meaning of "autonomy" is to be self-governed or self-controlled. Threats to autonomy can come from outside (i.e., other people) or from "inside". Autonomy in the first sense relates to the issues of political freedom, but our emphasis here is on the importance of autonomy from others in becoming what MacIntyre calls "independent practical reasoners".

What each of us has to do, in order to develop our powers as independent reasoners, and so to flourish *qua* members of our species, is to make the transition from accepting what we are taught by those earliest teachers to making our own independent judgments about goods, judgments that we are able to justify rationally to ourselves and to others as furnishing us with good reasons for acting in this way rather than that.[63]

This transition involves coming to realize at a certain point that it will please parents and teachers *not* to act so as to please them but to act "so as to achieve what is good and best, whether this pleases them or not".[64] So we are dependent, in becoming autonomous moral reasoners, on teachers who have the moral abilities themselves to allow for independent judgment.

The second sense of autonomy, better captured by the term "self-control", is the opposite of Aristotle's *akrasia*. In the tradition there has been a tendency to equate self-control with the rule of reason over passion. Alfred Mele describes self-controlled people as those who "have significant motivation to conduct themselves as they judge best and a robust capacity to do what it takes so to conduct themselves in the face of (actual or anticipated) competing motivation".[65] Aristotle had focused his discussion on temperance, but Mele rightly broadens the sphere of self-control beyond temperance to include the emotions and also belief. With regard to the latter, Mele points out that one can be *akratic* in one's believing—for

---

[63] MacIntyre, *Dependent Rational Animals*, 71.   [64] Ibid. 84.
[65] Alfred Mele, "Autonomy, Self-Control, and Weakness of Will", in Kane (ed.), *Oxford Handbook of Free Will*, 529–48, at p. 531.

example, allowing oneself to be self-deceived. He also objects to Aristotle's assumption that it is reason alone that is the arbiter of what one ought to do.

On an alternative, holistic view of human beings, the "self" of self-control is identified with the whole person rather than with reason. Even when one's passions and emotions run counter to one's better judgment, they often are not plausibly seen as alien forces. A conception of self-controlled individuals as, roughly, people who characteristically are guided by their better judgments even in the face of strong competing motivation does not commit one to viewing emotion, passion, and the like as having no place in the "self" of self-control. Self-control can be exercised in support of better judgments partially based on a person's appetites or emotional commitments. In some cases, our better judgments may indicate our evaluative ranking of competing *emotions* or *appetites*.[66]

This view is compatible with our account in Chapter 6. Responsible *reflection* involves evaluation of desires and impulses, but also of beliefs and perceptions. Morally responsible *action* involves acting in accord with the higher-order judgment, but there is no presumption here that reason *per se* is a "higher" faculty; "higher" in our sense is related to levels of self-transcendence.

8.1.3. Hierarchical Mesh Theories of Freedom   As noted above, Harry Frankfurt helpfully distinguishes between first- and second-order desires; second-order desires are desires about having or not having one's first-order desires. There is the common experience of desiring that we *not* have our own first-order desires, such as in the case of wanting to break a habit. Frankfurt argues that a person is responsible for his actions *and free* when his second-order desires are consistent with the lower level. Otherwise, he says, one is a passive victim of one's desires. So freedom consists in "motivational wholeness", regardless of the origin of one's desires.[67]

We endorse Frankfurt's recognition of the role of higher-order evaluation of one's desires, but we believe several modifications of his position are in order. First, as Charles Taylor has argued, we often act for desire-independent reasons. Taylor speaks of strong evaluation in contrast to weak evaluation, the latter based merely on something's being

---

[66] Alfred Mele, "Autonomy, Self-Control, and Weakness of Will", 532.

[67] Harry Frankfurt, "Alternative Possibilities and Moral Responsibility", *Journal of Philosophy*, 66 (1969), 829–89.

desirable. Strong evaluation invokes moral concepts.[68] Thus, we have adopted MacIntyre's account of moral responsibility in terms of evaluating "that which moves one to act"—he recognizes that desires are but one sort of motive—and whose evaluation is ultimately in terms of moral concepts.

Second, Frankfurt speaks of conforming one's higher-level desires to lower. We would emphasize, in contrast, the role of higher-order evaluation in allowing for the adjustment of lower-order desires (and other motives). Responsibility comes from having taken part in shaping one's own desires and attitudes. For example, inhibition of desired actions leads to habits, which are instantiated by means of neural changes. Such changes may result in making conscious inhibition unnecessary. We can also make changes in our environments now to forestall later desires and drives.[69]

8.1.4. Agent Causation

There are a vast number of positions on free will that invoke the notion of agent causation.[70] We shall not attempt to survey them here. One motive for developing the concept of agent causation has been the perceived impossibility of reconciling free will with ordinary physical causation. Thus, a special category of causation has been postulated whereby agents initiate sequences of events without that initiation being itself caused or determined.[71] Note that this apparent requirement comes from assuming a simplistic linear model of causation in the human sphere, which we criticized above (sec. 5).

Another, more legitimate, reason for such developments is recognition of the difference between mechanistic and purposive explanations; that is, explaining why an agent did something is clearly different from explaining a mechanical process that brought about some effect. Our argument to the effect that ordinary causal processes, appropriately structured, enable purposive behavior is relevant here. However, we recognize purposive

---

[68] Charles Taylor, "What is Human Agency?", in *Philosophical Papers*, 1 (Cambridge: Cambridge University Press, 1985), 15–44. See also John R. Searle's account of the creation of desire-independent reasons, in *Rationality in Action* (Cambridge, Mass.: MIT Press), ch. 6.

[69] See Ch. 6, sec. 3.6, for our report on George Ainslee's *Breakdown of Will* (Cambridge: Cambridge University Press, 2001).

[70] For an overview, see Timothy O'Connor, "Libertarian Views: Dualist and Agent-Causal Theories", in Kane (ed.), *Oxford Handbook of Free Will*, 337–55.

[71] Simon Blackburn, "Agent Causation", in *idem* (ed.), *The Oxford Dictionary of Philosophy* (Oxford: Oxford University Press, 1994), 9.

behavior in non-human animals, so a two-category distinction between mechanistic and purposive is not adequate. There is a spectrum from purely mechanical causation through the purposive behavior of primitive organisms, the intelligent goal seeking of higher animals, and finally to the reason-guided teleological action of humans.

8.2 The Achievement of Free Will

In our account of the differences separating mature humans from inanimate matter we have sketched a variety of levels of complexity, exhibiting increasing capacities for flexibility and self-direction. Even primitive organisms exhibit goal direction and action under evaluation. So what are the differences between humans and lower organisms? Unlike the lowly protozoa with only two possible courses of action—to swim ahead or turn—we have an extremely wide repertoire of behavioral possibilities. Unlike *Sphex*, we have the ability to learn from our past mistakes. As with nearly all other animals we can change from the pursuit of one goal to another in light of feedback from the environment. So increasing abilities to sense the environment, coupled with increasingly complex behavioral repertoires, result, in higher organisms, in what we call acting reasonably, as when a dog attempts to open a cupboard in which it smells food.

The development of human culture has resulted in the creation of external scaffolding, which leads to a remarkable increase in rational abilities. Language allows us to respond to the world around us in terms of abstract categories. The development of theories of rationality and logic, along with a symbolic concept of the self, allows us to engage in meta-level evaluation of our cognitive strategies. We argued in the previous chapter that such meta-evaluation of one's reasons for acting constitutes moral responsibility.

So our minimalist model of a moral agent is represented as in Figure 3.4. This is a picture of a person in her environment who, in Dennett's terms has "gone meta" in order to make her own lower-level cognitions, propensities, behavior, *and criteria for evaluation* (MC in the diagram) the object of evaluation. Juarrero says that "intentional human action is free to the degree that contextual constraints put the most complex levels of its neurological organization, those governing meaning, values, and morals, in control. Even as these levels regulate and close off options, they simultaneously free up qualitatively new possibilities for the expression of those values and morals."[72] As noted in the previous chapter, this process of self-transcendence can continue with the adding of additional levels of supervisory systems. It is interesting to note the grammatical fact that one associates the "I", the true self, with the highest-level supervisory system. I (nominative case) evaluate my motives.

The concepts of free will and moral responsibility are so closely linked in the philosophical literature and in ordinary discourse that many authors (e.g., Frankfurt) use them interchangeably in the course of their arguments. So is it reasonable to conclude that the criteria for one are indeed identical to those for the other? We have shown that our morally responsible actor fulfills all of the other traditional criteria for free will (to the extent that one should want). The one who is able to evaluate that which moves her to act (Frankfurt's lower-order desires included), on the basis of reason (Kant), especially moral reasons (Taylor, MacIntyre); who is furthermore not unduly influenced by the judgments of others (autonomy in the first sense), nor prevented from acting according to that evaluation by weakness of will or overpowering emotions (Mele; autonomy in the second sense) is indeed an agent, the primary, top-down cause (agent causation) of her own actions. Our suggestion, then, is that free will be understood as being the primary cause of one's own actions; this is a holistic capacity of mature, self-reflective human organisms acting within suitable social contexts.

9 Conclusion: An Agenda for Future Research

Our goal in this book has been the defeat of neurobiological reductionism, which we have taken to include the denial of a physical organism's ability to be the cause of its own action, to use language meaningfully, to act for a reason, and in a morally responsible way. In this chapter we addressed one aspect of the free-will problem, the worry that human behavior is biologically determined. In fact, we believe that greater understanding of our own neural and cognitive processes sheds valuable light on the

---

[72] Juarrero, *Dynamics in Action*, 249.

concept of free will itself. We suggest, then, that the problem of reconciling free will with neurobiology is *not* a particularly knotty philosophical problem, but rather an agenda for research—namely, to provide increasingly well-informed and cogent accounts of how our neural equipment provides for the cognitive and behavioral capacities that go into responsible action.

Postscript

We stated in the Introduction that one of our methodological commitments was *not* to lose sight of the deliverances of ordinary human experience. For example, if philosophical arguments or scientific conclusions lead to such non–commonsensical conclusions as our not being conscious, or our desires and plans not having any causal role in our actions, then something must have gone wrong with the argument.

The central purpose of this book has been to argue against the worry of neurobiological reductionism. In this book we have shown (attempted to show?) that it is almost never appropriate to say "My neurons made me do it". It is good news for us, then, that when we come to reflect on the practical implications of our work, we have almost nothing to say that would be at odds with the wisdom of the ages. Here are a few implications:

1. Teach children to ask themselves why they are doing what they are doing; teach them language for evaluating their actions and motives; help them to explore a wider range of possible thoughts and actions. The neurocognitive systems of young persons are very adaptive and in a constant process of organization and reorganization.

2. Go meta, regularly; remember the value of self-reflection. Through literature, discussion, psychotherapy and so forth, explore a broader range of possibilities for thought and action. Encounters with new ideas and perspectives offer opportunities for system reorganization, even in older adults.

3. It *is* harder to teach old dogs new tricks; it often takes a crisis. Nevertheless, in times of crisis, look for opportunities for a salutary reordering of the dynamic topography of motivations.

4. In legal and moral matters, remember that there is no such thing as total freedom; all human action is conditioned to a greater or lesser degree by both biology and environment.

5. At the same time, for complex self-determining systems such as human beings, there is no such thing as total biological determination. Neurons do not do things; *you* do whatever you do. Juries of our peers are pretty good at sorting out degrees of responsibility. One question to insert into the usual mix is to ask about the extent to which the person under consideration has the capacity for self-transcendence.

6. Because freedom is limited, take advantage of limited opportunities to increase freedom later; or decrease it—tie yourself to the mast when you are approaching the Sirens.

7. Go meta–meta: reflect regularly on the extent to which you are employing these strategies to increase the range of your own and your children's freedom, self-understanding, and ability to make fair judgments of others.

Bibliography

Ainslie, George, *Breakdown of Will* (Cambridge: Cambridge University Press, 2001).

Allman, John A., K. K. Watson, N. A. Tetreault, and A. Y. Hakeem, "Intuition and Autism: A Possible Role for Von Economo Neurons", *Trends in Cognitive Sciences*, 9 (2005), 367–73.

Alston, William P., "Meaning", in Paul Edwards (ed.), *The Encyclopedia of Philosophy* (New York: Macmillan Publishing Co., 1967).

Anderson, John R., *Cognitive Psychology and Its Implications* (New York: Worth Publishers, 2000).

Aquinas, Thomas, *Summa Theologiae*, Blackfriars edition (London: Eyre & Spottiswoode; New York: McGraw-Hill, 1963).

Arbib, Michael A., *The Metaphorical Brain, II: Neural Networks and Beyond* (New York: Wiley-Interscience, 1989).

Aronson, J., E. Dietrich, and E. Way, "Throwing the Conscious Baby Out with the Cartesian Bath Water", *Behavioral and Brain Science*, 15/2 (1992), 202–3.

Augustine, *Confessions*, trans. R. S. Pine-Coffin (Harmondsworth: Penguin, 1961).

Ayala, Francisco J., "Introduction", in *idem* and Theodosius Dobzhansky (eds.), *Studies in the Philosophy of Biology: Reduction and Related Problems* (Berkeley and Los Angeles: University of California Press, 1974).

——"Teleological Explanations versus Teleology", *History and Philosophy of the Life Sciences*, 20 (1998), 41–50.

Baker, Lynne Rudder, *Persons and Bodies: A Constitution View* (Cambridge: Cambridge University Press, 2000).

Bargh, J. A., and T. L. Chartrand, "The Unbearable Automaticity of Being", *American Psychologist*, 54 (1999), 462–79.

Baron-Cohen, S., A. Leslie, and U. Frith, "Does the Autistic Child Have a 'Theory of Mind'?", *Cognition*, 21 (1985), 37–46.

Baumeister, Roy F., and T. Heatherton, "Self-Regulation Failure: An Overview", *Psychological Inquiry*, 7 (1996), 1–5.

——and K. L. Sommer, "Consciousness, Free Choice, and Automaticity", in R. S. Wyer Jr. (ed.), *Advances in Social Cognition*, vol. X (Mahwah, NJ: Erlbaum, 1997).

Bechtel, William, "Representations: From Neural Systems to Cognitive Systems", in William Bechtel *et al.* (eds.), *Philosophy and the Neurosciences: A Reader* (Oxford: Blackwell, 2001).

Bennett, M. R., and P. M. S. Hacker, *Philosophical Foundations of Neuroscience* (Oxford: Blackwell, 2003).

Berridge, K. C., "Motivation Concepts in Behavioral Neuroscience", *Physiology & Behavior*, 81/2 (2004), 179–209.

Berry, D. C., and D. E. Broadbent, "On the Relationship between Task Performance and Associated Verbalizable Knowledge", *Quarterly Journal of Experimental Psychology*, 35A (1984), 209–31.

Blackburn, Simon, "Agent Causation", in *idem* (ed.), *The Oxford Dictionary of Philosophy* (Oxford: Oxford University Press, 1994).

Block, Ned, O. Flanagan, and G. Güzeldere (eds.), *The Nature of Consciousness: Philosophical Debates* (Cambridge, Mass.: MIT Press, 1997).

Bonevac, Daniel, "Reduction in the Mind of God", in Savellos and Yalçin.

Boysen, S., and G. Bernston, "Responses to Quantity: Perceptual versus Cognitive Mechanisms in Chimpanzees (Pan troglodytes)", *Journal of Experimental Psychology and Animal Behavior Processes*, 21 (1995), 82–6.

Braine, David, *The Human Person: Animal and Spirit* (Notre Dame, Ind.: University of Notre Dame Press, 1992).

Brand, M. D., "Top-Down Elasticity Analysis and its Application to Energy Metabolism in Isolated Mitochondria and Intact Cells", *Molecular and Cellular Biochemistry*, 184 (1998), 13–20.

Brothers, Leslie, *Friday's Footprint: How Society Shapes the Human Mind* (New York: Oxford, University Press, 1997).

——*Mistaken Identity: The Mind–Brain Problem Reconsidered* (Albany, NY: SUNY Press, 2001).

Brown, Warren S., "Cognitive Contributions to Soul", in Brown *et al.*

——, N. Murphy, and H. Newton Malony (eds.), *Whatever Happened to the Soul?: Scientific and Theological Portraits of Human Nature* (Minneapolis: Fortress Press, 1998).

Bunge, Mario, *Ontology, II: A World of Systems* (Dordrecht: D. Reidel, 1979).

Butterfield, Jeremy, "Determinism", in Edward Craig (ed.), *Routledge Encyclopedia of Philosophy* (London: Routledge, 1998).

Camille, Nathalie, *et al.*, "The Involvement of the Orbitofrontal Cortex in the Experience of Regret", *Science*, 304 (2004), 1167–70.

Campbell, Donald T., " 'Downward Causation' in Hierarchically Organised Biological Systems", in F. J. Ayala and T. Dobzhansky (eds.), *Studies in the Philosophy of Biology* (Berkeley and Los Angeles: University of California Press, 1974).

Cary, Phillip, *Augustine's Invention of the Inner Self: The Legacy of a Christian Platonist* (Oxford: Oxford University Press, 2000).

Chalmers, David J., *The Conscious Mind: In Search of a Fundamental Theory* (New York: Oxford University Press, 1996).

Chelazzi, L., J. Duncan, E. K. Miller, and R. Desimone, "Responses of Neurons in Inferior Temporal Cortex during Memory-Guided Visual Search", *Journal of Neurophysiology*, 80 (1998), 2918–40.

Churchland, Patricia S., "Self-Representation in Nervous Systems", *Science*, 296 (2002), 308–10.

Churchland, Paul M., "Eliminative Materialism and the Propositional Attitudes", *Journal of Philosophy*, 78 (1981), 67–90.

_____ *The Engine of Reason, the Seat of the Soul: A Philosophical Journey into the Brain* (Cambridge, Mass.: MIT Press, 1995).

Clark, Andy, *Being There: Putting Brain, Body, and World Together Again* (Cambridge, Mass.: MIT Press, 1997).

Damasio, Antonio R., *Descartes' Error: Emotion, Reason, and the Human Brain* (New York: G. P. Putnam's Sons, 1994).

Damasio, Hanna, *et al.*, "The Return of Phineas Gage: The Skull of a Famous Patient Yields Clues about the Brain", *Science*, 264 (1994), 1102–5.

Davidson, Donald, *Essays on Actions and Events* (Oxford: Clarendon Press, 1980).

_____ *Inquiries into Truth and Interpretation* (Oxford: Oxford University Press, 1984).

Deacon, Terrence W., *The Symbolic Species: The Co-evolution of Language and the Brain* (New York: Norton, 1997).

_____ "Three Levels of Emergent Phenomena", in Murphy and Stoeger.

de Gelder, B., J. Vroomen, *et al.*, "Non-Conscious Recognition of Affect in the Absence of Striate Cortex", *Neuroreport*, 10/18 (1999), 3759–63.

Dennett, Daniel C, *Elbow Room: The Varieties of Free Will Worth Wanting* (Cambridge, Mass.: MIT Press, 1984).

_____ *Consciousness Explained* (Boston: Little, Brown, and Co., 1991).

_____ *Brainchildren: Essays on Designing Minds* (Cambridge, Mass.: MIT Press, 1998).

_____ *Freedom Evolves* (New York: Viking, 2003).

_____ and M. Kinsbourne, "Time and the Observer: The Where and When of Consciousness in the Brain", *Behavioral and Brain Sciences*, 15 (1992), 183–247.

Descartes, René, *Meditations on First Philosophy*, in *The Philosophical Writings of Descartes*, ed. and trans. J. Cottingham, R. Stoothoff, and D. Murdoch (Cambridge: Cambridge University Press, 1985).

_____ *Discourse on Method*, in *The Philosophical Writings of Descartes*, ed. and trans. J. Cottingham, R. Stoothoff, and D. Murdoch (Cambridge: Cambridge University Press, 1985).

de Waal, Frans, *Good Natured: The Origins of Right and Wrong in Humans and Other Animals* (Cambridge, Mass.: Harvard University Press, 1996).

Donald, Merlin, *A Mind So Rare: The Evolution of Human Consciousness* (New York: Norton and Co., 2001).

Dretske, Fred, *Explaining Behavior: Reasons in a World of Causes* (Cambridge, Mass.: MIT Press, 1988).

—— "Fred Dretske", in Samuel Guttenplan (ed.), *A Companion to the Philosophy of Mind* (Oxford: Blackwell, 1994).

—— "Mental Events as Structuring Causes of Behavior", in Heil and Mele.

Edelman, Gerald M., *Neural Darwinism: The Theory of Neuronal Group Selection* (New York: Basic Books, 1987).

—— and G. Tononi, *A Universe of Consciousness: How Matter Becomes Imagination* (New York: Basic Books, 2000).

Ellis, George F. R., "Quantum Theory and the Macroscopic World", in Robert J. Russell *et al.* (eds.), *Quantum Mechanics: Scientific Perspectives on Divine Action* (Vatican City State and Berkeley: Vatican Observatory and Center for Theology and the Natural Sciences, 2001).

Ellis, R. R. and S. J. Lederman, "The Golf-Ball Illusion: Evidence for Top-Down Processing in Weight Perception", *Perception*, 27 (1998), 193–201.

Enç, Berent, "Nonreducible Supervenient Causation", in Savellos and Yalçin.

Farrer, Austin, *The Freedom of the Will*, The Gifford Lectures (1957) (London: Adam & Charles Black, 1958).

Feyerabend, Paul K., "Materialism and the Mind–Body Problem", in *Realism, Rationalism, and Scientific Method: Philosophical Papers*, I. (Cambridge: Cambridge University Press, 1981).

Fish, Stanley, *Is There a Text in this Class?: The Authority of Interpretive Communities* (Cambridge, Mass.: Harvard University Press, 1980).

Flanagan, Owen, *The Science of the Mind*, 2nd edn. (Cambridge, Mass.: MIT Press, 1991).

—— *Consciousness Reconsidered* (Cambridge, Mass.: MIT Press, 1992).

—— *The Problem of the Soul: Two Visions of Mind and How to Reconcile Them* (New York: Basic Books, 2002).

Fodor, Jerry, *The Language of Thought* (New York: Thomas Y. Crowell, 1975).

—— "Why Would Mother Nature Bother?", *London Review of Books*, 6 Mar. 2003, 17–18.

Frank, Robert H., *Passions within Reason: The Strategic Role of the Emotions* (New York: W. W. Norton and Co., 1988).

Frankfurt, Harry, "Alternate Possibilities and Moral Responsibility", *Journal of Philosophy*, 66 (1969), 829–39.

—— *The Importance of What We Care About* (Cambridge: Cambridge University Press, 1988).

—— *Necessity, Volition, and Love* (Cambridge: Cambridge University Press, 1999).

Frege, Gottlob, "*Über Sinn und Bedeutung*" (1892), trans. M. Black, "On Sense and Meaning", in B. McGuinness (ed.), *Collected Papers on Mathematics, Logic, and Philosophy* (Oxford: Oxford University Press, 1984).

Fuster, Joaquín M., *The Prefrontal Cortex: Anatomy, Physiology, and Neuropsychology of the Frontal Lobe* (New York: Raven Press, 1980).

——"Prefrontal Neurons in Networks of Executive Memory", *Brain Research Bulletin*, 42 (2000), 331–6.

——"Frontal Lobe and Cognitive Development", *Journal of Neurocytology*, 31 (2002), 373–85.

——*Cortex and Mind: Unifying Cognition* (Oxford: Oxford University Press, 2003).

Gatlin, Lila, *Information and Living Systems* (New York: Columbia University Press, 1972).

Gibbs, Raymond W. Jr., *Embodiment and Cognitive Science* (Cambridge: Cambridge University Press, 2006).

Giedd, J. N., "Structural Magnetic Resonauce Imaging of the Adolescent Brain", *Annals of the New York Academy of Science*, 1021 (2004), 105–9.

Gleick, James, *Chaos: Making a New Science* (New York: Penguin, 1987).

Globus, Gordon, "Kane on Incompatibilism: An Exercise in Neurophilosophy", unpublished paper, 1995.

Goetz, Stuart, "Naturalism and Libertarian Agency", in William Lane Craig and J. P. Moreland (eds.), *Naturalism: A Critical Analysis* (London and New York: Routledge, 2000).

Gordon, Deborah, *Ants at Work: How an Insect Society is Organized* (New York: Free Press, 1999).

Greeno, James G., "Gibson's Affordances", *Psychological Review*, 101 (1994), 336–42.

Grimes, Thomas R., "The Tweedledum and Tweedledee of Supervenience", in Savellos and Yalçin.

Grush, Rick, "The Architecture of Representation", in W. Bechtel *et al.* (eds.), *Philosophy and the Neurosciences: A Reader* (Oxford: Blackwell, 2001).

Güzeldere, Güven, "The Many Faces of Consciousness: A Field Guide", in Block *et al.*

Harak, G. Simon, *Virtuous Passions* (New York: Paulist Press, 1993).

Hare, R. M., *The Language of Morals* (New York: Oxford University Press, 1966; originally published in 1952).

Hasker, William, *The Emergent Self* (Ithaca, NY, and London: Cornell University Press, 1999).

——"Reply to My Friendly Critics", *Philosophia Christi*, 2/2 (2000), 197–207.

Hauerwas, Stanley, and L. Gregory Jones (eds.), *Why Narrative: Readings in Narrative Theology* (Grand Rapids, Mich.: Eerdmans, 1981).

Hebb, Donald O., *The Organization of Behavior: A Neuropsychological Theory* (New York: Wiley, 1949).

Heil, John, *The Nature of True Minds* (Cambridge: Cambridge University Press, 1992).

——— and A. Mele (eds.), *Mental Causation* (Oxford: Clarendon Press, 1995).

Heisenberg, Martin, "Voluntariness (*Willkürfähigkeit*) and the General Organization of Behavior", in R. J. Greenspan *et al.* (eds.), *Flexibility and Constraint in Behavioral Systems* (Hoboken, NJ: John Wiley & Sons, Ltd., 1994).

Helmuth, Laura, "Brain Model Puts Most Sophisticated Regions Front and Center", *Science*, 302 (2003), 1133.

Hempel, Carl G., and P. Oppenheim, "Studies in the Logic of Explanation", *Philosophy of Science*, 15 (1948), 135–76.

Hofstadter, D. R., "Can Creativity Be Mechanized?", *Scientific American*, 247 (1982), 18–34.

Horgan, Terence E., "Supervenience", in Robert Audi (ed.), *The Cambridge Dictionary of Philosophy* (Cambridge: Cambridge University Press, 1995).

Hutchins, E., and B. Hazelhurst, "Learning in the Cultural Process", in C. Langton *et al.* (eds.), *Artificial Life*. II (Reading, Mass.: Addison-Wesley, 1991).

Jeannerod, Marc, "To Act or Not to Act: Perspectives on the Representation of Actions", *Quarterly Journal of Experimental Psychology*, 52A (1999), 1–29.

Johnson, George, "Challenging Particle Physics as Path to Truth", *New York Times*, 4 Dec. 2001; reproduced by Metanexus Newsclippings, <www.metanexus.net>.

Johnson, Steven, *Emergence: The Connected Lives of Ants, Brains, Cities, and Software* (New York: Simon & Schuster, 2001).

Juarrero, Alicia, *Dynamics in Action: Intentional Behavior as a Complex System* (Cambridge, Mass.: MIT Press, 1999).

Kagan, Jerome, *The Nature of the Child* (New York: Basic Books, 1984).

Kandel, E. R., J. H. Schwartz, and T. M. Jessell, *Principles of Neural Science*, 3rd edn. (Norwalk, Conn.: Appleton & Lange, 1991).

Kane, Robert, *The Significance of Free Will* (Oxford: Oxford University Press, 1996).

——— "Free Will: New Directions for an Ancient Problem", in *idem* (ed.), *Free Will* (Oxford: Blackwell, 2002).

——— "Some Neglected Pathways in the Free Will Labyrinth", in *idem* (ed.), *The Oxford Handbook of Free Will* (Oxford: Oxford University Press, 2002).

Keller, Helen, *The Story of My Life* (New York: Penguin, 1988).

Kerr, Fergus, *Theology after Wittgenstein*, 2nd edn. (London: SPCK, 1997).

Kim, Jaegwon, "Concepts of Supervenience", *Philosophy and Phenomenological Research*, 45/2 (1984), 153–76.

—— *Supervenience and Mind: Selected Philosophical Essays* (Cambridge: Cambridge University Press, 1993).

—— "The Myth of Nonreductive Materialism", in Richard Warren and Tadeusz Szubka (eds.), *The Mind–Body Problem*, (Oxford: Blackwell, 1994).

—— "Causation", in Robert Audi (ed.), *The Cambridge Dictionary of Philosophy* (Cambridge: Cambridge University Press, 1995).

—— "The Non-Reductivist's Troubles with Mental Causation", in Heil and Mele.

—— *Physicalism, Or Something Near Enough* (Princeton: Princeton University Press, 2005).

—— "Being Realistic about Emergence", in Philip Clayton and Paul Davies (eds.), *The Re-Emergence of Emergence* (Oxford University Press, 2006).

Koechlin, E., C. Ody, and F. Kouneiher, "The Architecture of Cognitive Control in Human Prefrontal Cortex", *Science*, 302 (2003), 1181–5.

Köhler, Wolfgang, *The Mentality of Apes* (London: Routledge & Kegan Paul, 1956).

Kolb, B., and I. Q. Whishaw, *Fundamentals of Human Neuropsychology*, 4th edn. (New York: W. H. Freeman and Co., 1996).

Kuhn, Thomas, *The Structure of Scientific Revolutions*, 2nd edn. (Chicago: University of Chicago Press, 1970).

Küppers, Bernt-Olaf, "Understanding Complexity", in Robert J. Russell, Nancey Murphy, and Arthur R. Peacocke (eds.), *Chaos and Complexity: Scientific Perspectives on Divine Action*, (Vatican City State and Berkeley: Vatican Observatory and Center for Theology and the Natural Sciences, 1995).

Lakoff, George, and M. Johnson, *Philosophy in the Flesh: The Embodied Mind and Its Challenge to Western Thought* (New York: Basic Books, 1999).

Lash, Nicholas, *Easter in Ordinary: Reflections on Human Experience and the Knowledge of God* (Charlottesville, Va.: University Press of Virginia, 1986).

Lavond, D. G., "Role of the Nuclei in Eyeblink Conditioning", *Annals of the New York Academy of Sciences*, 978 (2002), 93–105.

——, J. J. Kim, *et al.*, "Mammalian Brain Substrates of Aversive Classical Conditioning", *Annual Review of Psychology*, 44 (1993), 317–42.

LeDoux, Joseph, *The Emotional Brain: The Mysterious Underpinnings of Emotional Life* (New York: Simon & Schuster, 1996).

Lewis, Michael, "The Emergence of Consciousness and Its Role in Human Development", in Joseph LeDoux, Jacek Debiec, and Henry Moss (eds.), *The Self: From Soul to Brain*, Annals of the New York Academy of Sciences, 1001, (New York: New York Academy of Sciences, 2003).

Locke, John, *An Essay Concerning Human Understanding* (1690), ed. P. H. Nidditch (Oxford: Clarendon Press, 1975).

Lorenz, E. N., *The Essence of Chaos* (Seattle: University of Washington Press, 1993).

Lovejoy, A. O., *The Great Chain of Being* (Cambridge, Mass.: Harvard University Press, 1936).

Luria, A. R., *The Man with the Shattered World* (New York: Basic Books, 1972).

MacIntyre, Alasdair, "Epistemological Crises, Dramatic Narrative, and the Philosophy of Science", *Monist*, 60/4 (1977), 453–72.

—— *After Virtue: A Study in Moral Theory*, 2nd edn. (Notre Dame, Ind.: University of Notre Dame Press, 1984).

—— *Dependent Rational Animals: Why Human Beings Need the Virtues* (Chicago: Open Court, 1999).

MacKay, Donald M., *Behind the Eye*, The Gifford Lectures, ed. Valerie MacKay (Oxford: Blackwell, 1991).

Martin, Jack, J. Sugarmann, and J. Thompson, *Psychology and the Question of Agency* (Albany: SUNY Press, 2003).

Matson, Wallace I., *A New History of Philosophy*, 2 vols. (San Diego: Harcourt Brace Jovanovich, 1987).

McClendon, James Wm., Jr. *Ethics: Systematic Theology, Volume 1*, 1st edn. (Nashville: Abingdon Press, 1986).

—— and James M. Smith, *Convictions: Defusing Religious Relativism* (Valley Forge, Pa.: Trinity Press International, 1994).

McGinn, Colin, "Consciousness and Content", in Block *et al.*

McLaughlin, Brian, "Varieties of Supervenience", in Savellos and Yalçin.

Mele, Alfred, "Autonomy, Self-Control, and Weakness of Will", in R. Kane (ed.), *The Oxford Handbook of Free Will* (Oxford: Oxford University Press, 2002).

Metzinger, Thomas, *Being No One: The Self-Model Theory of Subjectivity* (Cambridge, Mass.: MIT Press, 2003).

Midgley, Mary, *Beast and Man: The Roots of Human Nature* (Ithaca, NY: Cornell University Press, 1978).

—— "The Soul's Successors: Philosophy and the 'Body' ", in Sarah Coakley (ed.), *Religion and the Body* (Cambridge: Cambridge University Press, 1997).

Millikan, Ruth Garrett, *Language, Thought and Other Biological Categories* (Cambridge, Mass.: MIT Press, 1984).

—— "Pushmi–Pullyu Representations", in E. Tomberlin (ed.), *Philosophical Perspectives, IX: AI, Connectionism and Philosophical Psychology* (Atascadero, Calif.: Ridgeview Publishing Co., 1995).

Milner, B., "Memory and the Temporal Regions of the Brain", in K. H. Pribram and D. E. Broadbent (eds.), *Biology of Memory* (New York: Academic Press, 1970).

_____, S. Corkin, and H. L. Teuber, "Further Analysis of the Hippocampal Amnesic Syndrome: 14-year Follow-up Study of H. M.", *Neuropsychologia*, 6 (1968), 215–34.

Modell, Arnold H., *Imagination and the Meaningful Brain* (Cambridge, Mass.: MIT Press, 2003).

Moore, C., and P. Cavanagh, "Recovery of 3D Volume from 2-Tone Images of Novel Objects", *Cognition*, 67 (1998), 45–71.

Moreland, J. P., and Scott B. Rae, *Body and Soul: Human Nature and the Crisis in Ethics* (Downers Grove, Ill.: InterVarsity, 2000).

Murphy, Nancey, *Anglo-American Postmodernity: Philosophical Perspectives on Science, Religion, and Ethics* (Boulder, Colo.: Westview Press, 1998).

_____ "Nonreductive Physicalism", in Joel B. Green (ed.), *In Search of the Soul: Four Views* (Downers Grove, Ill.: InterVarsity, 2005).

_____ and George F. R. Ellis, *On the Moral Nature of the Universe: Theology, Cosmology, and Ethics* (Minneapolis: Fortress Press, 1996).

_____ and William R. Stoeger (eds.), *Evolution and Emergence: Systems, Organisms, Persons* (Oxford: Oxford University Press, 2007).

Noë, Alva, *Action in Perception* (Cambridge, Mass.: MIT Press, 2004).

O'Connor, Timothy, "Libertarian Views: Dualist and Agent-Causal Theories", in R. Kane (ed.), *The Oxford Handbook of Free Will* (Oxford: Oxford University Press, 2002).

O'Regan, J. K., and A. Noë, "A Sensorimotor Account of Vision and Visual Consciousness", *Behavior and Brain Science*, 25 (2001), 5.

O'Reilly, Randall C., "Biologically Based Computational Models of High-Level Cognition", *Science*, 314/5796 (2006), 91–94.

Ornstein, P. A., B. N. Gordon, and L. E. Baker-Ward, "Children's Memory for Salient Events: Implications for Testimony", in M. L. Howe, C. J. Brainerd, and V. F. Reyna (eds.), *Development of Long Term Retention* (New York: Springer Verlag, 1992).

Pattee, Harold, "The Physical Basis and Origin of Hierarchical Control", in *idem* (ed.), *Hierarchy Theory* (New York: George Braziller, 1973).

Peacocke, Arthur, *God and the New Biology* (Gloucester, Mass.: Peter Smith, 1986).

_____ *Theology for a Scientific Age: Being and Becoming—Natural, Divine, and Human*, 2nd enlarged edn. (Minneapolis: Fortress Press, 1993).

_____ "God's Interaction with the World: The Implications of Deterministic 'Chaos' and of Interconnected and Interdependent Complexity", in R. J. Russell, N. Murphy, and A. R. Peacocke (eds.), *Chaos and Complexity: Scientific Perspectives on Divine Action*.

Perner, J., and T. Ruffman, "Episodic Memory and Autonoetic Consciousness: Developmental Evidence and a Theory of Childhood Amnesia", *Journal of Experimental Child Psychology*, 59 (1995), 516–548.

Pinker, Stephen, *How the Mind Works* (New York: W.W. Norton, 1999).

Poincaré, Henri, *Science and Method* (1903) (Chicago: St. Augustine's Press, 2001).

Pojman, Louis, "Freedom and Determinism: A Contemporary Discussion", *Zygon* 22/4 (1987), 397–417.

Pols, Edward, *Mind Regained* (Ithaca, NY: Cornell University Press, 1998).

Popkin, Richard H., *The History of Skepticism: From Savonarola to Bayle*, rev. and expanded edn. (Oxford: Oxford University Press, 2003).

Popper, Karl R., *A World of Propensities* (Bristol: Thoemmes, 1990).

Putnam, Hilary, "Brains in a Vat", in *Reason, Truth, and History* (Cambridge: Cambridge University Press, 1981).

Quine, W. V. O., "Two Dogmas of Empiricism", *Philosophical Review*, 60 (1951); repr. in *From a Logical Point of View* (Cambridge, Mass.: Harvard University Press, 1953).

Ramachandran, V. S., "The Science of Art: How the Brain Responds to Beauty", in Warren S. Brown (ed.), *Understanding Wisdom: Sources, Science, and Society.* (Philadelphia and London: Templeton Foundation Press, 2000).

Reddy, Vasudevi, and P. Morris, "Participants Don't Need Theories: Knowing Minds in Engagement", *Theory and Psychology*, 14 (2004), 647–65.

Rizzolatti, G., and L. Craighero, "The Mirror–Neuron System", *Annual Review of Neuroscience*, 27 (2000), 169–92.

——— L. Fadiga, V. Gallese, and L. Fogassi, "Premotor Cortex and the Recognition of Motor Actions", *Cognitive Brain Research*, 3 (1996), 131–41.

Robinson, Howard (ed.), *Objections to Physicalism* (Oxford: Clarendon Press, 1993).

Rorty, Richard, *Philosophy and the Mirror of Nature* (Princeton: Princeton University Press, 1979).

Rose, Steven, *Life Lines: Life Beyond the Gene* (Oxford: Oxford University Press, 1997).

Rumbaugh, Duane (ed.), *Language Learning by a Chimpanzee: The Lana Project* (New York: Academic Press, 1977).

Russell, Robert J., "Special Providence and Genetic Mutation: A New Defense of Theistic Evolution", in *idem.*, William R. Stoeger, and Francisco J. Ayala (eds.), *Evolutionary and Molecular Biology: Scientific Perspectives on Divine Action* (Vatican City State and Berkeley: Vatican Observatory and Center for Theology and the Natural Sciences, 1998).

Ryle, Gilbert, *The Concept of Mind* (London: Hutchinson, 1949).

Sapire, David, "Propensity", in Robert Audi (ed.), *The Cambridge Dictionary of Philosophy* (Cambridge: Cambridge University Press, 1995).

Savage-Rumbaugh, E. Sue, *Ape Language: From Conditioned Response to Symbol* (New York: Columbia University Press, 1986).

Savellos, Elias E., and Ümit D. Yalçin (eds.), *Supervenience: New Essays* (Cambridge: Cambridge University Press, 1995).

Schulman, Adam, "Why Be Good?", *Books in Review*, May 2003, 71–3.

Scott, Alwyn, *Stairway to the Mind: The Controversial New Science of Consciousness* (New York: Springer Verlag, 1995).

——— "The Development of Nonlinear Science", *Revista del Nuovo Cimento*. 27/10-11 (2004), 1–115.

Scrivener, Alan B., "A Curriculum for Cybernetics and Systems Theory", <http://www.well.com/user/abs/curriculum.html> (accessed 19, Nov. 2004).

Searle, John R., *Speech Acts: An Essay in the Philosophy of Language* (Cambridge: Cambridge University Press, 1969).

——— *The Rediscovery of the Mind* (Cambridge, Mass.: MIT Press, 1992).

——— *Rationality in Action* (Cambridge, Mass.: MIT Press, 2001).

Sellars, Roy Wood, *Principles of Emergent Realism: The Philosophical Essays of Roy Wood Sellars*, ed. W. Preston Warren (St Louis: Warren H. Green, 1970).

——— *The Philosophy of Physical Realism* (1932); (New York: Russell and Russell, 1996).

Seyforth, Robert, *et al.*, "Monkey Responses to Three Different Alarm Calls: Evidence of Predator Classification and Semantic Communication", *Science*, 210 (1980), 801–3.

Silbersweig, D. A., and E. Stern, "Towards a Functional Neuroanatomy of Conscious Perception and its Modulation by Volition: Implications of Human Auditory Neuroimaging Studies", *Philosophical Transactions of the Royal Society of London*, Series B: *Biological Sciences*, 351 (1998), 1883–8.

Sperry, Roger W., "Hemisphere Deconnection and Unity in Conscious Awareness", *American Psychologist*, 23/10 (1968), 723–33.

——— "A Modified Concept of Consciousness", *Psychological Review*, 76/6 (1969), 532–6.

——— *Science and Moral Priority: Merging Mind, Brain, and Human Values* (New York: Columbia University Press, 1983).

——— "Psychology's Mentalist Paradigm and the Religion/Science Tension", *American Psychologist*, 43/8 (1988), 607–13.

——— "The Import and Promise of the Cognitive Revolution", *American Psychologist*, 48/8 (1993), 878–85.

Squire, Larry R., *Memory and Brain* (Oxford: Oxford University Press, 1987).

Stephan, Achim, "Emergence—A Systematic View on Its Historical Facets", in Ansgar Beckermann, Hans Flohr, and Jaegwon Kim (eds.), *Emergence or*

Reduction?: Essays on the Prospects of Nonreductive Physicalism (Berlin and New York: Walter de Gruyter, 1992).

Strawson, Galen, "Free Will", in Edward Craig (ed.), *Routledge Encyclopedia of Philosophy* (London and New York: Routledge, 1998).

——— "Evolution Explains It All for You", *New York Times Book Review*, 2 Mar. 2003, 11.

Taylor, Charles, "What is Human Agency?", in *Philosophical Papers*, I. (Cambridge: Cambridge University Press, 1985).

——— *Sources of the Self: The Making of Modern Identity* (Cambridge, Mass.: Harvard University Press, 1989).

Teller, Paul, "Reduction", in Robert Audi (ed.), *The Cambridge Dictionary of Philosophy* (Cambridge: Cambridge University Press, 1995).

Tomlin, D. T., *et al.*, "Agent-Specific Responses in the Cingulate Cortex during Economic Exchanges", *Science*, 312 (2006), 1047–50.

Toulmin, Stephen, *Cosmopolis: The Hidden Agenda of Modernity* (New York: Macmillan, 1990).

Van Gulick, Robert, "Who's in Charge Here? And Who's Doing All the Work?", in Heil and Mele.

——— "Reduction, Emergence and Other Recent Options on the Mind/Body Problem: A Philosophic Overview", *Journal of Consciousness Studies*, 8/9–10 (2001), 1–34.

van Inwagen, Peter, *An Essay on Free Will* (Oxford: Clarendon Press, 1983).

Weiskrantz, Lawrence, *Blindsight: A Case Study and Implications* (Oxford: Oxford University Press, 1986).

——— , E. K. Warrington, *et al.*, "Visual Capacity in the Hemianopic Field following a Restricted Occipital Ablation", *Brain: A Journal of Neurology*, 97/4 (1974), 709–28.

Wildman, Wesley J., and R. J. Russell. "Chaos: A Mathematical Introduction with Philosophical Reflections", in Robert John Russell, Nancey Murphy, and Arthur R. Peacocke (eds.), *Chaos and Complexity: Scientific Perspectives on Divine Action* (Vatican City State and Berkeley: Vatican Observatory and Center for Theology and the Natural Sciences, 1995).

Wilson, Edward O., and Bert Holldobler, *The Ants* (Cambridge, Mass.: Harvard University Press, 1990).

Wittgenstein, Ludwig, *Philosophical Investigations*, ed. G. E. M. Anscombe and R. Rhees, trans. G. E. M. Anscombe (Oxford: Blackwell, 1953).

——— *The Blue and Brown Books* ed. R. Rhees (New York: Harper & Row, 1958).

_____ *Zettel*, ed. G. E. M. Anscombe and G. H. von Wright, trans. G. E. M. Anscombe (Berkeley and Los Angeles: University of California Press, 1970).

_____ *Philosophical Grammar*, ed. R. Rhees, trans. A. Kenny (Berkeley and Los Angeles: University of California Press, 1974).

Woolridge, D., *Mechanical Man: The Physical Basis of Intelligent Life* (New York: McGraw-Hill, 1968).

Index

Made in the USA
San Bernardino, CA
17 December 2013